*lonely planet*

# CHINA

## TOP SIGHTS, AUTHENTIC EXPERIENCES

THIS EDITION WRITTEN AND RESEARCHED BY

Damian Harper, Piera Chen, Megan Eaves, David Eimer,
Helen Elfer, Trent Holden, Stephen Lioy, Emily Matchar,
Rebecca Milner, Kate Morgan, Tom Spurling, Phillip Tang

# Contents

Oriental Pearl TV Tower, Pǔdōng
(p125), Shànghǎi
KAPITONOV ILIA / SHUTTERSTOCK ©

# Plan Your Trip
# China's Top 12

GUOZHONGHUA / SHUTTERSTOCK ©

## Běijīng

*Běijīng is China's supreme historic capital*

It's so modern in parts it's easy to forget this ancient capital (p34) was home to Mongol, Ming and Manchu emperors. Few cities can boast a history so dramatic or turbulent as Běijīng: repeatedly razed and restored to reassert its authority as capital of a land that is today home to almost 1.4 billion people and with the Forbidden City (pictured above; p38) at its heart, Běijīng is the must-see city in China.

1

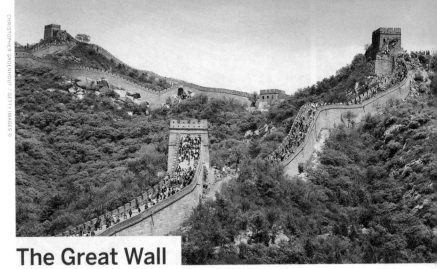

# The Great Wall

**China's greatest engineering feat meanders across the north of the land**

Spotting it from space is both tough and pointless: the only place you can truly put the Great Wall (p68) under your feet is in China. Select the Great Wall according to taste: perfectly chiselled, dilapidated, stripped of its bricks, overrun with saplings, coiling splendidly into the hills or returning to dust. Top: Jīnshānlǐng (p76); Above: Bādálǐng (p77)

HUNG_CHUNG_CHIH / GETTY IMAGES ©

# Xī'ān & the Terracotta Warriors

*Former Tang dynasty capital and one of China's most ancient cities*

Standing silent guard over their emperor for more than two millennia, the terracotta warriors (p98) are some of the most extraordinary archaeological discoveries ever made. Xī'ān (p94) itself stands among China's most appealing destinations, stuffed with dynastic history, boasting a superb city wall, and cooking up some of the best food in the land.

3

4

# Shànghǎi

*Shànghǎi typifies modern China, while being unlike anywhere else in the land*

More than just a city, Shànghǎi (p110) is the country's neon-lit beacon of change, opportunity and modernity. Whether it's your first stop in China, or you're pulling in after a 30-hour train journey from Gānsù, you'll find plenty to indulge in here. Start with the Bund (p114) and move on to the French Concession (p120), Shànghǎi's epicentre of food, fashion and fun.

5

# Guǎngxī & the Lí River

*Cycle, raft or hike the picture-perfect landscape*

It's hard to exaggerate the beauty of Yángshuò and the Lí River area (p190), renowned for classic images of mossy-green jagged limestone peaks providing a backdrop for tall bamboo fronds leaning over bubbling streams, wallowing water buffaloes and farmers sowing rice paddies.

DEA / G. DAGLI ORTI / GETTY IMAGES ©

# Gānsù & the Silk Road

*Boasting ancient Buddhist artefacts, geographic diversity and adventures galore*

An impressive length of the historic Silk Road runs through Gānsù province (p254), dotted with sublime fragments of Buddhist civilisations, including the outstanding Mògāo Grottoes (pictured; p258), and leading to the mighty desert fort of Jiāyùguān (p262), while also guiding travellers to the atmospheric Tibetan Buddhist enclave of Xiàhé and Labrang Monastery (p260).

# Hong Kong & Macau

*Past foreign rule lends these territories a unique feel and a different way of life*

Way down south in China's energetic Cantonese heartland, Hong Kong (pictured; p158) is an enticing fusion of traditional Chinese culture, international savoir faire and some of the best chow money can buy. The view across Victoria Harbour is stunning, too. And don't forget Macau (p180), a photogenic city with bundles of Portuguese heritage (and more of that excellent food).

7

# Yúnnán

*A combination of superlative sites and ethnic groups*

Yúnnán (p202) is China's most diverse province, both in its extraordinary mix of peoples and in the splendour of its landscapes, making it the trendiest destination for China's exploding domestic tourist industry. Most visitors are here for Lìjiāng (pictured; p208), Tiger Leaping Gorge (p210), Dàlǐ (p216) and the Yuányáng Rice Terraces (p206), and you should be too.

ELFIRED / SHUTTERSTOCK ©

BEIBAOKE / SHUTTERSTOCK ©

9

# Shānxī

## *Waist-deep in living history*

Shānxī (p80) brings you face to face with time-warped Píngyáo (pictured far left; p84) – an intact, walled Chinese town possessing an unbroken sense of continuity to its Qing dynasty heyday. The dusty province is also home to the astonishing Buddhist heritage of the Yúngāng Caves (pictured left; p86), while nearby Dàtóng (p90) is an increasingly handsome city worth several days of exploration.

ZZVET / SHUTTERSTOCK ©

REDCHOPSTICKS / GETTY IMAGES ©

CHRISTOPHE BOISVIEUX / ROBERT HARDING ©

# Huángshān & Huīzhōu Villages

*Home to archetypal granite peaks, graceful pines and picturesque hamlets*

Often shrouded in mist, Huángshān (pictured above right; p142) has a pull that attracts millions. Nearby are perfectly preserved Huīzhōu villages (p146), including Xīdì (pictured above left; p149) and Hóngcūn (pictured top; p148).

10

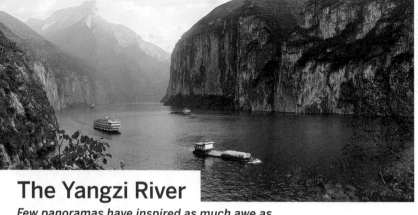

# The Yangzi River

*Few panoramas have inspired as much awe as China's longest, most scenic river*

The mighty Yangzi River (p238) reaches a crescendo with the Three Gorges (pictured; p242), carved out throughout the millennia by the inexorable persistence of its powerful waters. A Yangzi River cruise is a rare chance to hang up your travelling hat, take a seat and leisurely watch the drama unfold.

# Sìchuān

*A land of many guises, including China's most famous face – the giant panda*

Capital Chéngdū (p230) shows a modern face, but just beyond its bustling ring roads you'll find a more traditional landscape of mist-shrouded, sacred mountains, a countryside scattered with ancient villages, and cliffs of carved Buddhas. And don't overlook China's spiciest cuisine (not that you'll be able to miss it).

# Plan Your Trip
# Need to Know

## When to Go

- Warm to hot summers, mild winters
- Mild to hot summers, cold winters
- Mild summers, very cold winters
- Desert, dry climate
- Cold climate

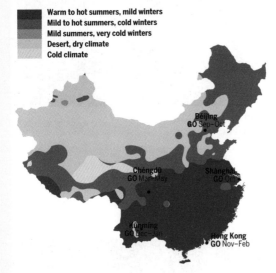

Běijīng
GO Sep–Oct

Chéngdū
GO Mar–May

Shànghǎi
GO Oct

Kūnmíng
GO Dec–Jan

Hong Kong
GO Nov–Feb

### High Season (May–Aug)

o Prepare for summer downpours and tourist crowds.

o Accommodation prices peak during the first week of the May holiday period.

### Shoulder (Feb–Apr, Sep & Oct)

o Expect warmer days in spring, cooler days in autumn.

o Optimal season in the north, with fresh weather and clear skies.

o Accommodation prices peak during holidays in early October.

### Low Season (Nov–Feb)

o Domestic tourism at a low ebb, but things are busy for Chinese New Year.

o Bitterly cold in the north and at altitude, and only warm in the far south.

## Currency
yuán (元; ¥)

## Language
Mandarin, Cantonese

## Visas
Needed for all visits to China except Hong Kong, Macau and trips of less than 72 hours to a number of cities including Běijīng, Shànghǎi, Xī'ān, Guìlín, Chéngdū, Kūnmíng and Chóngqìng.

## Money
Credit cards in big cities accepted, elsewhere less widely accepted. ATMs in cities and towns.

## Mobile Phones
Pay-as-you-go SIM cards can be bought locally for most mobile phones.

## Time
GMT/UTC plus eight hours

## Daily Costs

### Budget: Less than ¥200
- Dorm bed: ¥40 to ¥60
- Food markets, street food: ¥40
- Bike hire or other transport: ¥20

### Midrange: ¥200 to ¥1000
- Double room (midrange hotel): ¥200 to ¥600
- Lunch and dinner in local restaurants: ¥80 to ¥100
- Taxis: ¥60

### Top End: More than ¥1000
- Double room (top-end hotel): ¥600+
- Lunch and dinner in excellent local or hotel restaurants: ¥300
- Two tickets to Chinese opera: ¥300

## Useful Websites

**Lonely Planet** (www.lonelyplanet.com/china) Destination information, hotel bookings, traveller forum and more.
**Ctrip** (www.english.ctrip.com) Hotel booking, air and train ticketing.
**Chinasmack** (www.chinasmack.com) Human-interest stories and videos.
**Popupchinese** (www.popupchinese.com) Excellent podcasts.
**Far West China** (www.farwestchina.com) Indispensable resource for Silk Roaders.

## Opening Hours

China officially has a five-day working week; Saturday and Sunday are public holidays.
**Banks** Weekdays 9am to 5pm (or 6pm); may close for two hours in the afternoon. Many open Saturday and maybe Sunday.
**Bars** Late afternoon, shutting around midnight or later.
**Post offices** Generally open daily.
**Restaurants** 10.30am to 11pm; some shut at around 2pm and reopen at 5pm or 6pm.
**Shops** 10am to 10pm; same for department stores and shopping malls.

## Arriving in China

### Běijīng Capital Airport (p330)

**Train** Airport Express connects to subway lines 2, 10 and 13; every 10 minutes from 6am to 10.30pm.
**Buses** Express buses run to central Běijīng; every 10 to 20 minutes from 5am to midnight.
**Taxi** ¥90 to ¥120; 40 minutes to one hour into town.

### Hong Kong International Airport (p330)

**Train** Airport Express runs to Hong Kong Station in Central every 12 minutes.
**Bus** Spread out to many Hong Kong destinations.
**Taxi** HK$280 to Central; luggage is HK$5 extra.

### Pǔdōng International Airport (Shànghǎi; p330)

**Train** Maglev train connects to Longyang Rd metro station; every 20 minutes from 6.45am to 9.40pm. Metro Line 2 takes 45 minutes to People's Square.
**Bus** Shuttle buses run every 15 to 25 minutes from 7am to 11pm.
**Taxi** ¥160; one hour into town.

## Getting Around

**Train** Extensive modern network covers the nation; high-speed trains connect many cities.

**Bus** Extensive network; cheaper and slower than the train, but reaches extra destinations and runs more regularly.

**Air** Numerous domestic flights.

**Car** Limited but growing options; roads chaotic.

**Taxis** Cheap and plentiful in cities and big towns.

For more on **getting around**, see p331

# Plan Your Trip
# Hot Spots For...

**Chinese Food**

*Probably your first experience of China, Chinese cuisine has a global following, but if you want the real thing, you've simply got to visit the homeland of Chinese food.*

**Ancient Towns**

*North China is home to old dynastic capitals and walled towns that conjure up flavours of the China of yesteryear. If history floats your boat, you'll be spoiled for choice.*

**Hiking**

*China's epic landscapes are made for hiking so you'll never be short of reasons to get your walking shoes on. Mountains, gorges, terraced fields and the Great Wall: everything you could want.*

**Sacred China**

*China's sacred dimension can be easy to miss in the big cities, but a palpable atmosphere of religious devotion is not hard to find beyond town, on mountains and in caves.*

Běijīng (p59) Běijīng's most celebrated dish is Peking duck (pictured), and purists insist it must be cooked up in the capital to qualify.

Jīngzūn Peking Duck Mouthwatering roast fowl with a loyal fan base (p60).

Chéngdū (p233) You haven't tasted real Sìchuān food till you take your chopsticks out on home turf.

Chén Mápó Dòufu Signature dish – perfectly executed and loved by all (p233).

Hong Kong (p173) You could spend your whole holiday in Hong Kong feasting on dim sum and still demand more.

Lung King Heen Top-drawer dim sum from a three-star Michelin restaurant (p175).

Běijīng (p34) Disappear down the *hútòng*, explore the Forbidden City and marvel at the old city gates.

Qiánmén Size up Běijīng's mighty Front Gate, in the south of Tiān'ānmén Square (p47).

Píngyáo (p84) China's best preserved walled town (pictured) is almost perfect in every way.

City Walls For a bird's eye of the old town, bounded by its defensive walls (p84).

Xī'ān (p94) Site of the old Tang capital of Chang'an, Xī'ān is built from the soles up on history.

Xī'ān City Walls Walk or cycle the entire wall for a sense of the historic city (p103).

Tiger Leaping Gorge (p210) China's most legendary gorge walk along the Jīnshā River in Yúnnán.

Tiger Leaping Stone Scenic rock of the eponymous feline leaping the gorge (p211).

Lóngjǐ Rice Terraces (p192) When the sun catches the glistening water-filled rice terraces (pictured), it's a photo op made in heaven.

Nine Dragons & Five Tigers Viewing Point Stunning views to the valley below (p192).

The Great Wall (p68) The world's most famous wall, hikeable in its raw state.

Jiànkòu For the wall in its natural, dilapidated and most sublime form (p75).

Mògāo Grottoes (p258) These magnificent Buddhist grottoes outside Dūnhúang are the finest in the land.

The Two Big Buddhas The two big Buddhas, 34.5m and 26m tall (p259).

Huá Shān (p100) Go in search of *dào* (the way) climbing up one of China's most sacred Taoist peaks.

Sunrise Sleep on the mountain to celebrate the reappearance of the sun (p101).

Yúngāng Caves (p86) Spellbindingly beautiful gathering of ancient Buddhist statuary (pictured) outside Dàtóng.

Cave 6 It will simply bowl you over (p86).

# Plan Your Trip
# Local Life

SHUPIAN / SHUTTERSTOCK ©

## Activities

All manner of activities are available around China. Grab copies of expat magazines in Běijīng, Hong Kong and Shànghǎi for information on sports such as golf, running, horse riding, cycling, football, cricket, hiking and trekking, hot-air ballooning, martial arts, swimming, ice skating, skiing, skateboarding, waterskiing and rock climbing, as well as more Chinese-centric activities such as classes in cooking, Chinese herbal medicine, acupuncture, taichi, qì gōng and beyond.

## Shopping

You can find almost anything in China, and at low prices. Only imported goods and big-name electronics are more expensive than elsewhere (even if they're manufactured here). Antiques markets are good for curios, but never take anything at face value (it's best to treat items more as souvenirs). Check out the big garment markets in larger cities for cut-price clothing, while bird and flower markets are excellent for a taste of local life, with locals browsing for flowers, pet birds, crickets and fish. Bargaining in markets is crucial; be firm, but polite.

## Entertainment

Chinese opera – especially in Běijīng – is a colourful must-see (even if you don't understand it). International musicals are performed, though often in Chinese and usually in the big towns. Some local theatres in the largest cities perform in English or even bilingually. China's music stages feature everything from local bands to traditional performances and martial arts. To catch some informal singing, dancing, taichi or playing of traditional instruments, visit a public square or park in the evening or early morning.

## Eating

Snacking your way around China is a fine way to sample the different flavours of the land while on the move. Most towns have a street market or a night market (夜市; *yèshì*), a great place for good-value snacks and meals; you can either take it away or park yourself on a wobbly stool and grab a beer.

VICHIEBI / SHUTTERSTOCK ©

Chinese eateries come in every conceivable shape, size and type: from shabby, hole-in-the-wall noodle outfits with flimsy PVC furniture, blaring TV sets and well-worn plastic menus to gilded, banquet-style restaurants where elegant cheongsam-clad waitresses show you to your seat, straighten your chopsticks and bring you a warm hand towel and a gold-embossed wine list. In between are legions of very serviceable midrange restaurants serving cuisine from across China. English menus are on the increase and most reputable or popular places should have one, but they are vastly outnumbered by restaurants with menus solely in Chinese.

## Drinking & Nightlife

There are plenty of bars in larger cities, especially Hong Kong, Běijīng and Shànghǎi, many of them aimed at Western travellers or Chinese drinkers seeking a foreign vibe. Visit Western-style pubs to connect with travellers and homesick expats, listen to Western live music and often be treated to a non-Chinese menu. Hong Kong, Běijīng

## China's Best Bars

Great Leap Brewing (p61)

Glam (p131)

Long Bar (p131)

Club 71 (p176)

Ping Pong Gintoneria (p176)

and Shànghǎi have the most club options, with home-grown electronic music on the rise. Cocktail bars are very popular in the big cities, and even in smaller towns you can usually find a selection of bars serving the more cashed-up drinkers in town, even if they are in four- and five-star hotels.

Bars aimed specifically at Chinese are great for experiencing local life, but tend to be noisier and more aimed at the KTV crowd.

From left: Chinese opera (p307) performer; Food vendor, Chóngqìng (p246)

# Plan Your Trip
# Month by Month

MEIQIANBAO / SHUTTERSTOCK ©

## January

**North China is in deep freeze, but the south is less bitter; preparations for the Lunar New Year get under way well in advance of the festival, which arrives any time between late January and March.**

### ✹ Spring Festival

The Lunar New Year is family-focused, with dumpling feasts and *hóngbāo* (red envelopes stuffed with money) gifts. Most families eat together on New Year's Eve, then China goes on a big weeklong holiday. Expect fireworks, parades, temple fairs and lots of colour.

## February

**North China remains shockingly icy and dry, but things are slowly warming up in Hong Kong and Macau. The Lunar New Year could well be under way, but sort out your tickets well in advance.**

### ✹ Monlam Great Prayer Festival

Held during two weeks from the third day of the Tibetan New Year and celebrated with spectacular processions (except in Lhasa or the Tibet Autonomous Region); huge silk *thangka* (sacred art) are unveiled and, on the last day, a statue of the Maitreya Buddha is conveyed around.

### ✹ Lantern Festival

Held 15 days after the spring festival, this was traditionally a time when Chinese hung out highly decorated lanterns. Píngyáo in Shānxī is an atmospheric place to soak it up.

## March

**China comes to life after a long winter, although it remains glacial at high altitudes. The mercury climbs in Hong Kong and abrasive dust storms billow into Běijīng, scouring everything in their path. It's still low season.**

### ☂ Fields of Yellow

Delve into the countryside in the south to discover a landscape saturated in bright yellow rapeseed. In some parts of China, including lovely Yángshuò, it's a real tourist draw.

OSTILL / SHUTTERSTOCK ©

## April

**Most of China is warm and it's a good time to be on the road. The Chinese take several days off for the Qīngmíng festival, a traditional date for honouring their ancestors and now an official holiday.**

### 🎎 A Good Soaking

Flush away the dirt, demons and sorrows of the old year and bring in the new during the Dai New Year, with its water-splashing festival in Xīshuāngbǎnnà. Taking an umbrella is pointless.

### 🎎 Third Moon Festival

This Bai ethnic minority festival is an excellent reason to pitch up in the lovely north Yúnnán town of Dàlǐ. It's a week of horse racing, singing and merrymaking from the 15th day of the third lunar month (usually April) to the 21st.

### ☆ Formula One

Petrol heads and aficionados of speed, burnt rubber and hairpin bends flock to Shànghǎi for some serious motor racing at the track near Āntíng. Get your hotel room booked early: it's one of the most glamorous events on the Shànghǎi calendar.

**China's Best Festivals**

Spring Festival, January or February

Monlam Great Prayer Festival, February or March

Rapeseed fields around Yángshuò, mid-March

Dragon Boat Festival, June

Torch Festival, Dàlǐ, July

From left: Spring Festival decorations, Shǎnxī (p80); Dragon-boat racing, Hong Kong (p158)

## May

Mountainous regions, such as Sìchuān's Jiǔzhàigōu National Park, are in full bloom. For the first four days of May, China is on vacation (Labour Day). Buddha's Birthday falls on the 8th day of the fourth lunar month, usually in May.

### 🎎 Buddha's Birthday in Xiàhé

A fascinating time to enjoy the Tibetan charms of Gānsù province's Xiàhé, when Buddhist monks make charitable handouts to beggars and the streets throng with pilgrims.

### 🏃 Great Wall Marathon

Experience the true meaning of pain; not for the infirm or unfit. See www.great-wall-marathon.com for more details.

## June

Most of China is hot and getting hotter. Once-frozen areas, such as Jílín's Heaven Lake, are accessible – and nature springs instantly to life. Peak tourist season is cranking up.

### 🎎 Dragon Boat Festival

Head to Zhènyuǎn or the nearest large river and catch all the water-borne drama of dragon boat racers in this celebration of one of China's most famous poets. The Chinese traditionally eat zòngzi (triangular glutinous rice dumplings wrapped in reed leaves).

## July

Typhoons can wreak havoc with travel itineraries down south, lashing the Guǎngdōng and Fújiàn coastlines. Plenty of rain sweeps across China: the 'plum rains' give Shànghǎi a big soaking, and the grasslands of Inner Mongolia and Qīnghǎi turn green.

### 🎎 Torch Festival, Dàlǐ

Held on the 24th day of the sixth lunar month (usually July), this festival is held throughout Yúnnán by the Bai and Yi minorities. Making for great photos, flaming torches are paraded at night through streets and fields, and outside shops around town.

## August

The temperature gauge of the Yangzi's 'three ovens' – Chóngqìng, Wǔhàn and Nánjīng – gets set to blow. Rainstorms hit Běijīng, which is usually 40°C plus, as is Shànghǎi. Head uphill to Lúshān, Mògànshān, Huángshān or Guōliàngcūn.

## September

Come to Běijīng and stay put – September is part of the fleetingly lovely tiāngāo qìshuǎng (the sky is high and the air is fresh) autumnal season – an event in itself. It's also a pleasant time to visit the rest of North China.

### 🎎 Mid-Autumn Festival

Also called the moon festival; celebrated by devouring daintily prepared moon cakes – stuffed with bean paste, egg yolk, walnuts and more. With a full moon, it's a romantic occasion for lovers and a special time for families. On the 15th day of the eighth lunar month.

### 🎎 Confucius' Birthday

Head to the Confucius Temple in Qūfù for the 28 September birthday celebrations of axiom-quipping philosopher, sage and patriarch Confucius.

## October

The first week of October can be hellish if you're on the road: the National Day weeklong holiday kicks off, so everywhere is swamped. Go mid-month instead, when everywhere is deserted.

### 🍴 Hairy Crabs in Shànghǎi

Now is the time to sample delicious hairy crabs in Shànghǎi; they are at their best between October and December. Male and female crabs are eaten together with shots of lukewarm Shàoxīng rice wine.

## November

Most of China is getting pretty cold as tourist numbers drop and holidaymakers begin to flock south for sun and the last pockets of warmth.

# Plan Your Trip
# Get Inspired

## Read

**Country Driving: A Chinese Road Trip** (Peter Hessler; 2011) Hessler's amusing and insightful journey at the wheel around the highways and byways of China.

**Tiger Head, Snake Tails** (Jonathan Fenby; 2012) Compelling account of contemporary China's myriad challenges and contradictions.

**Diary of a Madman and Other Stories** (Lu Xun; 1918) Astonishing tales from the father of modern Chinese fiction.

**Wolf Totem** (Jiang Rong; 2009) An enthralling look at life on the grasslands of Inner Mongolia during the Cultural Revolution and the impact of modern culture on an ancient way of life.

## Watch

**Still Life** (Jia Zhangke; 2005) Bleak and hauntingly beautiful portrayal of a family devastated by the construction of the Three Gorges Dam.

**Raise the Red Lantern** (Zhang Yimou; 1991) Exquisitely fashioned tragedy from the sumptuous palette of the Fifth Generation.

**In the Mood for Love** (Wong Kar-Wai; 2000) Seductive, stylishly costumed and slow-burning Hong Kong romance.

**The House of Flying Daggers** (Zhang Yimou; 2004) Vibrantly coloured romantic martial-arts epic.

## Listen

**Eagle** (Mamer; 2009) Unique take on Kazakh folk music from northwest Xīnjiāng province.

**Nothing to My Name** (Cui Jian; 1986) Gutsy rock milestone from a different age.

**Lang Lang at Carnegie Hall** (2004) Astonishing display of virtuoso skill from China's leading pianist.

**Masterpieces of Chinese Traditional Music** (1995) Exquisite collection of traditional Chinese tunes.

Yuányáng Rice Terraces (p206), Yúnnán

# Plan Your Trip
# Five-Day Itineraries

## Hong Kong to Shànghǎi

Bookend two of the world's most famously modern, yet historic cities with a few days gently meandering the verdant dreamy landscape around Yángshuò.

FROM LEFT: CHINAFACE / GETTY IMAGES ©, LIUFUYU / GETTY IMAGES ©

**Shànghǎi** (p110) Discover Shànghǎi: the grandeur of the Bund, the stylish French Concession and the glass and steel skyscape of Pǔdōng.

**Yángshuò** (p190) Jump on a bike and discover the unmissable karst countryside around town.
🚌 1 hr to Guìlín then ✈ 2½ hrs to Shànghǎi

**Hong Kong** (p158) Hop aboard the Star Ferry, climb Victoria Peak and explore buzzing Central District.
✈ 1½ hrs to Guìlín then 🚌 1 hr to Yángshuò

# Běijīng to Xī'ān

Five days doesn't sound much, but you can do three of China's big-hitters at the very least: the Great Wall, ancient Píngyáo and the Terracotta Warriors outside Xī'ān (as well as the city walls).

**Běijīng** (p34) China's capital: home to the Forbidden City, Tiān'ānmén Square and the Great Wall – give the city two days. 🚆 4 ½ hrs to Píngyáo

**Píngyáo** (p84) China's best-preserved walled town needs a day of your attention and an overnight stay. 🚆 3 ¼ hrs to Xī'ān

**Xī'ān** (p94) Visit the awesome Terracotta Warriors outside town, climb the imposing city wall, snack your way through the bustling Muslim quarter and visit the Great Mosque.

# Plan Your Trip
# 10-Day Itinerary

## Shànghǎi to Lìjiāng

This colossal expedition sweeps from swinging Shànghǎi via the misty mountain of Huángshān and nearby Huīzhōu villages to Macau and the Naxi town of Lìjiāng in Yúnnán, via the capital of Sìchuān, Chéngdū.

**Chéngdū** (p230) Get a taste of Sìchuān food on home soil, take in the Giant Panda Breeding Research Base or consider an escape to sacred Éméi Shān. ✈ 1¾ hrs to Lìjiāng

**4**

**5**

**Lìjiāng** (p208) Wander the old town, photograph Yùlóng Xuěshān from Black Dragon Pool Park and plan a thrilling hike along spectacular Tiger Leaping Gorge.

**Shànghǎi** (p110) Put aside a couple of days to discover Shànghǎi, have a table booked for lunch at M on the Bund and visit the historic Yùyuán Gardens. 🚌 4 ½ hrs to Huángshān

**Huángshān** (p138) Climb Huángshān, spend the night on the mountain and traipse through the delightful Huīzhōu villages nearby. ✈ 2 hrs to Macau

**Macau** (p180) Admire the colonial remains of the former Portuguese enclave of Macau and plan a day trip to Hong Kong. ✈ 2¾ hrs to Chéngdū

Plan Your Trip
# Two-Week Itinerary

## To the Silk Road

This epic journey takes you on a dramatic voyage from the historic Chinese capital to the far northwest, stopping off in the Tibetan borderlands of Xiàhé before continuing to Shànghǎi via the ancient capital city of Xī'ān.

**Dūnhuáng** (p264) Travel out of town to the incredible Mògāo Grottoes and the Singing Sand Dunes and spend the night in Dūnhuáng.
🚌 4½ hrs to Jiāyùguān

**Jiāyùguān** (p262) Spend a day or two in Jiāyùguān to visit its splendid desert fort at the western end of the Great Wall. 🚌 4 hrs to Lánzhōu

**Lánzhōu** (p270) Lánzhōu has little of interest, but it's the launchpad for a four-hour bus trip to Labrang Monastery in Xiàhé, where you can spend the night. ✈ 1 hr to Xī'ān or 🚌 9 hrs to Xī'ān

**Běijīng** (p34) Spend three days exploring the Forbidden City, the Temple of Heaven and the Great Wall.
✈ 4 hrs to Dūnhuáng

**Xī'ān** (p94) Come face to face with the Terracotta Warriors before returning to town to walk around its magnificent city wall and dine in the Muslim Quarter. 🚆 6 hrs to Shànghǎi

**Shànghǎi** (p110) Shànghǎi's most grandiose sight is the Bund, but the Shànghǎi Museum is not to be missed, while the French Concession is the place for boutique shopping and charming bars.

FROM LEFT: VIEW STOCK / GETTY IMAGES ©; ONNES / SHUTTERSTOCK ©

# Plan Your Trip
# Family Travel

## The Low-Down

China is full of promise as a family-travel destination, but this potential remains largely unrealised. As a parent, an adventurous spirit is crucial, and you should treat any journey to China as a (potentially steep) learning curve.

## Travel Basics

Foreign children will feel more at home in the large cities of Hong Kong, Macau, Běijīng and Shànghǎi, where there is a service industry (hotels, restaurants and sights) attuned to the needs of parents, but in smaller towns and rural areas, little provision is made.

Travelling long distances with children in China has its own challenges. Hiring a car is problematic and remains an unrealistic way of travelling, partly because the car-hire network remains undeveloped, you cannot drive everywhere and China is simply too big. Trains (especially sleepers) are great fun, but can get crowded; on long-distance trains, food options are limited. Long-distance buses are also crowded and seatbelts are often not provided. Many taxis in provincial towns only have seatbelts in the front.

Food is another challenge. While larger towns will have Western restaurants, outside of fast food, smaller towns may only serve local food (fine for adults, not necessarily for young kids).

## Sightseeing

Teenagers may not share your enthusiasm for China's ancient sights, but they may fall for the great scenic outdoors.

There are some fantastic museums – especially in the large cities – and Shànghǎi, Běijīng, Hong Kong and other big towns have plenty of amusements to keep children occupied, from theme parks to high-altitude observation decks,

ice-skating rinks, aquariums, acrobatics shows, zoos and much more.

## Safety

The Chinese adore children and pay them a lot of attention; expect your children to receive even more attention for their colouring, especially if they are blond-haired or blue-eyed. China is generally very safe for non-Chinese children. Your biggest concerns may be what your children eat and keeping an eye on them when they cross the road.

## Need to Know

**Air travel** On domestic flights, infants under the age of two fly for 10% of the full airfare, while children between the ages of two and 11 pay half the full price.

**Infant supplies** Baby food, nappies and milk powder are widely available in supermarkets; few restaurants provide high chairs.

### Best Destinations for Kids

Star Ferry (p164)
Peak Tram (p162)
Yángshuò (p190)
Acrobatics show, Shànghǎi Centre Theatre (p132)

**Museums and sights** Many places have reduced admission prices for children under 1.1m or 1.3m in height.

**Train travel** Children shorter than 1.4m can get a hard sleeper for 75% of the full price or a half-price hard seat. Children shorter than 1.1m ride for free, but you have to hold them the entire journey.

From left: Star Ferry (p164), Hong Kong; Acrobats, Shànghǎi Centre Theatre (p132)

Běihǎi Park (p58)

National Museum
of China (p47)

*Kūnmíng Lake*

*West Lake*

**Běihǎi Park & Xīchéng North**
Beijingers' playground. With la and parks it's a spot to stroll b at night, carou crowded bars restaurants.

**Summer Palace & Hǎidiàn**
Enjoy a taste of the imperial high-life in this retreat of the emperors.

*Yùyuāntán*

**Forbidden City & Dōngchéng Central**
Prime district for culture vultures, shoppers and history buffs. Home to the extraordinary Forbidden City.

Beijing West Train Station

TIĀN SQ

**Dashilar & Xīchéng South**
Peking's former red-light district is now home to *hútòng*, many of the capital's Huí community and sites of worship.

0  5 km
0  3 miles

**Drum Tower & Dōngchéng North**
Historic, *hútòng*-rich neighbourhoods, with plenty of eating, drinking and entertainment options.

-
kes
great
day;
se the
nd

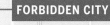

**Sānlǐtún & Cháoyáng**
Indulge your inner hedonist and shop at some of the best markets, eat at a staggering array of restaurants and party the night away.

*Béihǎi Lake*

*Zhōnghǎi Lake*

**FORBIDDEN CITY**

*Nánhǎi Lake*

ĀNMÉN
UARE

🚇 Beijing Train Station

*Tonghui River*

**TEMPLE OF HEAVEN PARK**

🚇 Beijing South Train Station

Dōngchéng, Drum Tower & Běihǎi Park Map (p56)
Forbidden City Map (p62)
Summer palace Map (p64)

Forbidden City
(p38)

Tiān'ānmén
Square (p46)

# BĚIJĪNG

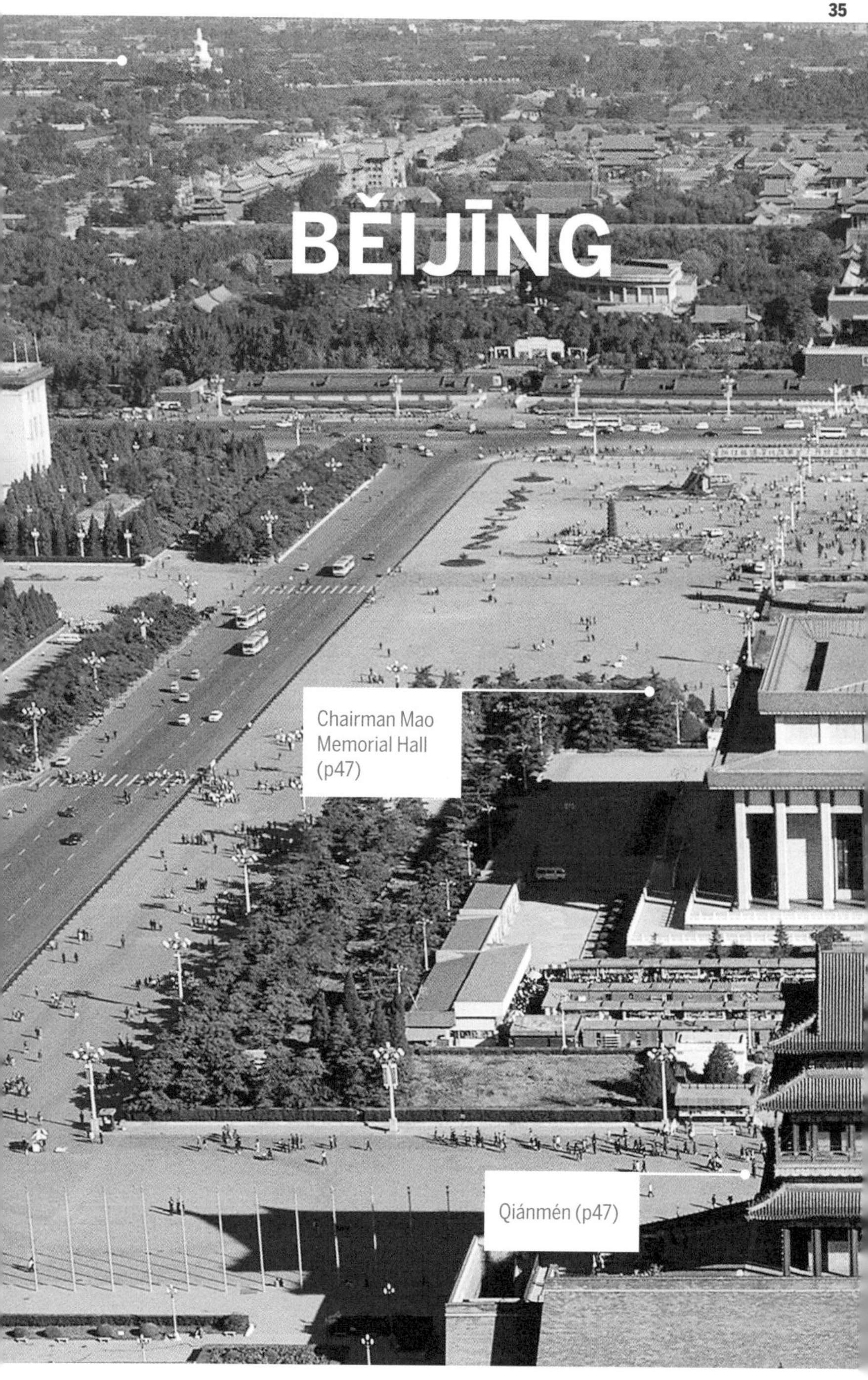

Chairman Mao
Memorial Hall
(p47)

Qiánmén (p47)

# Běijīng at a Glance...

*With six Unesco World Heritage Sites, few places on Earth can match the extraordinary historical panorama on display in Běijīng. At its heart is the magnificent Forbidden City, a royal palace on a scale like no other. Běijīng is also home to sublime temples that aspire to cosmological perfection, while the city centre is criss-crossed by enchanting hútòng: ancient alleyways that still teem with life today. And, to cap it all, the awe-inspiring Great Wall snakes its way across the hills north of town.*

### Two Days in Běijīng

Get up early for **Temple of Heaven Park** (p48), followed by a walk around **Tiān'ānmén Sq** (p46), with some roast duck lunch or dinner at **Jīngzūn Peking Duck** (p60). On day two, explore the **Forbidden City** (p38) in the morning before joining our *hútòng* **walk** (p54); call it a day with a beer at **Great Leap Brewing** (p61) or a cocktail at **Capital Spirits** (p61), after dining at **Crescent Moon Muslim Restaurant** (p59).

### Four Days in Běijīng

Visit the **Lama Temple** (p58) for flavours of Tibetan Buddhism before heading to the huge **Summer Palace** (p50), then charge yourself with caffeine at **Oasis Cafe** (p63). Hunt for goodies at **Pānjiāyuán Market** (p59) and go shopping along **Wangfujing Dajie** (p59). Discover gastronomic fare at **Georg** (p60) and catch an evening performance at the **National Centre for the Performing Arts** (p63).

Drummers in a Běijīng temple

### Arriving in Běijīng

**Běijīng Capital International Airport**
The Airport Express (¥25, 30 minutes, 6.30am to 11pm) links up with the subway system (Lines 2 and 10). Only use the official taxi rank to catch a cab (¥90 to ¥120).

**Běijīng train station** Subway Line 2.

**Běijīng West train station** Subway Line 9.

**Běijīng South train station** Subway Line 4.

### Sleeping

Hotel rooms are easy to find, although it's worth booking ahead during public holidays. It's always advisable to prebook courtyard hotels, as they often have only four or five rooms in total. You can book rooms directly through hotel websites, or over the phone.

For more information, see Where to Stay on p67.

# Forbidden City

*The astonishing Forbidden City (known as Gù Gōng; 故宫; ancient palace) is the largest palace complex in the world and a must-see sight for most visitors to Běijīng.*

Located at the geographical centre of China's capital, the palace occupies a primary position in the Chinese psyche.

## Layout

Ringed by a picturesque 52m-wide moat that freezes over in winter, the rectangular palace is laid out roughly symmetrically on a north–south axis, bisected by a line of grand gates and ceremonial halls that straddle the very axis that cleaves Běijīng in two. The palace is so unspeakably big (more than 1 million sq metres, with 800 buildings and 9000 rooms) that restoration is literally a never-ending work in progress, and despite the attentions of restorers, some of the hall rooftops still sprout tufts of grass.

## Great For...

☑ **Don't Miss**

The exquisite time pieces on display in the Clock Exhibition Hall.

Hall of Preserving Harmony (p40)

### ❶ Need to Know

紫禁城; Zǐjìn Chéng; Map p62; ☎010 8500 7114; www.dpm.org.cn; Nov-Mar ¥40, Apr-Oct ¥60, audio tour ¥40; ⏰8.30am-5pm Apr-Oct, to 4.30pm Nov-Mar, last entry 1hr prior to closing, closed Mon; Ⓢ Line 1 to Tian'anmen West or Tian'anmen East

### ✖ Take a Break

Exiting from the north gate, take a right and head towards **Oasis Cafe** (p63) for fantastic coffees.

### ★ Top Tip

In 2015 the palace introduced a cap of 80,000 visitors per day, so aim to get here early during peak season.

## Entering the Complex

After passing through **Meridian Gate** (午门; Wǔ Mén) – the only one of the four gateways now used as an entrance to the Forbidden City – you enter an enormous courtyard. Up top is the **Meridian Gate Gallery**, which hosts temporary cultural exhibitions of traditional Chinese arts and exhibitions from abroad.

From here, you cross the **Golden Stream** (金水; Jīn Shuǐ) – shaped to resemble a Tartar bow and spanned by five marble bridges – on your way to the magnificent **Gate of Supreme Harmony** (太和门; Tàihé Mén). This courtyard could hold an imperial audience of 100,000 people. Today it holds a tourist information desk where you can pick up an audio guide (¥40) and a handy free map.

## Three Great Halls

Raised on a three-tier marble terrace with balustrades are the **Three Great Halls** (三大殿; Sān Dàdiàn), the heart of the Forbidden City. The recently restored **Hall of Supreme Harmony** (太和殿; Tàihé Diàn) is the most important and largest structure in the Forbidden City. Built in the 15th century and restored in the 17th century, it was used for ceremonial occasions, such as the emperor's birthday, coronations and the nomination of military leaders. Inside the Hall of Supreme Harmony is a richly decorated **Dragon Throne** (龙椅; Lóngyǐ), from which the emperor would preside over trembling officials. The entire court had to touch the floor nine times with their foreheads (the custom known as kowtowing) in the emperor's presence.

Behind the Hall of Supreme Harmony is the **Hall of Central Harmony** (中和殿; Zhōnghé Diàn), which was used as the emperor's transit lounge. Here he would make last-minute preparations, rehearse speeches and receive ministers. On display are two Qing dynasty sedan chairs, the emperor's mode of transport around the Forbidden City.

The third of the Great Halls is the **Hall of Preserving Harmony** (保和殿; Bǎohé Diàn), used for banquets and later for imperial examinations. The hall has no support pillars, and to its rear is a 250-tonne marble imperial carriageway carved with dragons and clouds, which was transported into Běijīng on an ice path. The outer housing surrounding the Three Great Halls was used for storing gold, silver, silks, carpets and other treasures.

A string of side halls on the eastern and western flanks of the Three Great Halls

usually, but not always, houses a series of excellent exhibitions.

## Other Central Halls

The basic configuration of the Three Great Halls is echoed by the next group of buildings, which is accessed through the **Gate of Heavenly Purity**. Smaller in scale, these buildings were more important in terms of real power, which in China traditionally lies at the back door or, in this case, the back gate.

The first structure is the **Palace of Heavenly Purity** (乾清宫; Qiánqīng Gōng), a residence of Ming and early Qing emperors, and later an audience hall for receiving foreign envoys and high officials.

Immediately behind it is the **Hall of Union** (交泰殿; Jiāotài Diàn), which con-

tains a clepsydra – a water clock made in 1745 with five bronze vessels and a calibrated scale. There's also a mechanical clock built in 1797 and a collection of imperial jade seals on display. The **Palace of Earthly Tranquillity** (坤宁宫; Kūnníng Gōng) was the imperial couple's bridal chamber and the centre of operations for the palace harem.

## Western & Eastern Palaces

A dozen smaller palace courtyards lie to the west and east of the three lesser central halls. It was in these smaller courtyard buildings that most of the emperors actually lived and many of the buildings, particularly those to the west, are decked out in imperial furniture.

Of the six eastern palaces, the four that are open to the public have exhibitions displaying cultural relics from ceramics and temple musical instruments to ceremonial bronze vessels. The most unusual is the **Palace of Prolonging Happiness** (延禧宫; Yánxǐ Gōng), which features an unfinished 20th-century Western-style building with an intricately carved, white marble facade and iron-cast roof.

Many of the six western palaces were closed for renovation at the time of writing. The **Palace of Gathered Elegance** (储秀宫; Chǔxiù Gōng) contains some interesting photos of the last emperor, Puyi, who lived here as a child ruler at the turn of the 20th century.

## Clock Exhibition Hall

The **Clock Exhibition Hall** (钟表馆; Zhōngbiǎo Guǎn; admission ¥10; ☉8.30am-4pm summer, to 3.30pm winter) is one of the unmissable highlights of the Forbidden City. Located in the **Hall for Ancestral Worship** (奉先殿; Fèngxiān Diàn), the exhibition contains an astonishing array of elaborate timepieces, many of which were gifts to the Qing emperors from overseas. Many of the 18th-century examples are crafted by James Cox or Joseph Williamson (both of London) and imported through Guǎngdōng from England; others are from Switzerland, America and Japan. Exquisitely wrought, fashioned with magnificently designed elephants and other creatures, they all display astonishing artfulness and attention to detail.

Time your arrival for 11am or 2pm to see the clock performance in which choice timepieces strike the hour and give a display to wide-eyed children and adults.

## Treasure Gallery

In the northeastern corner of the complex is a mini Forbidden City known as the

> ★ **Top Tip**
>
> Before you pass through the Gate of Supreme Harmony, veer to the east of the huge courtyard to visit the exceptional Ceramics Gallery housed inside the Hall of Literary Brilliance.

**Treasure Gallery** (珍宝馆; Zhēn Bǎo Guǎn; admission ¥10) – also called the **Complete Palace of Peace and Longevity** (宁寿全宫; Níng Shǒu Quán Gōng). During the Ming dynasty, the Empress Dowager and the imperial concubines lived here. Today it comprises a number of atmospheric halls, pavilions, gardens and courtyard buildings that hold a collection of fine museums. Among the many exhibitions, highlights include the beautiful glazed **Nine Dragon Screen** (九龙壁; Jiǔlóng Bì), one of only three of its type left in China, and the **Belvedere of Pleasant Sounds** (畅音阁; Chàngyīn Gé), a three-storey wooden opera house, which was the palace's largest theatre. Across is the **Hall for Viewing Opera** where the emperor and empress watched the show, and today houses a collection of opera artefacts and clothing.

Enter the complex from the south – not far from the Clock Exhibition Hall; afterwards you'll be popped out at the northern end of the Forbidden City.

## Imperial Garden

At the northern end of the Forbidden City is the **Imperial Garden** (御花园; Yù Huāyuán), a classical Chinese garden with 7000 sq metres of fine landscaping, including rockeries, walkways, pavilions and ancient, carbuncular cypresses. At its centre is the double-eaved **Hall of Imperial Peace** (Qin'an dian). Before you reach the **Gate of Divine Prowess** (神武门; Shénwǔ Mén), note the pair of **bronze elephants** whose front knees bend in an anatomically impossible fashion, just before you reach **Shùnzhēn Gate** (顺贞门; Shùnzhēn Mén). They signify the power of the emperor; even elephants kowtow before him!

## A Centre for the Arts & Sciences

Following the Ming dynasty, Běijīng became the most important religious centre in Asia, graced by more than 2000 temples and shrines. Daoists and Buddhists vied for the favour of the emperor who, as a divine being, was automatically the patron of every approved religious institution in the empire. And as the residence of the emperor, Běijīng was regarded by the Chinese as the centre of the universe.

The best poets and painters also flocked here to seek court patronage. The Forbidden City required the finest porcelain, furniture and silverware, and its workshops grew in skill and design. Literature, drama, music, medicine, map-making, astrology and astronomy flourished, too, so the imperial city became a centre for arts and sciences.

## Palace Quirks

From the back of the Hall of Preserving Harmony slopes the largest of the city's

Bronze turtle statue

**marble imperial carriageways**. This beautifully carved, 250-ton block of marble, transported to the palace in winter on sheets of ice, was one of a few that acted as VIP access ramps for the raised hallways. Sedan-chair bearers would walk up the steps on each side, while the emperor was carried over a celestial scene of marble-carved clouds and dragons.

**Bronze turtles**, like the large one in front of the Hall of Supreme Harmony, symbolise longevity and stability. It has a removable lid, and on special occasions incense was lit inside it so that smoke billowed from its mouth.

**Sundials** also dot the complex. You can find one to the east of the Hall of Supreme Harmony. To the west of the hall, on a raised terrace, is a small pavilion with a bronze grain measure; both objects are symbolic of imperial justice.

Also look out for the round, football-sized **tether stones** dotted around the weed-covered corners of the large central courtyards. It is assumed that these were used for tethering horses to.

★ **Did You Know?**

'Forbidden City' is an approximation of the Chinese 紫禁城 (Zǐjìn Chéng), a moniker that references the colour purple and the cosmically significant North Star, 'celestial seat' of the emperor.

FOTOKON / SHUTTERSTOCK ©

# Forbidden City

## WALKING TOUR

After entering through the imperious Meridian Gate, resist the temptation to dive straight into the star attractions and veer right for a peek at the excellent **Ceramics Gallery ❶** housed inside the creaking Hall of Literary Glory.

Walk back to the central complex and head through the magnificent Gate of Supreme Harmony towards the Three Great Halls: first, the largest – the **Hall of Supreme Harmony ❷**, followed by the **Hall of Middle Harmony ❸** and the **Hall of Preserving Harmony ❹**, behind which slopes the enormous Marble Imperial Carriageway.

Turn right here to visit the fascinating **Clock Exhibition Hall ❺** before entering the **Complete Palace of Peace & Longevity ❻**, a mini Forbidden City constructed along the eastern axis of the main complex. It includes the beautiful **Nine Dragon Screen ❼** and, to the north, a series of halls, housing some excellent exhibitions and known collectively as The Treasure Gallery. Don't miss the **Pavilion of Cheerful Melodies ❽**, a wonderful three-storey opera house.

Work your way to the far north of this section, then head west to the **Imperial Garden ❾**, with its ancient cypress trees and pretty pavilions, before exiting via the garden's West Gate (behind the Thousand Year Pavilion) to explore the **Western Palaces ❿**, an absorbing collection of courtyard homes where many of the emperors lived during their reign.

Exit this section at its southwest corner before turning back on yourself to walk north through the Gate of Heavenly Purity to see the three final Central Halls – the **Palace of Heavenly Purity ⓫**, the **Hall of Union ⓬** and the **Palace of Earthly Tranquility ⓭** – before leaving via the North Gate.

### Water Vats

More than 300 copper and brass water vats dot the palace complex. They were used for fighting fires and in winter were prevented from freezing over by using thick quilts.

### ENTRANCE/EXIT

You must enter through the south gate (Meridian Gate), but you can exit via south, north or east.

← ticket offices →

### Guardian Lions

Pairs of lions guard important buildings. The male has a paw placed on a globe (representing the emperor's power over the world). The female has her paw on a baby lion (representing the emperor's fertility).

## Kneeling Elephants
At the northern entrance of the Imperial Garden are two bronze elephants kneeling in an anatomically impossible fashion, which symbolise the power of the emperor; even elephants kowtowed before him.

## Nine Dragon Screen
One of only three of its type left in China, this beautiful glazed dragon screen served to protect the Hall of Imperial Supremacy from evil spirits.

Forbidden City North Gate (exit only)

Thousand Year Pavilion

Forbidden City North Gate (exit only)

10

9

13

12

11

8

Marble Imperial Carriageway

Gate of Heavenly Purity

5

4

6

3

7

The Treasure Gallery

2

NORTH →

Gate of Supreme Harmony

1

Meridian Gate

Forbidden City East Gate (exit only)

## OFF-LIMITS
Only part of the Forbidden City is open to the public. The shaded areas you see here are off-limits.

## Opera House
The largest of the Forbidden City's opera stages; look out for the trap doors, which allowed supernatural characters to make dramatic entrances and exits during performances.

## Roof Guardians
The imperial dragon is at the tail of the procession, which is led by a figure riding a phoenix followed by a number of mythical beasts. The more beasts, the more important the building.

## Dragon-Head Spouts
More than a thousand dragon-head spouts encircle the raised marble platforms at the centre of the Forbidden City. They were – and still are – part of the drainage system.

# Tiān'ānmén Square

*Flanked by stern 1950s Soviet-style buildings and ringed by white perimeter fences, the world's largest public square (440,000 sq metres) is an immense flatland of paving stones at the heart of Běijīng.*

## Great For...

☑ **Don't Miss**

Qiánmén is one of the surviving gates of Běijīng, an imposing chunk of history in an otherwise more modern setting.

In the square, one stands at the symbolic centre of the Chinese universe. The rectangular arrangement, flanked by halls to both east and west, to some extent echoes the layout of the Forbidden City: the square employs a conventional plan that pays obeisance to traditional Chinese culture, but many of its ornaments and buildings are Soviet-inspired.

## The Gate of Heavenly Peace

Characterised by a giant portrait of Mao Zedong, and guarded by two pairs of Ming stone lions, the double-eaved Gate of Heavenly Peace, north of (and giving its name to) Tiān'ānmén Sq, is a potent national symbol. Built in the 15th century and restored in the 17th century, the gate was formerly the largest of the four gates

Statue of revolutionary soldiers and workers

FOTOKON / GETTY IMAGES ©

Xichang'an Jie

Tian'anmen West
天安门西

Tian'anmen East
天安门东

**Tiān'ānmén Square**

Qianmen
前门

Qianmen Xidajie
前门西大街

Qianmen Dongdajie

## ❶ Need to Know

天安门广场; Tiān'ānmén Guǎngchǎng; Map p62; S Line 1 to Tian'anmen West, Tian'anmen East, or Line 2 to Qianmen; FREE

## ✕ Take a Break

'Duck' into **Quánjùdé Roast Duck** (全聚德烤鸭店; Quánjùdé Kǎoyādiàn; east side Tiān'ānmén Sq; 天安门广场东边; mains from ¥35; ☉11am-3pm & 5-8pm) for a plate of the city's signature meal.

## ★ Top Tip

Get up early and catch the flag-raising ceremony at sunrise, performed by a troop of PLA soldiers.

of the Imperial City Wall. It was from here that Mao proclaimed the People's Republic of China on 1 October 1949.

## Qiánmén

Aka Front Gate, Qiánmén actually consists of two gates. The northernmost of the two gates is the 40m-high **Zhèngyáng Gate** (正阳门城楼; Zhèngyáng Mén Chénglóu), which dates from the Ming dynasty and was the largest of the nine gates of the Inner City Wall separating the inner, or Tartar (Manchu), city from the outer, or Chinese, city.

## Chairman Mao Memorial Hall

No doubt one of Běijīng's more surreal spectacles is the sight of Mao Zedong's embalmed corpse on public display within his mausoleum. The Soviet-inspired me-

morial hall was constructed soon after Mao died in September 1976, and is a prominent landmark in the middle of Tiān'ānmén Sq.

North of the mausoleum, the **Monument to the People's Heroes** (人民英雄纪念碑; Rénmín Yīngxióng Jìniànbēi) was completed in 1958. The 37.9m-high obelisk, made of Qīngdǎo granite, bears carvings of key patriotic and revolutionary events, as well as calligraphy from communist bigwigs Mao Zedong and Zhou Enlai.

## National Museum of China

Běijīng's premier **museum** (中国国际博物馆; Zhōngguó Guójì Bówùguǎn; en.chnmuseum. cn; Guangchangdongce Lu; 天安门, 广场东侧路; audio guide ¥30; ☉9am-5pm Tue-Sun, last entry 4pm) FREE is housed in an immense 1950s communist-style building on the eastern side of the square, and is well worth visiting. The Ancient China exhibition on the basement floor is outstanding.

ZHAO JIAN KANG / SHUTTERSTOCK ©

# Temple of Heaven Park

*Extraordinary to contemplate, the collection of halls and altars set within the delightful 276-hectare Temple of Heaven Park is the most perfect example of Ming architectural design.*

### Great For...

### ☑ Don't Miss

The Hall of Prayer for Good Harvests, the defining structure at the Temple of Heaven.

Each year, the Chinese emperors – the sons of heaven – came to the temple (more accurately an altar) to seek divine clearance and good harvests and to atone for the sins of their people in an esoteric ceremony of prayers and ritual sacrifices.

## Hall of Prayer for Good Harvests

The crowning structure of the Temple of Heaven Park is the Hall of Prayer for Good Harvests, magnificently mounted on a three-tiered marble terrace and capped with a triple-eaved umbrella roof of purplish-blue tiles. Built in 1420, it was burnt to cinders in 1889 and heads rolled in apportioning blame (although lightning was the most likely cause). A faithful reproduction based on Ming architectural methods was erected the following year; the builders chose Oregon fir for the support pillars.

Hall of Prayer for Good Harvests

Temple of Heaven Park
天坛公园

Tiantan Lu 天坛路

Tiantandongmen
天坛东门

Tiyuguan Lu

Tiantan Donglu

### ❶ Need to Know

天坛公园; Tiāntán Gōngyuán; ☑010 6702 9917; Tiantan Donglu; 天坛东路; park/through ticket Apr-Oct ¥15/35, Nov-Mar ¥10/30, audio tour ¥40 (deposit ¥50); ⊙park 6.30am-10pm, sights 8am-5.30pm Apr-Oct, park 6.30am-8pm, sights 8am-5pm Nov-Mar; Ⓢ Line 5 to Tiantandongmen, Exit A

### ✕ Take a Break

The delicious *shāomài* (dumplings) at **Dūyīchù** (都一处; ☑010 6702 1555; 38 Qianmen Dajie; 前门大街38号; dumplings ¥42-90; ⊙7.30am-9.30pm; Ⓢ Qianmen) are just a short subway ride away.

### ★ Top Tip

Get here as early as you can, preferably when the sights open at 8am.

You can't enter inside; you'll have to settle with viewing it through the open door.

## The Imperial Vault of Heaven

The octagonal Imperial Vault of Heaven was built at the same time as the Circular Mound Altar, and is structured along the same lines as the older Hall of Prayer for Good Harvests. The vault once contained spirit tablets used in the winter solstice ceremony.

## Echo Wall

Just north of the Round Altar, surrounding the Imperial Vault of Heaven, is Echo Wall, 65m in diameter. Its form has unusual acoustic properties, enabling a whisper to travel clearly from one end to the other (unless a tour group or a loud mouth with a mobile phone gets in the way).

## Round Altar

Constructed in 1530 and rebuilt in 1740, the 5m-high Round Altar once looked very different: its first incarnation was in deep-blue glazed stone before being redone in light green.

The current white marble structure is arrayed in three tiers; its geometry revolves around the imperial number nine. Odd numbers were considered heavenly, and nine is the largest single-digit odd number. The top tier, thought to symbolise heaven, contains nine rings of stones.

Each ring has multiples of nine stones, so that the ninth ring has 81 stones. The middle tier (earth) has the 10th to 18th rings. The bottom tier (humanity) has the 19th to 27th rings. The numbers of stairs and balustrades are also multiples of nine.

# Summer Palace

*This former playground for the imperial court fleeing the insufferable summer torpor of the old Imperial City is a marvel of landscaping: a wonderful, over-the-top mix of temples, gardens, pavilions, lakes and bridges.*

---

### Great For...

☑ **Don't Miss**

Walking around Kūnmíng Lake as the sun sets.

### Hall of Benevolence & Longevity

The main building at ground level, this **hall** (仁寿殿; Rénshòu Diàn) sits by the east gate and houses a hardwood throne. Look for the bronze animals that decorate the courtyard in front, including the mythical *qílín* (a hybrid animal that appeared on Earth only at times of harmony).

### The Long Corridor

Awesome in conception and execution, the **Long Corridor** (长廊; Cháng Láng) is absolutely unmissable. Open at the sides but covered with a roof to shield the emperors from the elements, and with four pavilions along the way, it stretches for more than 700m towards the foot of Longevity Hill. Its beams, the pavilion walls and some of the ceiling are decorated with 14,000 intricate paintings depicting scenes from Chinese

Long Corridor

HUNG_CHUNG_CHIH / SHUTTERSTOCK ©

## ❶ Need to Know

颐和园; Yíhé Yuán; Map p64; 19 Xinjian Gong-men; 新建宫门19号; Apr-Oct ¥30, through ticket ¥60, Nov-Mar ¥20, through ticket ¥50, audio guide ¥40; ⏰7am-7pm, sights 8am-5pm summer, 8.30am-4.30pm winter; Ⓢ Xiyuan or Beigongmen)

## ✕ Take a Break

Try afternoon tea in the suitably impe-rial surroundings of **Aman at Summer Palace** (颐和安缦; Yíhé Ānmàn; ☏010 5987 9999; www.amanresorts.com; 1 Gongmen Qianjie; 宫门前街 1号).

## ★ Top Tip

Visit in winter and get to see the splendid spectacle of a frozen Kūnmíng Lake.

history and myths, as well as classic literary texts. Your neck will ache from all that star-ing upwards, but the pain is worth it.

## Kūnmíng Lake

Three-quarters of the parkland in the palace is water, made up of Kūnmíng Lake (Kūnmíng Hú). Check out the extravagant **Marble Boat** (清晏舫; Qīngyuàn Chuán) moored on the northwestern shore. First built in 1755, it was restored in 1893 on the orders of Empress Cixi, using money meant to go towards building ships for the Chinese Navy. Boats ply the lake (¥15) be-tween April and October, running from the northern shore to South Lake Island, home to the **Dragon King Temple** (龙王庙; Lóng-wáng Miào), where royalty came to pray to the Dragon King's fearsome statue for rain in times of drought. You can also hire your

own pedalo (four/six people ¥80/100 per hour, ¥300 deposit) or electric-powered boat (¥120 per hour, ¥400 deposit) to sail around at your own pace.

## Longevity Hill

Rearing up by the side of Kūnmíng Lake and at the far end of the Long Corridor, the slopes of this 60m-high hill are covered in temples and pavilions, all arranged on a north–south axis. The most prominent and important are the **Buddhist Fragrance Pavilion** (佛香阁; Fóxiāng Gé) and the **Cloud Dispelling Hall** (排云殿; Páiyún Diàn), which are connected by corridors. Awaiting you at the peak of the hill is the **Buddhist Temple of the Sea of Wisdom** (智慧海; Zhìhuì Hǎi), featuring glazed tiles – many sadly damaged – depicting Buddha. On a clear day there are splendid views of Běijīng from here.

BEIBAOKE / SHUTTERSTOCK ©

# Ming Tombs

*The Unesco-protected Ming Tombs (十三陵; Shísān Líng) is the final resting place for 13 of the 16 Ming dynasty emperors and makes for a fascinating half-day trip from Běijīng.*

---

**Great For...**

☑ **Don't Miss**

Exploring Cháng Líng, the most iconic of the Ming Tombs.

---

The Ming Tombs follow a standard imperial layout. In each tomb the plan consists of a main gate, leading to the first of a series of courtyards and the main hall.

## Cháng Líng

The resting place of the first of the 13 emperors to be buried at the Ming Tombs, Cháng Líng (长陵) contains the body of Emperor Yongle (1402–24), his wife and 16 concubines. It's the largest, most impressive and most important of the tombs. Like all the tombs, it follows a standard imperial layout, a main gate (棱恩门; lín'ēn mén) leading to the first of a series of courtyards and the main hall (棱恩殿; líng'ēn diàn).

## Dìng Líng

The resting place of Emperor Wanli (1572–1620) and his wife and concubines,

Statue on the Spirit Way

KHIRMAN VLADIMIR / SHUTTERSTOCK ©

Nánkǒu · · ⊙ *Ming Tombs*
Chāngpíng

Shahe ·

Qinghe ·

✪ Běijīng   · Tōngzhōu

## ❶ Need to Know

十三陵; Shísān Líng; 📞010 6076 1643;
Changchi Lu, Chāngpíng; 昌平区昌赤路; per
site ¥20-60, through ticket ¥100 Nov-Mar,
¥135 Apr-Oct; ⊗8am-5.30pm; 🚍872, ⑤Ming
Tombs

## ✕ Take a Break

Both Dìng Líng and Cháng Líng have a
restaurant close to their ticket offices.

### ★ Top Tip

There are no hotels or guesthouses in
Cháng Líng, Dìng Líng or Zhāo Líng, so
sleep in Běijīng.

---

Dìng Líng (定陵) is at first sight less impressive than Cháng Líng because many of the
halls and gateways have been destroyed.
Many of the priceless artefacts were ruined
after being left in a huge, unsealed storage
room that leaked water. The treasures that
were left – including the bodies of Emperor
Wanli and his entourage – were looted and
burned by Red Guards during the Cultural
Revolution.

## Spirit Way

The road leading to the Ming Tombs is
a 7km stretch called **Spirit Way** (神道;
Shéndào). Commencing from the south
with a triumphal triple archway, known as
the **Great Palace Gate** (大宫门; Dàgōng
Mén), the path passes through **Stele Pavil-**
**ion** (碑亭; Bēi Tíng), which contains a giant
*bìxì* (mythical tortoise-like dragon) bearing
the largest stele in China. A guard of 12 sets
of giant stone animals and officials ensues.

## Getting there

The Ming Tombs are now on the subway,
although the station is almost at the end
of the Chángpíng Line – a long haul from
central Běijīng – and is inconveniently
located 3km from the entrance to the Spirit
Way, requiring you to either take a taxi
(¥13) there, or a bus (¥2) and then walk
another 1km.

A more direct way to get there is on bus
872 (¥9, one hour, 7.10am to 7.10pm) from
the north side of Déshèngmén Gateway
(德胜门; Déshèngmén; Map p56) in Běijīng.

# Historic Hútòng Walking Tour

Běijīng's *hútòng* are the heart and soul of the city and this walk conveys you through some of their most historic examples, while drawing you away from the crowds.

**Start** Nanluoguxiang subway station
**Distance** 2km
**Duration** one hour

**7** Follow this wonderfully winding alley to the back of the Bell Tower, then walk around the tower to the recently redeveloped **Drum & Bell Sq**.

Doufuchi Hutong 豆腐池胡同

Jiugulou Dajie

Caochang Hutong 草厂胡同

**6**

**7** END

Gulou Xidajie
鼓楼西大街

**5**

Di'anmen Waidajie
地安门外大街

Shichahai S
什刹海

Fangzhuanchang Hutong
方砖厂胡同

Qiánhǎi Lake

**5** Turn left at Gulou Dongdajie (鼓楼东大街). Straight ahead is the imperious red-painted **Drum Tower** (p59).

**3** Cross **Nanluogu Xiang** (p59) into **Mao'er Hutong** (帽儿胡同) where you can admire the entrance ways of this historic *hútòng*. No 37 is the former home of Wan Rong, who married China's last emperor, Puyi.

**1** Start at No 77 Chaodou Hutong (炒豆胡同): these courtyards were the former **mansion of Seng Gelinqin**, a Qing dynasty general.

Di'anmen Xidajie

Di'anmen Dongdajie
地安门东大街

N

0 _____ 400 m
0 _____ 0.2 miles

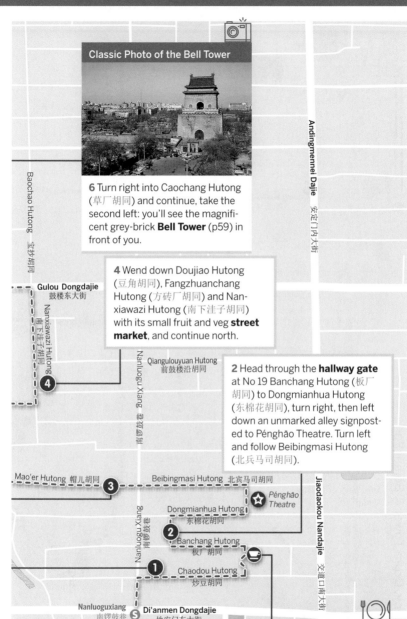

Classic Photo of the Bell Tower

**6** Turn right into Caochang Hutong (草厂胡同) and continue, take the second left: you'll see the magnificent grey-brick **Bell Tower** (p59) in front of you.

**4** Wend down Doujiao Hutong (豆角胡同), Fangzhuanchang Hutong (方砖厂胡同) and Nanxiawazi Hutong (南下洼子胡同) with its small fruit and veg **street market**, and continue north.

**2** Head through the **hallway gate** at No 19 Banchang Hutong (板厂胡同) to Dongmianhua Hutong (东棉花胡同), turn right, then left down an unmarked alley signposted to Pénghāo Theatre. Turn left and follow Beibingmasi Hutong (北兵马司胡同).

Baochao Hutong 宝钞胡同

Andingmennei Dajie 安定门内大街

Gulou Dongdajie 鼓楼东大街

Nanxiawazi Hutong 南下洼子胡同

Qianguoulouyuan Hutong 前鼓楼沿胡同

Nanluogu Xiang 南锣鼓巷

Mao'er Hutong 帽儿胡同

Beibingmasi Hutong 北兵马司胡同

Pénghāo Theatre

Dongmianhua Hutong 东棉花胡同

Nanluogu Xiang 南锣鼓巷

Banchang Hutong 板厂胡同

Chaodou Hutong 炒豆胡同

Jiaodaokou Nandajie 交道口南大街

Nanluoguxiang 南锣鼓巷

Di'anmen Dongdajie 地安门东大街

**START**

**Take a Break...** Stop off for some caffeine at **Coffee Fix** (20 Banchang Hutong; ⏰10am-8pm; coffee from ¥22).

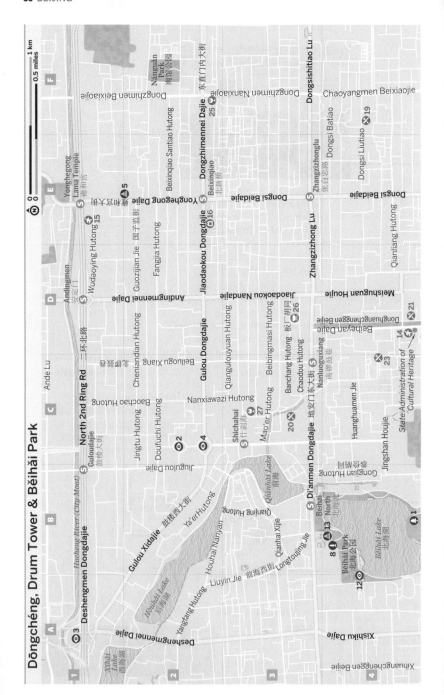

# Dōngchéng, Drum Tower & Běihǎi Park

Dongzhimen Beixiaojie

Nánguān Park 南馆公园

Nánguān
Dongzhimennei Dajie 25

Yonghegong
Lama Temple 雍和宫

Beixinqiao Santiao Hutong

Andingmen 安定门

Dongzhimen Nanxiaojie

Dongsishishitiao Lu

Chaoyangmen Beixiaojie

Beixinqiao 北新桥

Yonghegong Dajie 雍和宫大街 5

Wudaoying Hutong 15

Dongsi Batiao

Dongsi Liutiao 19

Guozijian Jie 国子监街

Fangjia Hutong

Zhangzizhonglu 张自忠路

Dongsi Beidajie

Qianliang Hutong

Jiaodaokou Dongdajie 16

Dongsi Beidajie

Andingmennei Dajie

Ande Lu

North 2nd Ring Rd 三环北路

Jiaodaokou Nandajie

Zhangzizhong Lu

Meishuguan Houjie

Chenianjian Hutong

Gulou Dongdajie

Beibingmasi Hutong

Beiyan Dajie

Beilouqu Xiang 北楼巷

Qianguolouyuan Hutong

Banchang Hutong 板厂胡同 26

Donghuangchenggen Beilie

Guloudajie 鼓楼大街

Baochao Hutong

Jingtu Hutong

Doufuchi Hutong

Nanxiawazi Hutong

Chaodou Hutong

Nanluoguxiang 南锣鼓巷

21

Huanghuamen Jie

State Administration of Cultural Heritage

Shichahai 什刹海

Mao'er Hutong

20

27

23

14

Jingshan Houjie

Gulou Xidajie

跨鼓西大街

Ya'er Hutong

Qianhai Lake 前海

Di'anmen Dongdajie 地安门东大街

Gongjian Hutong

北博胡同

Qianhai Hutong

Qianhai Xijie

2

4

Beihai North 北海北门

8 13

Liuyin Jie 前海西街

Longtoujing Jie

Jingshan Houjie

Deshengmennei Dajie

Houhai Nanyan

1

Deshengmen Dongdajie

Houhǎi Lake 后海湖

Yangtang Hutong

Xīhǎi Lake 西海湖

3

Beihai Park 北海公园

12

Běihǎi Lake 北海湖

Xishiku Dajie

Xihuangchenggen Beilie

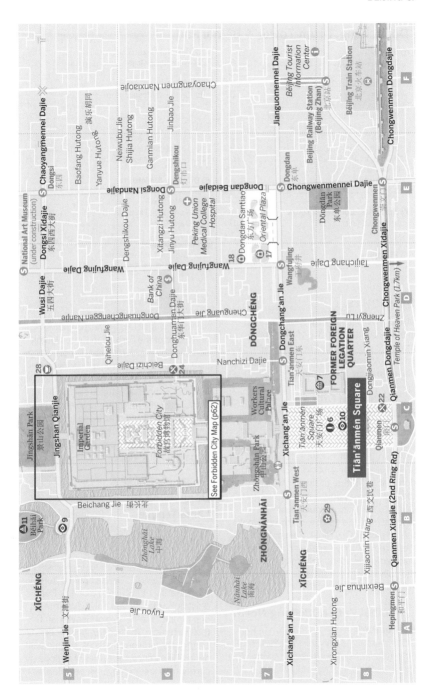

## Dōngchéng, Drum Tower & Běihǎi Park

## ◎ SIGHTS

Many of Běijīng's key sights are located in and around the centre of the capital, making it easy to move between them by subway and allowing you to see multiple places in a day.

### ◎ Forbidden City & Dōngchéng Central

**Jǐngshān Park**                                    Park

(景山公园; Jǐngshān Gōngyuán; Map p62; Jingshan Qianjie; adult/child ¥10/5; ⏰6.30am-9pm; Ⓢ Lines 6, 8 to Nanluoguxiang, exit A) The dominating feature of Jǐngshān – one of the city's finest parks – is one of central Běijīng's few hills; a mound that was created from the earth excavated to make the Forbidden City moat. Called Coal Hill by Westerners during Legation days, Jǐngshān also serves as a feng-shui shield, protecting the palace from evil spirits – or dust storms – from the north.

### ◎ Běihǎi Park & Xīchéng North

**Běihǎi Park**                                    Park

(北海公园; Běihǎi Gōngyuán; Map p56; 🕽010 6403 1102; www.beihaipark.com.cn/en; high/low season ¥10/5, through ticket high/low

season ¥20/15, audio guide ¥60; ⏰6am-9pm, sights to 5pm; Ⓢ Line 6 to Beihai North or Nanluogu Xiang; or Line 4 to Xisi) Běihǎi Park, northwest of the Forbidden City, is largely occupied by the North Sea (Běihǎi), a huge lake fringed by willows that freezes in winter and blooms with lotuses in summer. Old folk dance together outside temple halls and come twilight, young couples cuddle on benches. It's a restful place to stroll around, rent a rowing boat in summer and watch calligraphers practising characters on paving slabs with fat brushes and water.

### ◎ Drum Tower & Dōngchéng North

**Lama Temple**                     Buddhist Temple

(雍和宫; Yōnghé Gōng; Map p56; www.yonghegong.cn; 12 Yonghegong Dajie; 北新桥雍和宫大街12号; admission ¥25, English audio guide ¥50; ⏰9am-4.30pm; Ⓢ Lines 2, 5 to Yonghegong-Lama Temple, exit C) This exceptional temple is a glittering attraction in Běijīng's Buddhist firmament. If you only have time for one temple (the Temple of Heaven isn't really a temple) make it this one, where riveting roofs, fabulous frescoes, magnificent decorative arches, tapestries, eye-popping carpentry, Tibetan prayer wheels, Tantric statues and a superb pair of Chinese lions mingle with dense clouds of incense.

### Bell Tower
Historic Site

(钟楼; Zhōnglóu; Map p56; Gulou Dongdajie; 鼓楼东大街; admission ¥20, both towers through ticket ¥30; ⊙9am-5pm, last tickets 4.40pm; ⑤Line 8 to Shichahai, exit A2) The modest, grey-stone structure of the Bell Tower is arguably more charming than its resplendent other half, the Drum Tower, after which this area of Běijīng is named. It also has the added advantage of being able to view its sister tower from a balcony.

### Drum Tower
Historic Site

(鼓楼; Gǔlóu; Map p56; Gulou Dongdajie; 鼓楼东大街; admission ¥20, both towers through ticket ¥30; ⊙9am-5pm, last tickets 4.40pm; ⑤Line 8 to Shichahai, exit A2) Along with the older-looking Bell Tower, which stands behind it, the magnificent red-painted Drum Tower used to be the city's official timekeeper, with drums and bells beaten and rung to mark the times of the day. Originally built in 1272, the Drum Tower was once the heart of the Mongol capital of Dàdū, as Běijīng was then known. The current structure is a Qing dynasty version of that 1420 tower.

## 🅐 SHOPPING

**Pānjiāyuán Market** Antiques, Market

(潘家园古玩市场; Pānjiāyuán Gǔwán Shìchǎng; West of Panjiayuan Qiao; 潘家园桥西侧; ⊙8.30am-6pm Mon-Fri, 4.30am-6pm Sat & Sun; ⑤Line 10 to Panjiayuan, exit B) Hands down the best place in Běijīng to shop for *yìshù* (arts), *gōngyì* (crafts) and *gǔwán* (antiques). Some stalls open every day, but the market is at its biggest and most lively on weekends, when you can find everything from calligraphy and cigarette ad posters, to Buddha heads, ceramics, Qing dynasty–style furniture and Tibetan carpets.

**Wangfujing Dajie** Shopping Street

(王府井; Map p56; Wangfujing Dajie; ⑤Line 1 to Wangfujing, Exit C2 or B) Prestigious, but these days rather old-fashioned, this part-pedestrianised shopping street not far from Tiān'ānmén Sq, is generally known as Wángfǔjǐng. It boasts a strip of stores selling well-known, midrange brands, and a number of tacky souvenir outlets. At its south end, **Oriental Plaza** (东方广场; Dōngfāng Guǎngchǎng; Map p56; ☎010 8518 6363; 1 Dongchang'an Jie; 东长安街1号; ⊙10am-10.30pm; ⑤Line 1 to Wangfujing, exit B) is a top-quality, modern shopping mall.

### Běijīng's Best Shopping Streets

As well as Wangfujing Dajie, several of Běijīng's streets offer a unique shopping experience:

**Liulichang Xijie** (琉璃厂; Liúlíchǎng; 琉璃厂西街; ⊙9am-6pm; ⑤Hepingmen) Antiques, calligraphy and Chinese-ink and scroll paintings.

**Dashilar** (大栅栏; Dàzhàlan; Dazhalan Jie; ⑤Line 2 to Qianmen, exit B or C) Home to some of the capital's oldest stores.

**Nanluogu Xiang** (南锣鼓巷; ⑤Line 6, 8 to Nanluoguxiang, exit E) Crazy at weekends, but fine for souvenir-hunting.

**Qianmen Dajie** (前门大街; ⑤Qianmen) Increasingly busy, refurbished street with midrange brands and some silk.

**Yandai Xiejie** (烟袋斜街; off Di'anmen Neidajie; 地安门内大街烟袋斜街; ⑤Line 8 to Shichahai, exit A2) Souvenirs and fake antiques, as well as a few more quirky outlets, but fun browsing.

## 🅧 EATING

Běijīng is a magnificent place for culinary adventures. With upwards of 60,000 restaurants here, you can enjoy the finest local dishes, as well as eating your way through every region of China.

### Crescent Moon
### Muslim Restaurant
Xinjiang ¥

(新疆弯弯月亮维吾尔穆斯林餐厅; Xīnjiāng Wānwānyuèliàng Wéiwú'ěr Mùsīlín Cāntīng; Map p56; 16 Dongsi Liutiao Hutong; 东四六条胡同16号, 东四北大街; dishes from ¥18; ⊙11am-11pm; ❄️🛜; ⑤Line 5 to Zhangzizhonglu, exit C) You can find a Chinese Muslim restaurant on

# 798 Art District

Housed inside the cavernous buildings of a former electronics factory, **798** (798 艺术新区; Qī Jiǔ Bā Yìshù Qū; cnr Jiuxianqiao Lu & Jiuxianqiao Beilu; 酒仙桥路; ⊙galleries 10am-6pm, most closed Mon; 🚌403, 909, ⑤Line 14 to Jiangtai, exit A) has become the city's premier art district. You could easily spend half a day or longer here, and cafes dot the streets. Note that the galleries are mostly closed Mondays.

UCCA centre, 798 Art District
OSTILL / SHUTTERSTOCK ©

almost every street in Běijīng. Most are run by Huí Muslims, who are Hàn Chinese, rather than ethnic-minority Uighurs from the remote western province of Xīnjiāng. Crescent Moon is the real deal – owned and staffed by Uighurs, it attracts many Běijīng-based Uighurs and people from Central Asia, as well as a lot of Western expats.

### Little Yúnnán
Yunnan ¥¥

(小云南; Xiǎo Yúnnán; Map p56; ☑010 6401 9498; 28 Donghuang Chenggen Beijie; 东皇城根 北街28号; mains ¥26-60; ⊙10am-10pm; ⑤Lines 6, 8 to Nanluoguxiang, exit B or Line 5 to Zhang-zizhonglu, exit D) Run by young, friendly staff and housed in a cute courtyard conversion, Little Yúnnán is one of the more down-to-earth Yúnnán restaurants in Běijīng. The main room has a rustic feel to it, with wooden beams, flooring and furniture. The tables up in the eaves are fun, and there's also some seating in the small open-air courtyard by the entrance.

Dishes include some classic southwest China ingredients, with some tea-infused creations as well as river fish, mushroom dishes, fried goat's cheese and *là ròu* (腊肉; cured pork – south China's answer to bacon). It also serves a variety of Yúnnán wines (rice, pine and plum), rice wine–based cocktails and the province's local beer.

### Jīngzūn Peking Duck
Peking Duck ¥¥

(京尊烤鸭; Jīngzūn Kǎoyā; ☑010 6417 4075; 6 Chunxiu Lu; 春秀路6号; mains ¥26-98; ⊙11am-10pm; ⑤Line 2 to Dongsi Shitiao, exit B) Very popular place to sample Běijīng's signature dish. Not only is the Peking duck here extremely good value at ¥138/79 for a whole/half bird, but you can also sit outside on its atmospheric wooden-decked terrace decorated with red lanterns. Otherwise, head upstairs to its booth seating overlooking the leafy street. It has its own draft beer too.

There's also a big choice of dishes from across China. During the summer, book ahead if you want a spot on the terrace.

### Georg
International ¥¥¥

(Map p56; ☑010 8408 5300; www.thegeorg. com/en; 45 Dongbuyaqiao Hutong; 东不压桥胡 同45号; tasting plates from ¥130, set menu ¥450, cafe mains ¥58-78; ⊙restaurant 6.30-10.30pm Tue-Sun, cafe from 10.30am daily; ❄🔊; ⑤Lines 6, 8 to Nanluoguxiang, exit E or Line 8 to Shicha-hai, exit C) In a city glaringly short on international fine dining, the Georg delivers with its gastronomic menu of fusion cuisine. It's an enterprise by Copenhagen designer Georg Jensen, creating a refined, intimate space with Danish design and heritage silverware. Tasting plates with a Scandinavian twist are creative and original.

### Temple Restaurant Bites
European ¥¥¥

(TRB; Map p56; ☑010 8400 2232; www.trb-cn.com; 95 Donghuamen Dajie; 东华门大街95 号; 3/4/5 courses ¥198/258/298; ⊙11.30am-10.30pm Mon-Fri, 10.30am-10pm Sat & Sun; ⑤Line 1 to Tian'anmen East, exit A) A peerless location, housed in a Qing dynasty building beside the Forbidden City moat, Ignace Lecleir's new offering is a more casual version of his upmarket **Temple Restaurant** (嵩祝寺餐厅; Sōngzhù Sì Cāntīng; Map p56; ☎010 8400 2232; Sōngzhù Temple, 23 Shatanbei Jie, off Wusi Dajie; 五四大街沙滩北街23号, 嵩祝寺; 3/4/5/6 courses ¥388/488/588/688; ⊗11am-3pm & 5.30-11pm; ❀🛜; ⑤Lines 6, 8 to Nanluoguxiang, exit B or Lines 5, 6 to Dongsi, exit E). The service is flawless, and the contemporary European food – salmon, lobster, pigeon, veal – is sheer quality. Here you order by customising your own meals, picking three or more items from whatever section of the menu takes your fancy.

Reservations are recommended, especially if you want a table overlooking the moat (the walls beside it are lit up in the evening). There's rooftop terrace seating in the warmer months.

## 🍷 DRINKING & NIGHTLIFE

### Great Leap Brewing          Brewery
(GLB #6; 大跃啤酒, Dàyuè Píjiǔ; Map p56; www. greatleapbrewing.com; 6 Doujiao Hutong; 豆角胡同6号; beer per pint ¥25-50; ⊗2-11pm Sun-Thu,

to midnight Fri & Sat; ⑤Line 8 to Shichahai, exit C) Běijīng's original microbrewery, this refreshingly simple courtyard bar, set up by American beer enthusiast Carl Setzer, is housed in a hard-to-find, but beautifully renovated, 100-year-old Qing dynasty courtyard and serves up a wonderful selection of unique ales made largely from locally sourced ingredients. Sip on familiar favourites such as pale ales and porters, or choose from China-inspired tipples such as Honey Ma, a brew made with lip-tingling Sìchuān peppercorns.

### Capital Spirits          Cocktail Bar
(首都酒坊; Shǒudū Jiǔfāng; Map p56; www. capitalspiritsbj.com; 3 Daju Hutong; 大菊胡同3号; cocktails from ¥40; ⊗8pm-12.30am Tue-Sun; 🛜; ⑤Line 5 to Beixinqiao, exit C) Much maligned by non-Chinese drinkers, *báijiǔ* (白酒; literally 'white alcohol'; a face-numbing spirit) is often compared to consuming paint stripper. However, that's until you sample some of the top-shelf stuff, and that's where Capital Spirits step in with an entire speakeasy bar dedicated to quality *báijiǔs*.

Pānjiāyuán Market (p59)

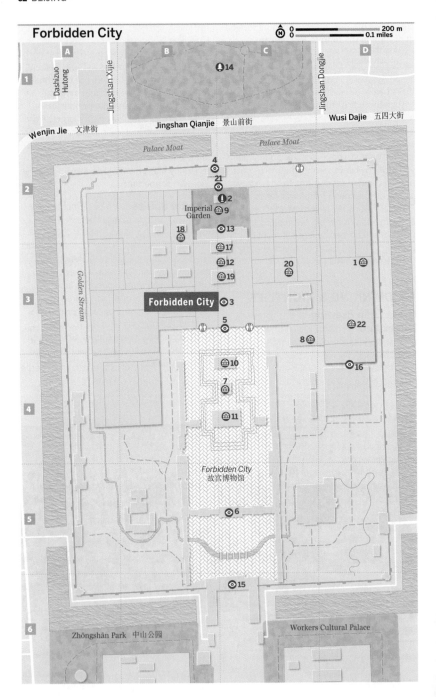

# Forbidden City

N

| 0 | 200 m |
| 0 | 0.1 miles |

Dashizuo Hutong

Jingshan Xijie

Jingshan Dongjie

14

Wenjin Jie 文津街

Jingshan Qianjie 景山前街

Wusi Dajie 五四大街

Palace Moat

Palace Moat

4

21

2

Imperial Garden

9

18

13

17

12

20

1

19

Golden Stream

**Forbidden City** 3

5

22

8

10

16

7

11

6

Forbidden City
故宫博物馆

15

Zhōngshān Park 中山公园

Workers Cultural Palace

# Forbidden City

## Oasis Cafe
Cafe

(绿洲咖啡; Lǜzhōu Kāfēi; Map p56; 2 Jingshan Qianjie; 景山前街2号; coffee from ¥15; ⊘9am-7pm; Ⓢ Lines 6, 8 to Nanluoguxiang, exit A, or Line 5, 6 to Dongsi, exit E) Oasis' award-winning owner/barista/coffee roaster, Duan, really knows his stuff. Not only does he nail the V60 drip-coffee pour overs, but he knocks out one of the best flat whites in the city.

## NBeer Pub
Bar

(牛啤堂; Niú Pí Táng; ☑010 8328 8823; www. nbcraftbrewing.com; Huguo Xintiandi, 85 Huguosi Dajie; 护国寺大街85号护国新天地一层; bottles from ¥25, draft ¥35-50; ⊘3pm-2am; 🛜; Ⓢ Lines 4, 6 to Ping'anli, exit B) In a scene dominated by North American expats, NBeer is an all-Chinese affair that produces some of Běijīng's best beers. It has a massive 37 ales on tap behind a bar made from Lonely Planet guidebooks! The majority are brewed on site and include a variety of IPAs, pale ales, stouts and European-style ales. It also boasts the biggest fridge of beers in Běijīng.

The food is also good, including excellent cheese burgers and enormous, juicy kebabs. Visit before 7pm for 30% discounts on all draft beers.

It's on the ground floor of a multifloor complex known as Xīntiāndì, at the western end of Huguosi Dajie. You can sometimes sit on the patio out the back in summer and spy **Jīngāng Hall** (金刚殿; Jīngāng Diàn), originally built in 1284 and the only surviving feature of Hùguó Temple, which this *hútòng* is named after.

## ★ ENTERTAINMENT

### National Centre for the Performing Arts
Classical Music

(国家大剧院; Guójiā Dàjùyuàn; Map p56; ☑010 6655 0000; www.chncpa.org/ens; 2 Xichang'an Jie; 西长安街2号; tickets ¥80-880; ⊘performances 7.30pm; Ⓢ Line 1 to Tian'anmen West, exit C) Sometimes called the National Grand Theatre, this spectacular Paul Andreu–designed dome, known to Beijingers as the 'Alien Egg', attracts as many architectural tourists as it does music fans. But it's *the* place to listen to classical music from home and abroad. You can also watch ballet, opera and classical Chinese dance here.

## ⓘ INFORMATION

**Bank of China** (中国银行; Zhōngguó Yínháng; Map p56; ☑010 6513 2214; 19 Dong'anmen Dajie, 东城区东安门大街19号) By the Dōnghuámén Night Market, this is one of dozens of branches around Běijīng with money-changing facilities.

**Běijīng Museum Pass** (博物馆通票; Bówùguǎn Tōngpiào; ☑010 6222 3793; www.bowuguan. com.cn; annual pass ¥120) An annual card that gets you into more than 112 sights, including 61 museums. A good investment.

**Běijīng Tourist Information Centers** (北京 旅游咨询; Běijīng Lǚyóu Zīxún Fúwù Zhōngxīn; ⊘9am-5pm) Branches in **Běijīng train station** (Map p56; ☑010 6528 4848; 16 Laoqianju Hutong; tours ¥260-400; ⊘8.30am-6pm; Ⓢ Line 2 to Beijing Railway Station, exit B) and **Capital Airport** (☑010 6459 8148; Terminal 3). Tourist information offices are aimed at domestic

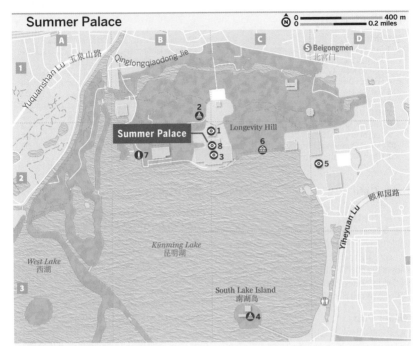

# Summer Palace

tourists; English skills are limited and information is basic, but you can grab a free tourist map of town and handfuls of free literature; some offices also have train-ticket offices.

**China Post** (Zhōngguó Yóuzhèng; ☑ 010 6512 8114; Jianguomen Beidajie; 建国门北大街; ⊙8.30am-6pm; ⑤ Lines 1, 2 to Jianguomen, exit B)

**Peking Union Medical College Hospital**
(PUMCH; 协和医院; Xiéhé Yīyuàn; Map p56; ☑010 6915 6699, emergency 010 6915 9180; www.pumch.cn; 1 Shuaifuyuan; 东城区 王府井帅府园1号; ⊙24hr; ⑤ Lines 1, 5 to Dongdan, exit A)

## ❶ GETTING THERE & AWAY

Běijīng can be reached by plane, train, bus, car or a combination of a ship and train, but most travellers coming from overseas fly into the city.

### AIR

Běijīng's main airport is **Běijīng Capital International Airport** (北京首都国际机场; Běijīng Shǒudū Guójì Jīchǎng, PEK; ☑010 6454 1100; www.en.bcia.com.cn). If coming from elsewhere in China, you may also fly into the small **Nányuàn Airport** (南苑机场; Nányuàn Jīchǎng, NAY; ☑010 6797 8899; Jingbeixi Lu, Nányuàn Zhèn, Fēngtái District; 丰台区南苑镇警备西路, 警备东路口).

Běijīng Capital International Airport has three terminals. Terminal 3 (三号航站楼; *sān hào hángzhànlóu*) deals with most long-haul flights, although international flights also use Terminal 2 (二号航站楼; *èr hào hángzhànlóu*). Both are connected to the slick **Airport Express** (机场快 轨; Jīchǎng Kuàiguǐ; one way ¥25; Ⓢ Lines 2, 13 to Dongzhimen, exit B), also written as ABC (Airport Běijīng City), which is quick and convenient and links to Běijīng's subway system at Sanyuanqiao station (Line 10) and Dongzhimen station (Lines 2 and 13).

The smaller Terminal 1 (一号航站楼; *yī hào hángzhànlóu*) is a 10-minute walk from Terminal 2. Free 24-hour shuttle buses connect all three terminals.

Aside from the airport express, there is an airport **shuttle bus** (机场巴士; Jīchǎng bāshì; one way ¥15.50-30) with 17 different routes, while a taxi should cost ¥90 to ¥120 from the airport to the city centre; bank on it taking 40 minutes to one hour to get into town.

## BUS

There are numerous long-distance bus stations, but no international bus routes to Běijīng.

**Liùlǐqiáo long-distance bus station** (六里桥长 途站; Liùlǐqiáo *chángtúzhàn*) In the southwest of town, adjacent to Liuliqiao subway station. Destinations include Dàtóng (大同; ¥133 to ¥150, 4½ hours, regular departures 7.10am to 6pm) and Xī'ān (西安; ¥278, 12 hours, daily at 5.45pm).

**Zhàogōngkǒu long-distance bus station** (赵 公口汽车站; Zhàogōngkǒu *qìchēzhàn*) In the south, 10 minutes walk west of Liujiayao subway station. Destinations include Shànghǎi (上海; ¥340, 16 hours, daily at 4.30pm).

## TRAIN

Běijīng has three major train stations for long-distance travel (Běijīng train station, Běijīng West station and Běijīng South station). Běijīng North station is used much less.

### BĚIJĪNG TRAIN STATION

The most central of Běijīng's four main train stations, Běijīng train station (北京站; Běijīng *zhàn*), which has its own subway stop, is mainly for T-class trains *(tèkuài)*, slow trains and

trains bound for the northeast; most fast trains heading south now depart from Běijīng South train station and Běijīng West train station. Destinations include Dàtóng (大同; K-series, hard seat ¥99, six hours, three daily) and Shànghǎi (上海; T-series, soft sleeper ¥476 to ¥879, 14 hours, daily).

### BĚIJĪNG WEST TRAIN STATION

The gargantuan Běijīng West train station (西站; Xī zhàn) accommodates fast Z-series trains, such as to Xī'ān (西安; Z- and T-series, hard sleeper ¥214 to ¥268, 11 to 12 hours, six daily) and Kowloon, Hong Kong (九龙; soft-sleeper ¥707 to ¥738, 24 hours, daily). Other destinations include Chéngdū (成都; Z-, T- and K-series, hard sleeper ¥399 to ¥456, 26 to 31 hours, five daily) and Chóngqìng (重庆; T- and K-class trains, hard sleeper ¥381 to ¥389, 25 to 30 hours, four daily).

### BĚIJĪNG SOUTH TRAIN STATION

The ultra-modern Běijīng South station (南站; Nán zhàn), which is linked to the subway system on Line 4, accommodates very high-speed 'bullet' trains to destinations such as Tiānjīn, Shànghǎi, Hángzhōu and Qīngdǎo.

 **GETTING AROUND**

### BICYCLE

Cycling is the most enjoyable way of getting around Běijīng. The city is as flat as a mah-jong table and almost every road has a bike lane, even if cars invade them. The quiet, tree-lined *hútòng* are particularly conducive to cycling.

### BIKE RENTAL

The following are good options for renting bicycles (租自行车; *zū zìxíngchē*):

**Bike Běijīng** (康多自行车租赁; Kāngduō Zìxíngchē Zūlìn; Map p56; ☏ 010 6526 5857; www. bikebeijing.com; 81 Beiheyan Dajie; 北河沿大街 81号; ◷ 8am-8pm; Ⓢ Lines 6, 8 to Nanluoguxiang, exit B or Line 5 to Zhangzizhonglu, exit D)

**Giant** (捷安特; Jié'āntè; Map p56; ☏ 010 6403 4537; www.giant.com.cn; 4-18 Jiaodaokou Dong-dajie; 交道口东大街4-18号; ◷ 9am-7pm; Ⓢ Line 5 to Beixinqiao, exit A)

**Natooke** (娃 (自行车店); Shuǎ (Zìxíngchē Diàn); Map p56; ☎010 8402 6925; www.natooke.com; 19-1 Wudaoying Hutong; 五道营胡同19—1号; ⊙11am-7pm; ⑤Lines 2, 5 to Yonghegong-Lama Temple, exit D)

Bike stands around the Hòuhái Lakes also rent bikes (¥10 per hour). Hostels typically charge ¥30 to ¥50 per day for a standard town bike.

## BUS

Běijīng's buses (公共汽车; gōnggòng qìchē) have always been numerous and cheap (from ¥2), but they're now easier to use for non-Chinese speakers, with swipe cards, announcements in English, and bus-stop signs written in pinyin as well as Chinese characters. Nevertheless, it's still a challenge to get from A to B successfully, and the buses are as packed as ever, so you rarely see foreigners climbing aboard.

If you use a travel card, you get a 50% discount on all journeys.

## TAXI

Taxis (出租车; chūzūchē) are everywhere, although finding one can be a problem during rush hour, rainstorms and between 8pm and 10pm – prime time for people heading home after eating out. Flag fall is ¥13, and lasts for 3km. After that it's ¥2 per kilometre. Rates increase slightly at night.

## TRAIN

Massive and getting bigger every year, with another 12 lines set to be in operation by 2021, the **Běijīng subway system** (地铁; dìtiě; www.bj subway.com; per trip ¥3-8; ⊙5am-11.30pm) is modern, safe, cheap and easy to use. Single fares are ¥3 to ¥8, depending on how far you are travelling.

It's worth getting a free **travel card** (一卡通; yīkǎtōng; deposit ¥20) at any subway station or large bus station. It makes subway travel more convenient and gives you 60% off all bus rides, including those out to the Great Wall.

You can recharge them at most (but not all) subway stations and bus-station ticket kiosks.

National Centre for the Performing Arts (p63)

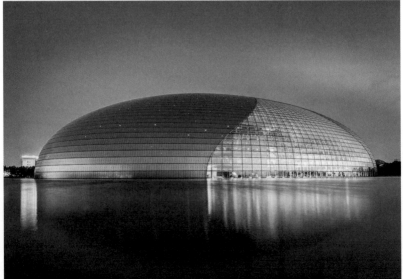

# Where to Stay

*Hostels are the best value, with traveller-friendly facilities and staff with good English-language skills. Courtyard hotels are wonderfully atmospheric, and you're right in the thick of the hútòng action, but they lack the facilities (pool etc) of top-end hotels in similar price brackets.*

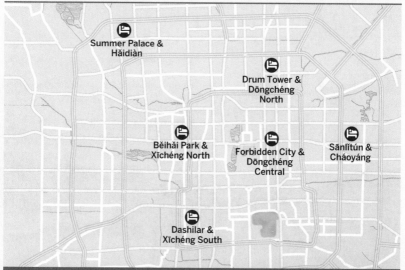

| Neighbourhood | Atmosphere |
| --- | --- |
| **Forbidden City & Dōngchéng Central** | Hugely historic; highest concentration of sights; good mix of ordinary hotels and *hútòng* accommodation. Some parts are less residential than other neighbourhoods, and so can be eerily quiet in the evenings. |
| **Drum Tower & Dōngchéng North** | Běijīng's most desirable neighbourhood; perfect for delving deep into the *hútòng*. Plenty of courtyard hotels; budget backpackers may be priced out. Cafes, bars and live music on your doorstep. |
| **Běihǎi Park & Xīchéng North** | Plenty of *hútòng* action; the area by the lakes sees little motorised traffic and so can be peaceful, although evening karaoke bars can ruin the ambience. Less touristy than Dōngchéng District. |
| **Dashilar & Xīchéng South** | Backpacker central with a great choice of hostels; *hútòng* vibe is still strong around Dashilar; extensive reconstruction has stolen some of the character from the area (particularly around Qiánmén) and seen restaurant prices rise. |
| **Sānlǐtún & Cháoyáng** | Great for shopping, eating and nightlife. Excellent choice of midrange and top-end places to stay, though the area lacks character and any historical narrative. |
| **Summer Palace & Hǎidiàn** | Less touristy than more central areas, and the presence of lots of students means there's nightlife, but it's a trek from the centre of town. |

# THE GREAT WALL

# The Great Wall at a Glance...

*China's greatest engineering triumph and must-see sight, the Great Wall (万里长城; Wànlǐ Chángchéng) wriggles haphazardly from its scattered Manchurian remains in Liáoníng province to wind-scoured rubble in the Gobi desert and faint traces in the unforgiving sands of Xīnjiāng. The most renowned and robust examples of the Wall undulate majestically over the peaks and hills of Běijīng municipality, but the Great Wall can be realistically visited in many north China provinces.*

### Two Days at the Great Wall

On your first day, and if time is tight, visit **Mùtiányù** (p76). Consider spending the night in Mùtiányù so you can take up the challenge of hiking to Jiànkòu the next day. On day two, visit **Jiànkòu** (p75) for its standout, raw scenery and Great Wall in its original and unrestored state, running along a ridge in the hills.

### Four Days at the Great Wall

**Bādálǐng** (p77) is easily reached from town and while the Wall here is heavily restored, it offers some superb panoramas and photo ops of the fortification snaking off into the hills. On your last day, take a day trip to distant **Jīnshānlǐng** (p76) and hike to your heart's content.

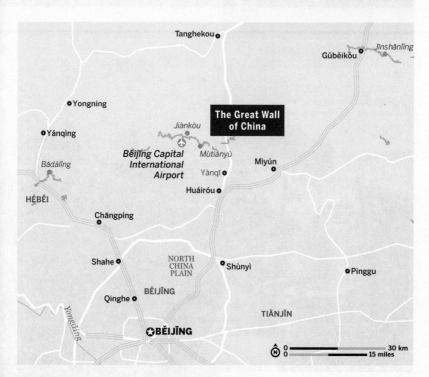

## Getting to the Great Wall

**Bādálǐng** Can be accessed by both bus and train or, of course, by taxi.

**Jīnshānlǐng**, **Jiànkòu & Mùtiányù** Can be reached by a combination of buses, or a bus and a taxi or minivan.

A number of taxi operators make day trips to the Wall, as do some ordinary Běijīng taxi drivers. Agree on the price beforehand.

## Where to Stay

You'll find places to stay at some parts of the Wall close to Běijīng, but most guesthouses and hotels cluster around the more remote sections, where staying overnight allows you to spend some proper time at the Wall. Jiànkòu has reasonable sleeping options. Remember, that most places close from November to March.

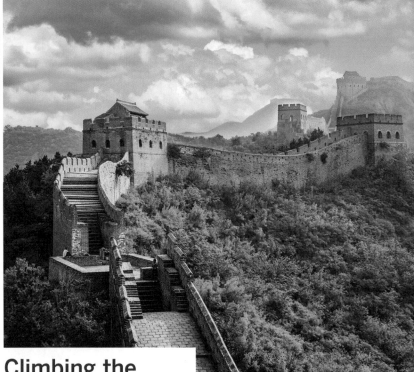

APHOTOSTORY / SHUTTERSTOCK ©

# Climbing the Great Wall

*The Great Wall has never been one continuous structure and snakes through 17 provinces, but nowhere is better than Běijīng for mounting your assault on this most famous of bastions.*

The most renowned and robust examples of the Wall undulate majestically over the peaks and hills of Běijīng municipality, but the Great Wall can be realistically visited in many north China provinces.

## History of the Great Wall

Official Chinese history likes to stress the unity of the Wall through the ages. In fact, there are at least four distinct Walls. Work on the 'original' was begun during the Qin dynasty (221–207 BC), when China was unified for the first time under Emperor Qin Shihuang. Hundreds of thousands of workers, many political prisoners, laboured for 10 years to construct it. An estimated 180-million cu metres of rammed earth was used to form the core of this Wall, and legend has it that the bones of dead workers were used as building materials, too.

**Great For...**

☑ **Don't Miss**

The astonishing views from Jiànkòu, where you can discover the Wall in its unrestored state.

Bǎdálǐng (p77)

LEONID ANDRONOV / SHUTTERSTOCK ©

Běijīng Capital International Airport · Jiànkòu · Jīnshānlǐng

Bǎdálǐng · Mùtiányù · **The Great Wall of China**

⊙ **BĚIJĪNG**

## ❶ Need to Know

Wear shoes with good grip and take a rucksack so you have both hands free for clambering.

## ✕ Take a Break

If you're hiking in more remote areas, make sure to bring food and water with you, as there are no restaurants.

### ★ Top Tip

Spring and autumn are good times to hike the Wall, when it's neither too hot nor cold.

installed in Běijīng as the Qing dynasty (1644–1911) and the Mongol threat long gone, there was little need to maintain the Wall, and it fell into disrepair.

## Visiting the Wall

The heavily reconstructed section at Bǎdálǐng is the most touristy part of the Wall. Mùtiányù and Jīnshānlǐng are also restored sections. These can feel less than authentic, but have the advantage of being much more accessible (with cable cars, handrails etc). Huánghuā Chéng and Zhuàngdàokǒu are part-restored, part-'wild' and offer some short but challenging hikes. Unrestored sections of 'Wild Wall' include Gǔběikǒu and Jiànkòu, but there are many others. All of these can be reached using public transport (you can even get to Bǎdálǐng by train), although some people choose to hire a car to speed things up. Staying overnight by the Wall is recommended.

Tours run by hostels, or by specialist tour companies, are far preferable to those run

After the Qin fell, work on the Wall continued during the Han dynasty (206 BC – AD 220). Little more was done until almost 1000 years later, during the Jin dynasty (1115–1234), when the impending threat of Genghis Khan spurred further construction. The Wall's final incarnation, and the one most visitors see today, came during the Ming dynasty (1368–1644), when it was reinforced with stone, brick and battlements over a period of 100 years and at great human cost to the two to three million people who toiled on it.

While the Wall was less than effective militarily, it was very useful as a kind of elevated highway for transporting people and equipment across mountainous terrain. Its beacon tower system, using smoke signals generated by burning wolves' dung, quickly transmitted news of enemy movements back to the capital. But with the Manchus

by ordinary hotels or general travel companies. Not only do they cater to the needs of adventurous Western travellers, they don't come with any hidden extras, such as a side trip to the Ming Tombs (a common add-on) or a tiresome diversion to a gem factory or traditional Chinese medicine centre. The following reputable companies and associations run trips to the Wall that we like.

**Bespoke Běijīng** (☑010 6400 0133; www.bespoketravelcompany.com; B510, 107 Dongsi Beidajie; 东四北大街107号B510楼; ⊙9am-6pm; Ⓢ Beixinqiao) High-end trips and tours.

**Great Wall Hiking** (www.greatwallhiking.com) Locally run hiking trips.

**China Hiking** (☑156 5220 0950; www.chinahiking.cn) Affordable hiking and camping trips run by a Chinese-Belgian couple.

**Běijīng Hikers** (☑010 6432 2786; www.beijinghikers.com; Galaxy Building, bldg A, room 4012, 10 Jiuxianqiao Zhonglu; 星科大厦A座4012室, 酒仙桥中路10号; per person from ¥380; ⊙9am-6pm) Organises some breathtaking outings out of town.

**Bike Běijīng** (☑010 6526 5857; www.bikebeijing.com; 81 Beiheyan Jie; 北河沿大街81号; ⊙8am-8pm; Ⓢ Nanluoguxiang) For cycling trips.

**Běijīng Sideways** (☑139 1133 4947; www.beijingsideways.com; Xingfu Cun Zhonglu, Jieizuo Dasha Xibian, Lishihongye Zhiyeyouxiangongsi Duimian; 幸福村中路杰座大厦西边利世鸿业置业有限公司对面; ⊙9am-9pm; Ⓢ Dongsishitiao) For trips in a motorbike sidecar.

## Camping on the Wall

Although, strictly speaking, camping on the Great Wall is not allowed, many people do

Camping on the Wall

it; some of the watchtowers make excellent bases for pitching tents, or just laying down a sleeping bag. Remember, though; don't light fires and don't leave anything behind. You'll find fun places to camp at Zhuàngdàokǒu, Jiànkòu and Gǔběikǒu.

There are plenty of places to buy camping equipment in Běijīng, but one of the best in terms of quality and choice is **Sanfo** (三夫户外; Sānfū Hùwài; ☏010 6201 5550; www.sanfo.com/en; 3-4 Madian Nancun; 北三环中路马甸南村4之3—4号; ☺9am-9pm; Ⓢ Line 10 to Jiandemen, exit D). There are branches across the city, but this location on a side road of the middle section of the North 3rd Ring Rd stands out because it has three outlets side by side, as well as a few smaller cheaper camping shops next door. Turn right out of exit D of Jiandemen subway station (Line 10) and walk south for about 800m, then cross under the 3rd Ring Rd and the camping shops will be on your right.

There's a smaller, easier-to-get-to **branch** (9-4 Fuchengmen Dajie; 阜城门大街9—4号; ☺10am-8.30pm; Ⓢ Line 2 to Fuchengmen, exit C), about 200m south of Fuchengmen subway station.

## Jiànkòu

For stupefying hikes along perhaps Běijīng's most incomparable section of 'Wild Wall', head to the rear section of the Jiànkòu Great Wall (后箭扣长城; Hòu Jiànkòu Chángchéng), accessible from Xīzhàzi village (西栅子村; Xīzhàzi Cūn), via the town of Huáiróu. Tantalising panoramic views of the Great Wall spread out in either direction from here, as the crumbling brickwork meanders dramatically along a mountain ridge; the setting is truly sublime. But this is completely unrestored wall, so it is both dangerous and, strictly speaking, illegal to hike along it. On summer weekends especially, crowds can render it even more risky. Footwear with very good grip is required, and never attempt to traverse this section in the rain, particularly during thunderstorms.

### ⓘ GETTING TO JIÀNKÒU

Take bus 916 (快) from the Dōngzhímén Transport Hub to its terminus at **Huáiróu bus station** (怀柔汽车站; Huáiróu qìchēzhàn; ¥12, 90 minutes; ☺6.30am-7.30pm). Turn left out of the station, right at the crossroads and take bus 862 from the first bus stop to Yújiāyuán (于家园; ¥2, five stops), then take the H25 to Xīzhàzi (西栅子; ¥8, 70 minutes). Note, the H25 only runs twice a day, at 11.30am and 4.30pm. The return

### Visiting from Běijīng

While the Great Wall can be visited at many locations in northern China, this chapter shows how it can be visited in a day trip from Běijīng. Please refer to the Běijīng chapter (p34) for listings for the capital.

AZEMEGEA / GETTY IMAGES ©

H25 bus leaves Xīzhàzi at 6.30am and 1.15pm, so you can't do this in a day trip on public transport alone.

A taxi costs around ¥700 to ¥900 for a return day trip from Běijīng.

### ⓘ SLEEPING AT JIÀNKÒU

There are an ever-increasing number of guest-houses in Xīzhàzi village, but Jiànkòu is now a very popular destination for local visitors, so book ahead at weekends, especially in summer. Expect to pay ¥120 and up for a room with a bathroom.

## Jīnshānlǐng

The **Jīnshānlǐng** (金山岭长城; Jīnshānlǐng Chángchéng; ☎0314 883 0222; Apr-Oct ¥65, Nov-Mar ¥55; ☺8am-5pm; ⛟Luánpíng) section of the Great Wall is a completely restored and, in places, very steep stretch, but it's so far from Běijīng that it sees far fewer tourists than other fully restored sections. It contains some unusual features, such as Barrier Walls (walls within the Wall), and each watchtower comes with an inscription, in English, detailing the historic significance of that part of the Wall. This is the finish point of an adventurous 6½-hour hike from Gǔběikǒu.

### ⓘ GETTING TO JĪNSHĀNLǏNG

From April to November, direct buses run from Wàngjīng West subway station (Line 13) to the Jīnshānlǐng ticket office. Come out of exit C of the subway station and look over your right shoulder to see the red sign for the 'Tourist Bus to Jīnshānlǐng Great Wall' (金山岭长城旅游班车; Jīnshānlǐng Chángchéng lǚyóu bānchē) on the other side of the road. The bus leaves at 8am and returns to Běijīng at 3pm (¥32, 100 minutes).

A taxi costs around ¥1000 to ¥1200 for a return day trip from Běijīng.

## Mùtiányù

Famed for its Ming-era guard towers and excellent views, this 3km-long section of wall is largely a recently restored Ming dynasty structure that was built upon an earlier Northern Qi dynasty edifice. With 26 watchtowers, the Wall is impressive and manageable and, although it's popular, most souvenir hawking is reserved to the lower levels.

From the ticket office at Mùtiányù, shuttle buses (¥15 return, 7.20am to 7pm April to October, 8.20am to 6pm November to December) run the 3km to the Wall, where there are three or four stepped pathways leading up to the Wall itself, plus a **cable car** (缆车; lǎn chē; one way/return ¥80/100, kids half-price), a **chairlift** (索道; suǒdào; combined ticket with toboggan ¥80) – called a 'ropeway'

Mùtiányù

on the signs here – and a **toboggan ride** (滑道; *huá dào*; one way ¥80), making this ideal for those who can't manage too many steps, or who have kids in tow.

### ℹ️ GETTING TO MÙTIÁNYÙ

From Dōngzhímén Wai bus stand, bus 867 makes a special detour to Mùtiányù twice every morning (¥16, 2½ hours, 7am and 8.30am, 15 March to 15 November only) and returns from Mùtiányù twice each afternoon (2pm and 4pm).

A taxi costs around ¥600 to ¥700 for a return day trip from Běijīng.

### ℹ️ SLEEPING AT MÙTIÁNYÙ

There are half a dozen village guesthouses about 500m downhill from the Mùtiányù entrance. All have English signage. Expect to pay around ¥100 for a simple room.

## Bādálǐng

The mere mention of **Bādálǐng** (八达岭长城; Bādálǐng Chángchéng; Apr-Oct ¥45, Nov-Mar ¥35; ⏱6am-7pm Apr-Oct, 7am-6pm Nov-Mar; 🚌877, 🚆from Běijīng North) sends a shudder down the spine of hard-core Wall walkers, but this is the easiest part of the Wall to get to – you can even get here by train – and as such, if you are really pushed for time, this may be your only option. You'll have to put up with huge crowds of domestic tourists, a lot of souvenir hawkers and a Wall that was completely renovated in the 1980s and so lacks a true sense of historical authenticity. But the Bādálǐng Wall is highly photogenic, as well as authentically steep, has good

tourist facilities (restaurants, disabled access, cable cars etc) and can be visited on a half-day trip from Běijīng.

## GETTING TO BĀDÁLǏNG

Getting here by train is the cheapest and most enjoyable option. Bādálǐng train station is a short walk downhill from the west car park; come out of the train station and turn left for the Wall (about 1km).

Trains (¥6, 70 to 80 minutes) leave from Běijīng North train station, which is connected to Xizhimen subway station.

By bus, the 877 (¥12, one hour, 6am to 5pm) leaves for Bādálǐng from the northern side of the Déshèngmén Gateway (德胜门; Déshèngmén; Map p56), about 400m east of Jishuitan subway station. Buses return to Běijīng from just south

of where they drop you: you'll see the queue of people waiting for them. The last bus back leaves at 5pm (4.30pm November to March).

Expect to pay around ¥600 to ¥700 for a round trip by taxi.

## Three Great Wall Hikes

### Jiànkòu to Mùtiányù

⊙ **Two hours (plus one-hour climb to the Wall)** Unrivalled for pure 'Wild Wall' scenery, the Wall at Jiànkòu is very tough to negotiate. This short stretch, which passes through the 180-degree U-turn known as the Ox Horn, is equally hairy, but it soon links to an easier, restored section at Mùtiányù. Access the Wall from hamlet No 1 in Xīzhàzi village (西栅子村一队; Xīzhàzi

Hiking the Wall, near Jīnshānlǐng (p76)

Cūn Yīduì). It takes an hour to reach the Wall from the village; from the sign that says 'this section of the Great Wall is not open to the public', follow a narrow dirt path uphill and through a lovely pine forest. When you reach a small clearing, go straight on (and down slightly), rather than up to the right. Later, when you hit the Wall, turn left. You'll climb/clamber up to, and round, the Ox Horn before descending (it's very slippery here) all the way to Mùtiányù where cable cars, toboggan rides and transport back to Běijīng await.

## Zhuàngdàokǒu to Shuǐ Chángchéng

○ **Two hours (plus 20-minute climb to the Wall)** Climb up to the Wall from Zhuàngdàokǒu village, and turn left at the

Wall to be rewarded with this dangerous but fabulous stretch of crumbling bastion. The Wall eventually splits at a corner tower: turn left. Then, soon after you reach another tower from where you can see the reservoir far below you, the Wall crumbles down the mountain, and is impassable. Instead of risking your life, take the path that leads down to your left, just before the tower. This path eventually links up with the Wall again, but you may as well follow it all the way down to the road from here, where you'll be able to catch the H21 bus back to Huáiróu from the lower one of the two large car parks.

## Coiled Dragon Loop

○ **2½ hours** This scenic but manageable hike starts and finishes in the town of Gǔběikǒu and follows a curling stretch of the Wall known as the Coiled Dragon. From the Folk Customs Village (the southern half of Gǔběikǒu), walk up to the newly reconstructed Gǔběikǒu Gate (古北口关; Gǔběikǒu Guān) but turn right up a dirt track just before the gateway. You should start seeing yellow-painted blobs, left over from an old marathon that was run here: follow them. The first section of Wall you reach is a very rare stony stretch of Northern Qi dynasty Wall (1500 years old). It soon joins up with the Ming dynasty bricked version, which you should continue to walk along (although at one stage, you need to follow yellow arrows down off the Wall to the left, before rejoining it later). Around 90 minutes after you set off, you should reach a big sweeping right-hand bend in the Wall (the coil), with three towers on top. The first and third of these towers are quite well preserved, with walls, windows and part of a roof (great for camping in). At the third tower (called Jiangjun Tower), turn left, skirting right around it, then walk down the steps before turning right at a point marked with a yellow 'X' (the marathon went straight on here). Follow this pathway all the way back to Gǔběikǒu (30 minutes), turning right when you reach the road.

SHĀNXĪ

# Shānxī at a Glance...

*Waist-deep in handsome history, Shānxī (山西) is home to an impressive roll call of must-see, ancient sights. Start with the walled city of Píngyáo, from where you can encounter time-worn temples, traditional Qing dynasty courtyard architecture and some of the warmest people in the Middle Kingdom, then head to Dàtóng, a forward-thinking city with a brand-new city wall and a great-looking old town. Outside town, the astonishing cave sculptures at Yúngāng give expression to the province's rich vein of Buddhist heritage.*

### Two Days in Shānxī

Arrive in **Píngyáo** (p84) and spend at least a night here. Climb the city walls, pass beneath the City Tower and admire the Nine Dragon Screen. Pay a visit to the **Shuānglín Temple** (p85), dine at **Déjūyuán** (p88) and have evening drinks in the courtyard of your traditional hotel or explore the tranquil alleyways of town.

### Four Days in Shānxī

After Píngyáo travel by train to **Dàtóng** (p90) and spend the afternoon exploring the old town and walking along the reconstructed **city wall** (p91). Dine at **Fènglín Gé** (p92) and stay overnight in town. Visit the **Yúngāng Caves** (p86) early the next day and in the afternoon journey to the church ruins at **Bā Táizi** (p91) before dinner at **Tónghé Dàfàndiàn** (p93).

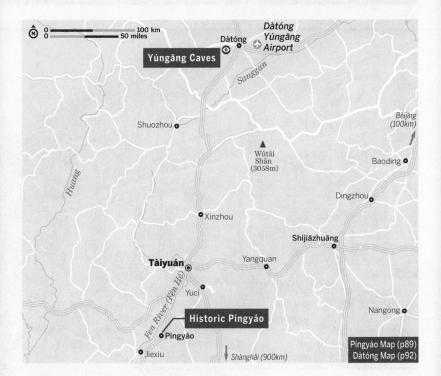

## Arriving in Shānxī

**Píngyáo Gǔchéng train station** Take public bus 108 (¥1), a rickshaw (¥10) or a taxi (¥30) to the old town. Note that taxis are not allowed to enter the old town; you will be dropped outside the gates of the city wall.

**Dàtóng Yúngāng Airport** Connected to Dàtóng by taxi (¥50).

## Where to Stay

Shānxi's best accommodation options centre on Píngyáo, where most old-town hotels are conversions of old courtyard homes, and finding a bed isn't hard. Other fine choices can also be found, especially in Dàtóng, which has a reasonable choice of well-priced midrange options, as well as a few hostels. Hoteliers in the area are increasingly aware of the needs of Western travellers, some English is spoken and they can make a passable Western breakfast.

# Historic Píngyáo

*With red lantern–hung lanes set against a night-time silhouette of imposing town walls, elegant courtyard architecture, ancient towers and creaking temples, Píngyáo (平遥) is China's best-preserved ancient walled town.*

## Great For...

### ☑ Don't Miss

Walking above Píngyáo along its magnificent city walls.

If you have even the remotest interest in Chinese history, culture or architecture, you could easily spend a couple of days wandering the pinched lanes of Píngyáo, stumbling across hidden gems while ticking off all the well-known sights.

## City Walls

A good place to start your Píngyáo experience is the magnificent **city walls** (城墙; *chéng qiáng*); they date from 1370 and are among the most complete in the nation. At 10m high and more than 6km in circumference, they are punctuated by 72 watchtowers, each containing a paragraph from Sunzi's *The Art of War*.

## Píngyáo City Tower

The **City Tower** (市楼; Shì Lóu; Nan Dajie; 南大街) is the signature structure standing

Thousand Buddha Hall, Shuānglín Temple

MARTIN MOOS / GETTY IMAGES ©

the interiors of the Sakyamuni Hall and flanking buildings are exquisite. The Four Heavenly Kings date to the Tang dynasty and the Thousand Buddha Hall contains an astonishing 1000-arm Guanyin. Dark-faced Buddha statues hide within the Great Treasure Hall, while young sculptors come here to cast their likeness from clay.

A rickshaw or taxi from town will cost ¥50 return, or you could cycle the 7km here.

## Rìshēngchāng Financial House Museum

Not to be missed, this **museum** (日升昌; Rìshēngchāng; 38 Xi Dajie; 西大街38号; ⊗8am-7pm) began life as a humble dye shop in the late 18th century before its tremendous success as a business saw it transform into China's first draft bank (1823), eventually expanding to 57 branches nationwide.

## Cultural Revolution Slogans

Stop by 153 Xi Dajie to see two red-blooded Cultural Revolution slogans that have survived on buildings within the courtyard. The one on the left intones: 工业学大庆 ('Industry should learn from Dàqìng'); the rarer slogan on the right proclaims: 认真搞好斗批改 ('Earnestly undertake struggle, criticism and reform'). They are of little interest to Chinese people, but are of heritage value in their own right.

proud above Píngyáo, the tallest building in the old town – snap a photo before passing under it en route to other sites. Sadly, you can no longer climb it for city views and a gate bars its stone steps.

## Nine Dragon Screen

The old Píngyáo Theatre (大戏堂; Dàxì Táng) has been converted into a hotel's banquet hall, but it is fronted by the magnificent **Nine Dragon Screen** (九龙壁; Jiǔlóng Bì; Chenghuangmiao Jie; 城隍庙街).

## Shuānglín Temple

Within easy reach of Píngyáo, this astonishing Buddhist **temple** (双林寺; Shuānglín Sì; ¥40; ⊗8.30am-6.30pm) houses many incredibly rare, intricately carved Tang, Song and Yuan painted statues. Rebuilt in 1571, it's an impressive complex of ancient halls:

CORLAFFRA / SHUTTERSTOCK ©

# Yúngāng Caves

*One of China's most supreme examples of Buddhist cave art, these 5th-century caves are simply magnificent. With 51,000 ancient statues and celestial beings, they put virtually everything else in the Shānxī shade.*

### Great For...

### ☑ Don't Miss

The stunning interior of Cave 6.

Carved by the Turkic-speaking Tuoba, the Yúngāng Caves drew their designs from Indian, Persian and even Greek influences that swept along the Silk Road. Work began in AD 460, continuing for 60 years, before all 252 caves – the oldest collection of Buddhist carvings in China – had been completed.

### Caves 5 & 6

Eight of the caves contain enormous Buddha statues; the largest can be found in Cave 5, an outstanding 17m-high seated effigy of Sakyamuni with a gilded face. As with many here, the frescoes in this cave are badly scratched and vandalised, but note the painted vaulted ceiling. Bursting with colour, Cave 6, the Cave of Sakyamuni, is also stunning, resembling an overblown set from an Indiana Jones epic with legions

Section of China's oldest Buddhist carvings

### ❶ Need to Know

云冈石窟; Yúngāng Shíkū; ☑0352
302 6230; Dec-Feb ¥80, Mar-Nov ¥125;
⊙8.30am-5.30pm 1 Apr–15 Oct, to 4.50pm
16 Oct-31 Mar

### ✖ Take a Break

There are no restaurants at the caves,
so return to Dàtóng for a bite to eat and
a drink.

### ★ Top Tip

To get to the caves, take bus 603 (¥3,
45 minutes, every 10 to 15 minutes)
from Dàtóng's train station to the
terminus.

of Buddhist angels, Bodhisattvas and other
celestial figures. In the middle of the cave,
a square block pagoda or column fuses
with the ceiling, with Buddhas on each side
across two levels.

### Cave 9

The dual-chamber Cave 9, the Aksokhya
Buddha Cave, is also an astonishing spec-
tacle, with its vast seated and gold-faced
Buddha.

### Caves 16 to 20

Caves 16 to 20 are the earliest caves at
Yúngāng, carved under the supervision
of monk Tanyao. Cave 16, the Standing
Buddha Cave, contains a huge standing
Buddha whose middle section is badly
eroded. The walls of the cave are perforat-
ed with small niches containing Buddhas.

Cave 17 houses a colossal 15.6m seated
Maitreya Buddha, badly weathered, but
intact. Examine the exceptional quality of
the carvings in Cave 18; some of the faces
are perfectly presented. Cave 19 contains a
vast 16.8m-high effigy of Sakyamuni.

### Cave 20

Entirely exposed to the elements, Cave
20 (AD 460–470) is similar to the Losana
Buddha Statue Cave at Lóngmén, originally
depicting a trinity (past, present and future) of Buddhas. The huge seated Buddha
in the middle is the representative icon at
Yúngāng, while the Buddha on the left has
somehow vanished.

### The Museum

Past the last set of caves, you can head
down to the slick and highly informative
**museum** (⊙9.30am-5pm) detailing the Wei
Kingdom and the artwork at the caves.
Sadly, English captions are very limited.

# Píngyáo

While other 'ancient' cities in China will rustle together an unconvincing display of old city walls, sporadic temples or the occasional ragged alley, Píngyáo has managed to keep its beguiling narrative largely intact.

## ◉ SIGHTS

### Confucius Temple
Confucian Site

(文庙; Wén Miào; Wenmiao Jie; 文庙街; ⊙8am-7pm) Píngyáo's oldest surviving building is **Dàchéng Hall** (大成殿; Dàchéng Diàn), dating from 1163. It can be found in the Confucius Temple, a huge complex where bureaucrats-to-be came to take the imperial exams. Within the hall, beneath the roosting and cooing pigeons, is the seated sage with his fellow disciples.

### Wang Family Courtyard
Courtyard

(王家大院; Wángjiā Dàyuàn; ¥55; ⊙8am-7pm) More castle than cosy home, this grand Qing dynasty former residence has been very well maintained (note the wooden galleries fronting many of the courtyard buildings). Due to the sheer size, the seemingly endless procession of courtyards (123 in all) become a little repetitive, but it's still beautiful and the complex is interspersed with gardens.

Four direct buses (¥17, one hour, 7.10am, 8.40am, 12.40pm and 2.20pm) leave from Píngyáo's bus station, returning at 10.50am, 12.30pm, 3.30pm and 5.20pm.

### Zhāngbì Underground Castle
Cave

(张壁古堡; Zhāngbì Gǔbǎo; ¥60; ⊙8am-6.30pm) This 1400-year-old network of defence tunnels, stretching underground for 10km, is the oldest and longest series of such tunnels in China. Built at the end of the Sui dynasty in case of attack by Tang dynasty invaders, they were never used and subsequently fell into disrepair. Today, 1500m of tunnels on three levels have been restored.

You descend as low as 26m in places and tour narrow and stooped subterranean passages, which were once storage rooms, guardhouses and bedrooms. Holes cut into the side of shafts leading to the surface indicate escape routes and places where soldiers stood sentry to spy on would-be attackers.

You can only get here on a tour or by private car (per day ¥350). Check with your accommodation in Píngyáo.

## ☉ TOURS

Most hostels and guesthouses will arrange transport to the surrounding sights. Day tours to the Wang Family Courtyard and Zhāngbì Underground Castle are ¥80 per person (excluding the admission price and food) and depart at 8.30am, returning late afternoon. You can also hire a private car for ¥350 per day.

## ✖ EATING

### Déjūyuán
Shānxī ¥

(德居源; Petit Resto; 82 Nan Dajie; 南大街 82号; mains from ¥25; ⊙8.30am-10pm; 🛜) Traveller-friendly, but no worse for that, this welcoming and popular little restaurant has a simple and tasty menu (in English) of northern Chinese dishes such as dumplings (¥25), plus all the local faves. Try the famed Píngyáo beef (¥45), the mountain noodles (¥15) or the fried shrimps with green pepper (¥48). It's often packed, so you may have to share a table.

### Tianyuankui Guesthouse
Shānxī ¥¥

(天元奎客栈; Tiānyuánkuí Kèzhàn; ☎0354 568 0069; 73 Nan Dajie; 南大街73号; dishes ¥10-68; ⊙7.30am-10pm; 🛜) With warm wooden furnishings and floral cushions, friendly staff, free wi-fi and soft music, this restaurant has an easygoing vibe that invites travellers to linger over their meals. The English iPad menu has photos of the dishes – a range of traditional favourites such as Píngyáo

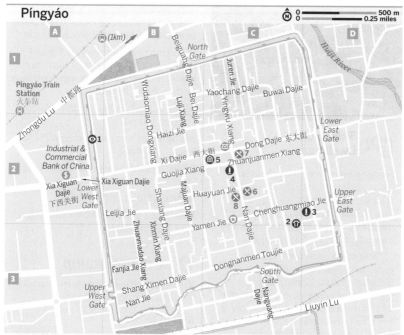

# Píngyáo

beef sit next to the usual meat, veg and tofu offerings – making ordering a snap.

### Sakura Cafe                                       Cafe ¥¥

(櫻花屋西餐酒吧; Yīnghuāwū Xīcān Jiǔbā; 6 Dong Jie; 东大街6号; mains from ¥30, beers from ¥15; ⊙8am-11pm; 🛜🅿) This eclectic and fun cafe-bar attracts both locals and foreigners with its daily food and drink specials. It does decent, if pricey, pizzas (from ¥65), burgers, sandwiches and omelettes, plus breakfasts, coffee, beer and cocktails. Staff are welcoming. There's another equally popular branch at 86 Nan Dajie, which is more aimed at Chinese (this branch is aimed at Westerners).

## ℹ INFORMATION

**China Post** (中国邮政; Zhōngguó Yóuzhèng; Xi Dajie; 西大街; ⊙8am-6pm) Handily located at the centre of the old town.

**Industrial & Commercial Bank of China** (ICBC; 工商银行; Gōngshāng Yínháng; Xia Xiguan Dajie; 下西关大街) ATM just west of the old city wall.

## ℹ GETTING THERE & AWAY

### BUS

Píngyáo's **bus station** (汽车新站; qìchēxīn zhàn; ☎0354 569 0011; Zhongdu Dongjie; 中都东街) has buses to Tàiyuán (¥26, two hours, frequent

## Shānxī Cave Dwellings

People have been living in **cave houses** (窑洞; *yáodòng*) in Shānxī for almost 5000 years; it's believed that at one stage a quarter of the population lived underground and the countryside is still littered with *yáodòng*, especially around the Yellow River area.

These days most lie empty and abandoned, but almost three million people in Shānxī (and around 30 million in total in China) still live in caves. And who can blame them? Compared to modern houses, they're cheap, far better insulated against freezing winters and scorching summers, more soundproof, and they afford better protection from natural disasters such as earthquakes or forest fires. Furthermore, with far fewer building materials needed to construct them, they're a lot more environmentally friendly. So why isn't everyone living in them? Well, although most are now connected to the national grid, the vast majority of cave communities have no running water or sewerage system, turning simple daily tasks such as washing or going to the toilet into a mission. Suddenly, even the ugliest tower block seems attractive.

Cave houses
BAMBOOME / GETTY IMAGES ©

6.30am to 7.40pm) and the Qiao Family Courtyard (¥13, 45 minutes, half-hourly).

### TRAIN

Píngyáo has two train stations – the older Píngyáo station (平遥站; Píngyáo *zhàn*) just north of the city walls and the new Píngyáo Gǔchéng train station (平遥古城站; Píngyáo Gǔchéng *zhàn*) further away to the south; the latter mainly services high-speed trains. Check to see which station your train is pulling in at.

Tickets for trains (especially to Xī'ān) are tough to get in summer, so book ahead. Your hotel/hostel should be able to help. Trains depart for the following destinations.

**Běijīng** D-class train 2nd/1st class ¥183/255, 4½ hours, two daily

**Běijīng** G-class train 2nd/1st class ¥226/323, four hours, one daily

**Dàtóng** hard seat/sleeper ¥61/122, six to eight hours, four daily

**Tàiyuán** ¥18, 1½ hours, frequent

**Xī'ān** D-class train 2nd/1st class ¥150/188, three hours, six daily

### ℹ️ GETTING AROUND

Many hotels and hostels arrange pick-up from the train station, so check upfront.

### BICYCLE

Píngyáo can be easily navigated on foot or by bicycle (¥10 per day). Bike rental is available all over; most guesthouses offer it and there are many spots along Nan Dajie and Xi Dajie.

### BUS

From Píngyáo Gǔchéng train station, take bus 108 (¥1) to the old town.

### TAXI

A rickshaw will run from Píngyáo train station and the bus station to the old town for ¥10. A taxi from Píngyáo Gǔchéng train station to the old town costs ¥30. Note that taxis are not allowed to enter the old town (to keep traffic under control), so you will be dropped outside the gates of the city wall.

## Dàtóng

Dàtóng (大同) today is fascinating, and charming to boot. Come evening, the old-town sensations – with red lanterns swinging in the breeze and wind chimes tinkling on the illuminated city walls – are hard to beat. No matter that most of this has been recreated from scratch by an overambitious mayor: a mountain of cash – an estimated ¥50 billion – has been ploughed into a colossal renovation of the old quarter. What's more, the town is the gateway to the awe-inspiring Yúngāng Caves, one of China's most outstanding Buddhist treasures.

## ◎ SIGHTS

### Dàtóng City Wall
Fortress

(大同城墙; Dàtóng Chéngqiáng; admission ¥30; ⊙8am-9.30pm) This incredible city wall has been rebuilt from the soles up in what must be one of the greatest feats of engineering to hit Dàtóng since, well, since the last time it was built. Prior to the rebuild, the wall had been denuded of bricks and reduced to earthen stumps. At present, you can only walk around three sides of the wall – the gate in the west is still under construction. The wall is not the original, but looks sublime.

### Nine Dragon Screen
Wall

(九龙壁; Jiǔlóng Bì; Da Dongjie; 大东街; admission ¥10; ⊙8am-6.30pm) With its nine beautiful multicoloured coiling dragons, this 45.5m-long, 8m-high and 2m-thick Ming dynasty spirit wall was built in 1392. One of the finest in China (there are two more in Běijīng), it's the largest glazed-tile yǐngbì (影壁) spirit wall in China and is a truly amazing sight; the palace it once protected belonged to the 13th son of a Ming emperor and burnt down in 1644. Amazingly, the palace is being rebuilt in its entirety, covering a vast area of town.

### Bā Táizi
Ruins

(八台子; Bā Táizicūn; 八台子村; ⊙24hr) FREE Alongside magnificently dilapidated earthen sections of the Great Wall that disappear over the top of Horsehead Hill (马头山; Mǎtóu Shān), this fabulous Gothic church ruin is quite a sight. All that remains of the **Holy Mother Church** (圣母堂; Shèngmǔ Táng), built in 1876, is its front gate and bell tower and lopped-off spire above it.

 **Rebuilding Dàtóng's Old Town**

Much of Dàtóng's **old town** (老城区; Lǎochéngqū) has been recreated in an astonishingly ambitious program commenced by former city mayor Geng Yanbo, which aimed to restore its ancient grandeur and charm. While much, including the amazing city wall, is now largely finished, further re-creations were ongoing at the time of writing, including the simply colossal Dài Wángfǔ palace. While much of this rebuild looks good, it has unfortunately involved a huge and deliberate loss of the original city to re-create something better looking.

Buildings rebuilt from the ground up include the **mosque** (清真大寺; Qīngzhēn Dà Sì; admission ¥10; ⊙8am-8pm), a Taoist temple, and many former courtyard houses, while portions of Huayan Jie, Da Beijie and Da Nanjie have become pedestrian-only shopping streets.

The vast cost of the old-town refit has been partially passed onto visitors, with admission prices to key sights doubling or more. Other costs include the resettling of tens of thousands of residents to accommodate the great rebuild. Mayor Geng Yanbo (nicknamed 'Geng Chai Chai', or 'Geng the Demolisher') moved on to become Tàiyuán mayor in 2013, greatly slowing the pace of the program. The city walls still have a western section waiting to be rebuilt and work on the Dài Wángfǔ palace has slowed, although it's gradually nearing completion.

Reconstructed city gate, Dàtóng
HECKEPICS / GETTY IMAGES ©

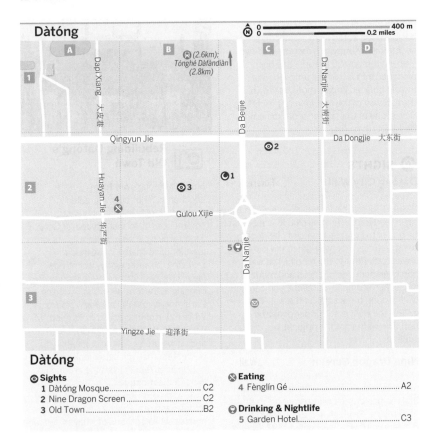

# Dàtóng

Qingyun Jie

Da Dongjie 大东街

Dapi Xiang 大皮巷

Da Beijie

Da Nanjie 大南街

Huayan Jie 华严街

Gulou Xijie

Da Nanjie

Yingze Jie 迎泽街

(2.6km);
*Tónghé Dàfàndiàn*
(2.8km)

## Dàtóng

### ◉ Sights
1 Dàtóng Mosque.............................................C2
2 Nine Dragon Screen .................................C2
3 Old Town .......................................................B2

### 🍴 Eating
4 Fènglín Gé .....................................................A2

### 🍸 Drinking & Nightlife
5 Garden Hotel..................................................C3

No explanation for the church's demise is given in the blurb on the board alongside, nor how the church arrived in such a remote spot.

This entire area is very near the border with Inner Mongolia. To reach Bā Táizi, hop on a bus (¥18, 80 minutes, regularly 6.15am to 6.20pm) from Dàtóng's main bus station to Zuǒyún (左云), then negotiate with a taxi driver to take you to Bā Táizicūn (八台子村), around 20km away. Expect to pay between ¥80 and ¥100 return; the driver will wait for you for around 30 minutes.

The last bus to Dàtóng leaves Zuǒyún at 6.30pm.

## 🍴 EATING

Dàtóng has some excellent dining options, from packed and popular noodle diners to elegant, traditional-style restaurants.

### Fènglín Gé          Chinese ¥

(凤临阁; ☎0352 205 9799; near cnr Gulou Xijie & Huayan Jie; 鼓楼西街华严街路口; mains from ¥25; ◷6.30-9.30am, 11.30am-2pm & 5.30-9pm; ❄🅸) Exquisite and delectable *shāomai* (steamed dim-sum dumpling) is the star of the show at this traditionally styled restaurant at the heart of the old town. Order by the steamer (笼; *lóng*) or half steamer. The crab *shāomai* are succulent and gorgeous, but not cheap (¥15 each, half steamer ¥45); there's lamb too (¥7 each, half steamer ¥26) and other tempting fillings.

### Tónghé Dàfàndiàn                    Chinese ¥

(同和大饭店; Zhanqian Jie; dishes ¥16-40; ⏰11am-2pm & 6-9pm) This fantastic, bright and cheery spot alongside the Hongqi Hotel can look a little intimidating with its big round tables better suited to functions, but solo diners can pull up a chair no problem. There's a huge range of tasty, well-presented dishes on the picture menu, suiting all budgets.

## 🍷 DRINKING & NIGHTLIFE

Dàtóng is a rather quiet place come nightfall and doesn't have much of a bar or clubbing culture. The lounge bar of the **Garden Hotel** (花园大饭店; Huāyuán Dàfàndiàn; ☑0352 586 5888; www.garden hoteldatong.com; 59 Da Nanjie; 大南街59号) is a restful place for a drink.

## ℹ INFORMATION

**China Post** (Da Nanjie) A short walk south from the Garden Hotel.

**Industrial & Commercial Bank of China** (ICBC; 工商银行; Gōngshāng Yínháng; Weidu Dadao)

## ℹ GETTING THERE & AWAY

### AIR

Located 20km east of the city, Dàtóng's small airport has flights to Běijīng (¥450, one hour), Shànghǎi (¥1450, 2½ hours) and Guǎngzhōu (¥1650, 4½ hours). Buy tickets at www.ctrip.com or www.elong.net.

### BUS

Buses from the South bus station (新南站; *xīnnán zhàn*), located 9km from the train station, include those to Běijīng (¥120, four hours, hourly 8am to 5.30pm) and Tàiyuán (¥100, 3½ hours, four daily). You can also catch minibuses to some destinations from outside the train station.

### TRAIN

Train departures from Dàtóng include Běijīng (hard seat/sleeper ¥48/108, six hours, 11 daily), Píngyáo (hard seat/sleeper ¥63/122, seven to eight hours, four daily), Tàiyuán (hard seat/sleeper ¥44/98, four hours, seven daily) and Xī'ān (hard seat/sleeper ¥114/223, 16½ hours, daily).

## ℹ GETTING AROUND

Bus routes are being readjusted owing to the massive construction all around town, so expect changes. Bus 4 and 15 run from the train station to the main bus station. Bus 30 takes 30 minutes to run from the train station to the new south bus station. Buses 27 and 35 go to the old town from Weidu Dadao. Taxi flagfall is ¥7.

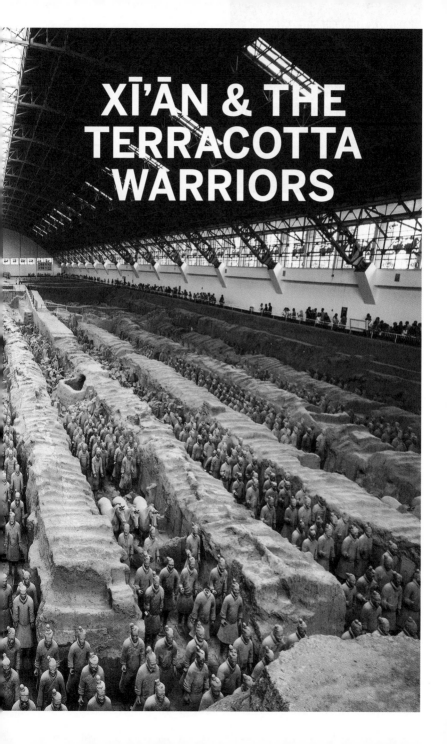

# XĪ'ĀN & THE TERRACOTTA WARRIORS

# Xī'ān & the Terracotta Warriors at a Glance...

*Once the terminus of the Silk Road and a melting pot of cultures and religions, as well as home to emperors, courtesans, poets, monks, merchants and warriors, the glory days of Xī'ān (西安; pronounced 'see-an') may have ended in the early 10th century, but a considerable amount of ancient Cháng'ān, the former city, still survives. Xī'ān's Ming-era city walls remain intact, vendors of all descriptions still crowd the narrow lanes of the Muslim Quarter, and there are enough places of interest to keep even the most amateur historian riveted.*

### Two Days in Xī'ān

Journey out of town on the bus to see the **Terracotta Warriors** (p98), then walk the amazing **city wall** (p103) of Xī'ān in the afternoon to put the city in perspective. Dine at **Hǎiróng Guōtiēdiàn** (p105) or **Sānjiěmèi Jiǎozi** (p106). On day two, snack your way through the **Muslim Quarter** (p103) and then explore the astonishing **Great Mosque** (p103) before discovering the secrets of the **Forest of Stelae Museum** (p104).

### Four Days in Xī'ān

Pack some supplies and hop on an early bus for Huá Shān. Climb the mountain, explore its temples and either spend the night on the mountain or catch the last bus back to Xī'ān. Earmark the **Shaanxi History Museum** (p104) for a morning visit, then discover Xī'ān's temple brood: **Big Goose Pagoda** (p103), **Little Goose Pagoda** (p103) and Tibetan Buddhist **Guǎngrén Temple** (p104).

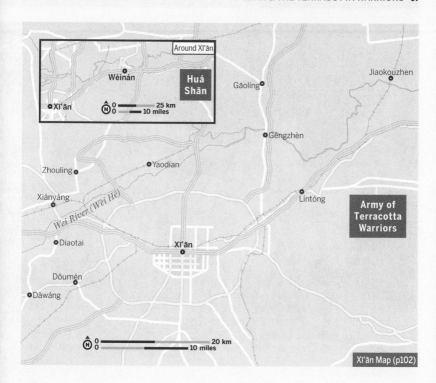

Around Xī'ān

Wèinán

Huá
Shān

Xī'ān

Gāolíng

Jiaokouzhen

0 — 25 km
0 — 10 miles

Gěngzhèn

Zhouling

Yáodian

Xiányáng

Wei River (Wei Hé)

Lìntóng

Diaotai

Xī'ān

Army of
Terracotta
Warriors

Dòumén

Dàwáng

0 — 20 km
0 — 10 miles

Xī'ān Map (p102)

### Arriving in Xī'ān

**Xiányáng Airport** Shuttle buses run
every 20 to 30 minutes from 5.40am to
8pm between the airport and the city.
Metered taxis into the city charge more
than ¥100.

**Main train station** Just outside the
northern city walls; well connected to
the rest of the country.

**Long-distance bus station** Opposite
the train station, with buses throughout
the region.

### Where to Stay

Xī'ān has a very good choice of accommodation in every budget from basic
to top-end. All hostels in the city offer
similar services, including bike hire,
wi-fi, laundry, restaurant and travel services. Ask about free pick-up from the
train station and book ahead at popular
places.

In Huá Shān, you can either stay in Huá
Shān village or on one of the peaks.
Mountain hotels are basic, with no
showers and shared bathrooms.

CONTAX66 / SHUTTERSTOCK ©

# The Terracotta Warriors

*The Terracotta Army isn't just Xī'ān's premier site, it's one of the most famous archaeological finds in the world.*

### Great For...

☑ **Don't Miss**

The pair of bronze chariots and horses in the Qin Shi Huang Emperor Tomb Artefact Exhibition Hall.

This subterranean life-size army of thousands has silently stood guard over the soul of China's first unifier for more than two millennia. Either Qin Shi Huang was terrified of the vanquished spirits awaiting him in the afterlife or, as most archaeologists believe, he expected his rule to continue in death as it had in life.

The discovery of the army of warriors was entirely fortuitous. In 1974, peasants drilling a well uncovered an underground vault that eventually yielded thousands of terracotta soldiers and horses in battle formation. Throughout the years the site became so famous that many of its unusual attributes are now well known, in particular the fact that no two soldier's faces are alike.

### Pits 3 & 2

Start with the smallest pit, Pit 3, containing

Terracotta Warriors

DANIEL GILBEY PHOTOGRAPHY - MY PORTFOLIO / SHUTTERSTOCK ©

### ⓘ Need to Know

兵马俑; Bīngmǎyǒng; www.bmy.com.cn; adult/student Mar-Nov ¥150/75, Dec-Feb ¥120/60; ⊙8.30am-5.30pm Mar-Nov, to 5pm Dec-Feb

### ✕ Take a Break

There's a decent cafe in the theatre building. There's also an assortment of restaurants beyond the exit on the way back to the parking lot.

### ★ Top Tip

The site is easily reached by public bus 914 or 915 (¥8, one hour), which depart from Xī'ān train station every four minutes from 6am to 7pm.

72 warriors and horses; it's believed to be the army headquarters due to the number of high-ranking officers unearthed here. It's interesting to note that the northern room would have been used to make sacrificial offerings before battle.

In the next pit, Pit 2, containing around 1300 warriors and horses, you can examine five of the soldiers up close: a kneeling archer, a standing archer, a cavalryman and his horse, a mid-ranking officer and a general. The level of detail is extraordinary: the expressions, hairstyles, armour and even the tread on the footwear are all unique.

### Pit 1

The largest pit, Pit 1, is the most imposing. Housed in a building the size of an aircraft hangar, it is believed to contain 6000 warriors (only 2000 are on display) and horses,

all facing east and ready for battle. The vanguard of three rows of archers (both crossbow and longbow) is followed by the main force of soldiers, who originally held spears, swords, dagger-axes and other long-shaft weapons. The infantry were accompanied by 35 chariots, though these, made of wood, have long since disintegrated.

### Qin Shi Huang Emperor Tomb Artefact Exhibition Hall

Almost as extraordinary as the soldiers is a pair of bronze chariots and horses unearthed just 20m west of the Tomb of Qin Shi Huang. These are now on display, together with some of the original weaponry and a mid-ranking officer you can see up close in this huge modern **museum** (秦始皇帝陵文物陈列厅; Qínshǐhuángdìlíng Chénliètīng).

# Huá Shān

*One of Taoism's five sacred mountains, the granite domes of Huá Shān (华山) used to be home to hermits, sages and Taoist mystics (some of whom, they say, could fly).*

---

**Great For...**

☑ **Don't Miss**

The heart-in-your-mouth, white knuckle Plank Walk.

The mountain routes feature knife-blade ridges and twisted pine trees poking from crevices and clinging to ledges, while the summits of the mountain offer transcendent panoramas of hills and countryside stretching away to the horizon.

## The Route to the Peaks

There are three ways up the mountain to the **North Peak** (北峰; Běi Fēng), the first of five summit peaks. Two of these options start from the eastern base of the mountain, at the North Peak cable-car terminus. The first option is handy if you don't fancy the climb: an Austrian-built **cable car** (北峰索道; *běifēng suǒdào*; one way/return ¥80/150; ☉7am-7pm) will lift you silently to the North Peak in eight scenic minutes, though you may face long queues at busy times.

Plank Walk

NICHOLAS BILLINGTON / SHUTTERSTOCK ©

Wèinán

Huá Shān

Xī'ān

### ❶ Need to Know

Admission is ¥180 (students ¥90).

### ✕ Take a Break

At the end of your slog, sit down for coffee and superb views at **Huá Shān Coffee** (华山咖啡; Huàshān Kāfēi; North Peak Hotel; coffee from ¥38; ⏲8.30am-5pm, 24hr in summer).

> ★ **Top Tip**
> Some locals make the climb at night, using torches (flashlights); the idea is to start around 11pm and be at the East Peak for sunrise.

**West Peak** (西峰; Xī Fēng), the way has been cut along a narrow rock ridge with impressive sheer cliffs on either side.

## Plank Walk

At the South Peak, thrill-seekers can try the **Plank Walk** (长空栈道; Chángkōng Zhàndào; adult ¥30); a metal ladder leads down to a path made from wooden boards that hover above a 2000m vertical drop. Thankfully, the admission fee includes a harness and carabiners that you lock onto cables, but even with these safety features it's scary as hell. At peak times, and even in the slow season, queues can get seriously long here.

## Getting There

From Xī'ān to Huá Shān, catch one of the private buses (¥36, two hours, 6am to 8pm) that depart when full from in front of Xī'ān train station. You'll be dropped off on Yuquan Lu, which is also where buses back to Xī'ān leave from 7.30am to 7pm; they depart from the lot opposite the post office.

The second option is to work your way to the North Peak under the cable-car route. This takes two sweaty hours, and two sections of 50m or so are literally vertical, with nothing but a steel chain to grab onto and tiny chinks cut into the rock for footing.

The third option is the most popular, but it's still hard work, taking between three and five hours. A 6km path leads to the North Peak from the village of Huá Shān, at the base of the mountain (the other side of the mountain from the cable car). It's pretty easy for the first 4km, but after that it's all steep stairs.

## Blue Dragon Ridge

Along **Blue Dragon Ridge** (苍龙岭; Cānglóng Lǐng), which connects the **North Peak** with the **East Peak** (东峰; Dōng Fēng), **South Peak** (南峰; Nán Fēng) and

# Xī'ān

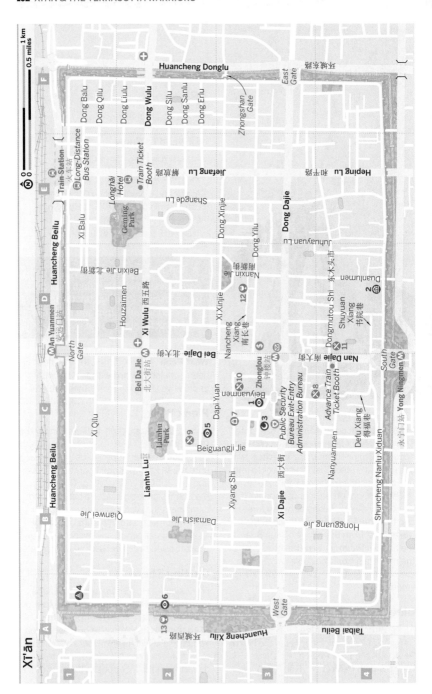

Huancheng Beilu

Huancheng Beilu

M An Yuanmen
安远门站

North
Gate

Xi Qilu

Lianhu Lu 莲湖路

Lianhu
Park

Qianwei Jie

Damaishi Jie

Xiyang Shi

Xi Dajie 西大街

Beiguangji Jie

Huancheng Xilu 环城西路

West
Gate

Taibai Beilu

Houzaimen

Xi Wulu 西五路

Bei Da Jie
北大街站 M

Bei Dajie 北大街 M

Dapi Yuan

9

5

Beiyuanmen

10

Zhonglou
钟楼

1

7

3

Public Security
Bureau Exit-Entry
Administration Bureau

Nanyuanmen

Hongguang Jie

Shuncheng Nanlu Xiduan

4

13

6

Geming
Park

Lónghăi
Hotel

Shangde Lu

Dong Xinjie

Beixin Jie 北新街

Nanjie
Xiang
南长巷

Xi Xinjie

12

Naxin Jie
南新街

Dong Yilu

S

M

8

Advance Train
Ticket Booth

Defu Xiang
得福巷

Train Station
Long-Distance
Bus Station

Train Ticket
Booth

Dong Balu

Dong Qilu

Dong Liulu

**Dong Wulu**

Dong Silu

Dong Sanlu

Dong Erlu

Zhongshan
Gate

Jiefang Lu 解放路

**Dong Dajie**

Juhuayuan Lu

Dongmutou Shi 东木头市

Shuyuan
Xiang
书院巷

Dongcang
Xiang

Dunlunmen

2

South
Gate

Yong Ningmen M
永宁门站

**Huancheng Donglu**

East
Gate

Heping Lu 和平路

M South
Gate

1 km
0.5 miles

N

# Xī'ān

# Xī'ān

## ◉ SIGHTS

The ranging plains and flat ochre farmland around Xī'ān are strewn with early imperial tombs, many of which have yet to be excavated. Unless you have a particular fascination for imperial burial sites, you can probably come away satisfied after visiting a couple of them.

### Xī'ān City Walls                    Historic Site

(西安城墙; Xī'ān Chéngqiáng; ¥54; ⊗8am-8.30pm Apr-Oct, to 7pm Nov-Mar) Xī'ān is one of the few cities in China where the imposing old city walls still stand. Built in 1370 during the Ming dynasty, the magnificent 12m-high walls are surrounded by a dry moat and form a rectangle with a perimeter of 14km. Most sections have been restored or rebuilt, and it is possible to walk the walls in their entirety in a leisurely four hours (or around two hours by bike, or at a slow jog).

### Muslim Quarter                    Historic Site

(回族区; Ⓜ Zhonglou (Bell Tower)) The backstreets leading north from the **Drum Tower** (鼓楼; Gǔ Lóu; Beiyuanmen; ¥35, combined Bell Tower ticket ¥50; ⊗8.30am-9.30pm Mar-Oct, to 6.30pm Nov-Feb, last admission 30min before closing; Ⓜ Zhonglou (Bell Tower)) have been home to the city's Huí community (non-Uighur Chinese Muslims) for centuries, perhaps as far back as the Ming dynasty or further still. The narrow lanes are full of butcher shops, sesame-oil factories, smaller mosques hidden behind enormous wooden doors, men in white skullcaps and women with their heads covered in colour-ed scarves. It's a great place to wander and especially atmospheric at night.

### Great Mosque                    Mosque

(清真大寺; Qīngzhēn Dàsi; Huajue Xiang; 化觉巷; Mar-Nov ¥25, Dec-Feb ¥15, Muslims free; ⊗8am-7.30pm Mar-Nov, to 5.30pm Dec-Feb; Ⓜ Zhonglou (Bell Tower)) Bigger than many temples in China, the Great Mosque is a gorgeous blend of Chinese and Islamic architecture and one of the most fascinating sacred sights in the land. The present buildings are mostly Ming and Qing, though the mosque was founded in the 8th century. Arab influences extend from the central minaret (cleverly disguised as a stumpy pagoda) to the enormous turquoise-roofed Prayer Hall (not open to visitors) at the back of the complex, dating to the Ming dynasty.

### Big Goose Pagoda                    Pagoda

(大雁塔; Dàyàn Tǎ; Yanta Nanlu; 雁塔南路; grounds ¥50, pagoda ¥40; ⊗8am-7pm Apr-Oct, to 6pm Nov-Mar) This pagoda, Xī'ān's most famous landmark, 4km southeast of the South Gate and formerly within the old (and huge) Tang dynasty city wall, dominates the surrounding modern buildings. One of China's best examples of a Tang-style pagoda (squarish rather than round), it was completed in AD 652 to house Buddhist sutras brought back from India by the monk Xuan Zang. His travels inspired one of the best-known works of Chinese literature, *Journey to the West*.

### Little Goose Pagoda                    Pagoda

(小雁塔; Xiǎoyàn Tǎ; grounds free, pagoda ¥30; ⊗8.30am-7pm Wed-Mon; Ⓜ Nanshaomen) Little Goose Pagoda is in the pleasant grounds of

## Muslim Quarter Eats

Hit the Muslim Quarter for tasty eating in Xī'ān. Common dishes here include *májiàng liángpí* (麻酱凉皮; cold noodles in sesame sauce), *fěnzhēngròu* (粉蒸肉; chopped mutton fried in a wok with ground wheat), the 'Chinese hamburger' *ròujiāmó* (肉夹馍; fried pork or beef in pitta bread, sometimes with green peppers and cumin), *càijiāmó* (菜夹馍; the vegetarian version of *ròujiāmó*) and the ubiquitous *ròuchuàn* (肉串; kebabs).

Best of all is the delicious *yángròu pàomó* (羊肉泡馍), a soup dish that involves crumbling a flat loaf of bread into a bowl and adding noodles, mutton and broth; discover it at **Lǎo Sūn Jiā** (老孙家; ☏ 029 8240 3205; 5th fl, 364 Dong Dajie; 东大街364号5层; dishes ¥12-49; ⊗ 8am-9.30pm; ⓜ Zhonglou (Bell Tower)).

You can also pick up mouth-watering desserts such as *huāshēnggāo* (花生糕; peanut cakes) and *shìbǐng* (柿饼; dried persimmons), which can be found at the market or in Muslim Quarter shops.

The food market around Xiyangshi Jie (西羊市街) is excellent for everything from lamb skewers to walnuts, cakes, pomegranate juice, flat breads of all sorts, fried potatoes, fragrant tofu and much more.

---

Jiànfú Temple. Its top was shaken off by an earthquake in the middle of the 16th century, but the rest of the 43m-high structure is intact.

Jiànfú Temple was built in AD 684 to bless the afterlife of the late Emperor Gaozong. The pagoda, a rather delicate building of 15 progressively smaller tiers, was built in AD 707–709 and housed Buddhist scriptures brought back from India by the pilgrim Yi Jing.

### Forest of Stelae Museum  Museum

(碑林博物馆; Bēilín Bówùguǎn; www.beilin-museum.com; 15 Sanxue Jie; 三学街15号; Mar-Nov ¥75, Dec-Feb ¥50; ⊗ 8am-6.45pm Mar-Nov, to 5.45pm Dec-Feb, last admission 45min before closing) Housed in Xī'ān's Confucius Temple, this museum holds more than 1000 stone stelae (inscribed tablets), including the nine Confucian classics and some exemplary calligraphy. The highlight is the fantastic sculpture gallery (across from the gift shop), where animal guardians from the Tang dynasty, pictorial tomb stones and Buddhist statuary muster together. To reach the museum, follow Shuyuan Xiang east from the South Gate. The second gallery holds a Nestorian tablet (AD 781), the earliest recorded account of Christianity in China. The fourth gallery displays a collection of ancient maps and portraits, and rubbings (copies) are made here, an absorbing process to observe.

### Shaanxi History Museum  Museum

(陕西历史博物馆; Shǎnxī Lìshǐ Bówùguǎn; 91 Xiaozhai Donglu; 小寨东路91号; ⊗ 8.30am-6pm Tue-Sun Apr-Oct, last admission 4.30pm, 9.30am-5pm Tue-Sun Nov-Mar, last admission 4pm) FREE This museum naturally overlaps with Xī'ān's surrounding sights but makes for a comprehensive stroll through ancient Cháng'ān. Most exhibits offer illuminating explanations in English. Don't miss the four original terracotta warrior statues on the ground floor. In the Sui and Tang section, unique murals depict a polo match, and you'll find a series of painted pottery figurines with elaborate hairstyles and dress, including several bearded foreigners, musicians and braying camels.

Go early and expect to queue for at least 30 minutes.

### Guǎngrén Temple  Buddhist

(广仁寺; Guǎngrén Sì; Guangren Si Lu; 广仁寺路; ¥20; ⊗ 8am-5.30pm; ⓜ Sajinqiao or Yuxiangmen) The sole Tibetan Buddhist temple in the entire province, Guǎngrén Temple originally dates to the early 18th century, but was largely rebuilt in the 20th century. As a sacred Tibetan Buddhist place of worship, the temple hums with mystery and spiritual energy. Perhaps the most valuable object in the temple resides in the final hall, a golden

Street-food vendors, Xī'ān

representation of Sakyamuni that rests upon a Tang dynasty pedestal. There is only one other like it, housed at the Jokhang Temple in Lhasa.

## 🕑 TOURS

Most hostels run their own tours, but make sure you find out what is included (admission fees, lunch, English-speaking guide) and try to get an exact itinerary, or you could end up being herded through the Terracotta Warriors before you have a chance to get your camera out. Tours may also include stops you may wish not to include, such as terracotta warrior figurine factories, where you may feel coerced into buying things you don't want.

## 🔒 SHOPPING

### Xiyang Market                    Market
(西羊市; Xīyáng Shì) This narrow alley running north of the Great Mosque is a great central stop for souvenirs. With vocal vendors, bargaining is a way of life here.

You'll get everything from terracotta warriors to shadow puppets, lanterns, tea ware, 'antiques', jade, T-shirts, paintings, Cultural Revolution memorabilia and whatnot. Quality varies a lot, so look for defects, but bargains can be had.

## 🍴 EATING

Xī'ān has a wide range of restaurants serving cuisine from across China and the world. The Muslim Quarter is an excellent place for snacking, while a good street to wander for a selection of more typically Chinese restaurants is Dongmutou Shi, east of Nan Dajie.

### Hǎiróng Guōtiēdiàn     Dumpling ¥
(海荣锅贴店; 67 Zhubashi; 竹笆市67号; mains from ¥12; ⏰10.30am-10pm) A civilised and restful choice, this place specialises in *guōtiē* (锅贴) 'pot-sticker' fried dumplings and they are simply delicious. There's six different types to choose from, including a vegetarian choice. There are other dishes on the menu too, including the lovely *tiáozi*

*ròu* (条子肉; ¥32), soft chunks of pork that you squeeze into white buns to consume together.

### Mǎ Hóng Xiǎochǎo Pàomóguǎn
Muslim ¥

(马洪小炒泡馍馆; ☎133 5918 5583; 46 Hongbu Jie; 红埠街46号; ¥17; Ⓜ Bei Da Jie) At this superb choice for lamb or beef *pàomó*, you need to grab a seat before 11am, otherwise it's all elbows. Pay for your dish, take your seat and then break the round bread into a myriad tiny pieces (they *must* be small) to drop them in the bowl and wait for your meat broth to arrive, splashed over the crumbs for a filling and fine meal. Ask either for mild (清淡; *qīngdàn*) or spicy (辣; *là*).

### Muslim Family Restaurant
Chinese, Muslim ¥

(回文人家; Huiwen Renjia; Beiyuanmen; 北院门; dishes ¥10-98; ◷9am-10.30pm; ⓂZhonglou (Bell Tower)) Right on Beiyuanmen in the heart of the Muslim Quarter, this smart establishment serves classic Muslim dishes such as *ròujiāmó* (beef in flat bread; ¥15), lamb kebabs (¥10 each), beef or lamb-filled *xiàbǐng* (fried, crispy bread; ¥18 to ¥20),

dumplings (¥15 to ¥18) and lovely grilled golden needle mushrooms (¥18).

There's no English sign so look for the veil-adorned female waiting staff in the doorway.

### Sānjiěmèi Jiǎozi
Dumpling ¥

(三姐妹饺子, Three Sisters Dumplings; ☎029 8725 2129; 140 Dongmutou Shi; 东木头市140 号; dumplings from ¥14; ◷10.30am-2.30pm & 5-9.30pm) Weary diners with dumpling fatigue will be inspired by the rustic two-room Three Sisters, with its well-done twist on classics. Try succulent carrot and lamb dumplings blanketed in crisp peanuts and fried chives. Or for vegetarians, the winning texture of dry and marinated tofu (yes, two types) with the zing of crunchy coriander and a lashing of chilli.

## 🍷 DRINKING & NIGHTLIFE

### ParkQin
Bar

(秦吧; Qínbā; 2 Shuncheng Nanlu Xiduan; 南门里顺城南路西段2号; ⓂYongningmen) In the basement bowels of the **Shūyuàn Youth Hostel** (书院青年旅舍; Shūyuàn Qīngnián

From left: Golden Buddha statue; Shaanxi History Museum (p104); Great Mosque (p103)

Lùshè; ☏029 8728 0092), this music bar is a tip-top riot and a fun night out. Staff are excellent and very mindful: look for lovely Kathy with her perfect English. It has lots of coloured terracotta-warrior statues, Blues music, balloons and delicious savoury snacks delivered to your table.

A live singer takes to the stand every night save Tuesday. Hoegaarden is on draft at ¥55 a pint. It's candlelit at night.

### Jamaica Blue                         Bar
(蓝色牙买加; Lánsè Yámǎijiā; Nanchang Xiang; ⓂZhonglou (Bell Tower)) Doubling as a good restaurant, enterprising Jamaica Blue gets a daily workout come sundown as a fine and sociable bar, with live crooning nightly at around 9pm. Moreish, finger-lickin' savoury snacks are delivered free to tables. The layout is a squarish mezzanine, looking down into the lobby of a youth hostel below. Staff are polite and efficient.

The singing finishes at around 11pm to allow guests in the attached hostel to get some kip.

### King Garden Bar                       Bar
(老城根; Lǎo Chénggēn; ☏029 8797 3366; ⊙7pm-2am; 🛜; ⓂYuxiangmen) Picturesquely located just outside the gate of Yuxiang Men, this slick bar is a cool spot to hang out with Xī'ān's high rollers. With illuminated bar top, snappily attired bar staff, subdued lights and chill-out sounds, the setting is sharp. A lovely outside garden area awaits for the warmer months. A small Tsingtao beer is ¥55, so it's not cheap.

## ❂ ENTERTAINMENT

### Tang Dynasty                    Dinner Show
(唐乐宫; Tángyuè Gōng; ☏029 8782 2222; www.xiantangdynasty.com; 75 Chang'an Beilu; 长安北路75号; performance with/without dinner ¥500/220) The most famous dinner theatre in the city stages an over-the-top spectacle with Vegas-style costumes, traditional dance, live music and singing. It's dubbed into English. Book online for discounts. Buses can take you to the theatre 1.5km directly south of the South Gate, or walk five minutes south of South Shaomen metro.

## The Man Behind the Army

Qin Shi Huang (秦始皇), China's first emperor, has gone down in history as the sort of tyrant who gives tyrants a bad name. It might be because he outlawed Confucianism, ordering almost all its written texts to be burnt and, according to legend, burying 460 of its leading scholars alive.

Or perhaps it was his enslaving of hundreds of thousands of people to achieve his (admittedly monumental) accomplishments during his 36 years of rule (which began when he was just 13).

In recent years, the Chinese Communist Party (CCP) has tried to rehabilitate him, by emphasising both his efforts to unify China and the far-sighted nature of his policies. A classic overachiever, he created an efficient, centralised government that became the model for later dynasties; he standardised measurements, currency and, most importantly, writing. He built more than 6400km of new roads and canals and, of course, he conquered six major kingdoms before turning 40.

Nevertheless, he remains a hugely controversial figure in Chinese history, but also one whose presence permeates popular culture. The first emperor pops up in video games, in literature and on TV shows. He's also been the subject of films by both Chen Kaige and Zhang Yimou (*The Emperor and the Assassin* and *Hero*).

 ## INFORMATION

**Bank of China** (中国银行; Zhōngguó Yínháng; 29 Nan Dajie; ⏱8am-6pm) For ATMs and changing cash.

**China Post** (中国邮政; Zhōngguó Yóuzhèng; Bei Dajie; ⏱8am-8pm) Right across from the Bell Tower; Western Union is here too.

**Xī'ān Central Hospital** (西安市中心医院; Xī'ān Shì Zhōngxīn Yīyuàn; www.xaszxyy.com; 161

Xi Wulu; 西五路161号; Ⓜ Bei Da Jie) Centrally located and a short walk from Bei Da Jie metro station.

 ## GETTING THERE & AWAY

### AIR

Xī'ān's **Xiányáng Airport** (西安咸阳国际机场; Xī'ān Xiányáng Guójì Jīchǎng; ✆029 96788; www.xxia.com/en) is one of China's best connected – you can fly to almost any major Chinese destination from here, as well as several international ones. Most hostels and hotels and all travel agencies sell airline tickets.

The airport is about 40km northwest of Xī'ān. Shuttle buses (¥26, one hour) run every 20 to 30 minutes from 5.40am to 8pm between the airport and several points in the city, including the **Lónghǎi Hotel** (龙海大酒店; Lónghǎi Dàjiǔdiàn; 306 Jiefang Lu; 解放路306好). Metered taxis into the city charge more than ¥100.

### BUS

The **long-distance bus station** (长途汽车站, chángtú qìchēzhàn) is opposite Xī'ān's train station. It's a chaotic place. Note that buses to Huá Shān (6am to 8pm) depart from in front of the train station.

Buses from Xī'ān's East bus station include to Huá Shān (one way ¥36, two hours, hourly from 7.30am to 7pm) and Píngyáo (¥160, six hours, five daily).

### TRAIN

Xī'ān's main train station (huǒchē zhàn) is just outside the northern city walls. It's always busy, so arrive early for your departure to account for queues and poor signage. Try to buy your onward tickets as soon as you arrive.

Most hotels and hostels can get you tickets (¥40 commission); there's also an **advance train ticket booking booth** (代售火车票; dàishòu huǒchēpiào; Nan Dajie; 南大街; ⏱8.50am-noon & 1.30-4.30pm) in the ICBC Bank's south entrance and another **train ticket booth** (代售火车票; dàishòu huǒchēpiào; Xiwu Lu; 西五路; ⏱8am-5pm & 5.30pm-midnight) just west of Wulukou metro station on Xiwu Lu.

CANGHAI76 / SHUTTERSTOCK ©

Guǎngrén Temple (p104)

This is much easier than the hectic crowds in the main ticket hall and commission is only ¥5.

For an overnight journey, deluxe Z trains run to/from Běijīng West (hard/soft sleeper ¥273/416, 11½ hours), the later departures leaving Xī'ān at 7.21pm and 7.27pm and Běijīng at 8.12pm and 8.40pm. The Z94 to Shànghǎi departs 4.46pm and arrives 7.53am (hard/soft sleeper ¥332/510, 15 hours).

From Xī'ān's North train station (Běihuǒchē zhàn), high-speed 'bullet' G trains zip to Běijīng west (2nd/1st class ¥825/516, 5½ hours, 10 daily). Other destinations include Guìlín (hard/soft sleeper ¥377/582, 28 hours), Píngyáo (2nd/1st class ¥150/188, 2½ hours, seven daily), Shànghǎi (2nd-class seat/soft sleeper ¥338/834, 11 hours, daily at 8.35pm), Tàiyuán (2nd/1st class ¥179/222, 3½ hours, several daily) and Ürümqi (hard/soft sleeper ¥497/768, 25 to 35 hours).

## ❶ GETTING AROUND

Tourist buses run to almost all the sites from in front of Xī'ān's main train station, with the notable exception of the Tomb of Emperor Jingdi.

### METRO

The Xī'ān metro system (西安地铁, Xī'ān dìtiě) started in 2011 with Line 2, followed by Line 1 in 2013 – Line 3 opened in late 2016, with more lines under construction or in the planning stages. Rides cost ¥2 to ¥5 depending on distance. Useful stations on Line 2 include Beihuoche zhan (North train station) and Xiaozhai (near the Shaanxi History Museum). Line 1 has a stop at the Bànpō Neolithic Village. Trains run between around 6.10am and 11.15pm.

### TAXI

Taxi flagfall is ¥9. It can be very difficult to get a taxi in the late afternoon, when the drivers change shifts. Bicycles are a good alternative.

SHÀNGHǍI

# Shànghǎi at a Glance...

*Rapidly becoming a world metropolis, Shànghǎi typifies modern China while being unlike anywhere else in the nation. Awash with cash, ambition and economic vitality, Shànghǎi is, for the movers and shakers of business, the place to be. For all its modernity and cosmopolitanism, however, Shànghǎi is part and parcel of the People's Republic of China, and its challenges are multiplying as fast as cocktails are mixed and served on the Bund.*

### Two Days in Shànghǎi

Rise early to stroll the **Bund** (p114) and watch the taichi enthusiasts. Have a spot reserved at **M on the Bund** (p129) for lunch before an afternoon seeking skyscrapers in Pǔdōng and evening cocktails at **Flair** (p131). Save the next morning for the standout **Shànghǎi Museum** (p124), followed by an afternoon shopping in Xīntiāndì, Tiánzǐfáng and the **French Concession** (p120), rounding off the day with drinks at **Long Bar** (p131).

### Four Days in Shànghǎi

Enjoy an early morning **Yùyuán Gardens & Bazaar** (p118) stroll, followed by a promenade along **Yuanmingyuan Rd** (p124). Wander west along **East Nanjing Road** (p124) to People's Square for the **Shànghǎi Urban Planning Exhibition Hall** (p125), then dine at **Dī Shuǐ Dòng** (p130). The next day visit the **Jade Buddha Temple** (p125), go art-hunting at **M50** (p125) and explore the new **Shànghǎi Natural History Museum** (p125).

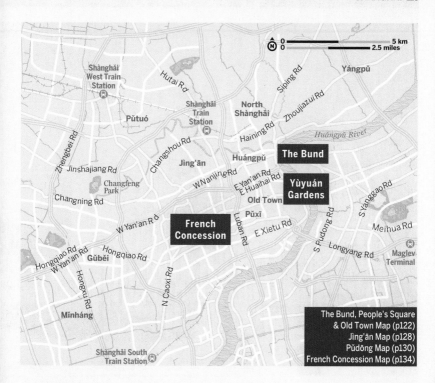

The Bund, People's Square
& Old Town Map (p122)
Jìng'ān Map (p128)
Pŭdōng Map (p130)
French Concession Map (p134)

## Arriving in Shànghăi

**Pŭdōng International Airport** Connected to town by Maglev, metro (Line 2), airport bus and taxi (¥160).

**Hóngqiáo International Airport**
Linked to the rest of town by metro, bus and taxi.

**Shànghăi Hóngqiáo railway station**
The largest of three train stations, each connected to the city metro system.

## Where to Stay

There's never been a better time to find a bed in Shànghăi. From ultrachic, carbon-neutral boutique rooms to sumptuous five-star hotels housed in glimmering towers, grand heritage affairs and snappy, down-to-earth backpacker haunts, the range of accommodation in town is just what you would expect from a city of this stature.

For more information see Where to Stay on p137.

# Exploring the Bund

*Symbolic of colonial Shànghǎi, the Bund was once the city's Wall St, a place of feverish trading and fortunes made and lost. Today, it's the bars, restaurants and hypnotising views that pull the crowds.*

### Great For...

### ☑ Don't Miss

The astonishing evening view across the Huángpǔ River to Pǔdōng.

### Peace Hotel

Lording it over the corner of East Nanjing and East Zhongshan Rds is the most famous building on the Bund, the landmark **Peace Hotel** (费尔蒙和平饭店, Fèi'ěrmēng Hépíng Fàndiàn; ☎021 6321 6888; www.fairmont. com; 20 East Nanjing Rd; 南京东路20号; Ⓜ Line 2,10 to East Nanjing Rd), constructed between 1926 and 1929. It was originally built as Sassoon House, with Victor Sassoon's famous Cathay Hotel on the 4th to 7th floors. It wasn't for the hoi polloi, with a guest list running to Charlie Chaplin, George Bernard Shaw, and Noel Coward, who penned *Private Lives* here in four days in 1930 when he had the flu. Sassoon himself spent weekdays in his personal suite on the top floor, just beneath the green pyramid. The building was renamed the Peace Hotel in 1956.

Peace Hotel

JON ARNOLD / GETTY IMAGES ©

## ❶ Need to Know

The Bund gets its Anglo-Indian name from the embankments built up to discourage flooding (a *band* is an embankment in Hindi).

## ✕ Take a Break

Five on the Bund is home to **M on the Bund** (p129) and the **Glam** (p131).

### ★ Top Tip

Arrive before 7.30am to witness locals partaking in their early morning exercises, including taichi.

## Custom House

The neoclassical **Custom House** (自订的房子; Zì Dìng De Fángzi; Map p122; 13 East Zhongshan No 1 Rd; 中山东一路13号; [M] Line 2, 10 to East Nanjing Rd, exit 1), established at this site in 1857 and rebuilt in 1927, is one of the most important buildings on the Bund. Capping it is Big Ching, a bell modelled on London's Big Ben. Clocks were by no means new to China, but Shànghǎi was the first city in which they gained widespread acceptance and the lives of many became dictated by a standardised, common schedule.

## Hongkong & Shanghai Bank Building

Adjacent to the Custom House, the **Hongkong & Shanghai Bank Building** (HSBC Building, 汇丰大厦; Map p122; 12 East

Zhongshan No 1 Rd; 中山东一路12号; [M] Line 2, 10 to East Nanjing Rd) was constructed in 1923. The bank was first established in Hong Kong in 1864 and in Shànghǎi in 1865 to finance trade, and soon became one of the richest in Shànghǎi, arranging the indemnity paid after the Boxer Rebellion. The magnificent mosaic ceiling inside the entrance was plastered over until its restoration in 1997 and is therefore well preserved.

## Promenade

The Bund offers a host of things to do, but most visitors head straight for the riverside promenade to pose for photos in front of Pǔdōng's ever-changing skyline. The area is essentially open around the clock, but it's at its best in the early morning, when locals are out practising taichi, or in the early evening, when both sides of the river are lit up and the romance of the waterfront reaches a crescendo.

# The Bund

The best way to get acquainted with Shànghǎi is to take a stroll along the Bund.

This illustration shows the main sights along the Bund's central stretch, beginning near the intersection with East Nanjing Rd.

The Bund is 1km long and walking it should take around an hour.

Head to the area south of the Hongkong & Shanghai Bank Building to find the biggest selection of drinking and dining destinations.

### Hongkong & Shanghai Bank Building (1923)

Head into this massive bank to marvel at the beautiful mosaic ceiling, featuring the 12 zodiac signs and the world's (former) eight centres of finance.

### Custom House (1927)

One of the most important buildings on the Bund, Custom House was capped by the largest clock face in Asia and 'Big Ching', a bell modelled on London's Big Ben.

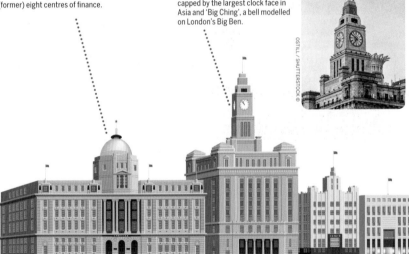

OSTILL / SHUTTERSTOCK ©

**Former Bank of Communications (1947)**

**Bund Public Service Centre (2010)**

SEAN PAVONE / SHUTTERSTOCK ©

### North China Daily News Building (1924)

Known as the 'Old Lady of the Bund'. The *News* ran from 1864 to 1951 as the main English-language newspaper in China. Look for the paper's motto above the central windows.

### Fairmont Peace Hotel (1929)

Originally built as the Cathay Hotel, this art deco masterpiece was *the* place to stay in Shànghǎi and the crown jewel in Victor Sassoon's real-estate empire.

JON ARNOLD / GETTY IMAGES ©

### Former Chartered Bank Building (1923)

Reopened in 2004 as the upscale entertainment complex Bund 18; the building's top-floor Bar Rouge is one of the Bund's premier late-night destinations.

GREG ELMS / GETTY IMAGES ©

**Russo-Chinese Bank Building (1902)**

**Former Bank of Taiwan (1927)**

PHILIPPE LOPEZ / AFP / GETTY IMAGES ©

### Former Palace Hotel (1906)

Now known as the Swatch Art Peace Hotel (an artists' residence and gallery, with a top-floor restaurant and bar), this building was completed in 1908 and hosted Sun Yatsen's victory celebration in 1911 following his election as the first president of the Republic of China.

### Bank of China (1942)

This unusual building was originally commissioned to be the tallest building in Shànghǎi but, probably because of Victor Sassoon's influence, wound up being 1m shorter than its neighbour.

# Yùyuán Gardens & Bazaar

*With its shaded corridors, glittering pools and whispering bamboo, the Yùyuán Gardens are a delightful escape from Shànghǎi's glass-and-steel modernity.*

### Great For...

### ☑ Don't Miss

Hunting out the delightfully ornate inner garden stage.

### The Gardens

The Yùyuán Gardens were founded by the Pan family, who were rich Ming dynasty officials. The gardens took 18 years (from 1559 to 1577) to be nurtured into existence, only to be ransacked during the Opium War in 1842, when British officers were barracked here, and again during the Taiping Rebellion, this time by the French.

### Three Ears of Corn Hall & Rockeries

Today the restored gardens are a fine example of Ming garden design. As you enter, **Three Ears of Corn Hall** (三穗堂; Sānsuìtáng) is the largest of the halls in the gardens. The **rockeries** (假山; jiǎshān) attempt to recreate a mountain setting within the flatland of the garden, so when combined with **ponds** (池塘; chítáng) they

Yùyuán Gardens

GREIR / GETTY IMAGES ©

## ❶ Need to Know

豫园、豫园商城, Yùyuán & Yùyuán Shāngchéng; Map p122; Anren St; 安仁街; high/low
season ¥40/30; ◉8.30am-5.15pm; Ⓜ Line 10
to Yuyuan Garden

## ✕ Take a Break

Grab a tray of dumplings from the famed
**Nánxiáng Steamed Bun Restaurant** (南
翔馒头店, Nánxiáng Mántou Diàn; 12 dumplings
on 1st fl ¥22; ◉1st fl 10am-9pm, 2nd fl 7am-
8pm, 3rd fl 9.30am-7pm) in the Bazaar.

---

### ★ Top Tip

Aim to arrive at 8.30am; from 10am
onwards the crowds get increasingly
dense.

---

suggest the 'hills and rivers' (*shānshuǐ*) of
China's landscapes.

## Hall of Heralding Spring & Inner Garden

In the east of the gardens, keep an eye out
for the **Hall of Heralding Spring** (点春
堂; Diǎnchūn Táng), which in 1853 was the
headquarters of the Small Swords Society,
a rebel group affiliated with the Taiping
rebels. To the south, the **Exquisite Jade
Rock** (玉玲珑; Yù Línglóng) was destined
for the imperial court in Běijīng until the
boat carrying it sank outside Shànghǎi.

South of the Exquisite Jade Rock is the
**inner garden** (内园; *nèiyuán*), where you
can also find the beautiful **stage** (古戏台;
*gǔxìtái*) dating from 1888, with a gilded,
carved ceiling and fine acoustics, as well as

the charming **Hall for Watching Waves**
(观涛楼; Guāntāo Lóu).

## The Bazaar

Next to the Yùyuán Gardens entrance rises
the **Mid-Lake Pavilion Teahouse** (湖心亭;
Húxīntíng; tea ¥50; ◉8am-9pm; Ⓜ Line 10 to
Yuyuan Garden), once part of the gardens
and now one of the most famous teahouses
in China. Surrounding all this is the restored
bazaar area, where scores of speciality
shops and restaurants jostle over narrow
laneways and small squares in a mock 'ye
olde Cathay' setting. There are some choice
gift-giving ideas in the souvenir shops,
from painted snuff bottles to Chinese kites.
At the heart of the melee, south of the
Yùyuán Gardens exit, is the venerable
**Temple of the Town God** (城隍庙; Chéng-
huáng Miào; off Middle Fangbang Rd; 豫园商城
方浜中路; admission ¥10; ◉8.30am-4.30pm;
Ⓜ Line 10 to Yuyuan Garden), dedicated to the
protector of the city of Shànghǎi.

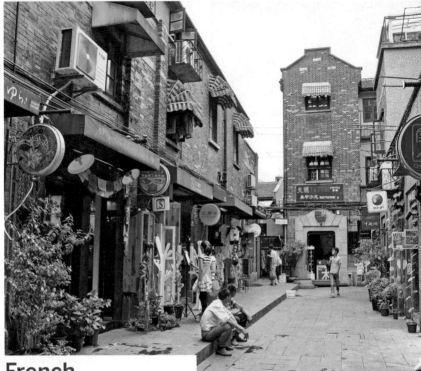

GIFTOGRAPHY / SHUTTERSTOCK ©

# French Concession

*For local boutiques, head along leafy backstreets such as Nanchang, Changle, Fumin or Xinle Rds. Xīntiāndì has high-end brands, while Tiánzǐfáng is home to a number of cool gift stores.*

## Great For...

☑ **Don't Miss**

Getting thoroughly lost down the disorientating alleyways of Tiánzǐfáng.

## Tiánzǐfáng

A shopping complex housed within a grid of tiny alleyways, Tiánzǐfáng is probably the most accessible, authentic and vibrant example of Shànghǎi's trademark traditional back-lane architecture. A community of design studios, local families, cafes and boutiques, it's a much-needed counterpoint to Shànghǎi's mega-malls and skyscrapers.

There are three main north–south lanes (Nos 210, 248 and 274) criss-crossed by irregular east–west alleyways, which makes exploration disorienting and fun. Most shops and boutiques are slim and bijoux. One gallery to seek out is **Beaugeste** (比极影像; Bǐjí Yǐngxiàng; Map p134; ☏021 6466 9012; www.beaugeste-gallery.com; 5th fl, No 5, Lane 210, Taikang Rd; 泰康路210弄5号520室 田子坊; ⊙10am-6pm Sat & Sun; MDapuqiao) FREE, which has thought-provoking contemporary photography exhibits.

Xīntiāndì

ALAN COPSON / GETTY IMAGES ©

## ℹ Need to Know

For Xīntiāndì, take metro Line 1 to South Huangpi Rd or Line 10 to Xintiandi. For Tiánzǐfáng, take metro Line 9 to Dapuqiao.

## ✕ Take a Break

Drop into **East** (Map p134; ☎021 6467 0100; www.east-eatery.com; No 39, Lane 155, Middle Jianguo Rd, Tiánzǐfáng; 建国中路155弄39号田子坊; bao 1/3 pieces ¥12/30, dishes from ¥50; ⊗11am-11pm; ☎; Ⓜ Dapuqiao Rd) for tasty *bao* (steamed filled buns).

### ★ Top Tip

Try to go shopping during the week, as crowds are at their worst on weekends.

Just outside the complex at 25 Taikang Rd, an enormous peony bloom covers the exterior of the **Liúli China Museum** (琉璃艺术博物馆; Liúli Yìshù Bówùguǎn; Map p134; ☎021 6461 3189; www.liulichinamuseum.com; adult/child under 18yr ¥20/free; ⊗10am-5pm Tue-Sun; Ⓜ Dapuqiao), dedicated to the art of glass sculpture.

## Xīntiāndì

With its own namesake metro station, Xīntiāndì has been a Shànghǎi icon for a decade or more. An upscale entertainment and shopping complex modelled on traditional *lòngtáng* (alleyway) homes, this was the first development in the city to prove that historic architecture makes big commercial sense.

The heart of the complex, cleaved into a pedestrianised north and south block, consists of largely rebuilt traditional *shíkùmén*

(stone-gate houses), brought bang up to date with a stylish, modern spin. But while the layout suggests a flavour of yesteryear, don't expect too much historic magic or cultural allure.

Serious shoppers – and diners – will eventually gravitate towards the malls at the southern tip of the south block. Beyond the first **mall** (Xīntiāndì South Block, 2nd fl, Bldg 6; 兴业路123弄新天地南里6号楼2楼; Ⓜ South Huangpi Rd), which holds three top-notch restaurants on the 2nd floor – **Din Tai Fung** (鼎泰丰; Dǐng Tài Fēng; ☎021 6385 8378; www.dintaifung.com.cn; 10 dumplings ¥60-96; ⊗10am-midnight), **Crystal Jade** (翡翠酒家; Fěicuì Jiǔjiā; ☎021 6385 8752; dim sum ¥20-42; ⊗11am-10.30pm) and **Shànghǎi Min** (小南国; Xiǎo Nán Guó; ☎400 820 9777; dishes ¥35-198; ⊗11am-10pm) – is the **Xīntiāndì Style** (新天地时尚; Xīntiāndì Shíshàng; Map p134; 245 Madang Rd; 马当路245号; ⊗10am-10pm; Ⓜ Xintiandi) mall showcasing local brands and chic pieces at the vanguard of Shanghainese fashion.

# The Bund, People's Square & Old Town

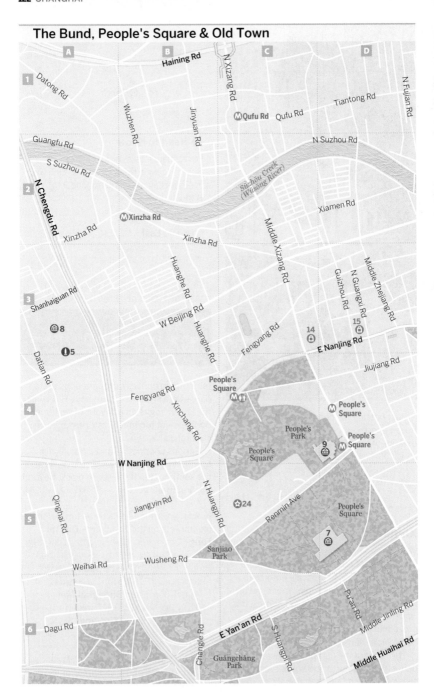

| | A | B | C | D |
|---|---|---|---|---|

**Haining Rd**

Datong Rd

N Xizang Rd

Wuzhen Rd

Jinyuan Rd

Ⓜ Qufu Rd   Qufu Rd

Tiantong Rd

N Fujian Rd

Guangfu Rd

N Suzhou Rd

S Suzhou Rd

Sūzhōu Creek (Wúsōng River)

N Chengdu Rd

Xiamen Rd

Ⓜ Xinzha Rd

Xinzha Rd

Xinzha Rd

Middle Xizang Rd

Middle Zhejiang Rd

Huanghe Rd

Shanhaiguan Rd

W Beijing Rd

Huanghe Rd

Fengyang Rd

Guizhou Rd

N Guangxi Rd

🏛 8

14
🔒

15
🔒

**E Nanjing Rd**

Datian Rd

❶ 5

Jiujiang Rd

Fengyang Rd

Xinchang Rd

People's
Square
Ⓜ🚇

Ⓜ People's
Square

People's
Park

People's
Square
🏛 9 Ⓜ Square

W Nanjing Rd

People's
Square

Qinghai Rd

Jiangyin Rd

N Huangpi Rd

♨ 24

Renmin Ave

People's
Square

🏛 7

Weihai Rd

Wusheng Rd

Sanjiao
Park

Pu'an Rd

Middle Jinling Rd

Dagu Rd

Changle Rd

**E Yan'an Rd**

S Huangpi Rd

**Middle Huaihai Rd**

Guǎngchǎng
Park

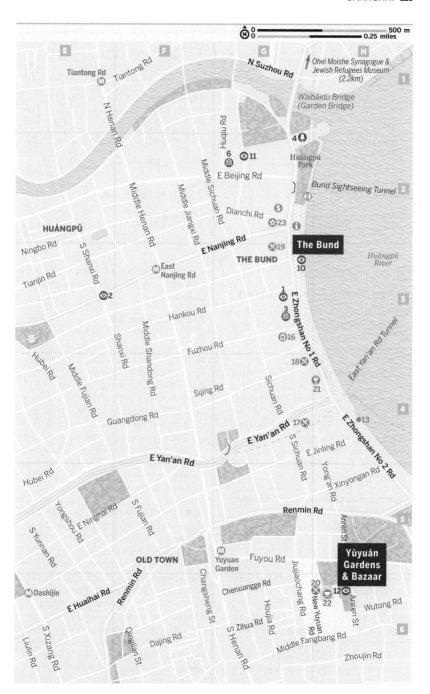

N 0 ___ 500 m
0 ___ 0.25 miles

Ohel Moishe Synagogue &
Jewish Refugees Museum
(2.2km)

Tiantong Rd [M] Tiantong Rd

N Suzhou Rd [G]

Wàibáidù Bridge
(Garden Bridge)

N Henan Rd

Huqiu Rd

4

6 11

E Beijing Rd

Huángpǔ
Park

Middle Sichuan Rd

Middle Jiangxi Rd

Dianchi Rd

Bund Sightseeing Tunnel [2]

HUÁNGPǓ

Middle Henan Rd

$
23

Ningbo Rd

S Shanxi Rd

E Nanjing Rd

19

THE BUND

**The Bund**

*Huángpǔ
River*

East
Nanjing Rd [M]

Tianjin Rd

THE BUND

10

2

Hankou Rd

Shanxi Rd

Middle Shandong Rd

1

3

[3]

Hubei Rd

Middle Fujian Rd

Fuzhou Rd

16

E Zhongshan No 1 Rd

Sijing Rd

18

East Yan'an Rd Tunnel

Guangdong Rd

Sichuan Rd

21

Hubei Rd

E Yan'an Rd

S Sichuan Rd

17

E Zhongshan No 2 Rd

13 [4]

E Yan'an Rd

E Jinling Rd

Yong'an Rd

Yongshou Rd

E Ninghai Rd

S Fujian Rd

Xinyongan Rd

S Yunnan Rd

Renmin Rd

Anren St

[5]

OLD TOWN

[M] Yuyuan
Garden

Fuyou Rd

**Yùyuán
Gardens
& Bazaar**

[M] Dashijie

E Huaihai Rd

Renmin Rd

Changsheng St

Chenxiangge Rd

Jiujiaochang Rd

New Yuyuan Rd

20

12

22

Anren St

Wutong Rd

S Xizang Rd

Qinglian St

Dajing Rd

Houjia Rd

S Zihua Rd

S Henan Rd

Middle Fangbang Rd

[6]

Liulin Rd

Zhoujin Rd

# The Bund, People's Square & Old Town

## ◎ SIGHTS

### ◎ The Bund & People's Square

West of the Bund, People's Square is ground central for Shànghǎi sightseeing, with world-class museums, art galleries and a beautiful park.

### East Nanjing Road     Area

(南京东路, Nánjīng Dōnglù; Map p122; Ⓜ Line 2, 10 to East Nanjing Rd) Linking the Bund with People's Square is East Nanjing Rd, once known as Nanking Rd. A glowing forest of neon at night, it's no longer the cream of Shànghǎi shopping, but its pedestrian strip remains one of the most famous and crowd-ed streets in China.

### Rockbund Art Museum     Museum

(RAM, 上海外滩美术馆, Shànghǎi Wàitān Měishùguǎn; Map p122; www.rockbundart museum.org; 20 Huqiu Rd; 虎丘路20号; adult/ child ¥30/15; ⊙ 10am-6pm Tue-Sun; Ⓜ Line 2, 10 to East Nanjing Rd) Housed in the magnificent former Royal Asiatic Society building (1932) – once Shànghǎi's first museum – this world-class gallery behind the Bund focuses on contemporary Chinese and international art, with rotating exhibits year-round and no permanent collection. One of the city's top modern-art venues, the building's interior and exterior are both sublime. Check out the unique art-deco eight-sided *bāguà* (trigram)

windows at the front, a fetching synthesis of Western modernist styling and traditional Chinese design.

### Yuanmingyuan Rd     Area

(圆明园路, Yuánmíngyuán Lù; Map p122; Ⓜ Line 2, 10 to East Nanjing Rd) Like a smaller, con-densed version of the Bund, the pedestri-anised, cobblestone Yuanmingyuan Rd is lined with a mishmash of colonial architec-ture. Running parallel with the Bund, just one block back, some fine examples of renovated red-brick and stone buildings dating from the 1900s include the art-deco YWCA Build-ing (No 133) and Chinese Baptist Publication building (No 209), the ornate 1907 red-brick Panama Legation building (No 97) and the 1927 neoclassical Lyceum Building.

### Shànghǎi Museum     Museum

(上海博物馆, Shànghǎi Bówùguǎn; Map p122; www.shanghaimuseum.net; 201 Renmin Ave; 人民大道201号; ⊙ 9am-5pm, last entry 4pm; ♿; Ⓜ Line 1, 2, 8 to People's Square) **FREE** This must-see museum escorts you through the craft of millennia and the pages of Chinese history. It's home to one of the most impressive collections in the land: take your pick from the archaic green patinas of the Ancient Chi-nese Bronzes Gallery through to the silent solemnity of the Ancient Chinese Sculpture Gallery; from the exquisite beauty of the ceramics in the Zande Lou Gallery to the measured and timeless flourishes captured in the Chinese Calligraphy Gallery.

## Shànghǎi Urban Planning Exhibition Hall    Museum

(上海城市规划展示馆, Shànghǎi Chéngshì Guīhuà Zhǎnshìguǎn; Map p122; www.supec.org; 100 Renmin Ave, entrance on Middle Xizang Rd; 人民大道100号; adult/child ¥30/15; ☺9am-5pm Tue-Sun, last entry 4pm; ⓂLine 1, 2, 8 to People's Square, exit 2) Set over five levels, this modern museum covers Shànghǎi's urban planning history, tracing its development from swampy fishing village to modern-day megacity. Its mix of photography, models, and interactive multimedia displays keeps things entertaining. The 1st floor covers the city's rise, including the establishment of the international settlement and profiles its colonial architecture and *shíkùmén* housing. The most popular feature is on the 3rd floor – a visually stunning model showing a detailed layout of this megalopolis-to-be, plus an impressive Virtual World 3D wraparound tour.

## ◉ Jing'an

### Jade Buddha Temple    Buddhist Temple

(玉佛寺, Yùfó Sì; Map p128; cnr Anyuan & Jiangning Rds; 安远路和江宁路街口; high/low season ¥20/10; ☺8am-4.30pm; ⓂLine 7, 13 to Changshou Rd, exit 5) One of Shànghǎi's active Buddhist monasteries, this temple was built between 1918 and 1928. The highlight is a transcendent Buddha crafted from pure jade, one of five shipped back to China by the monk Hui Gen at the turn of the 20th century.

### M50    Gallery

(M50创意产业集聚区, M50 Chuàngyì Chǎnyè Jíjùqū; Map p128; www.m50.com.cn/en; 50 Moganshan Rd; 莫干山路50号; ⓂLine 3, 4 to Zhongtan Rd, exit 5; Line 1, 3, 4 to Shànghǎi Railway Station, exit 3) FREE Shànghǎi may be known for its glitz and glamour, but it's got an edgy subculture too. The industrial M50 art complex is one prime example, where galleries have been set up in disused factories and cotton mills, utilising the vast space to showcase contemporary Chinese emerging and established artists. There's a lot to see,

so plan to spend half a day poking around the site.

## Shànghǎi Natural History Museum    Museum

(上海自然博物馆, Shànghǎi Zìrán Bówùguǎn; Map p122; ☑021 6862 2000; www.snhm.org.cn; 510 West Beijing Rd; 北京西路510号; adult/teen/under 13 yr ¥30/12/free; ☺9am-5.15pm Tue-Sun; ⓂLines 2, 12, 13 to West Nanjng Rd) Perhaps not quite on the same scale as the Smithsonian, Shànghǎi's new sleek space would nevertheless be a fitting choice for a *Night at the Museum* movie. As comprehensive as it is entertaining and informative, the museum is packed with displays of taxidermied animals, dinosaurs and cool interactive features. Its architecture is also a highlight with a striking design that is beautifully integrated in its art-filled **Jìng'ān Sculpture Park** (静安雕塑公园, Jìng'ān Diāosù Gōngyuán; 128 Shimen 2nd Rd; 石门二路128号; ☺6am-8.30pm) FREE setting.

## ◉ Pǔdōng

### Shànghǎi Tower    Notable Building

(上海中心大厦; Shànghǎi Zhōngxīn Dàshà; Map p130; www.shanghaitower.com.cn; cnr Middle Yincheng & Huayuanshiqiao Rds; admission ¥160; ☺9am-9pm; ⓂLujiazui) China's tallest building dramatically twists skywards from its footing. The 121-storey, 632m-tall, Gensler-designed Shànghǎi Tower topped out in August 2013 and opened in mid-2016. The observation deck on the 118th-floor is the world's highest.

### Jīnmào Tower    Notable Building

(金茂大厦; Jīnmào Dàshà; Map p130; ☑021 5047 5101; 88 Century Ave; 世纪大道88号; adult/student/child ¥120/90/60; ☺8.30am-10pm; ⓂLujiazui) Resembling an art-deco take on a pagoda, this crystalline edifice is a beauty. It's essentially an office block with the high-altitude **Grand Hyatt** (金茂君悦大酒店; Jīnmào Jūnyuè Dàjiǔdiàn; ☑021 5049 1234; www.shanghai.grand.hyatt.com) renting space from the 53rd to 87th floors. You can zip up in the elevators to the 88th-floor observation deck, accessed from the separate podium building to the side of the main tower (aim for clear days at dusk for both day and night views).

## Shànghǎi World Financial Center — Notable Building

(上海环球金融中心; Shànghǎi Huánqiú Jīnróng Zhōngxīn; Map p130; 📞021 5878 0101; www. swfc-observatory.com; 100 Century Ave; 世纪大道100号; observation deck adult 94th fl/94th, 97th & 100th fl ¥120/180, child under 140cm ¥60/90; ⏱8am-11pm, last entry 10.30pm; Ⓜ Lujiazui) Although trumped by the adjacent Shànghǎi Tower as the city's most stratospheric building, the awe-inspiring 492m-high Shànghǎi World Financial Center is an astonishing sight, even more so come nightfall when its 'bottle opener' top dances with lights. There are three observation decks with head-spinningly altitude-adjusted ticket prices and wow-factor elevators thrown in.

## Aurora Museum — Museum

(震旦博物馆; Zhèn Dàn Bówùguǎn; Map p130; 📞021 5840 8899; www.auroramuseum.cn; Aurora Building, 99 Fucheng Rd; 浦东新区富城路99号震旦大厦; admission ¥60; ⏱10am-5pm Tue-Sun, to 9pm Fri, last entry 1hr before closing; Ⓜ Lujiazui) Designed by renowned Japanese architect, Andō Tadao, the Aurora Museum is set over six floors of the Aurora building and houses a stunning collection of Chinese treasures. Artifacts and antiquities on display include pottery from the Han dynasty; jade dating back from the Neolithic to the Qing dynasty; blue and white porcelain spanning the Yuan, Ming and Qing dynasties; as well as Buddhist sculptures from the Gandharan and Northern Wei period. Don't miss the jade burial suit of 2903 tiles sewn with gold wire.

## Shànghǎi History Museum — Museum

(上海城市历史发展陈列馆; Shànghǎi Chéngshì Lìshǐ Fāzhǎn Chénlièguǎn; Map p130; 📞021 5879 8888; 1 Century Ave; 世纪大道1号, Oriental Pearl TV Tower basement; admission ¥35, English audio tour ¥30; ⏱8am-9.30pm; Ⓜ Lujiazui) The entire family will enjoy this informative museum with a fun presentation on old Shànghǎi. Learn how the city prospered on the back of the cotton trade and junk transportation, when it was known as 'Little Sūzhōu'. Life-sized models of traditional shops are staffed by realistic waxworks, amid a wealth of historical detail, including a boundary stone from the International Settlement and one of the bronze lions that originally guarded the entrance to the HSBC bank on the Bund.

Shànghǎi Natural History Museum (p125)

##  Hóngkǒu & North Shànghǎi

### Ohel Moishe Synagogue & Jewish Refugees Museum  Museum

(摩西会堂; Móxī Huìtáng; ☏021 6512 6669; 62 Changyang Rd; 长阳路62号; admission ¥50; ⊙9am-5pm, last entry 4.30pm; Ⓜ Tilanqiao) Built by the Russian Ashkenazi Jewish community in 1927, this synagogue lies in the heart of the 1940s Jewish ghetto. Today it houses the synagogue and the Shànghǎi Jewish Refugees Museum, with exhibitions on the lives of the approximately 20,000 Central European refugees who fled to Shànghǎi to escape the Nazis. There are English-language tours every hour, from 9.30am to 11.30am and 1pm to 4pm.

## ✈ ACTIVITIES

### Huángpǔ River Cruise  Cruise

(黄浦江游览, Huángpǔ Jiāng Yóulǎn; Map p122; 219-239 East Zhongshan No 2 Rd; 中山东二路 219-239号; tickets ¥120; ⊙11am-9.30pm; Ⓜ Line 2, 10 to East Nanjing Rd) The Huángpǔ River offers intriguing views of the Bund, Pǔdōng and riverfront activity. The night cruises are arguably more scenic, though boat traffic during the day is more interesting. Most cruises last 50 minutes.

## 🔒 SHOPPING

### Spin  Ceramics

(旋, Xuán; Map p128; www.spinceramics.com; 360 Kangding Rd; 康定路360号; ⊙11am-8pm; Ⓜ Line 7 to Changping Rd, exit 2) High on creative flair, Spin brings Chinese ceramics up to speed with oblong tea cups, twisted sake sets and all manner of cool plates, chopstick holders and 'kung fu' vases. Pieces are never overbearing, but trendily lean towards the whimsical, geometric, thoughtful and elegant.

### Sūzhōu Cobblers  Fashion & Accessories

(上海起想艺术品, Shànghǎi Qǐxiǎng Yìshùpǐn; Map p122; www.suzhou-cobblers.com; Unit 101, 17 Fuzhou Rd; 福州路17号101室; ⊙10am-6.30pm; Ⓜ Line 2, 10 to East Nanjing Rd) Right off the Bund, this cute boutique sells exquisite hand-embroidered silk slippers, bags, hats

 **Shànghǎi Disneyland**

After a decade of planning and diplomatic wrangling, the Magic Kingdom finally arrived in the Middle Kingdom in 2016, offering up a spectacular serving of **Disney** (上海迪士尼乐园; Shànghǎi Díshìní Lèyuán; ☏021 3158 0000; www.shanghaidisneyresort.com; Shànghǎi Disney Resort, Pǔdōng; adult/child 1.0-1.4m & senior ¥499/375; ⊙9am-9pm; Ⓜ Disney Resort) seasoned with a dash of Chinese culture. 'Main Street USA' has become the locally inspired yet rather sterile 'Gardens of the Imagination', and you can gnaw the ears off a steamed Mickey Mouse pork bun at snack vendors throughout the park.

Much has been said about the queues; if you're serious about packing in all the big rides in a day, aim to arrive at least 30 minutes before the park opens, and play a tactical Fast Pass game (the longest lines are at Roaring Rapids, Soaring Over the Horizon and TRON). Alternatively, for groups of up to six, a cool ¥12,500 gets you a 'Premier Tour' with fast access to all the rides.

With younger kids in tow you can takes things at a more leisurely pace, and there are plenty of roving musical performances, costumed characters to meet and the excellent parade (3.30pm) and fireworks display (8.30pm), which don't require any waiting.

Fireworks, Enchanted Storybook Castle

and clothing. Patterns and colours are based on the fashions of the 1930s, and as far as the owner, Huang 'Denise' Mengqi, is

# Jìng'ān

0        500 m
0        0.25 miles

**A**  **B**  **C**  **D**

**1**

Panjiawan Rd

Yichang Rd

Moganshan Rd

Jiaotong Rd

Shànghǎi Long-Distance Bus Station

Zhongxing Rd

Shanghai Train Station Ⓜ

Shànghǎi Train Station Ⓔ

Shanghai Train Station Ⓜ

Datong Rd

Gonghexin Rd

Moling Rd

**2**

Aomen Rd

Suzhou Creek (Wúsōng River)

Changshou Rd

Meiyuan Rd

W Tianmu Rd

**3**

Yutong Rd

Hengfeng Rd

Minli Rd

Hanzhong Rd

Hengtong Rd

Chang'an Rd

Ⓜ Hanzhong Rd

Guangfu Rd

S Suzhou Rd

1 Anyuan Rd

Jiangning Rd

Haifang Rd

Huai'an Rd

Changhua Rd

Datian Rd

**4**

N Shaanxi Rd

JÌNG'ĀN

Changping Rd

4 ✗ Kangding Rd

Shimen No 2 Rd

Shanhaiguan Rd

Xikang Rd

🔒 3

Wuding Rd

**5**

Changde Rd

Xinzha Rd

N Shaanxi Rd

5 ✗

6 ♨

W Beijing Rd

Taixing Rd

Fengxian Rd

W Nanjing Rd

Fengxian Rd

West Nanjing Rd Ⓜ

N Maoming Rd

Wujiang Rd

Shimen No 1 Rd

**6**

Nanyang Rd

# Jìng'ān

concerned, the products are one of a kind. Slippers start at ¥650 and the shop can make to order.

## Pīlíngpālāng – Anfu Lu    Ceramics

(噼呤啪唥; Map p134; www.pilingpalang.com; 183 Anfu Rd; 安福路183号; ◷10am-9.30pm; ⓜChangshu Rd) You'll find gorgeous vibrant coloured ceramics, cloisonné and lacquer, in pieces that celebrate traditional Chinese forms while adding a modern and deco-inspired slant here at Pīlíngpālāng. Tea caddies and decorative trays make for great gifts or souvenirs.

## Lolo Love Vintage    Vintage

(Map p134; 2 Yongfu Rd; 永福路2号; ◷noon-9pm; ⓜShanghai Library, Changshu Rd) There's rock and roll on the stereo and a huge white rabbit, stuffed peacock and plastic cactus outside at this wacky shrine to vintage 1940s and '50s glad rags, behind the blue steel door on Yongfu Rd. It's stuffed with frocks, blouses, tops, shoes, brooches and sundry togs spilling from hangers, shelves and battered suitcases.

# ✖ EATING

As much an introduction to regional Chinese cuisine as a magnet for talented chefs from around the globe, Shànghǎi has staked a formidable claim as the Middle Kingdom's hottest dining destination.

## ✖ The Bund & People's Square

### Lost Heaven    Yunnan ¥¥

(花马天堂, Huāmǎ Tiāntáng; Map p122; 2021 6330 0967; www.lostheaven.com.cn; 17 East Yan'an Rd; 延安东路17号; dishes ¥50-160; ◷11.30am-3pm & 5.30-10.30pm; ⓜLine 2, 10 to East Nanjing Rd) Lost Heaven might not have the views that keep its rivals in business, but why go

to the same old Western restaurants when you can get sophisticated Bai, Dai and Miao folk cuisine from China's mighty southwest? Specialities are flowers (banana and pomegranate), wild mushrooms, chillies, Burmese curries, Bai chicken and superb *pǔ'ěr* teas, all served up in gorgeous Yúnnán-meets-Shànghǎi surrounds. The rooftop bar and lounge is a popular spot for a drink.

### Mr & Mrs Bund    French ¥¥¥

(先生及夫人外滩; Xiānshēng Jí Fūrén Wàitān; Map p122; 2021 6323 9898; www.mmbund.com; 6th fl, Bund 18, 18 East Zhongshan No 1 Rd; 中山东一路18号6楼; mains ¥160-800, 2-/3-course set lunch ¥200/250; ◷11.30am-2pm Mon-Fri, 6-10.30pm Sun & Mon, 6pm-2am Tue-Sat; ⓜLine 2, 10 to East Nanjing Rd) French chef Paul Pairet's casual eatery aims for a space that's considerably more playful than your average fine-dining Bund restaurant. The mix-and-match menu has a heavy French bistro influence, reimagined and served up with Pairet's ingenious presentation. But it's not just the food you're here for: it's the post-midnight menu deal (two-/three-course meals ¥250/300), the bingo nights and the wonderfully wonky atmosphere. Ring the doorbell for entry.

### M on the Bund    European ¥¥¥

(米氏西餐厅, Mǐshì Xīcāntīng; Map p122; 2021 6350 9988; www.m-restaurantgroup.com/mbund/home.html; 7th fl, 20 Guangdong Rd; 广东路20号7楼; mains ¥200-400, 2-course set lunch ¥188, weekend brunch 2-/3-course ¥268/298; ◷11.30am-2.30pm & 6-10.30pm; ⓜLine 2, 10 to East Nanjing Rd) M exudes a timelessness and level of sophistication that eclipses the razzle-dazzle of many other upscale Shànghǎi restaurants. The menu ain't radical, but that's the question it seems to ask you – is breaking new culinary ground really so crucial? Crispy suckling pig and tajine with

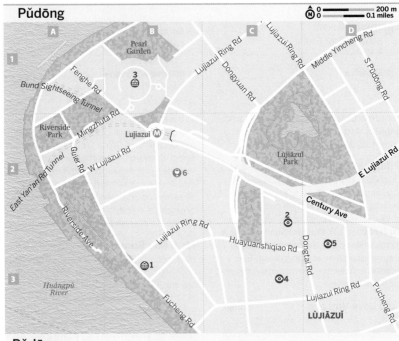

# Pǔdōng

## Pǔdōng

### ⊚ Sights
1 Aurora Museum ............................................ B3
2 Jīnmào Tower ............................................... C2
3 Shànghǎi History Museum ...................... B1
4 Shànghǎi Tower ......................................... C3
5 Shànghǎi World Financial Center ............ D3

### ☉ Drinking & Nightlife
100 Century Avenue ..........................(see 5)
Cloud 9 ...............................................(see 2)
6 Flair ............................................................. B2

saffron are, after all, simply delicious just the way they are.

## ❌ French Concession

### Jian Guo 328          Shanghai ¥
(建国; Jiànguó; Map p134; ☎021 6471 3819; 328 West Jianguo Rd; 建国西路328号; mains ¥22-58; ☉11am-2pm & 5-9.30pm; Ⓜ Jiashan Rd) Frequently crammed, this boisterous narrow two-floor MSG-free spot tucked away on Jianguo Rd does a roaring trade on the back of excellent well-priced Shànghainese cuisine. You can't go wrong with the menu, but highlights include the deep-fried duck legs,

eggplant casserole, scallion oil noodles and yellow croaker fish spring rolls. Reserve.

### Dī Shuǐ Dòng          Hunanese ¥¥
(滴水洞; Map p134; ☎021 6253 2689; 2nd fl, 56 South Maoming Rd; 茂名南路56号2楼; dishes ¥25-128; ☉11am-1am; Ⓜ South Shaanxi Rd) Until the chilled lagers arrive, the faint breeze from the spreading of the blue-and-white tablecloth by your waiter may be the last cooling sensation at Dī Shuǐ Dòng, a rustic upstairs shrine to the volcanic cuisine of Húnán. Loved by Shanghainese and expats in equal measure, dishes are ferried in by sprightly peasant-attired staff to tables stuffed with enthusiastic, red-faced diners.

## Jìng'ān

### Commune Social
Tapas ¥¥

(食社, Shíshè; Map p128; www.communesocial. com; 511 Jiangning Rd; 江宁路511号; tapas ¥38- 198, lunch 3/5 courses ¥178/218; ⊘noon-2.30pm & 6-10.30pm Tue-Fri, noon-3pm & 6-10.30pm Sat, to 3pm Sun; MLine 7 to Changping Rd) A venture by UK celebrity chef Jason Atherton, this natty Neri & Hu–designed restaurant blends a stylish, yet relaxed, vibe with sensational tasting dishes, exquisitely presented by chef Scott Melvin. It's divided neatly into upstairs cocktail bar with terrace, downstairs open-kitchen tapas bar and dessert bar. It's the talk of the town, but has a no-reservations policy, so prepare to queue.

### Fù 1088
Shanghai ¥¥¥

(福1088; Map p134; ☑021 5239 7878; 375 Zhenning Rd; 镇宁路375号; ⊘11am-2pm & 5.30- 11pm; MLine 2, 11 to Jiangsu Rd) In a 1930s villa, exclusive Fu 1088 has 17 rooms filled with Chinese antiques. Rooms are rented out privately, with white-gloved service and an emphasis on elegant Shanghainese fare with a modern twist such as shredded crab and drunken chicken. There's a minimum charge of ¥300 per person for lunch, and ¥400 for dinner, excluding drinks.

## 🍷 DRINKING & NIGHTLIFE

### 🍸 The Bund & People's Square

#### Glam
Lounge

(魅力, Mèilì; Map p122; 7th fl, 20 Guangdong Rd; 广东路20号7楼; cocktails ¥80-100; ⊘5pm-late; MLine 2, 10 to East Nanjing Rd) The decor here is decidedly bohemian – full of art and curiosities – and its cool retro feel makes it one of the Bund's most atmospheric spots for a drink. Cocktail prices are accessible, as is the bar menu, ranging from truffle cheese toasties to soft-serve ice cream.

#### Long Bar
Bar

(廊吧, Láng Bā; Map p122; ☑021 6322 9988; 2 East Zhongshan No 1 Rd; 中山东一路2号; ⊘4pm-1am Mon-Sat, 2pm-1am Sun; 🛜; MLine 2, 10 to East Nanjing Rd) For a taste of colonial-era

Shànghǎi's elitist trappings, you'll do no better than the Long Bar. This was once the members-only Shànghǎi Club, whose most spectacular accoutrement was a 33.7m-long wooden bar. Foreign businessmen would sit here according to rank, comparing fortunes, with the taipans (foreign heads of business) closest to the view of the Bund. Drinks start from ¥70.

### 🍷 French Concession

#### Boxing Cat Brewery
Brewery

(拳击猫啤酒屋; Quánjīmāo Píjiǔwū; Map p134; www.boxingcatbrewery.com; 82 West Fuxing Rd; 复 兴西路82号; ⊘5pm-midnight Mon-Wed, 5pm-2am Thu, 3pm-2am Fri, 10am-midnight Sat & Sun; 🛜; MShanghai Library, Changshu Rd) A deservedly popular three-floor microbrewery, with a rotating line-up of top-notch beers that range from the Standing 8 Pilsner to the Right Hook Helles. But that's not all – the omnipresent restaurateur Kelley Lee has paired Southern home cooking (gumbo, blackened fish tacos), burgers and beer snacks to go with the drinks. Come for a pint; stay for dinner.

### 🍷 Jìng'ān

#### Dogtown
Bar

(狗镇; Gǒu Zhèn; Map p128; 409 N Shaanxi Rd; 陕西北路409号; ⊘4-10pm Mon-Fri, noon-11pm Sat & Sun; MLine 2, 7 to Jing'an Temple; Line 2, 12, 13 to West Nanjing Rd) Run by the team from

#### Sumerian
(苏美尔人; Sū Měi Ěr Rén; Map p128; www.sumeriancoffee.com; 415 North Shaanxi Rd; 陕西北路415号; mains from ¥20; ⊘7am-8pm; 🛜; MLine 2, 12, 13 to West Nanjing Rd, exit 1) next door, this pocket-sized bar is literally a streetside shack with a few stools at its bar, though most revellers stand on the pavement with beer in hand. It's a great place to get chatting to random strangers. For early starters, there's a free keg of Asahi going on weekends from noon until it runs out.

### 🍷 Pǔdōng

#### Flair
Bar

(Map p130; 58th fl, Ritz-Carlton Shanghai Pudong, 8 Century Ave; 世纪大道8号58楼; cocktails from

Work by Xu Zhen, M50 (p125)

¥95; ⊙5.30pm-late; 🛜; MLujiazui) Wow your date with Shànghǎi's most intoxicating nocturnal visuals from the outdoor terrace on the 58th floor of the Ritz-Carlton, where Flair nudges you closer to the baubles of the Oriental Pearl TV Tower. If it's raining, you'll end up inside, but that's OK as the chilled-out interior, designed by Super Potato, is very cool. Book well in advance for the terrace.

## ⭐ ENTERTAINMENT

Shànghǎi is no longer the decadent city that slipped on its dancing shoes as the revolution shot its way into town, but entertainment options have blossomed again during the past decade.

### Shànghǎi Centre
### Theatre — Acrobatics

(上海商城剧院, Shànghǎi Shāngchéng Jùyuàn; Map p134; ☎021 6279 8948; Shànghǎi Centre, 1376 West Nanjing Rd; 南京西路1376号; tickets ¥120-300; MLine 2, 7 to Jing'an Temple) Spend an evening with the acrobats.

### Shànghǎi Circus
### World — Acrobatics

(上海马戏城; Shànghǎi Mǎxìchéng; ☎021 6652 7501; www.era-shanghai.com/era/en/; 2266 Gonghexin Rd; 共和新路2266号; admission ¥120-600; MShanghai Circus World) Venue of the amazing acrobatics event *Era: Intersection of Time*.

### Fairmont Peace
### Hotel Jazz Bar — Jazz

(爵士吧, Juéshì Bā; Map p122; ☎021 6138 6883; 20 East Nanjing Rd; 南京东路20号费尔蒙和平饭店; ⊙5.30pm-2am, live music from 7pm; MLine 2, 10 to East Nanjing Rd) Swing with Shànghǎi's most famous – and oldest – jazz band.

### Shànghǎi Grand
### Theatre — Classical Music

(上海大剧院, Shànghǎi Dàjùyuàn; Map p122; ☎021 6386 8686; www.shgtheatre.com; 300 Renmin Ave; 人民广场人民大道300号; ⊙box office 9am-8pm; MLine 1, 2, 8 to People's Square) Ballet, opera and classical music on the biggest stage in town.

#  INFORMATION

**Bank of China** (中国银行; Zhōngguó Yínháng; Map p122; East Zhongshan No 1 Rd; 中山东一路; ⊘9am-noon & 1.30-4.30pm Mon-Fri, 9am-noon Sat; Ⓜ Line 2, 10 to East Nanjing Rd) **Right next to the Peace Hotel. Tends to get crowded, but is better organised than Chinese banks elsewhere around the country (it's worth a peek for its grand interior). Take a ticket and wait for your number. For credit-card advances, head to the furthest hall (counter No 2).**

**China Post** (中国邮政; Zhōngguó Yóuzhèng; Map p134; Xingye Lu; 兴业路) **Opposite site of the 1st National Congress of the CCP in Xīntiāndì.**

**Huàshān Hospital** (华山医院国际医疗中心; Huàshān Yīyuàn Guójì Yīliáo Zhōngxīn; Map p134; 🕿021 5288 9998; www.sh-hwmc.com.cn; 12 Middle Wulumuqi Rd; 乌鲁木齐中路12号; Ⓜ Changshu Rd) **Hospital treatment and outpatient consultations are available at the 8th-floor foreigners' clinic, the Huashan Worldwide Medical Center** (华山医院国际医疗中心; Huàshān Yīyuàn Guójì Yīliáo Zhōngxīn; 🕿021 6248 3986; ⊘8am-10pm;), **and there's 24-hour emergency treatment on the 15th floor in building 6.**

**Transport Card** (交通卡; jiāotōng kǎ). **Available at metro stations and some convenience stores, cards can be topped up with credit and used on the metro, some buses and ferries, and all taxis; credit is electronically deducted. Cards don't save you money, but will save you from queuing for tickets or hunting for change. A refundable deposit of ¥20 is required.**

#  GETTING THERE & AWAY

## AIR

**Pǔdōng International Airport** (PVG; 浦东国际机场; Pǔdōng Guójì Jīchǎng; 🕿021 6834 7575, flight information 96990; www.shairport.com) **is located 30km southeast of Shànghǎi, near the East China Sea. Most international flights (and some domestic flights) operate from here. If you're making an onward domestic connection, it's crucial that you find out whether the domestic flight leaves from Pǔdōng or Hóngqiáo, as it will take at least an hour to cross the city.**

 ### No Dogs or Chinese

A notorious sign at **Huángpǔ Park** (黄浦公园, Huángpǔ Gōngyuán; Map p122; Ⓜ Line 2, 10 to East Nanjing Rd), then called the Public Gardens, apocryphally declared 'No dogs or Chinese allowed'. Although this widely promoted notice never actually existed, the general gist of the wording hits the mark. A series of regulations was indeed posted outside the gardens listing 10 rules governing use of the park. The first regulation noted that 'The gardens are for the use of the foreign community', while the fourth ruled that 'Dogs and bicycles are not admitted'. Chinese were barred from the park (as expressed in the first regulation), an injustice that gave rise to the canard.

The bluntly worded sign has, however, become firmly embedded in the Chinese consciousness. Bruce Lee destroys a Shànghǎi park sign declaring 'No dogs and Chinese allowed' with a flying kick in *Fist of Fury* and Chinese history books cite the insult as further evidence of Chinese humiliation at the hands of foreigners. For an academic examination of the subject, hunt down *Shanghai's 'Dogs and Chinese not Admitted' Sign: Legend, History and Contemporary Symbol* by Robert A Bickers and Jeffrey N Wasserstrom, published in the *China Quarterly*, No 142 (June 1995).

**Hóngqiáo International Airport** (SHA; 虹桥国际机场; Hóngqiáo Guójì Jīchǎng; 🕿021 5260 4620, flight information 021 6268 8899; www.shairport.com; Ⓜ Hongqiao Airport Terminal 1, Hongqiao Airport Terminal 2), **18km west of the Bund, has two terminals: the older and less-used Terminal 1 (east terminal; halls A and B), and the new and sophisticated Terminal 2 (west terminal; attached to Shànghǎi Hóngqiáo railway station), where most flights arrive.**

# French Concession

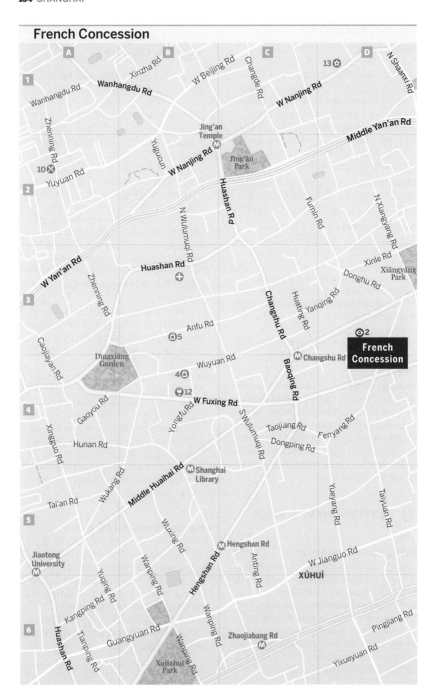

A1 · B1 · C1 · D1

Xinzha Rd
W Beijing Rd
Changde Rd
**Wanhangdu Rd**
Wanhangdu Rd
W Nanjing Rd
**W Nanjing Rd**
13 ✪
N Shaanxi Rd
Wanhangdu Rd

Zhenning Rd
Yugucun
Jing'an Temple
Jing'an Park
Middle Yan'an Rd

10 ✖
Yuyuan Rd
W Nanjing Rd
Huashan Rd
Funmin Rd
N Xiangyang Rd

A2 · B2 · C2 · D2

**W Yan'an Rd**
Zhenning Rd
N Wulumuqi Rd
Xinle Rd
Xiāngyáng Park

**Huashan Rd**
Changshu Rd
Huating Rd
D, Donghu Rd

Caojiayan Rd
✚
Yanqing Rd

A3 · B3 · C3 · D3

Dīngxiāng Garden
Anfu Rd
5 🔒
Baojing Rd
◉2
Changshu Rd Ⓜ
**French Concession**

Gaoyou Rd
Wuyuan Rd
4 🔒
12 🍴
Yongfu Rd
S Wulumuqi Rd
**W Fuxing Rd**

A4 · B4 · C4 · D4

Xinguo Rd
Hunan Rd
Taojiang Rd
Fenyang Rd
Dongping Rd

Tai'an Rd
Wukang Rd
**Middle Huaihai Rd**
Ⓜ Shanghai Library
Yueyang Rd
Taiyuan Rd

A5 · B5 · C5 · D5

Jiaotong University
Ⓜ
Wuxing Rd
Hengshan Rd Ⓜ Hengshan Rd
Anting Rd
W Jianguo Rd
**XÚHUÌ**

Yuqing Rd
Wanping Rd
Kangping Rd
**Huashan Rd**
Tianping Rd
Guangyuan Rd
Zhaojiabang Rd
Ⓜ
Pingjiang Rd

A6 · B6 · C6 · D6

Xujiahui Park
Wanping Rd
Yixueyuan Rd

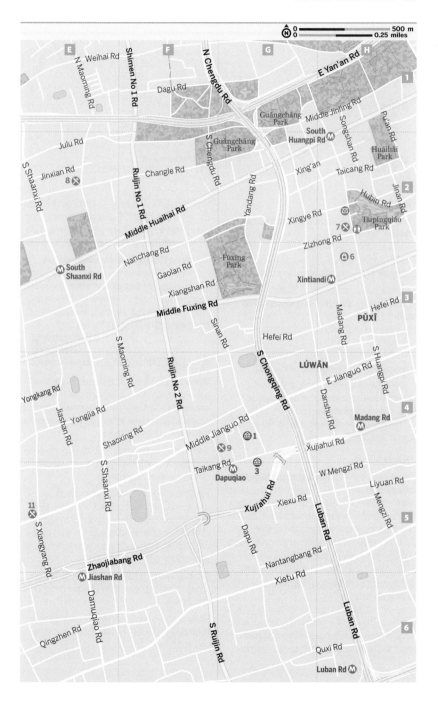

N

0       500 m
0       0.25 miles

E

F

G

H

1

Weihai Rd

N Maoming Rd

Shimen No 1 Rd

Dagu Rd

N Chengdu Rd

E Yan'an Rd

Guǎngchǎng Park

Middle Jinling Rd

Songshan Rd

Pǔ'an Rd

Julu Rd

S Chengdu Rd

Guǎngchǎng Park

South Huangpi Rd M

Xing'an

Huáihǎi Park

Jinxian Rd

Ruijin No 1 Rd

Changle Rd

Yandang Rd

Xingye Rd

Taicang Rd

2

S Shaanxi Rd

8 X

Middle Huaihai Rd

Hubin Rd

Jinan Rd

7 X

Tàipíngqiáo Park

Nanchang Rd

Fùxing Park

Zizhong Rd

South Shaanxi Rd M

Gaolan Rd

6

Xiangshan Rd

Xintiandi M

3

Middle Fuxing Rd

Hefei Rd

Madang Rd

PǓXĪ

Sinan Rd

Hefei Rd

S Chongqing Rd

LÚWĀN

S Huangpi Rd

S Maoming Rd

E Jianguo Rd

4

Yongkang Rd

Ruijin No 2 Rd

Danshui Rd

Madang Rd M

Jiashan Rd

Yongjia Rd

Shaoxing Rd

Middle Jianguo Rd

1

Xujiahui Rd

S Shaanxi Rd

9 X

Taikang Rd

3

W Mengzi Rd

Liyuan Rd

11 X

Dapuqiao

Xujiahui Rd

Xiexu Rd

Luban Rd

Mengzi Rd

5

S Xiangyang Rd

Dapu Rd

Zhaojiabang Rd

Nantangbang Rd

Jiashan Rd M

Xietu Rd

Damuqiao Rd

Qingzhen Rd

S Ruijin Rd

Luban Rd

6

Quxi Rd

Luban Rd M

# French Concession

## BUS

The huge **Shànghǎi South long-distance bus station** (上海长途客运南站; Shànghǎi chángtú kèyùn nánzhàn; ☎021 5436 2835; www.ctnz.net; 666 Shilong Rd; Ⓜ Shanghai South Railway Station) has buses largely to destinations in south China.

Although it appears close to Shànghǎi railway station, the vast **Shànghǎi long-distance bus station** (上海长途汽车客运总站, Shànghǎi chángtú qìchē kèyùn zǒngzhàn; Map p128; ☎021 6605 0000; www.kyzz.com.cn; 1666 Zhongxing Rd; 中兴路1666号; Ⓜ Shanghai Railway Station) is a pain to get to, but has buses to everywhere.

Buses for Hángzhōu, Sūzhōu and a host of destinations also leave from the **Hóngqiáo long-distance bus station** (长途客运虹桥站; Hóngqiáo chángtú kèyùn zhàn) at Hóngqiáo Airport Terminal 2.

## TRAIN

The new and sophisticated **Shànghǎi Hóngqiáo railway station** (上海虹桥站; Shànghǎi Hóngqiáo zhàn; Ⓜ Hongqiao Railway Station) is Asia's largest train station. It's the terminus for the high-speed G-class trains and other trains, and includes services to Běijīng (from ¥555, very regular), Hángzhōu (from ¥73, very regular), Nánjīng South (from ¥95, frequent) and Sūzhōu (from ¥25, regular).

The vast, hectic and sprawling **Shànghǎi railway station** (上海火车站; Shànghǎi huǒchē zhàn; ☎in Chinese 12306; 385 Meiyuan Rd; 梅园路 385号; Ⓜ Shanghai Railway Station), located in the north of town, is easily reached by metro lines 1, 3 and 4 and has G-class, D-class and express trains

to Běijīng (¥309, three daily), Hángzhōu (¥95, four daily), Hong Kong (¥226, daily at 6.20pm), Huáng-shān (¥93, two daily), Nánjīng (¥144, frequent), Sūzhōu (¥40, frequent) and Xī'ān (¥180, frequent).

Modern **Shànghǎi South railway station** (上海南站; Shànghǎi nánzhàn; ☎021 9510 5123; 200 Zhaofeng Rd) is easily accessed on metro lines 1 and 3. It has trains largely to southern and southwestern destinations including Guìlín (¥190, four daily) and Hángzhōu (¥29, frequent).

## ⓘ GETTING AROUND

**Metro** The rapidly expanding metro and light railway system works like a dream; it's fast, efficient and inexpensive. Rush hour on the metro operates at overcapacity, however, and you get to savour the full meaning of the big squeeze.

**Taxi** Ubiquitous and cheap, but flagging one down during rush hour or during a rainstorm requires staying power of a high order.

**Bus** With a wide-ranging web of routes, buses may sound tempting, but that's before you try to decipher routes and stops or attempt to squeeze aboard during the crush hour. Buses also have to contend with Shànghǎi's traffic, which can slow to an agonising crawl.

**Bicycle** Good for small neighbourhoods, but distances are too colossal for effective transport about town.

**Walking** This is only really possible within neighbourhoods, and even then the distances can be epic and tiring.

# Where to Stay

*You'll need to book your Shànghǎi accommodation well in advance to secure your top choice. Be prepared for surprisingly rudimentary English-language ability, except at the very best hotels (and youth hostels).*

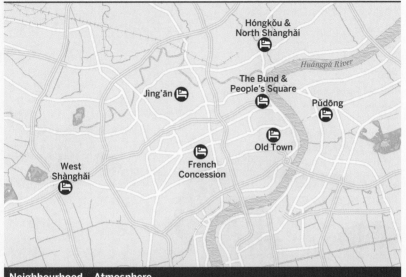

| Neighbourhood | Atmosphere |
| --- | --- |
| **The Bund & People's Square** | Luxury hotels on the Bund, iconic views and exclusive restaurants; ubercentral with good transport links but busy and expensive. |
| **Old Town** | Traditional part of town; river views from stylish and happening South Bund area; transport options are limited and the area is ramshackle in parts. |
| **French Concession** | Dapper neighbourhood with heritage architecture; vibrant, leafy and central; tip-top range of hotels and restaurants; fab transport links; can be expensive. |
| **Jìng'ān** | Good transport links; fine range of accommodation choices; shopping zone; central and stylish but light on sights. |
| **Pǔdōng** | Luxury, stylish and high-altitude hotels and fantastic restaurants; good transport links but big distances; little character. |
| **Hóngkǒu & North Shànghǎi** | Heritage and stylish long-stay options; good transport links; parts close to centre; grittier and less fashionable. |
| **West Shànghǎi** | Close to Hóngqiáo International Airport; some good-value options but not much character. |

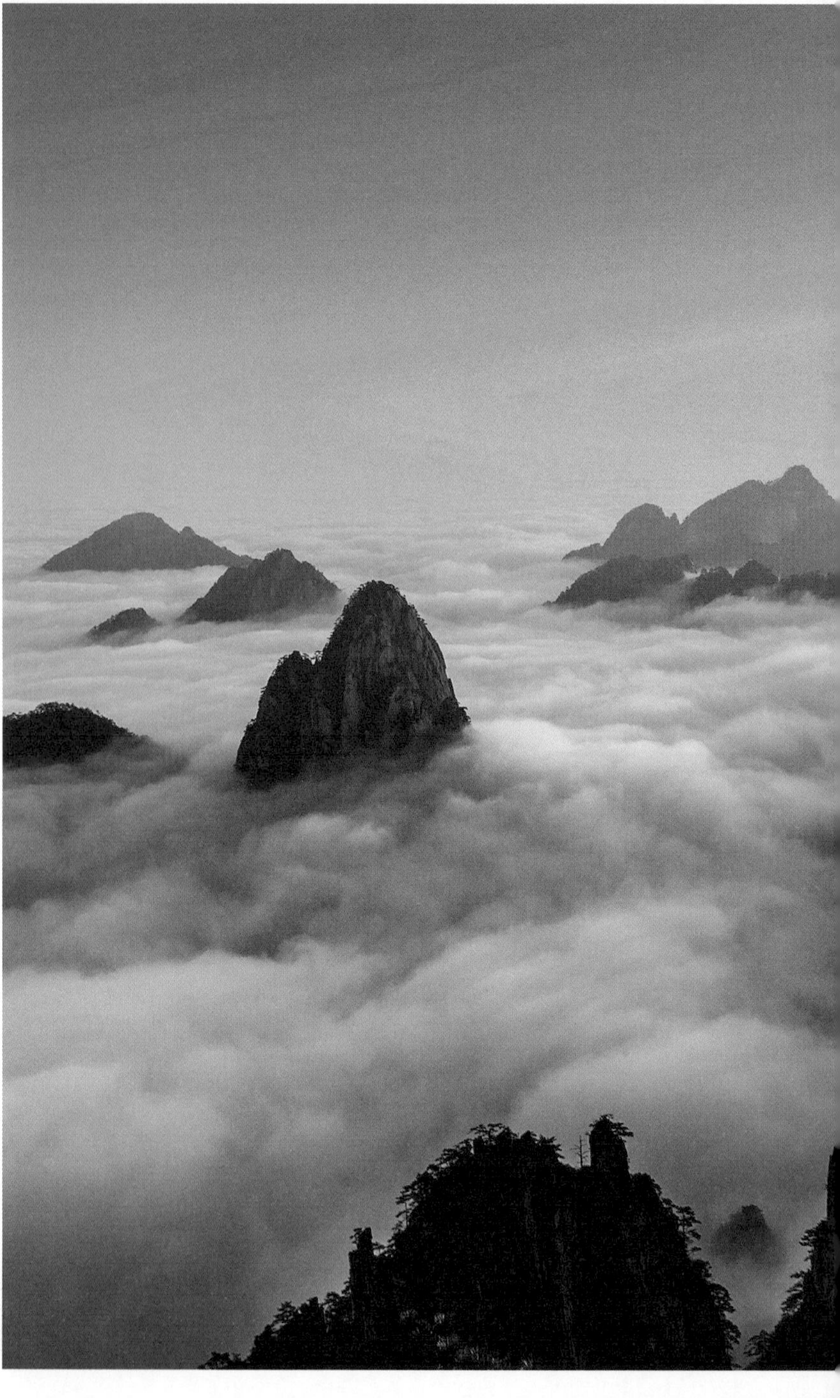

HUÁNGSHĀN (P142): OBBCHAO / SHUTTERSTOCK ©

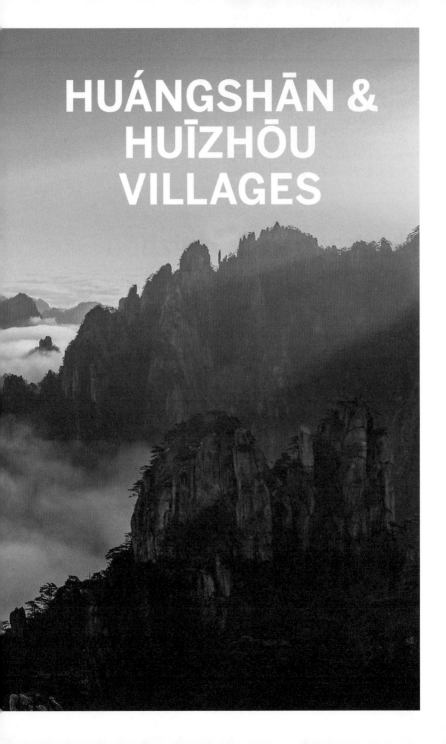

# HUÁNGSHĀN &
# HUĪZHŌU
# VILLAGES

# Huángshān & Huīzhōu Villages at a Glance...

*Fantastical mountainscapes and well-preserved villages make Ānhuī (安徽) the perfect antidote to the brashness of China's larger cities. The main attraction is unquestionably Huángshān, a jumble of sheer granite cliffs wrapped in cottony clouds that inspired an entire school of ink painting during the 17th and 18th centuries. At the foot of these ranges are strewn the ancient villages of the province formerly known as Huīzhōu. With distinctive whitewashed walls and black-tiled roofs, they are among the most picturesque in the country.*

### Two Days in Huángshān & Huīzhōu Villages

Make an early start at climbing the mountain and exploring the peak area before spending the night on **Huángshān** (p142). Rise early to catch the sunrise and spend the day hiking the West Canyon and slowly descending to spend the night either in Tángkǒu or Túnxī.

### Four Days in Huángshān & Huīzhōu Villages

Explore the villages of **Hóngcūn** (p148), **Xīdì** (p149) and **Píngshān** (p150) around Yīxiàn and consider spending the night here. The next morning climb **Qíyún Shān** (p152), before continuing on to **Shèxiàn** (p150) to visit the riverside town of **Yúliáng** (p153), the village of **Chéngkǎn** (p150) and the astonishing decorative arches of **Tángyuè** (p147).

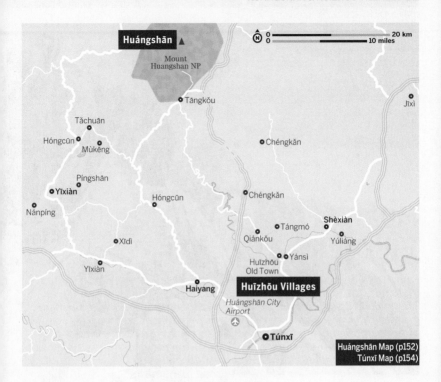

## Arriving in Huángshān & Huīzhōu Villages

**Huángshān City Airport** Take a taxi (¥30) the 5km to Túnxī (Huángshān City).

**Túnxī long-distance bus station** On the outskirts of town; bus 2 (¥2) runs to Old St.

**Huángshān train station** In central Túnxī; bus 12 (¥2) runs to Old St.

## Where to Stay

Huángshān has numerous hotels, ranging from cheap and not-so-cheerful places devoid of views to well-equipped properties with spectacular outlooks. Book ahead to secure a bed, particularly for dormitories and summit properties.

Túnxī's Old St is an established traveller base, with excellent hostels and boutique hotels in restored wooden homes.

# Climbing Huángshān

*When its granite peaks and twisted pines are wreathed in spectral folds of mist, Huángshān's idyllic views easily nudge it into the select company of China's top five sights.*

### Great For...

☑ **Don't Miss**

Hiking along the West Sea Canyon.

Legions of poets and painters have drawn inspiration from Huángshān's iconic beauty. Yesterday's artists seeking an escape from the hustle and bustle of the temporal world have been replaced by crowds of tourists, who bring the hustle and bustle with them: the mountain is inundated with tourist traffic at points, so the magic can rapidly evaporate, especially during holiday periods and weekends. But Huángshān still rewards visitors with moments of tranquillity, and the unearthly views are simply breathtaking.

## Orientation

Buses from Túnxī drop you off at the Tourist Distribution Center (p145) in the tourist village 2km south of Tāngkǒu, the town at the southern foot of Huángshān. The area around the bus station is a base for

West Sea Canyon (p144)

HUANG XIN / GETTY IMAGES ©

◉ *Huángshān*

▲ Lotus Flower Peak
(1873m)

Mount
Huangshan NP

Tāngkŏu ○

### ℹ Need to Know

黄山; Yellow Mountain; www.chinahuangshan.
gov.cn; Mar-Nov ¥230, Dec-Feb ¥150, child
1.2-1.4m ¥115, under 1.2m free

### ✕ Take a Break

Most hotel restaurants offer buffets
(breakfast ¥60, lunch and dinner ¥100
to ¥140).

### ★ Top Tip

Make sure to take plenty of food to
the summit. Autumn days are best for
climbing.

climbers; you can stock up on supplies
(maps, rain gear and food), store luggage
(¥10 per bag per day) and arrange onward
transport here. Tangchuan Lu runs north to
the town itself, where you can find ameni-
ties such as the post office and banks with
international ATMs. Tāngkŏu Town is small,
basically two streets, Yanxi Zonglu and
Yanxi Xilu, on either side of a river; look for
the stairs leading down from the bridge on
Tangchuan Lu.

## Ascending & Descending
## the Mountain

Regardless of how you ascend Huángshān,
you will be stung by a dizzying entrance
fee. You can pay at the eastern steps near
the **Cloud Valley Station** (Map p152; 云谷站;
Yúngǔ Zhàn) or at the **Mercy Light Pavilion**

**Station** (Map p152; 慈光阁站; Cíguānggé Zhàn),
where the western steps begin. Shuttle
buses (¥19) run to both places from
Tāngkŏu.

Three basic routes will get you up to
the summit: the short, hard way (eastern
steps); the longer, harder way (western
steps); and the very short, easy way (cable
car). It's possible to do a 10-hour circuit going up the eastern steps and then down the
western steps in one day, but you'll have to
be slightly insane, in good shape and you'll
definitely miss out on some of the more
spectacular, hard-to-get-to areas.

A basic itinerary would be to take an
early morning bus from Túnxī, climb the
eastern steps, hike around the summit
area, spend the night at the top, catch
the sunrise and then hike back down the
western steps the next day, giving you time
to catch an afternoon bus back to Túnxī.
Most travellers do opt to spend more than
one night on the summit to explore all of
the various trails. Don't underestimate

the hardship involved; the steep gradients and granite steps can wreak havoc on your knees, both going up and down.

Most sightseers are packed (and we mean *packed*) into the summit area above the upper cable-car stations, consisting of a network of trails running between various peaks, so don't go expecting peace and quiet. The number of visitors is mounting every year and paths are being widened at bottleneck points where scrums develop. The highlight of the climb for many independent travellers is the lesser-known **West Sea Canyon** (西海大峡谷; Xīhǎi Dàxiágǔ) hike, a more rugged, exposed section where most tour groups do not venture.

Make sure to bring enough water, food, warm clothing and rain gear before climbing. Bottled water and food prices increase the higher you go as porters carry everything up. As the mountain paths are easy to follow and English signs are plentiful, guides are unnecessary.

## Porters on the Mountain

When climbing Huángshān, spare a thought for the long-suffering, muscular and suntanned porters (挑山工; *tiāoshāngōng*) who toil slowly uphill with all manner of goods from rice to water and building materials for the hotels and hawkers that populate the higher levels. They then descend with rubbish. Going up, they earn ¥1.80 per kilogram hauled aloft, downhill it's ¥1.50 per kilogram. They ferry around 100kg each trip (and only ascend once per day), balanced on two ends of a stout pole across their shoulders. Remember to give way to them on your way up (and down).

Trail, West Sea Canyon

## Sleeping

Huángshān has clusters of hotels. Prices and availability vary according to season; book ahead for summit accommodation, especially for dorms and at peak times. If you're on a tight budget you can stay in Tāngkǒu, but otherwise you might as well stay on the mountain, though dorm rooms on the summit do cost twice as much as doubles in town.

### ⓘ Need to Know

Locals claim it rains more than 200 days a year on the mountain. Autumn (September to October) is generally considered to be the best travel period.

On the Mountain

Huángshān visits should ideally include nights on the summit. Room prices rise on Saturday and Sunday, and are astronomical during major holiday periods.

It's possible to camp at select, though not scenic, points on the mountain, such as the plaza in front of the **Běihǎi Hotel** (Map p152; 北海宾馆; Běihǎi Bīnguǎn; ☏0559 558 2555; www.hsbeihaihotel.com; dm/d ¥300/1480; ❄@☎). You'll need to ask for permission and pay a fee of ¥180.

Tāngkǒu

In the tourist village around the bus station, chain hotels, such as 7 Days Inn and Green Tree Inn, offer rooms for around ¥200. Mediocre midrange hotels geared for tour groups line Tangchuan Lu all the way to Tāngkǒu Town, where rooms are a little cheaper; remember to look at rooms first and ask for discounts before committing. Many hotels in town offer transport to and from the Tourist Distribution Center.

## Getting There

Buses from Túnxī (aka Huángshān Shì) take around one hour to reach Tāngkǒu from either the long-distance bus station (¥20, frequent, 6am to 5pm) or the train station (¥20, departures when full, 6.30am to 5.30pm, may leave as late as 8pm in summer).

Buses back to Túnxī (¥20) from Tāngkǒu depart over roughly the same schedule, and can be flagged down on the road to Túnxī. The last bus back leaves at 5.30pm.

The main bus depot for both long-distance buses to and from Tāngkǒu and tourist buses around Huángshān is the **Tourist Distribution Center** (新国线 客车站; Xīnguóxiàn Kèchēzhàn; Tangchuan Lu; 汤川路).

Destinations include Hángzhōu (¥110, 3½ hours, seven daily), Shànghǎi (¥148, 6½ hours, five daily) and Yīxiàn (¥17, one hour, four daily; stops at Hóngcūn and Xīdì).

A taxi between Túnxī and the Huángshān Scenic Area should cost around ¥200; to the villages of Yīxiàn, ¥110 to ¥140.

CORNELIA DOERR / GETTY IMAGES ©

Memorial archway, Tángyuè

# Huīzhōu Villages

*Boasting elegant architecture augmented by lush surroundings of buckling earth, bamboo and pine forest, the Huīzhōu villages offer a delightful slice of historical China.*

## Great For...

### ☑ Don't Miss

The decorative Húwénguāng Páifāng arch at the entrance to Xīdì.

Huīzhōu (徽州) is the old name for the region of southeastern Ānhuī (a portmanteau of Ānqìng and Huīzhōu) and northern Jiāngxī. It developed into a mercantile powerhouse in the 13th century, and with that developed a unique culture. Fortunes were made in lumber, tea and salt (and a string of lucrative pawnshops throughout the empire). And yet success was a double-edged sword: the life of a merchant was essentially one of exile. At age 13, many young men were shunted out the door for the remainder of their lives to do business elsewhere, sometimes returning home only once per year. Rather than uproot their families and disrespect their ancestral clans, these merchants remained attached to the home towns they rarely saw, funnelling their profits into the construction of lavish residences, ancestral halls and

Stone gateway, Xīdì (p149)

TRAVELGAME / GETTY IMAGES ©

TRAVELGAME / GETTY IMAGES ©

### ℹ Need to Know

Avoid visiting during weekends and public holidays.

### ✕ Take a Break

Hóngcūn has a smattering of cafes that serve good coffee and morph into bars in the evening.

### ★ Top Tip

Pack a camera to catch the flowering yellow rapeseed in the villages around Shèxiàn.

memorial arches – and making the ancient villages of Huīzhōu among the most spectacular in China.

## Memorial Archways & Social Prestige

Wealthy merchants didn't just turn their profits into material luxuries: they also invested heavily in their children's education. As a result, Huīzhōu produced a significant number of high-ranking imperial officials, which in turn bought the region influence. Such achievements were commemorated in archways, called *páifāng* (牌坊). Women who led lives of exemplary chastity were honoured with similar arches called *páilóu* (牌楼), though roads were built to pass under a *páifāng* but around a *páilóu*, so that a man would never feel that his status was beneath that of a woman's.

Archways are common throughout China, but in Huīzhōu they carry a great significance, giving the merchants – who occupied the bottom rung of the Confucian social ladder (under artisans, peasants and scholars) – much-desired social prestige. Only the imperial government could approve the construction of a memorial archway. The most elaborate examples are in Tángyuè, just outside Shèxiàn.

With the fall of the Qing dynasty, the influence and prestige that the merchants of Huīzhōu had spent generations accruing instantly vanished. Yet the lavish constructions, rich in symbolism, that they bequeathed to their descendants have indeed bestowed prosperity – now in the form of tourism.

## Distinctive Architecture & Decorative Carvings

Whitewashed homes with high, narrow windows and slate-tiled roofs face inwards around open courtyards – to protect the residents from thieves – can also be found in Huīzhōu, along with horse-head gables, originally designed to prevent fire from travelling along a line of houses, and which evolved into decorative motifs. In grander homes, exterior doorways are overhung with decorative eaves and carved brick or stone lintels, and sometimes flanked by drum stones (鼓石; *gǔshí*).

The exteriors, however, pale in comparison to the interiors: inner courtyards, delightfully illuminated by light wells (天井; *tiānjǐng*), reveal intricately carved wood panels on inner corridors and doorways. Carvings are also rich in intent: a bat picking up coins, for example, promises fortune; a *qílín* (麒麟; mythical chimera) looking up at a magpie suggests a blessing.

Furnishings hold meaning, too. You might notice semicircular half-tables against the walls: if the master of the house is in, the tables would be combined; if they are split, it's a subtle hint for male visitors to not intrude upon the wife. Mantels are invariably decorated with a clock, vase and mirror, which symbolises peace and harmony in the house. The village of Xīdì has the best preserved residential architecture.

## Hóngcūn

**Hóngcūn** (宏村; admission ¥104; ⊘7am-5.30pm), a Unesco World Heritage Site, is the most-visited of the Huīzhōu villages. It is a standout example of ancient feng-shui planning, a perfect marriage of symbolism and function, predicated on a sophisticated network of waterways. Founded in the Song

Courtyard, merchant's house, Hóngcūn

dynasty, the village was remodelled in the Ming dynasty by village elders, under the direction of a geomancer, to suggest an ox; its still-functioning waterway system represents the animal's entrails.

The village has crescent-shaped **Moon Pond** (月沼; Yuè Zhǎo) at its heart, or rather at its stomach – as that's what the pond represents in the village's ox-shaped layout. Larger **South Lake** (南湖; Nán Hú), built later, is another stomach; **Léigǎng Mountain** (雷岗山; Léigǎng Shān), to the north, is the head. The busy square by **Hóngjì**

> ★ **Top Tip**
> Alleyway channels flush water through the village from West Stream to Moon Pond and from there on to South Lake. Lost? Just follow the water flow.

KARL JOHAENTGES / LOOK FOTO / GETTY IMAGES ©

**Bridge** (宏际桥; Hóngjì Qiáo) on the West Stream is shaded by two ancient trees (the 'horns' of the ox), a red poplar and a ginkgo.

Tourist bus 1 runs to Hóngcūn (¥20, 1½ hours) via Xīdì from Túnxī's Huángshān Tourist Distribution Center (p156), leaving hourly from 8am to 4pm. Return buses run hourly from 8am to 5pm. The fare from Hóngcūn to Xīdì (30 minutes) and Píngshān (15 minutes) is ¥6.

## Xīdì

Typical of the elegant Huīzhōu style, Xīdì's 124 surviving buildings reflect the wealth and prestige of the prosperous merchants who settled here. Its Unesco World Heritage Site status means **Xīdì** (西递; admission ¥104; ⏰7am-5pm) enjoys a lucrative tourist economy, yet it remains a picturesque tableau of slender lanes, cream-coloured walls topped with horse-head gables, roofs capped with dark tiles, and doorways ornately decorated with carved lintels.

Dating to AD 1047, the village has for centuries been a stronghold of the Hu (胡) clan, descended from the eldest son of the last Tang emperor who fled here in the twilight years of the Tang dynasty. Xīdì's magnificent three-tiered Ming dynasty decorative arch, the Húwénguāng Páifāng (胡文光牌坊), at the entrance to the village, is an ostentatious symbol of Xīdì's former standing.

## Tǎchuān

Tǎchuān is a favourite among photographers, especially in the early spring, when the rapeseed blooms, and in the autumn, when the leaves of the old-growth trees turn vivid colours. Year-round you can stroll the flagstone walking path through the village, past residents tending their rice and tea fields.

Tǎchuān is 5km northwest of Hóngcūn, on the road to Huángshān.

## Nánpíng

Labyrinthine Nánpíng has a history of more than 1100 years. However, it's relatively recent history that draws most visitors, particularly film fans: much of Zhang Yimou's 1989 tragedy *Judou* was filmed inside the village's **Xùzhì Hall** (叙秩堂; Xùzhì Táng). Props from the film and behind-the-scenes photographs from the filming are on display inside the dramatic 530-year-old hall. Parts of Ang Lee's 1999 *Crouching Tiger, Hidden Dragon* were filmed next door in the Ming dynasty **Kuíguāng Hall** (奎光堂; Kuíguāng Táng).

Nánpíng is 5km west of Yīxiàn. Minibuses (¥3) depart for Nánpíng every 30 minutes (7am to 4pm) from Yīxiàn; a taxi from Xīdì costs ¥40.

## Píngshān

**Píngshān** (屏山; admission ¥50; ⏱7.30am-5pm), first settled in the Tang dynasty, was once the largest village in the county, with 38 ancestral halls and 13 archways. Its stature made it a target during the Cultural Revolution; only a handful of these structures remain. The lack of grand halls means that Píngshān sees few visitors; most who do come are art students sitting with easels in shady corners.

## Shèxiàn

**Shèxiàn** (歙县) is 25km east of Túnxī and can be visited as a day trip. The town was formerly the grand centre of the Huīzhōu culture, serving as its capital.

The entrance to Shèxiàn's old town (known as Huīzhōu Old Town) is marked by Yánghé Mén (阳和门), a double-eaved, wooden gate tower that dates to the Song dynasty. To the left are two stone *xièzhì* (獬豸; a legendary beast) and straight ahead, the main attraction: the magnificent **Xǔguó Archway** (许国石坊; Xǔguó Shífáng).

Continue in the same direction to reach the alleyway (on the left) to the old residential area of **Doushan Jie** (斗山街古民居; Dòushānjiē Gǔmínjū), a street of Huīzhōu houses, with several courtyard residences decorated with exquisitely carved lintels,

beautiful interiors and occasional pairs of leaping-on blocks for mounting horses.

There are five trains daily from Huángshān station in Túnxī to Shèxiàn (¥2 to ¥9, 20 to 40 minutes), departing at 6.30am, 8.05am, 10.57am, 7.50pm and 8.45pm; the last train returns at 6.36pm. Buses from Túnxī's long-distance bus station run regularly to Shèxiàn (¥7, 45 minutes, frequent 6am to 5pm). You can walk from Shèxiàn bus station to the old town in about 20 minutes: cross the bridge over the river and turn right at the end of the road.

Tourist shuttle 2 runs from Túnxī's Huángshān Tourist Distribution Center (p156) – at 8am, 10am, 2pm and 4pm – to Huīzhōu Old Town (¥8, 75 minutes). The last bus returns to Túnxī at 4pm.

Traditional architecture, Chéngkǎn

## Chéngkǎn

Chéngkǎn is a photogenic village, with arched bridges over waterways cloaked with lilies, that hasn't yet been completely restored: buildings are in various states of repair and its visitors are far fewer than those at villages more firmly on the tourist map. Chéngkǎn is designed around the *bāguà*, the eight trigrams of the *I-Ching*, which match up with eight surrounding hills. An S-shaped stream snakes through the middle, carving the symbol for yin and yang deep into the heart of the village.

Most visitors are here to see southern China's largest ancestral temple, **Luó Dōngshū Temple** (罗东舒祠; Luó Dōngshū Cí), a massive wooden complex several courtyards deep that took 71 years

(1539–1610) to build. Also worth a peek is the three-storey Yànyì Táng (燕翼堂), nearly 600 years old.

Tourist bus 3 runs from Túnxī's Huáng-shān Tourist Distribution Center (p156) (¥10, 40 minutes, hourly 8am to 11am and 1pm to 4pm). To get the return bus from the exit, walk up the commercial street for 10 minutes; the last bus departs at 4pm.

### ⓘ Did you Know?

Traditionally Hóngcūn villagers followed a strict time regimen: collecting water before 6am, washing vegetables from 6am to 7am and doing laundry afterwards.

PINGGR / SHUTTERSTOCK ©

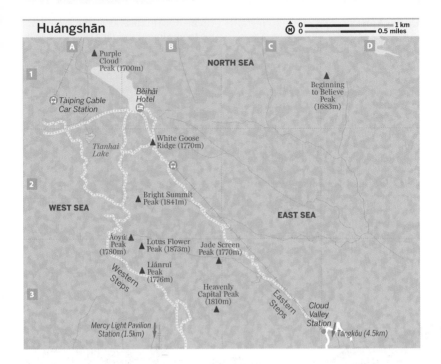

## Huángshān

NORTH SEA

▲ Purple Cloud Peak (1700m)

▲ Beginning to Believe Peak (1683m)

🚡 Tàipíng Cable Car Station

*Běihǎi Hotel*

*Tianhai Lake*

▲ White Goose Ridge (1770m)

▲ Bright Summit Peak (1841m)

WEST SEA

EAST SEA

Aoyú ▲ Peak (1780m)

▲ Lotus Flower Peak (1873m)

Jade Screen Peak (1770m) ▲

*Western Steps*

Liánruǐ ▲ Peak (1776m)

Heavenly Capital Peak (1810m) ▲

*Eastern Steps*

Cloud Valley Station

Mercy Light Pavilion Station (1.5km)

Tāngkǒu (4.5km)

## Túnxī

Ringed by low-lying hills, the old trading town of Túnxī (屯溪), also called Huángshān Shì (黄山市), is the main springboard for trips to Huángshān and the surrounding Huīzhōu villages. Compared with the region's capital, Héféi, Túnxī makes for a far, far better base. Particularly as Túnxī's Old St is an established traveller base, with excellent hostels and boutique hotels in restored wooden homes.

## ◎ SIGHTS

Túnxī's historic heart is the restored **Old St** (老街; Lao Jie). Unless you're travelling outwards, to nearby villages or the atmospheric Taoist center Qíyún Shān, there's little else to see.

### Túnxī Old Street                Street

(屯溪老街; Túnxī Lǎojiē) Running a block in from the river, Old St is lined with restored Ming-style Huīzhōu buildings. It's definitely touristy – every block is a repetitive loop of tea shops and snack vendors – but it's pretty nonetheless, and nice for an evening stroll.

### Wàncuìlóu Museum                Museum

(万粹楼博物馆; Wàncuìlóu Bówùguǎn; 143 Lao Jie; 老街143号; admission ¥50; ◎8.30am-9.30pm) This is a fascinating private collection of ceramics, painted scrolls and religious carvings displayed as they were meant to be – in the halls of a wealthy merchant's house. The house itself, three storeys, with an open-air atrium over a fishpond, is something to behold as well.

### Qíyún Shān                Mountain

(齐云山; Mar-Nov ¥75, Dec-Feb ¥55; ◎8am-5pm Mon-Fri, 7.30am-5.30pm Sat & Sun) Qíyún Shān means 'mountain as high as the clouds' and it's an apt description; though not actually that high (just 585m), its peaks do pierce the low-lying, ghostly puffs of mists that regularly envelop the region. Long venerated by Taoists, the reddish sandstone rock provides a mountain home to temples, many built into the mountain itself, and the monks who tend to them. Qíyún Shān is a 45-minute bus trip west of Túnxī.

## TOURS

Youth hostels offer day trips to the villages of Xīdì and Hóngcūn (expect to pay around ¥250 including transport, admission fees and lunch) and to Huángshān (around ¥350). They can also arrange tickets for a shuttle bus from Old St to Huángshān (¥22, one hour, 6.15am) and pack you a lunch.

The **Huángshān Tourist Distribution Center** (黄山市旅游集散中心; 31 Qiyun Lu; 齐云路31号; ☑0559 255 8358; ⊙8.30am-5.30pm), located inside the long-distance bus station, runs day trips and tourist shuttles to surrounding villages, and sells discounted tickets.

## SHOPPING

**Xiè Yù Dà Tea**                    Food & Drinks

(谢裕大茶行; Xiè Yù Dàchāháng; 149 Lao Jie; 老街149号) Old St is lined with tea shops but Xiè Yù Dà Tea is the real deal, founded by Xie Zhengan (1838–1910) – the man who first marketed Huángshān's now famous *máofēng* (毛峰) tea. Literally 'fur peak', the subtle, slightly floral green tea gets its name from an almost indiscernible peach fuzz.

While 50g of the premium stuff costs more than a plane ticket, 'standard' first-grade starts at ¥85 for 150g. Local *qímén hóngchá* (祁门红茶), a rich, malty and also highly regarded black tea, and *júhuāchá* (菊花茶; chrysanthemum tea) are available too – all packaged in highly collectable tins.

## EATING

Old St is full of restaurants and stalls selling classic local snacks such as *xièké huáng* (蟹壳黄; yellow crab shells) – actually baked buns stuffed with meat or vegetables that just look like crab shells.

### Off-the-beaten-track to Yúliáng

Little-visited **Yúliáng** (渔梁; adult ¥30, child & senior free; ⊙9am-5pm) is a historic riverine port village on the Liàn River (练江; Liàn Jiāng). The cobbled and picturesque alley of Yuliang Jie (渔梁街) houses former transfer stations for the wood, salt and tea that plied the river; the tea shop at No 87 is an example. Note the firewalls separating the houses along the road. The attraction with most historical significance is the 138m-long granite Yúliáng Dam (渔梁坝; Yúliáng Bà) across the river; it's believed to be 1400 years old.

Boat operators can take you on excellent 20-minute return river trips (¥20). A pedicab from Shèxiàn's bus station or Huīzhōu Old Town to Yúliáng costs ¥10.

Yúliáng village and dam
XIA YUAN / GETTY IMAGES ©

There are cheaper street eats and fast-food restaurants just east of the eastern entrance and also along the river on Binjiang Xinlu.

**Gāotāng Húndūn**                    Dumplings ¥

(高汤馄饨; 1 Haidi Xiang; 海底巷1号; wontons ¥10; ⊙7am-10pm; ✐) Duck down a little alley opposite 120 Lao Jie for what is essentially an ancient food cart inside an even more ancient Qing dynasty home – run by a 12th-generation *húndūn* (wonton) seller and his family. The speciality is obviously the wontons, made to order and with super-thin skin, though there are other

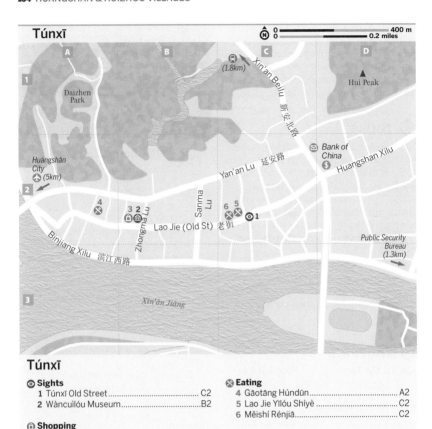

# Túnxī

dishes, including fried *jiǎozi* (stuffed dumplings), on the menu too.

### Měishí Rénjiā                    Huizhou ¥
(美食人家; 245 Lao Jie; 老街245号; dishes ¥5-108; ⏰10.30am-2pm & 5-10.30pm) Měishí Rénjiā is designed to please everyone: if you want to dig in deep on local specialities, you can find *chòu guìyú* (臭鳜鱼; fermented mandarin fish; ¥108) here. If you just want something light and cheap, you can snack on various *bāozi* (steamed buns stuffed with meat or vegetables, from ¥5). Belly-warming claypots cost ¥25 to ¥40.

All the dishes are on display; pick up a pen and pad and mark down the ones you want cooked up.

### Lao Jie Yīlóu Shíyè      Huizhou ¥¥¥
(老街一楼食业; ☎0559 235 9999; 247 Lao Jie; 老街247号; mains ¥28-88; ⏰11am-1.30pm & 5-8.30pm) Considered the best restaurant on Old St, this is the place to splash out on Huīzhōu delicacies, such as *tiánluó* (田螺; pond snails), here braised in a plate-licking concoction of soy sauce and spices. Also excellent is the Huīzhōu *wēisānbǎo* (徽州煨三宝), a stew of 'three treasures' – salt-cured pork, thin skins of tofu tied in

decorative knots, and puffs of fried tofu stuffed with meat. There's a picture menu.

## 🍷 DRINKING & NIGHTLIFE

Zhongma Lu off Old St has a string of cute coffee shops and bars, all with free wi-fi; coffee and beer starts at about ¥20. Most open around 10am and close up around 10pm.

## ℹ️ INFORMATION

**Bank of China** (中国银行; Zhōngguó Yínháng; cnr Xin'an Beilu & Huangshan Xilu; 新安北路黄山西路的路口; ⊙8am-5.30pm) Changes travellers cheques and major currencies; 24-hour ATM.

**China Post** (中国邮局; Zhōngguó Yóuqú; cnr Xin'an Beilu & Yan'an Lu; 新安北路延安路的路口; ⊙8am-5pm)

## ℹ️ GETTING THERE & AWAY

### AIR

Daily flights from Huángshān City Airport (黄山市飞机场; Huángshānshì Fēijīchǎng), located 5km west of town, include Běijīng (¥1140, 2½ hours) and Shànghǎi (¥630, one hour). Flights usually depart late in the evening.

The 5km taxi from the airport to Old St should cost ¥30.

### BUS

The **long-distance bus station** (客运总站; kèyùn qǒngzhàn; ☎0559 256 6666; 31 Qiyun Dadao; 齐云大道31号; ⊙5.45am-5.50pm) is roughly 2km west of the train station on the outskirts of town. Destinations include Hángzhōu (¥85, three hours, hourly 7.10am to 5.50pm), Jǐngdézhèn (¥61, 3½ hours, three daily), Nánjīng (¥122, 5½ hours, four daily), Shànghǎi (¥135, five hours, 10 daily, last bus 4.20pm), Sūzhōu (¥132, six hours, three daily) and Wùyuán (¥45, two hours, daily).

Within Ānhuī, buses go to Héféi (¥114, four hours, hourly 7.30am to 4pm), Shèxiàn (¥7, 45 minutes, frequent services 6am to 5pm) and Yīxiàn (¥13, one hour, frequent services 6am to 5pm).

## Sacred Mountain

The Tang dynasty Buddhists who determined **Jiǔhuá Shān** (九华山; Jiǔhuá Mountain; Nine Lotus Mountain; Mar-Nov ¥190, Dec-Feb ¥140) to be the earthly abode of the Bodhisattva Dizang (Ksitigarbha), Lord of the Underworld, chose well. Often shrouded in a fog that pours in through the windows of its cliff-side temples, it has a powerful gravitas, heightened by the devotion of those who come here to pray for the souls of the departed. It is among the four most sacred peaks in China, with a population of some 500-plus monks and nuns.

The mountain is not untouched by commercialism; however, the hawkers of over-priced joss sticks and jade carvings come together with the ochre-coloured monasteries, flickering candles and low, steady drone of Buddhist chanting emanating from pilgrims' MP3 players to create an atmosphere that is both of this world and of another one entirely.

Buses (from Túnxī ¥70, 3½ hours, 7.20am and 1.30pm or Huángshān ¥54, three hours, 7.20am and 2.30pm) will let you off at Jiǔhuáshān bus station (九华山气车站; Jiǔhuàshān qìchēzhàn), where you purchase your ticket for the mountain. You'll need to buy a return shuttle bus ticket (¥50, 20 minutes, half-hourly) from the counters on the left of the admission-ticket windows. The shuttle bus goes to Jiǔhuá village (九华镇), halfway up the mountain and terminates at the bus station just before the gate (大门; dàmén) leading to the village.

Buses to Huángshān go to the main base at Tāngkǒu (¥20, one hour, every 20 minutes 6am to 5pm) and on to the north entrance, Tàipíng (¥20, two hours).

There are also minibuses to Tāngkǒu (¥20) from in front of the train station (6.30am to 5pm) that leave when full.

# Huīzhōu Cuisine

Huīzhōu cuisine is one of China's eight major culinary traditions, though it lacks the household name of, say, Sìchuān. Large sections of the mountainous terrain in this southeastern section of Ānhuī remain uncultivated and Huīzhōu cooking makes use of foraged shoots, roots, fungi and herbs (many untranslatable). Look for dishes of bracken (蕨菜; *juécài*), day lily (黄花菜; *huánghuācài*), bamboo shoots (竹笋; *zhúsǔn*) and wood ear mushrooms (黑木耳; *hēi mù'ěr*). Jiǔhuá Shān, one of China's four Buddhist mountains, has a long tradition of vegetarian cooking. Meat often appears stewed or braised, rather than steamed or fried. Time-honoured preservation techniques, such as fermenting and dry-curing, are still very much in use.

**Máo dòufu** (毛豆腐) 'Furry' tofu aged to the point where long wispy mould spores grow over the surface; the Roquefort of tofu.

**Chòu guìyú** (臭鳜鱼) 'Stinky' (but not) mandarin fish preserved for days in salted water, then braised in soy sauce.

**Jìxī yīpǐn guō** (绩溪一品锅) 'One pot' stew of seasonal vegetables with savoury chunks of ham, chicken or beef.

**Làbā dòufu** (腊八豆腐) Tofu hung up to dry on the eighth day of the 12th lunar month (*làbā*) until it turns a golden brown; a speciality of Yìxiàn.

**Chǎo tiánluó** (炒田螺) Tender pond snails stir-fried in soy sauce; best in spring.

*Dòufu*
HELLDORF ZCOOL / SHUTTERSTOCK ©

Inside the bus station (to the right as you enter) is the separate **Huángshān Tourist Distribution Center** (黄山市旅游集散中心; Huángshān Lǚyóu Jísàn Zhōngxīn; ☑0559 255 8358; 31 Qiyun Lu; 齐云路31号; ◷8.30am-5.30pm) with tourist buses following three routes to popular destinations:

**Bus 1** Qíyún Shān (¥10, 45 minutes), Xīdì (¥14, one hour) and Hóngcūn (¥18, 1½ hours); hourly 8am to 4pm, last return bus 5pm.

**Bus 2** Tángmó (¥5.50, 45 minutes), Tángyuè (¥6, one hour), Huīzhōu Old Town (¥8, 75 minutes) and Yúliáng (¥9, 90 minutes); 8am, 10am, 2pm and 4pm, last return bus 4pm.

**Bus 3** Chéngkǎn (¥10, 40 minutes); hourly 8am to 11am and 1pm to 4pm, last return bus 4pm.

## TRAIN

At the time of writing, there was one direct high-speed train departing at 2.33pm from Huángshān North station (黄山北站; Huángshān *běizhàn*) for Hángzhōu East (¥304, 3½ hours) and Shànghǎi (¥549, 6½ hours). Otherwise, it's necessary to first take one of the frequent trains to Shàngráo (上饶; ¥74, one hour) and transfer. When the Huángshān–Hángzhōu rail line is completed, the trip between the two will take just 1½ hours.

Regular-service trains depart from the older Huángshān station in central Túnxī to Běijīng (hard/soft sleeper from ¥262/489, 20 hours, 9am and 4.30pm), Nánjīng (hard/soft sleeper ¥100/153, six to seven hours, six daily) and Shànghǎi (hard/soft sleeper ¥163/251, 12 hours, 8.45pm and 10.17pm).

## ❶ GETTING AROUND

Bus 2 (¥2) runs between the bus station and Old St; bus 12 (¥2) runs between Huángshān train station and Old St.

Taxi flag-fall is ¥7, but most drivers who hang out around Old St refuse to use the meter. Grab one from Binjiang Xilu instead, or pay the accepted fares from Old St: long-distance bus station or main train station ¥10; high-speed train station (Huángshān *běizhàn*) ¥50.

Huángshān (p142)

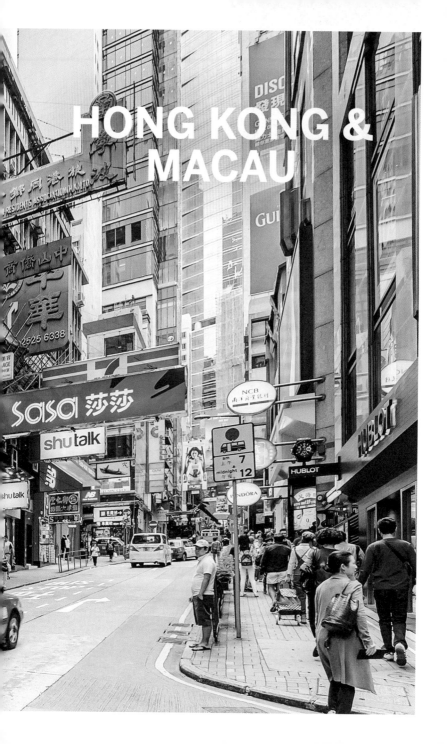

# HONG KONG & MACAU

# Hong Kong & Macau at a Glance...

*Hong Kong's enchanting neighbourhoods and islands offer a sensory feast – sway on a historic double-decker tram, cheer with the hordes at the city-centre horse races or simply gaze at the glorious harbour. A short journey west of Hong Kong and best known globally as the 'Vegas of China', the Macau Special Administrative Region is indeed a mecca of gambling and glitz. A Portuguese colony for more than 300 years, it is also a fascinating city of blended cultures, where ancient Chinese temples sit on streets paved with traditional Portuguese tiles.*

## Two Days in Hong Kong & Macau

Explore Hong Kong's impressive **Central District** (p166) and its stand-out historic and architectural sights, before climbing aboard the **Peak Tram** (p162) to **Victoria Peak** (p162) for breathtaking views of the territory. Wind down with dinner at **Fortune Kitchen** (p175). The next morning, take the **Star Ferry** (p164) to Kowloon to walk along the promenade and visit the **Hong Kong Museum of History** (p171).

## Four Days in Hong Kong & Macau

Take an early morning TurboJet to Macau to explore its colonial quarter – make sure to have a room booked for the night. Meditate upon the **Ruins of the Church of St Paul** (p166) and explore the **Mandarin's House** (p167) before devouring dim sum at **Lung Wah Tea House** (p180). Put some time aside the next day to visit Macau's islands and in the evening enjoy a drink at **Macau Soul** (p181).

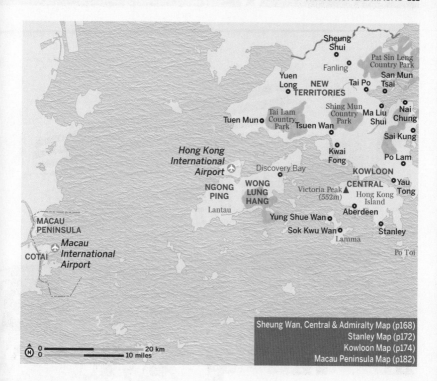

Sheung Shui

Fanling

Pat Sin Leng Country Park

Yuen Long   NEW   Tai Po   San Mun Tsai

TERRITORIES

Shing Mun   Ma Liu   Nai

Tai Lam   Country   Shui   Chung
Country   Park
Tuen Mun   Park   Tsuen Wan

Sai Kung

Kwai   Po Lam
Fong

Hong Kong   Discovery Bay   KOWLOON
International
Airport   WONG   CENTRAL   Yau
NGONG   LUNG   Victoria Peak ▲   Tong
PING   HANG   (552m)   Hong Kong
Island
Lantau   Aberdeen

Yung Shue Wan   Stanley

Sok Kwu Wan

Lamma

MACAU
PENINSULA

COTAI   Macau
International
Airport

Po Toi

Ⓝ 0 ___ 20 km
0 ___ 10 miles

Sheung Wan, Central & Admiralty Map (p168)
Stanley Map (p172)
Kowloon Map (p174)
Macau Peninsula Map (p182)

### Arriving in Hong Kong & Macau

**Hong Kong International Airport** Take the Airport Express MTR train (HK$9 to HK$100), an airport bus (HK$19 to HK$48) or a taxi (HK$220 to HK$360) to the city centre.

**Hong Kong-Macau ferry terminal** MTR train (Sheung Wan) to the city centre (HK$4.50 to HK$13).

**Macau International Airport** Buses 21 and 26 run to Coloane. Airport bus AP1 (MOP$4.20) runs to Taipa. A taxi to the centre should cost about MOP$65.

### Where to Stay

Hong Kong offers a full range of accommodation, from closet-sized rooms to palatial suites. For more info see p185.

Macau Peninsula options run from dated, but serviceable, business hotels to international luxury brands. The high-end casino hotels generally occupy the southeast and the centre of town, while cheap guesthouses occupy central Macau, on and around Rua das Lorchas and Avenida de Almeida Ribeiro, with options aplenty on Rua da Felicidade.

TESTING / SHUTTERSTOCK ©

# Victoria Peak

*Standing at 552m, Victoria Peak is the highest point on Hong Kong Island, with sweeping views of the vibrant metropolis and easy but spectacular walks.*

### Great For...

### ☑ Don't Miss

Heading up Victoria Peak on the vertigo-inducing Peak Tram.

## The Peak Tram

The best way to reach the Peak is by the 125-year-old gravity-defying **Peak Tram** (Map p168; ☎852 2522 0922; www.thepeak. com.hk; Lower Terminus, 33 Garden Rd, Central; one way/return adult HK$28/40, child 3-11yr & seniors over 65yr HK$11/18; ⊗7am-midnight; ⓂCentral, exit J2). The Peak Tram is not really a tram but a cable-hauled funicular railway that has been scaling the 396m ascent to the highest point on Hong Kong Island since 1888. Rising almost vertically above the high-rises nearby, Asia's oldest funicular clanks its way up the hillside to finish at the Peak Tower. The lower terminus in Central has an interesting gallery that houses a replica of the earliest carriage. A ride on the tram is a classic Hong Kong experience, with vertiginous views over the city as you ascend the steep mountainside.

Peak Tram

LEUNGCHOPAN / GETTY IMAGES ©

### ℹ Need to Know

維多利亞山頂; Map p168; ☑852 2522 0922;
www.thepeak.com.hk; ⊙24hr; ⊟Bus 15 from
Central, below Exchange Sq, ⊟Peak Tram
Lower Terminus

### ✕ Take a Break

Grab a bite at the **Peak Lookout** (太平
山餐廳; Map p168; ☑852 2849 1000; www.
peaklookout.com.hk; 121 Peak Rd; lunch/
dinner from HK$250/350; ⊙10.30am-
11.30pm Mon-Fri, from 8.30am Sat & Sun;
⊟15, ⊟Peak Tram).

### ★ Top Tip

The Lion Pavilion, just east of the Peak
Tram terminus, is the best place to get
a free view of Victoria Harbour.

## Exploring the Peak

Some 500m to the northwest of the upper
terminus, up steep Mt Austin Rd, is the site
of the old governor's summer lodge, which
was burned to the ground by Japanese
soldiers during WWII. The beautiful gardens
remain, however, and have been refurbished with faux-Victorian gazebos and
stone pillars. They are open to the public.

The dappled Morning Trail, a 3.5km
circuit formed by Harlech Rd on the south,
just outside the Peak Lookout, and Lugard
Rd on the northern slope, which it runs into,
takes about 45 minutes to cover. A further
2km along Peak Rd will lead you to Pok Fu
Lam Reservoir Rd. Hatton Rd, reachable by
Lugard or Harlech Rd, on the western slope
goes all the way down to the University of
Hong Kong. The 50km Hong Kong Trail also
starts on the Peak.

## Peak Tower

The anvil-shaped **Peak Tower** (凌霄閣; Map
p168; ☑852 2849 0668; 128 Peak Rd; ⊙10am-
11pm Mon-Fri, 8am-11pm Sat, Sun & public holidays; ⊟Peak Tram) makes a good grandstand
for great views of the city and harbour. On
Level P1 there's an outpost of Madame
Tussauds, with eerie wax likenesses of
international stars and local celebrities.
There is an open-air viewing **terrace** (adult/
child $30/15) on Level 5.

## High West

Just west of Victoria Peak is the 494m High
West, a mountain offering tremendous
panoramic views with a fraction of the
crowds. The only caveat? You have to hike
to get here. Take the path from the junction
of Hatton, Harlech and Lugard Rds, and
prepare for a steep climb. Bring water and
decent shoes and expect a one- to 1½-hour
round trip.

MARCO WONG / GETTY IMAGES ©

# Central District

*The minted heart of Asia's financial hub comes replete with corporate citadels, colonial relics and massive monuments to consumerism. Dynamic during the day, it retires soon after sundown.*

## Great For...

☑ **Don't Miss**

Taking a journey on the legendary Star Ferry from Tsim Sha Tsui to Central.

## Star Ferry

You can't say you've 'done' Hong Kong until you've taken a ride on a **Star Ferry** (天星小輪; Map p168; ☎852 2367 7065; www.starferry.com.hk; adult HK$2.50-3.40, child HK$1.50-2.10; ⊗every 6-12min, 6.30am-11.30pm; ⓂHong Kong, exit A2), that wonderful fleet of electric-diesel vessels with names such as *Morning Star*, *Celestial Star* and *Twinkling Star*. Try to take your first trip on a clear night from Kowloon to Central.

## HSBC Building

This stunning **building** (滙豐銀行總行大廈; Map p168; www.hsbc.com.hk/1/2/about/home/unique-headquarters; 1 Queen's Rd; ⊗escalator 9am-4.30pm Mon-Fri, 9am-12.30pm Sat; ⓂCentral, exit K) **FREE**, designed by British architect Sir Norman Foster in 1985, is a masterpiece of precision and innovation. And so it should be; on completion it was

St John's Cathedral

TUOMAS LEHTINEN / SHUTTERSTOCK ©

Lung Wui Rd

Connaught Rd Central

Tim Wa Ave

**Central District**

Tim Mei Ave

### ⓘ Need to Know

Shops in Central close relatively early (6pm or 7pm).

### ✖ Take a Break

Cross the street for cocktails with a view at **Sevva** (Map p168; ☏852 2537 1388; www.sevva.hk; 25th fl, Prince's Bldg, 10 Chater Rd, Central; ☺noon-midnight Mon-Thu, to 2am Fri & Sat; ☎; Ⓜ Central, exit H).

### ★ Top Tip

To enjoy Central's top-notch French and Italian restaurants without breaking the bank, go for the midday specials.

the world's most expensive building. Don't miss the pair of bronze lions guarding the harbourside entrance of the building.

## Hong Kong Maritime Museum

Relocation and expansion have turned this **museum** (香港海事博物館; Map p168; ☏852 3713 2500; www.hkmaritimemuseum.org; Central Ferry Pier 8; adult/child & senior HK$30/15; ☺9.30am-5.30pm Mon-Fri, 10am-7pm Sat & Sun; ♿; Ⓜ Hong Kong, exit A2) into one of the city's strongest, with 15 well-curated galleries detailing more than 2000 years of Chinese maritime history and the development of the Port of Hong Kong. An eye-opening painted scroll depicting piracy in China in the early 19th century is one of Hong Kong's most important historical artefacts.

## Bank of China Tower

The awesome 70-storey **Bank of China Tower** (中銀大廈; 1 Garden Rd; Ⓜ Central, exit K), designed by IM Pei, rises from the ground like a cube, and is then successively reduced, quarter by quarter, until the south-facing side is left to rise on its own. Some geomancers believe the four prisms are negative symbols; being the opposite of circles, these triangles contradict what circles suggest – money, union and perfection.

## St John's Cathedral

Services have been held at this Anglican **cathedral** (聖約翰座堂; Map p168; ☏852 2523 4157; www.stjohnscathedral.org.hk; 4-8 Garden Rd; ☺7am-6pm; ☐12A, 40, 40M; Ⓜ Central, exit K) since it opened in 1849, with the exception of 1944, when the Japanese army used it as a social club. It suffered heavy damage during WWII, and the doors were subsequently remade using timber salvaged from HMS *Tamar*, a British warship that guarded Victoria Harbour. Enter from Battery Path.

Mandarin's House

# Colonial Macau

*For a small place (just 29 sq km), Macau is packed with important cultural and historical sights, including eight squares and 22 historic buildings that have been Unesco heritage-listed.*

### Great For...

### ☑ Don't Miss

Contemplating and meditating upon the sublime Ruins of the Church of St Paul.

## Ruins of the Church of St Paul

The towering facade and stairway are all that remain of this early-17th-century Jesuit **church** (大三巴牌坊, Ruinas de Igreja de São Paulo; Travessa de São Paulo; 🚌8A, 17, 26, disembark at Luís de Camões Garden) **FREE**, the most treasured icon in Macau. With its statues, portals and engravings that effectively make up a 'sermon in stone' and a *Biblia pauperum* (Bible of the poor), the church was one of the greatest monuments to Christianity in Asia, intended to help the illiterate understand the Passion of Christ and the lives of the saints.

## Monte Fort

Just east of the ruins, **Monte Fort** (大炮台, Fortaleza do Monte; ⏱7am-7pm; 🚌7, 8, disembark at Social Welfare Bureau) **was built by the Jesuits between 1617 and 1626 as part of the**

Ruins of the Church of St Paul

WIBOWO RUSLI / GETTY IMAGES ©

College of the Mother of God. Barracks and storehouses were designed to allow the fort to survive a two-year siege, but the cannons were fired only once, during the aborted attempt by the Dutch to invade Macau in 1622.

## Mandarin's House

Built around 1869, the **Mandarin's House** (鄭家大屋, Caso do Mandarim; ☏853 2896 8820; www.wh.mo/mandarinhouse; 10 Travessa de Antonio da Silva; ⊙10am-5.30pm Thu-Tue; ☐28B, 18) FREE, with more than 60 rooms, was the ancestral home of Zheng Guanying, an influential author-merchant whose readers included emperors, Dr Sun Yatsen and Chairman Mao.

## Leal Senado & Senate Library

Facing Largo do Senado is Macau's most important historical building, the 18th-

century **Leal Senado** (民政總署大樓; ☏853 2857 2233; 163 Avenida de Almeida Ribeiro; ⊙9am-9pm Tue-Sun; ☐3, 6, 26A, 18A, 33, disembark at Almeida Ribeiro), which houses the Instituto para os Assuntos Cívicos e Municipais (IACM; Civic and Municipal Affairs Bureau).

Located in the Leal Senado, Macau's oldest and most lavish **library** (民政總署圖書館; ☏853 2857 2233; ⊙1-7pm Tue-Sat) FREE is a beautiful adaptation of the 18th-century library in the Convento de Mafra outside Lisbon. Though much smaller, with only two rooms, it features a baroque style with scrolling on the ceiling, and dark wood bookcases surmounted by cartouches. The library's 19,000-book collection includes antique publications in Portuguese, French and English.

## St Lazarus Church District

A lovely **neighbourhood** (瘋堂斜巷, Calcada da Igreja de Sao Lazaro; www.cipa.org.mo; ☐7, 8) with colonial-style houses and cobbled streets makes for some of Macau's best photo ops.

Designers and other creative types like to gather here, setting up shop and organising artsy events.

# Sheung Wan, Central & Admiralty

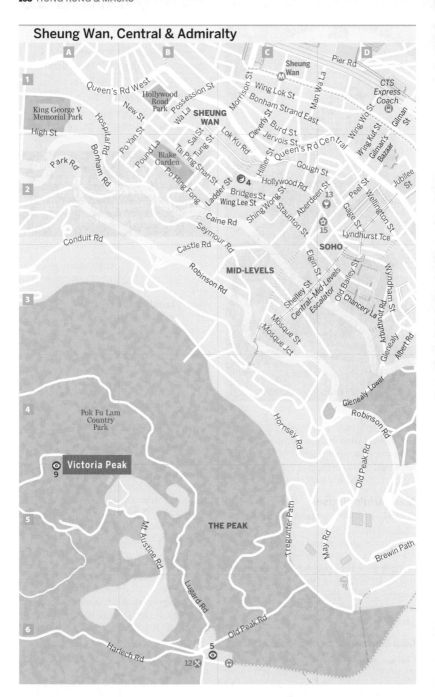

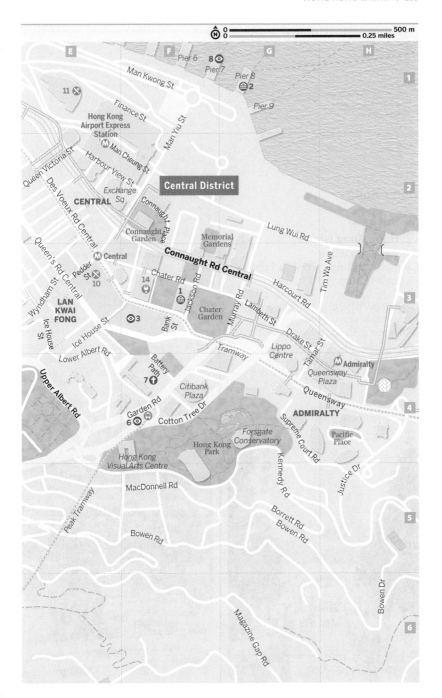

▲ N 0 ——— 500 m
0 ——— 0.25 miles

**1**

Pier 6
Man Kwong St
Pier 7 **8**
Pier 8 **2**
Pier 9

E

F

G

H

**11**

Finance St

Hong Kong
Airport Express
Station
Man Cheung St

Man Yiu St

Harbour View St

Des Voeux Rd Central

Queen Victoria St

Exchange
Sq

**CENTRAL**

Connaught Place

Connaught
Garden

**Central District**

Memorial
Gardens

Lung Wui Rd

**2**

Queen's Rd Central

Pedder
St
**10**

**Central**

Chater Rd

Jackson Rd

**Connaught Rd Central**

Harcourt Rd

Tim Wa Ave

**3**

Wyndham St

**LAN
KWAI
FONG**

Ice House St

**14**

**1**

Chater
Garden

Bank St

Murray Rd

Lambeth St

Drake St

Tamar St

Ice House
St

**3**

Lower Albert Rd

Tramway

Lippo
Centre

**Admiralty**

**Upper Albert Rd**

Battery
Path
**7**

Citibank
Plaza

Queensway
Plaza

Queensway

**4**

Garden Rd
**6**
Cotton Tree Dr

**ADMIRALTY**

Supreme Court Rd

Pacific
Place

Hong Kong
Visual Arts Centre

Hong Kong
Park

Forsgate
Conservatory

Kennedy Rd

Justice Dr

Peak Tramway

MacDonnell Rd

Bowen Rd

Borrett Rd
Bowen Rd

Bowen Dr

**5**

Magazine Gap Rd

**6**

## Sheung Wan, Central & Admiralty

# Hong Kong

## ◉ SIGHTS

### ◉ Hong Kong Island

#### Former Legislative
#### Council Building    Historic Building
(前立法會大樓; Map p168; 8 Jackson Rd,
Central; MCentral, exit G) The colonnaded
and domed building (c 1912) was built of
granite quarried on Stonecutters Island,
and served as the seat of the Legislative
Council from 1985 to 2012. During WWII it
was a headquarters of the Gendarmerie,
the Japanese version of the Gestapo, and
many people were executed here. Standing
atop the pediment is a blindfolded statue of
Themis, the Greek goddess of justice and
natural law.

#### Man Mo Temple    Taoist Temple
(文武廟; Map p168; ☎852 2540 0350; 124-126
Hollywood Rd, Sheung Wan; ☺8am-6pm; 🚌26)
FREE One of Hong Kong's oldest temples
and a declared monument, atmospheric
Man Mo Temple is dedicated to the gods of
literature ('Man'), holding a writing brush,
and of war ('Mo'), wielding a sword. Built in
1847 during the Qing dynasty by wealthy
Chinese merchants, it was, besides a place

From left: Tian Tan Giant Buddha, Po Lin Monastery
(p172); Sik Sik Yuen Wong Tai Sin Temple (p172); incense
coils, Man Mo Temple

of worship, a court of arbitration for local disputes when trust was thin between the Chinese and the colonialists.

### Aberdeen Promenade     Waterfront
(香港仔海濱公園; Aberdeen Praya Rd, Aberdeen) FREE Tree-lined Aberdeen Promenade runs from west to east on Aberdeen Praya Rd across the water from Ap Lei Chau. On its western end is the sprawling **Aberdeen Wholesale Fish Market** (香港仔魚市場; Aberdeen Promenade) with its industrial-strength water tanks teeming with marine life. It's pungent and grimy, but 100% Hong Kong. Before reaching the market, you'll pass berthed house boats and seafood-processing vessels. (We detected a karaoke parlour or two as well.)

### Stanley     Village
(赤柱; Map p172) This crowd pleaser is best visited on weekdays. **Stanley Market** (赤柱市集; Map p172; Stanley Village Rd; ☉9am-6pm; ☒6, 6A, 6X or 260) is a maze of alleyways that has bargain clothing (haggling is a must!), while **Stanley Main Beach** (赤柱正灘; Map p172; ☒6A, 14) is for beachbumming and windsurfing. With graves

dating back to 1841, **Stanley Military Cemetery** (赤柱軍人墳場; Map p172; ☒852 2557 3498; Wong Ma Kok Rd; ☉8am-5pm; ☒14, 6A), 500m south of the market, is worth a visit.

### ⊙ Kowloon

### Tsim Sha Tsui
### East Promenade     Harbour
(尖沙嘴東部海濱花園; Map p174; Salisbury Rd, Tsim Sha Tsui; Ⓜ Tsim Sha Tsui, exit E) One of the finest city skylines in the world has to be that of Hong Kong Island, and the promenade here is one of the best ways to get an uninterrupted view. It's a lovely place to stroll around during the day, but it really comes into its own in the evening, during the nightly **Symphony of Lights** (Kowloon waterfront; ☉8-8.20pm), a spectacular sound-and-light show involving 44 buildings on the Hong Kong Island skyline.

### Hong Kong
### Museum of History     Museum
(香港歷史博物館; Map p174; ☒852 2724 9042; http://hk.history.museum; 100 Chatham Rd South, Tsim Sha Tsui; adult/concession HK$10/5, Wed free; ☉10am-6pm Mon & Wed-Sat, to 7pm Sun; ♿; Ⓜ Tsim Sha Tsui, exit B2) For

WIBOWO RUSLI / GETTY IMAGES ©

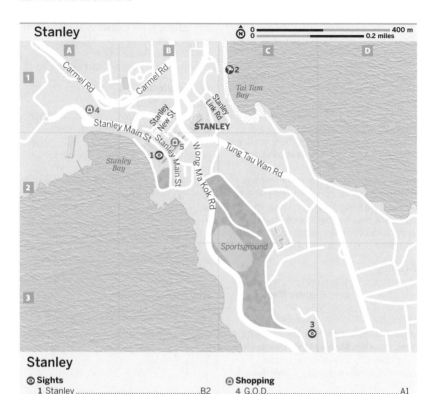

## Stanley

a whistle-stop overview of the territory's archaeology, ethnography, and natural and local history, this museum is well worth a visit, not just to learn more about the subject but also to understand how Hong Kong presents its stories to the world.

### Sik Sik Yuen Wong Tai Sin Temple    Taoist Temple

(嗇色園黃大仙祠; ☑852 2351 5640, 852 2327 8141; www.siksikyuen.org.hk; 2 Chuk Yuen Village, Wong Tai Sin; donation HK$2; ☺7am-5.30pm; Ⓜ Wong Tai Sin, exit B2) An explosion of colourful pillars, roofs, lattice work, flowers and incense, this busy temple is a destination for all walks of Hong Kong society, from pensioners and businesspeople to parents and young professionals. Some come simply to pray, others to divine the future with

*chìm* – bamboo 'fortune sticks' that are shaken out of a box on to the ground and then read by a fortune-teller (they're available free from the left of the main temple).

### ◉ Outlying Islands

The sheer size of **Lantau**, Hong Kong's largest island, makes for days of exploration. The north tip of the island, home to the airport, Disneyland and the high-rise Tung Chung residential and shopping complex, is highly developed. Much of the rest of Lantau is still entirely rural. Here you'll find traditional fishing villages, empty beaches and a mountainous interior crisscrossed with quad-burning hiking trails.

**Po Lin Monastery** (寶蓮禪寺; ☑852 2985 5248; Lantau Island; ☺9am-6pm) is a huge

Buddhist monastery and temple complex that was built in 1924. Today it seems more of a tourist honeypot than a religious retreat, attracting hundreds of thousands of visitors a year and still being expanded. Most of the buildings you'll see on arrival are new, with the older, simpler ones tucked away behind them. The big draw is the enormous seated bronze Buddha, a must-see on any Hong Kong trip.

If you are after a quick island escape from downtown Hong Kong, laid-back **Lamma** exudes a bohemian charm and is home to many a commuter who prefers more space and greenery. It's got decent beaches, great walks and a cluster of restaurants.

Pocket-sized **Cheng Chau** is a bustling isle with great windsurfing beaches and temples dedicated to water deities. The annual Bun Festival is a highlight.

 **Hong Kong's Best Hikes**

**Lion Rock Country Park** A steep climb past forests of monkeys to a craggy, lion-shaped peak.

**Dragon's Back** Hong Kong Island's best scenery.

**Morning Trail** Shady, paved path around the Peak, with stunning city views.

**Sunset Peak** On Lantau; Hong Kong's third-highest peak.

**Lamma Island Family Trail** A two-hour stroll between this outer island's two main villages.

Lion Rock Country Park
STRIPPED PIXEL / SHUTTERSTOCK ©

# 🔒 SHOPPING

Everyone knows Hong Kong as a place of neon-lit retail pilgrimage. This city is positively stuffed with swanky shopping malls and brand-name boutiques.

### Shanghai Street                    Market
(上海街; Map p174; Yau Ma Tei; Ⓜ Yau Ma Tei, exit C) Wander Kowloon's kitchen district for food-related souvenirs such as wooden mooncake moulds, chopsticks, woks and ceramic teapots.

### Yue Hwa Chinese Products
### Emporium              Department Store
(裕華國貨; Map p174; ☎ 852 3511 2222; www.yuehwa.com; 301-309 Nathan Rd, Jordan; ⏱ 10am-10pm; Ⓜ Jordan, exit A) This five-storey behemoth is one of the few old-school Chinese department stores left in the city. Items here include silk scarves, traditional Chinese baby clothes and embroidered slippers, jewellery both cheap and expensive, pretty patterned chopsticks and ceramics, plastic acupuncture models and calligraphy equipment (to name a few). The top floor is all about tea, with various vendors offering free sips. Food is in the basement.

### G.O.D.              Clothing, Housewares
(Goods of Desire; Map p172; ☎ 852 2673 0071; www.god.com.hk; Shop 105, Stanley Plaza, 22-23 Carmel Rd, Stanley; ⏱ 10.30am-8pm Mon-Fri, to 9pm Sat; 🚌 6, 6A, 6X, 260) One of the coolest Hong Kong–born shops around, G.O.D. does irreverent takes on classic Hong Kong iconography. Think mobile-phone covers printed with pictures of Hong Kong housing blocks, light fixtures resembling the ones in old-fashioned wet markets, and pillows covered in lucky koi print. There are a handful of G.O.D. shops in town, but this is one of the biggest.

# ✖ EATING

One of the world's most delicious cities, Hong Kong offers culinary excitement whether you're spending HK$20 on a bowl of noodles or HK$2000 on a seafood feast.

# Kowloon

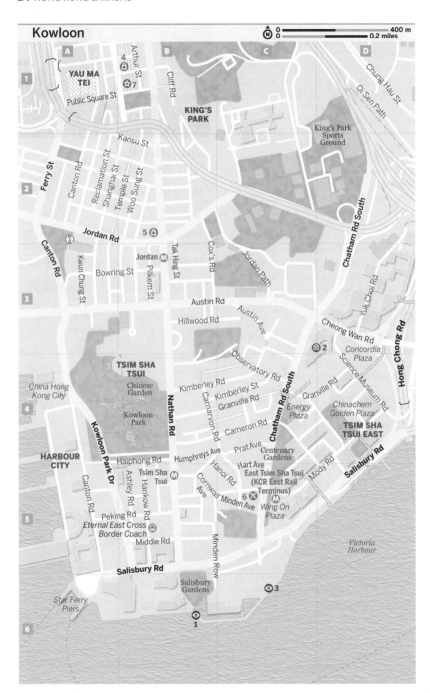

0        400 m
0        0.2 miles

**A**    **B**    **C**    **D**

**YAU MA TEI**

4

7

Arthur St

Public Square St

Cliff Rd

Chung Hau St

Oi Sen Path

**KING'S PARK**

King's Park Sports Ground

Kansu St

Ferry St

Canton Rd

Reclamation St

Shanghai St

Temple St

Woo Sung St

**Jordan Rd**

5

Chatham Rd South

Canton Rd

Kwun Chung St

Bowring St

Pilkem St

Tak Hing St

Cox's Rd

Jordan Path

**Jordan** M

Yuk Choi Rd

Hong Chong Rd

Austin Rd

Austin Ave

Hillwood Rd

Cheong Wan Rd

2

Concordia Plaza

**TSIM SHA TSUI**

Chinese Garden

Kowloon Park

Observatory Rd

Science Museum Rd

China Hong Kong City

Kimberley Rd

Kimberley St

Granville Rd

Carnarvon Rd

Cameron Rd

Granville Rd

Energy Plaza

Chinachem Golden Plaza

**TSIM SHA TSUI EAST**

Nathan Rd

**HARBOUR CITY**

Kowloon Park Dr

Haiphong Rd

Humphreys Ave

Prat Ave

Hart Ave

Centenary Gardens

Chatham Rd South

Mody Rd

Salisbury Rd

Ashley Rd

Hankow Rd

**Tsim Sha Tsui** M

Hanoi Rd

**East Tsim Sha Tsui (KCR East Rail Terminus)**

6

Wing On Plaza

Canton Rd

Peking Rd

**Eternal East Cross Border Coach**

Middle Rd

Cornwall Ave

Minden Ave

Minden Row

**Victoria Harbour**

**Salisbury Rd**

Salisbury Gardens

Star Ferry Piers

3

1

# Kowloon

## Tim Ho Wan, the Dim Sum Specialists  Dim Sum $

(添好運點心專門店; ☎852 2332 3078; www.
timhowan.com; Shop 12a, Podium Level 1, 8
Finance St, IFC Mall, Central; dishes HK$50;
⊙9am-8.30pm; Ⓜ Hong Kong, exit E1) Opened
by a former Four Seasons chef, Tim Ho Wan
was the first ever budget dim sum place to
receive a Michelin star. Many relocations
and branches later, the star is still tucked
snugly inside their tasty titbits, including
the top-selling baked barbecue-pork bun.
Expect to wait 15 to 40 minutes for a table.

## Choi's Kitchen  Cantonese $$

(私房蔡; ☎852 3485 0501; Shop C, ground fl,
Hoi Kok Mansion, 9 Whitfield Rd, Tin Hau; mains
from HK$128; ⊙11am-3pm & 6-10pm; Ⓜ Tin Hau,
exit A) This charming shop refines common
Cantonese dishes by using only fresh,
high-quality ingredients and restraint in seasoning. The signature claypot rice is made
to order and is only available at dinner. Decor is understated faux-retro to reflect the
restaurant's origin as a *dai pai dong* (大牌檔;
food stall). Prices are a far cry from those
days, but the (well-heeled) customers keep
coming. Booking advised or go early.

## Fortune Kitchen  Cantonese $$

(盈福小廚; ☎852 2697 7317; 5 Lan Fong Rd,
Causeway Bay; mains HK$100-500; ⊙11.30am-
5pm & 6-10.30pm; Ⓜ Causeway Bay, exit A)
Despite the old-fashioned Chinatown
name, Fortune Kitchen is decorated like
an old teahouse and serves homey but
sophisticated Cantonese at wallet-friendly
prices. The owner was a sous-chef at a
Michelin-star restaurant and his culinary
skills are evident in dishes such as the

signature steamed chicken with dried
scallops and the eponymous fried rice.
Booking advised.

## Spring Deer  Northern Chinese $$

(鹿鳴春飯店; Map p174; ☎852 2366 4012; 1st
fl, 42 Mody Rd, Tsim Sha Tsui; meals HK$80-500;
⊙noon-3pm & 6-11pm; Ⓜ East Tsim Sha Tsui,
exit N2) Hong Kong's most authentic
northern-style roasted lamb is served
here. Better known is the Peking duck,
which is very good. That said, the service
can be about as welcoming as a Běijīng
winter, c 1967. Booking is essential.

## L'Atelier de Joël Robuchon  Modern French $$$

(Map p168; ☎852 2166 9000; www.robuchon.
hk; Shop 401, 15 Queen's Rd Central, Landmark,
Central; set lunch HK$598-858, set dinner
HK$2080, à la carte mains HK$440-1000;
⊙noon-2.30pm & 6.30-10.30pm; 📶; Ⓜ Central,
exit G) One-third of celebrity chef Joel de
Robuchon's Michelin-crowned wonder
in Hong Kong, this red-and-black work-
shop has a tantalising list of tapas (from
HK$350) and a 70-page wine list. If you
prefer something more formal, visit Le Jar-
din in the next room. Le Salon de The, one
floor down, has the best sandwiches and
pastries in town for dine-in or takeaway.

## Lung King Heen  Cantonese, Dim Sum $$$

(龍景軒; Map p168; ☎852 3196 8888; www.
fourseasons.com/hongkong; Four Seasons Hotel,
8 Finance St, Central; lunch HK$200-500, dinner
HK$500-2000; ⊙noon-2.30pm & 6-10.30pm; 📶;
Ⓜ Hong Kong, exit E1) The world's first Chinese
restaurant to receive three Michelin stars

From left: dim sum dishes; Ozone bar; Tim Ho Wan, the Dim Sum Specialists (p175)

still retains them. The Cantonese food, though by no means peerless in Hong Kong, is excellent in both taste and presentation, and when combined with the harbour views and the impeccable service, provides a truly stellar dining experience. The signature

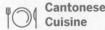

### Cantonese Cuisine

The dominant cuisine in Hong Kong is Cantonese and it's easily the best in the world. Many of China's top chefs fled to the territory around 1949; it was therefore here and not in its original home, Guǎngzhōu, that Cantonese cuisine flourished.

This style of cooking is characterised by an insistence on freshness. Seafood restaurants display tanks full of finned and shelled creatures enjoying their final moments. Flavours are delicate and balanced, obtained through restrained use of seasoning and light-handed cooking techniques such as steaming and quick stir-frying.

steamed lobster and scallop dumplings sell out early.

## 🍷 DRINKING & NIGHTLIFE

### Ping Pong Gintoneria
Bar

(📞852 9835 5061; www.pingpong129.com/; 135 Second St, Sai Ying Pun; ⏱6-11.30pm; Ⓜ Sai Ying Pun, exit B2) An unmarked red door leads you downstairs into a cavernous former ping-pong hall, now one of Hong Kong's coolest bars. The drink here is gin – the bar stocks more than 50 types from across the globe, served in a variety of cocktails both classic and creative.

### Club 71
Bar

(Map p168; Basement, 67 Hollywood Rd, Soho; ⏱3pm-2am Mon-Sat, 6pm-1am Sun, happy hour 3-9pm; 🚌26, Ⓜ Central, exit D1) This friendly bar with a bohemian vibe is named after a protest march on 1 July 2003. It's a favourite haunt of local artists and activists who come for the beer and jamming sessions. In the garden out the front, revolutionaries plotted to overthrow the Qing dynasty a hundred years ago. Enter from the alley next to 69 Hollywood.

JOE FOX / AGE FOTOSTOCK ©

### Tai Lung Fung    Bar
(大龍鳳; ☑852 2572 0055; 5-9 Hing Wan St, Wan Chai; ☺noon-1am Mon-Thu, to 1.30am Fri & Sat, happy hour noon-9pm; Ⓜ Wan Chai, exit A3) This capriciously retro bar takes its name from a 1960s Cantonese opera troupe. In common parlance, Tai Lung Fung (Big Dragon Phoenix) means 'much ado'. Appropriately the decor is fabulously over-the-top. Tai Lung Fung attracts artsy types who prefer its funky aesthetics and quiet environment to a more conventional partying vibe. Cocktails, less adventurous than the decor, are the speciality.

### Ozone    Bar
(☑852 2263 2263; www.ritzcarlton.com; 118th fl, ICC, 1 Austin Rd, Tsim Sha Tsui; ☺5pm-1am Mon-Wed, to 2am Thu, to 3am Fri, 3pm-3am Sat, noon-midnight Sun; ☜; Ⓜ Kowloon, exit U3) Ozone is the highest bar in Asia. The imaginative interiors, created to evoke a cyber-esque Garden of Eden, have pillars resembling chocolate fountains in a hurricane and a myriad of refracted glass and colour-changing illumination. Equally dizzying is the wine list, with the most expensive bottle selling for more than HK$150,000. Offers potential for a once-in-a-lifetime experience, in more ways than one. Oh, that temptingly empty corner table? That's HK$10k just to sit there.

## ✪ ENTERTAINMENT
The increasingly busy cultural calendar includes music, drama and dance hailing from a plethora of traditions.

### Hong Kong Arts Centre    Dance, Theatre
(香港藝術中心; ☑852 2582 0200; www.hkac. org.hk; 2 Harbour Rd, Wan Chai; Ⓜ Wan Chai, exit C) A popular venue for dance, theatre and music performances, the Arts Centre has theatres, a cinema and a gallery.

### Canton Singing House    Live Music
(艷陽天; Map p174; 49-51 Temple St, Yau Ma Tei; HK$20; ☺3-7pm & 8pm-5am; Ⓜ Yau Ma Tei, exit C) The oldest and most atmospheric of the singalong parlours, Canton resembles a film set with its mirror balls and glowing shrines. Each session features 20 singers, all with fan followings. Patrons tip a minimum of HK$20 (per patron) if they like a song.

## Peel Fresco Jazz

(Map p168; 852 2540 2046; www.peelfresco.com; 49 Peel St, Soho; ☺5pm-late Mon-Sat; 🚌13, 26, 40M) Charming Peel Fresco has live jazz six nights a week, with local and overseas acts performing on a small but spectacular stage next to teetering faux-Renaissance paintings. The action starts around 9.30pm, but get there at 9pm to secure a seat.

 **INFORMATION**

**American Express** (emergency 852 2811 6122, general card info 852 2277 1010; www.americanexpress.com/hk)

**Discover Hong Kong** (www.discoverhongkong.com) The Hong Kong Government's user-friendly website for travel information.

**Hong Kong Observatory** (www.hko.gov.hk) Weather information including forecasts.

**Princess Margaret Hospital** (瑪嘉烈醫院; 852 2990 1111; www.ha.org.hk; 2-10 Princess Margaret Hospital Rd, Lai Chi Kok) Public hospital.

**Time Out Hong Kong** (www.timeout.com.hk) What to eat, drink and do in Hong Kong and Macau.

**Urbtix** (www.urbtix.hk) Tickets to movies, shows and exhibitions.

 **GETTING THERE & AWAY**

### AIR

Designed by British architect Sir Norman Foster, the **Hong Kong International Airport** (HKG; 852 2181 8888; www.hkairport.com) is on Chek Lap Kok, a largely reclaimed area off Lantau's northern coast. Highways, bridges (including the 2.2km-long Tsing Ma Bridge, one of the world's longest suspension bridges) and a fast train link the airport with Kowloon and Hong Kong Island.

The two terminals have a wide range of shops, restaurants, cafes, ATMs and money changers.

The **Airport Express** (852 881 8888; www.mtr.com.hk; one way Central/Kowloon/Tsing Yi HK$100/90/60; ☺every 10min) line is the fastest (and most expensive, other than a taxi) way to get to and from the airport.

There are good bus links to/from the airport. For more details on the routes, check the transport section at www.hkairport.com. Buses run every 10 to 30 minutes from about 6am to

Lamma island (p173)

between midnight and 1am. There are also quite a few night buses (designated 'N'). Major hotel and guesthouse areas on Hong Kong Island are served by the A11 (HK$40) and A12 (HK$45) buses; the A21 (HK$33) covers similar areas in Kowloon. Bus drivers in Hong Kong do not give change, but it is available at the ground transportation centre at the airport, as are Octopus cards. Buy your ticket at the booth near the airport bus stand.

## BUS

**CTS Express Coach** (Map p168; ☑852 2764 9803; http://ctsbus.hkcts.com) Buses to mainland China.

**Eternal East Cross-Border Coach** (Map p174; ☑852 3760 0888, 852 3412 6677; www.eebus. com; 13th fl, Kai Seng Commercial Centre, 4-6 Hankow Rd, Tsim Sha Tsui; ⊗7am-8pm) Mainland destinations from Hong Kong include Dōngguǎn, Fóshān, Guǎngzhōu, Huìzhōu, Kāipíng, Shēnzhèn's Bǎoān airport and Zhōngshān.

## TRAIN

One-way and return tickets for Guǎngzhōu, Běijīng and Shànghǎi can be booked 30 to 60 days in advance at Mass Transit Railway (MTR) stations in Hung Hom, Mong Kok East, Kowloon Tong and Sha Tin, at Tourist Services at Admiralty station. Tickets to Guǎngzhōu can also be booked with a credit card on the **MTR website** (www.it3.mtr.com.hk) or via the **Tele-Ticketing Hotline** (☑bookings 852 2947 7888, enquiries 852 2314 7702; www.lcsd.gov.hk/en/leisurelink/ ls_booking_5.html)

#  GETTING AROUND

Hong Kong is small and crowded, and public transport is the only practical way to move people. The ultramodern Mass Transit Railway (MTR) is the quickest way to get to most urban destinations.

## BUS

Hong Kong's extensive bus system will take you just about anywhere in the territory. Since Kowloon and the northern side of Hong Kong Island are so well served by the MTR, most visitors use the buses primarily to explore the southern side

of Hong Kong Island, the New Territories and Lantau Island.

## MTR

The **Mass Transit Railway** (MTR; ☑852 2881 8888; www.mtr.com.hk; fares HK$4-25) is the name for Hong Kong's rail system comprising underground, overland and light rail (slower tram-style) services. Universally known as the MTR, it is clean, fast and safe, and transports around four million people daily.

## OUTLYING ISLANDS FERRIES

Regular ferry services link the main Outlying Islands to Hong Kong.

### Central (Pier 6)–Mui Wo on Lantau

**Island** Adult ordinary/deluxe class/ fast ferry HK$15.20/25.40/29.90 (HK$22.50/37.20/42.90 on Sunday and public holidays); 50 to 55 minutes with large ferry and 31 minutes with fast ferry; departures around every half-hour from 6.10am (from 7am Sunday and public holidays). The last ferry from Mui Wo to Central departs at 11.30pm.

### Central (Pier 4)–Yung Shue Wan on Lamma

**Island** Adult HK$17.10 (HK$23.70 on Sunday and public holidays); 30 to 35 minutes; departures approximately every half-hour to an hour. The last boat to Central from Yung Shue Wan departs at 11.30pm.

### Central (Pier 4)–Sok Kwu Wan on Lamma

**Island** Adult HK$21 (HK$29.80 on Sunday and public holidays); 40 minutes; departures every 1½ hours or so from 7.20am to 11.30pm. The last ferry to Central from Sok Kwu Wan is at 10.40pm.

### Central (Pier 5)–Cheung Chau

Adult ordinary/ deluxe class/fast ferry HK$13.20/20.70/25.80 (HK$19.40/30.72/27.20 on Sunday and public holidays); 55 to 60 minutes with large ferry and 35 minutes with fast ferry; departures approximately every half-hour from 6.10am. The last boat to Central from Cheung Chau departs at 11.45pm.

## STAR FERRY

There are two Star Ferry routes, but by far the most popular is the one running between Central (Pier 7) and Tsim Sha Tsui. Quite frankly, there's no other trip like it in the world. Star Ferry also links Wan Chai with Tsim Sha Tsui.

### TAXI

With more than 18,000 taxis cruising the streets of the territory, they're easy to flag down, except during rush hour, when it rains or during the driver shift-change period (around 4pm daily).

Taxis are colour-coded:

**Red with silver roofs** Urban taxis in Kowloon and Hong Kong Island; go anywhere except Lantau

**Green with white tops** New Territories taxis

**Blue** Lantau taxis

### TRAM

Hong Kong's venerable old trams, operated by **Hong Kong Tramways** (📞852 2548 7102; www.hktramways.com; fares HK$2.30; �
6am-midnight), are tall, narrow double-deckers. They're slow, but cheap, and a great way to explore the city.

### TICKETS & PASSES

**Octopus Card** (www.octopuscards.com; adult/concession HK$150/70, incl refundable deposit). A rechargeable smartcard valid on the MTR and most forms of public transport.

**Airport Express Travel Pass** (one way/return HK$250/350) As well as travel to/from the airport, it allows three consecutive days of unlimited travel on the MTR.

**MTR Tourist Day Pass** (adult/child 3-11yr HK$65/35) Valid on the MTR for 24 hours after the first use.

**Tourist Cross-Boundary Travel Pass** (1/2 consecutive days HK$85/120) Allows unlimited travel on the MTR and two single journeys to/from Lo Wu or Lok Ma Chau stations.

## Macau

### ⊙ SIGHTS

#### Guia Fortress & Guia Chapel                    Fort, Church

(東望洋炮台及聖母雪地殿聖堂, Fortaleza da Guia e Capela de Guia; ☉fortress 6am-6pm, chapel 10am-5.30pm; 🚌2, 2A, 6A, 12, 17, 18, Flora Garden stop) **FREE** As the highest point on the peninsula, Guia Fort affords panoramic

views of the city and, when the air is clear, across to the islands and China. At the top is the stunning Chapel of Our Lady of Guia, built in 1622 and retaining almost 100% of its original features, including some of Asia's most important frescoes. Next to it stands the oldest modern **lighthouse** on the China coast (1865) – an attractive 15m-tall structure that is closed to the public.

#### Taipa & Coloane                    Islands

Taipa was once two islands that were slowly joined together by silt from the Pearl River. A similar physical joining has happened to Taipa and Coloane because of land reclamation from the sea. The new strip of land joining the two islands is known as Cotai (from Co-loane and Tai-pa). Today the most interesting part of the area for visitors is the well-preserved streets around Taipa Village. A haven for pirates until the start of the 20th century, Coloane (路環), considerably larger than Taipa or Cotai, is the only part of Macau that doesn't seem to be changing at a head-spinning rate. Today it retains Macau's old way of life, though luxurious villas are finding their way onto the island. All buses stop at the roundabout in Coloane Village.

###  EATING

#### Lung Wah Tea House    Cantonese $

(龍華茶樓; 📞853 2857 4456; 3 Rua Norte do Mercado Aim-Lacerda; dim sum from MOP$14, tea MOP$10, meals MOP$50-180; ☉7am-2pm; ☝; 🚌23, 32) There's grace in the retro furniture and the casual way it's thrown together in this airy Cantonese teahouse (c 1963). Take a booth by the windows overlooking the Red Market, where the teahouse buys its produce every day. There's no English menu; just point and take. Lung Wah sells a fine array of Chinese teas.

#### Clube Militar de Macau          Portuguese $$

(陸軍俱樂部; 📞853 2871 4000; 975 Avenida da Praia Grande; meals MOP$150-400; ☉1.45-2.30pm & 7-10.30pm Mon-Fri, noon-2.30pm & 7-10pm Sat & Sun; 🚌6, 28C) Housed in a distinguished colonial building, with fans

Guia Chapel and lighthouse, Macau

spinning lazily above, the Military Club takes you back in time to a slower and quieter Macau. The simple and delicious Portuguese fare is complemented by an excellent selection of wine and cheese from Portugal. The MOP$153 buffet is excellent value. Reservations are required for dinner and weekend lunches.

##  DRINKING & NIGHTLIFE

**Macau Soul**  Bar
(澳感廊; ☑ 853 2836 5182; www.macausoul.com; 31a Rua de São Paulo; ☺3-10pm Wed & Thu, to midnight Fri-Sun; ☒8A, 17, 26) An elegant haven in wood and stained glass, where a jazz band plays twice a month to a packed audience. On most nights, though, Thelonious Monk fills the air as customers chat with the owners and dither over their 430 Portuguese wines. Opening hours vary; phone ahead.

## ☆ ENTERTAINMENT

**Live Music Association**  Live Music
(LMA; 現場音樂協會; www.facebook.com/LMA.Macau; 11b San Mei Industrial Bldg, 50 Avenida do Coronel Mesquita; ☒3, 9, 32, 12, 25) The go-to place for indie music in Macau, this excellent dive inside an industrial building has hosted local and overseas acts, including Cold Cave, Buddhistson, Mio Myo and Pet Conspiracy.

## ⓘ INFORMATION

**Hospital Kiang Wu** (鏡湖醫院; ☑ 853 2837 1333; Rua de Coelho do Amaral) Private hospital with 24-hour emergency service.

**Post Office** (☑ 853 2872 8079; Macau Ferry Terminal; ☺10am-7pm Mon-Sat) Post office branch inside the ferry terminal.

**Tourist Office** (☑ 853 8397 1120, tourism hotline 853 2833 3000; www.macautourism.gov.mo; Edifício Ritz, Largo de Senado; ☺9am-1pm & 2.30-5.35pm Mon-Fri) The central location of the Macau Government Tourism Office.

## ⓘ GETTING THERE & AWAY

### AIR

**Air Macau** (澳門航空; NX; ☑ 853 8396 5555; www.airmacau.com.mo; ground fl, 398 Alameda Doutor Carlos d'Assumpção; ☺9am-6pm) Flies

# Macau Peninsula

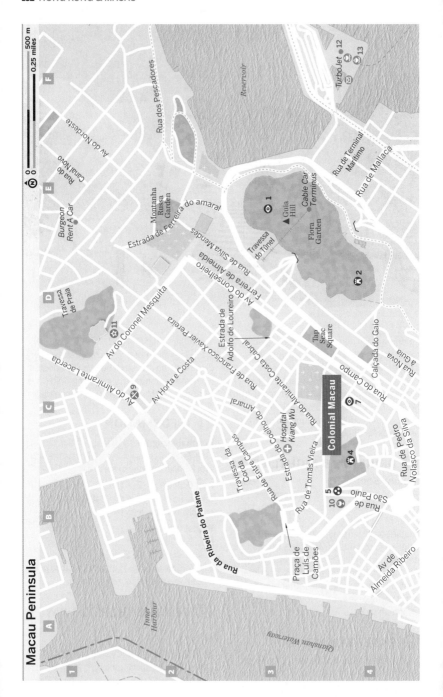

500 m
0.25 miles

**Colonial Macau**

Inner Harbour

Qianshan Waterway

Rua da Ribeira do Patane

Praça de Luís de Camões

Rua de São Paulo

Rua de Tomás Vieira

Av de Almeida Ribeiro

Estrada de Coelho do Amaral

Hospital Kiang Wu

Travessa da Corda

Rua de Entre Campos

Rua de Francisco Xavier Pereira

Rua do Almirante Costa Cabral

Estrada de Adolfo de Loureiro

Av do Conselheiro Ferreira de Almeida

Rua de Silva Mendes

Estrada de Ferreira do amaral

Av do Coronel Mesquita

Av do Almirante Lacerda

Av Horta e Costa

Travessa de Praia

Burgeon Rent A Car

Montanha Russa Garden

Rua do Canal Novo

Av do Nordeste

Rua dos Pescadores

Reservoir

Guia Hill

Flora Garden

Cable Car Terminus

Travessa do Túnel

Tap Seac Square

Rua do Campo

Calçada do Gaio

Rua Nova à Guia

Rua de Pedro Nolasco da Silva

Rua de Terminal Marítimo

Rua de Malaca

TurboJet

A1
B1
C1
D1
E1
F1
A2
B2
C2
D2
E2
F2
A3
B3
C3
D3
A4
B4

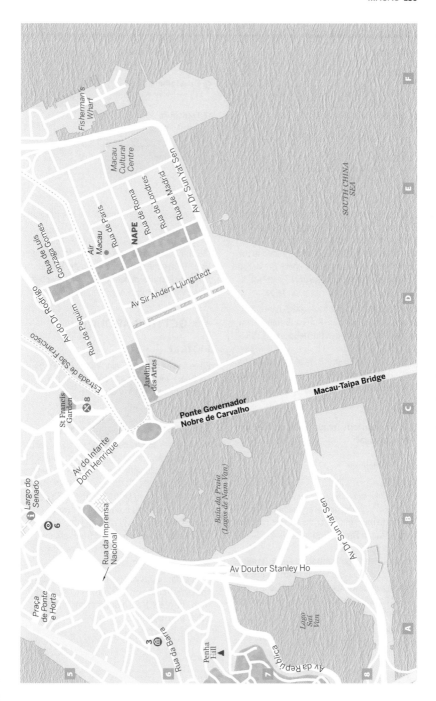

Fisherman's Wharf

Macau Cultural Centre

Rua de Paris
Rua de Roma
Rua de Londres
Rua de Madrid
Av Dr Sun Yat Sen

Air Macau

**NAPE**

Rua de Luís Gonzaga Gomes

Av do Dr Rodrigo

Rua de Pequim

Estrada de São Francisco

Av Sir Anders Ljungstedt

SOUTH CHINA SEA

Jardim des Artes

St Francis Garden

Macau-Taipa Bridge

**Ponte Governador Nobre de Carvalho**

Av do Infante Dom Henrique

Largo do Senado

Rua da Imprensa Nacional

Baía da Praia (Lagos de Nam Van)

Av Sun Yat Sen

Av Doutor Stanley Ho

Praça de Ponte e Horta

Rua da Barra

Penha Hill

Lago Sai Van

Av da República

# Macau Peninsula

to more than a dozen destinations in mainland China and has codeshare flights to South Korea, Taiwan, Vietnam, Thailand and Japan. The departure tax is MOP$110, and is added to the ticket fee. For further details, check the website of **Macau International Airport** (☑853 2886 1111; www.macau-airport.com) on Taipa.

**Sky Shuttle** (☑in Hong Kong 852 2108 9898; www.skyshuttlehk.com) Runs a 15-minute helicopter shuttle between the **heliport** (☑853 2872 7288; Macau Maritime Ferry Terminal, Avenida da Amizade; ◷8.15am-11pm) at Macau Maritime Ferry Terminal and Hong Kong (HK$4500, every 30 minutes from 9am to 11pm).

### BOAT

Macau's main ferry terminal, **Macau Maritime Ferry Terminal** (外港客運碼頭; Terminal Maritimo de Passageiros do Porto Exterior), is in the outer harbour.

**CotaiJet** (☑853 2885 0595; www.cotaijet.com. mo; weekdays to Hong Kong regular/1st class MOP$154/267) Departs every half-hour from 7.30am to midnight, and runs between the **Hong Kong–Macau Ferry Terminal** (Shun Tak Centre; Shun Tak Centre, 200 Connaught Rd, Sheung Wan) and the **Taipa Temporary Ferry Terminal** (☑853 2885 0595); a feeder shuttle-bus service drops off at destinations along the Cotai Strip. Check CotaiJet's website for services to Hong Kong International Airport.

**TurboJet** (☑bookings 852 2921 6688, in Hong Kong 852 790 7039, information 852 2859 3333; www.turbojet.com.hk; economy/superclass Mon-Fri HK$153/315, Sat & Sun HK$166/337, night crossing HK$189/358) Has the most sailings; the one-hour trip departs from the Hong Kong–Macau Ferry Terminal and runs to the Macau Maritime Ferry Terminal; see TurboJet's website for services to Hong Kong International Airport.

##  GETTING AROUND

### BICYCLE

Bikes can be rented in Taipa Village (MOP$20 per hour). You are not allowed to cross the Macau–Taipa bridges on a bicycle.

### BUS

Public buses and minibuses run by **TCM** (www.tcm.com.mo) and **Transmac** (☑853 2827 1122; www.transmac.com.mo) operate from 6am until shortly after midnight. Fares – MOP$3.20 on the peninsula, MOP$4.20 to Taipa Village, MOP$5 to Coloane Village and MOP$6.40 to Hác Sá beach – are dropped into a box upon entry (exact change needed), or you can pay with a Macau Pass, which can be purchased from various supermarkets and convenience stores. Expect buses to be very crowded.

The *Macau Tourist Map* has a full list of bus company routes and it's worth picking one up from one of the Macau Government Tourist Office (MGTO) outlets.

# Where to Stay

*Most hotels on Hong Kong Island are between Central and Causeway Bay; in Kowloon, they fall around Nathan Rd, where you'll also find budget places. Booking a room is not essential outside peak periods.*

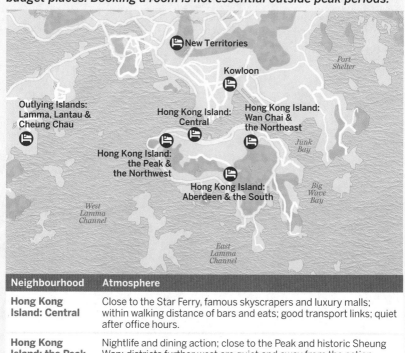

| Neighbourhood | Atmosphere |
|---|---|
| **Hong Kong Island: Central** | Close to the Star Ferry, famous skyscrapers and luxury malls; within walking distance of bars and eats; good transport links; quiet after office hours. |
| **Hong Kong Island: the Peak & the Northwest** | Nightlife and dining action; close to the Peak and historic Sheung Wan; districts further west are quiet and away from the action. |
| **Hong Kong Island: Wan Chai & the Northeast** | Good for Hong Kong Park, Happy Valley Racecourse and shopping; abundant eating and drinking options; great transport links; Wan Chai and Causeway Bay can be traffic-choked and crowded. |
| **Hong Kong Island: Aberdeen & the South** | Great for Aberdeen Typhoon Shelter, Stanley Market, Horizon Plaza, swimming and hiking around Repulse Bay and Shek O; limited sleeps, eats, bars and shops. |
| **Kowloon** | Convenient for museums, shopping and eating; best views of the harbour; great transport links; crowded and traffic-choked around Nathan Rd; some areas can be touristy and/or a little seedy. |
| **New Territories** | Fewer crowds, fresher air; handy for outdoor sports, nature tours, walled villages; prices generally lower but far from the action with fewer eats, sleeps, bars and shops. |
| **Outlying Islands: Lamma, Lantau & Cheung Chau** | Laid-back vibe; good for seafood on Lamma, windsurfing on Cheung Chau, hiking the Lantau Trail, and beaches; longer time spent commuting; fewer eats, sleeps, bars and shops. |

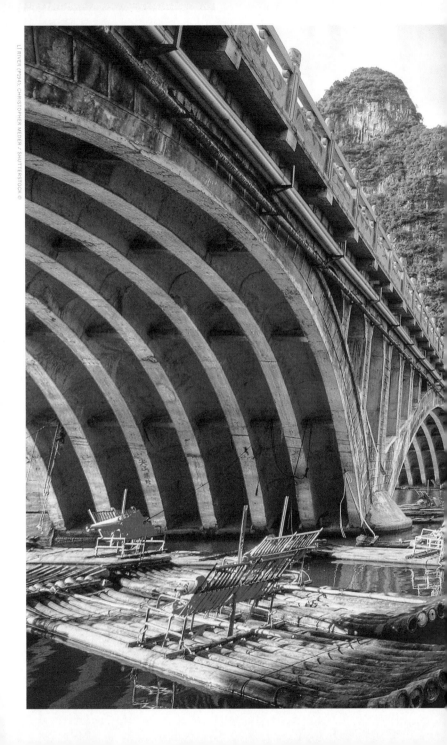

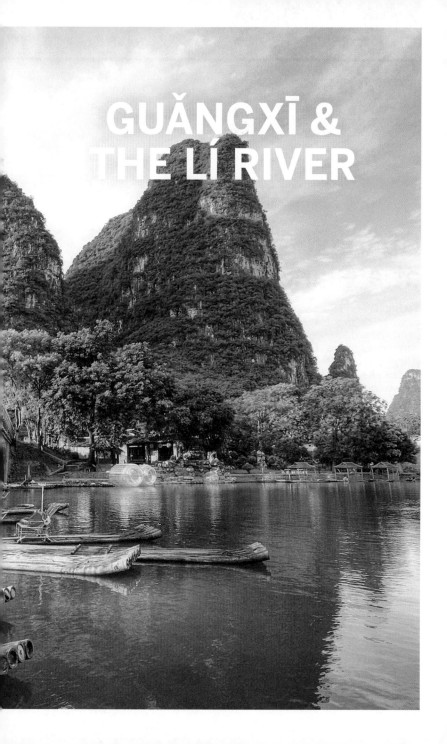

# GUĂNGXĪ &
# THE LÍ RIVER

# Guăngxī & the Lí River at a Glance...

*Guăngxī (广西) conjures up visions of cycling gentle pathways or bamboo-rafting the Yùlóng River past scenery straight out of a painting. Indeed, Yángshuò's sublime karst landscape is one of China's don't-miss draws. Don't forget, of course, hiking between ethnic villages in the lofty Lóngjǐ Rice Terraces, where fields cascade down the slopes like giant stairs. The town of Guìlín, also blessed with a raft of natural endowments, makes a great jumping-off point – particularly for a cruise down the magical Lí River.*

### Two Days in Guăngxī & the Lí River

Spend a morning exploring the sights in **Guìlín** (p197) before taking a cruise down the **Lí River** (p198) to **Yángshuò** (p190) to spend the night in the town and devote a day at least to exploring the surrounding karst scenery. Don't miss Liúgōng, Xìngpíng, Moon Hill and the Yùlóng River. In the evening, dine at **Echo Cafe** (p195) or **Lucy's** (p195).

### Four Days in Guăngxī & the Lí River

Further explore the region around Yángshuò for half a day before returning to Guìlín and continuing north to the **Lóngjǐ Rice Terraces** (p192), to spend the night in one of the plentiful accommodation options. The next day, set out early on the walk from Dàzhài, via Tiántóuzhài to Píng'ān and get your camera out for the **Nine Dragons & Five Tigers Viewing Point** (p192).

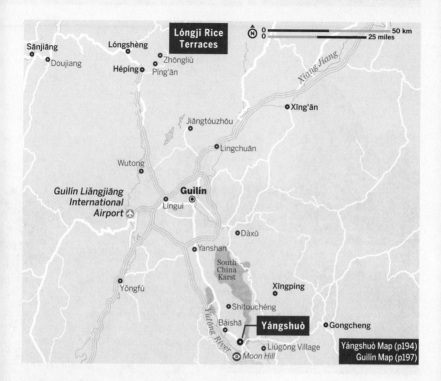

## Arriving in Guăngxī & the Lí River

**Guìlín Liăngjiāng International Airport** Situated 30km west of the city; shuttle buses (¥20) meet every arrival; a taxi to the centre (40 minutes) costs about ¥120.

Long-distance buses are very handy for accessing nearby towns in closer provinces. High-speed rail, centred in Nánníng, connects Guăngxī to provincial neighbours, but Guìlín also has trains to Běijīng, Chóngqìng, Kūnmíng, Shànghăi and Xī'ān.

## Where to Stay

Guăngxī is spilling over with accommodation choices, especially in the drawcard regions of Guìlín, Yángshuò, Huángyáo, Lóngjǐ Rice Terraces and Běihăi, although sleeping options vary enormously in type and choice between these destinations. The environs of Yángshuò have the best choice, where you can escape into bucolic bliss and never look back.

XUANLU WANG / SHUTTERSTOCK ©

# Exploring Yángshuò

*Outside town, which is the reason you will be here, the karst landscape becomes surreal and otherworldly. Take a bamboo-raft ride or cycle through the dreamy valleys to discover a different world.*

### Great For...

### ☑ Don't Miss

Jumping on a bike and following the Yùlóng River.

The countryside of Yángshuò and the region through which the Lí River and its tributary waterways flow offer weeks of exploration by bike, boat, foot or any combination thereof. Scenes that inspired generations of Chinese painters are the standard here: wallowing water buffalo and farmers tending their crops against a backdrop of limestone peaks.

## Yùlóng River

The scenery along this small, quiet river about 6km southwest of Yángshuò is breathtaking. It is visited by hiring a boatman in Yángshuò for the lazy float up the river. Tell the boatman you want to visit the fairy-tale **Dragon Bridge** (遇龙桥; Yùlóng Qiáo), about 10km upstream from

Rock climbing, Moon Hill

HENN PHOTOGRAPHY / GETTY IMAGES ©

Yángshuò. This 600-year-old, stone, arched structure overhung with old gnarly trees is among Guǎngxī's largest, and comes with crooked steps and leaning parapets.

## Moon Hill

A 30-minute – extremely sweaty – climb up steps to the magnificent natural arch that adorns Moon Hill is rewarded with both lost calories and some exhilarating views of surrounding peaks and the tapestry of flat fields in the lowlands. Load up with liquids in hot weather, and be prepared to be pounced on by hawkers flogging water to anything that moves at the top. Moon Hill is easily reached by bike; just set off down Kangzhan Lu (抗战路), keep going and follow the signs.

## Xìngpíng

Some say Xìngpíng (兴坪) is just like Yángshuò before the latter became a honeypot, for better or worse. This 1750-year-old town has loads of history and is certainly attractive; in fact, the landscape you see when you disembark from the raft is printed on the back of China's ¥20 banknote. Travellers come here for its yesteryear flavours; with the recent opening of nearby Yángshuò train station, however, it is set to get a lot busier.

## Liúgōng

The very quiet 400-year-old village of Liúgōng (留公村; Liúgōng Cūn), 13km from Yángshuò, was a trading hub on the Lí River during the Ming and Qing dynasties. Traces of its former affluence are visible in the handsome buildings (of which the walls of some still blush with slogans painted during the Cultural Revolution). You can stroll from the village to the hills behind it, where the only things punctuating the silence are cockerels and murmurs of the past.

KEREN SU / GETTY IMAGES ©

# Lóngjǐ Rice Terraces

*This part of Guǎngxī is famous for its breathtaking vistas of terraced paddy fields cascading in swirls down into a valley.*

### Great For...

### ☑ Don't Miss

The astonishing photo ops at Nine Dragons & Five Tigers Viewing Point.

Rising to 1000m, the rice terraces of Lóngjǐ (literally 'Dragon's Back') are an amazing feat of farm engineering on hills dotted with minority villages.

## Rice Terrace Villages

You'll find spectacular views around the villages of Píng'ān (平安), a Zhuang settlement; Dàzhài (大寨), a mesmerising Yao village; and Tiántóuzhài (田头寨), which sits slightly further above Dàzhài. You can take a number of short, clearly signposted walks from each village to various fabulous viewing points. One of the most sublime is the **Nine Dragons & Five Tigers Viewing Point** (九龙五虎观景点; Jiǔlóng Wǔhǔ Guānjǐngdiǎn), with its astonishing, curvaceous layers of terraces; it's around a 30-minute walk above Píng'ān.

Lóngjĭ Rice Terraces

The three- to four-hour trek between these three villages is also highly recommended; get a local to guide you for around ¥100 or ask for directions frequently along the way, as there are almost no signposts for this hike and you will meet numerous sign-less forks in the path.

## Accommodation

Although Lóngjĭ can be done as a day trip from Guìlín, it's an excellent plan to spend the night so you can catch the terraces at their best at dusk and dawn. You can stay in traditional wooden homes for around ¥30 to ¥40 a night (per bed) or grab a dorm bed for a little bit more; hostels also have double rooms. There are also several hotels offering further comfort.

## Getting There

Hotels in Dàzhài and Tiántóuzhài arrange direct shuttle services from Guìlín to Dàzhài (8am, 10.30am and 2pm) and from Dàzhài to Guìlín (10am, 1pm and 4pm) for their guests. The price is usually ¥50 per person. They also take other passengers if seats are available. Reservations are a must. All hotels in Píng'ān provide a similar service.

For public transport from Guìlín, head to the city's North Bus Station (p200) or Qíntán Bus Station (p200). From there, take a bus to Lóngshèng (龙胜; ¥34, two hours, every 30 minutes 7am to 7pm) and ask to get off at Hépíng (和平). From the road junction (or the ticket office three minutes' walk away), minibuses trundle between Lóngshèng and the rice terraces, stopping to pick up passengers to Dàzhài (¥10, one hour, every 30 minutes 7am to 5pm) and Píng'ān (¥10, 30 minutes, every 20 minutes to one hour 7am to 5pm).

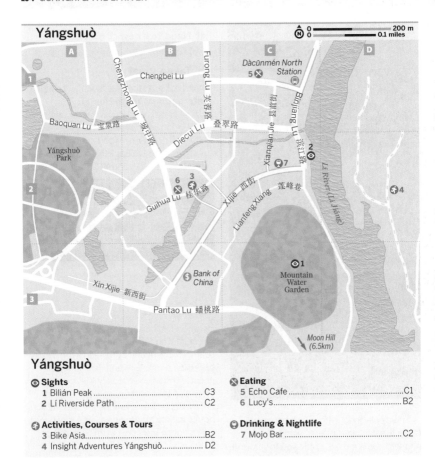

## Yángshuò

### ⊙ Sights

### ⊕ Activities, Courses & Tours

### ⊗ Eating

### ⊕ Drinking & Nightlife

## Yángshuò

### ⊙ SIGHTS

#### Lí Riverside Path — River

(Líjiāng Jiāngbīn Dào; 漓江江滨道; Binjiang Lu; 滨江路) When Xijie, the crowds and postcard hawkers get too much, head down the steps to the Lí River. Unfolding before you is a beautiful panorama of karst peaks, glittering river water and green bamboo. It's a stunning sight, and you can walk for a fair distance along the bank of the river, past folk practising taichi or playing with their children.

#### Bìlián Peak — Mountain

(碧莲峰; Bìlián Fēng; admission ¥30) Located in the southeastern corner of town, this is Yángshuò's main peak; it's also the most accessible (it can be climbed in half an hour). Because it has a flat northern face that is supposed to resemble an ancient bronze mirror, it is also called Bronze Mirror Peak (Tóngjìng Fēng). The peak rises up next to the Lí River, in the Mountain Water

Garden (Shānshuǐ Yuán); look for the sign that says 山水园.

## ACTIVITIES

Yángshuò is one of the hottest climbing destinations in Asia. There are eight major peaks in regular use, already providing more than 250 bolted climbs. **Insight Adventures Yángshuò** (☎0773 881 1033; www.insight-adventures.com; 12 Furong Lu; 芙蓉路12号; ☯9am-9pm) offers guided climbs, while Bike Asia (p196) hires out bicycles, and offers maps and English-speaking guides.

## SHOPPING

Souvenir shops run the length of Xijie, while stalls set up daily along Binjiang Lu. You'll find silk scarves, trinkets, knitted shoes and all manner of other goods here. Bargain your socks off and fend off the relentless hawkers.

## EATING

You can find anything from wood-fired pizza and chicken korma to full English breakfasts, frankfurters served by German chefs and outposts of US fast-food empires.

### Echo Cafe
Cafe ¥

(2 Fuqian Jie; 府前街2号; mains from ¥30; ☯9am-midnight) This lovely cafe is tucked a long way from the tourist maelstrom, despite being just around the corner from Xijie. Very relaxing and tranquil, guitars and ukuleles lie around randomly, awaiting musical fingers. Sounds are (ballpark) classic jazz ballads. Staff are sweet and a small library rounds it off. There's a tasty and changing German/Western menu, too, and breakfasts (9am to midday). Great cheesecake.

### Lucy's
International ¥

(露茜; Lùxī; 30 Guihua Lu; 桂花路30号; mains from ¥25; ☯7am-midnight; ☎) With graffiti-splattered walls, Lucy's is quite an institution. Western and Chinese food are done with equal aplomb – aim for one of the terrace seats upstairs overlooking the tourist traffic below. There's shepherd's pie (¥40), beer fish (¥88), sizzling beef platter (¥40), tuna spaghetti (¥35) and more, plus full English brekkies (¥38).

## DRINKING & NIGHTLIFE

Yángshuò is stuffed with bars, but there are few of character and taste, and many are cheesy.

Several restaurants double as decent bars, and many hotels, hostels and guesthouses have relaxing bar areas. Just off Xijie is where German beer gardens sit alongside generic Western-style cafes.

### Mojo Bar
Bar

(露天酒吧; Lùtiān Jiǔbā; 6th fl, Alshan Hotel, 18 Xijie; 西街18号阿里山大酒店六楼; ☯7pm-3am; ☎) Way above the throngs choking Xijie, Mojo Bar – on the 6th floor and roof of the Alshan Hotel – has the most amazing outdoor terrace with wraparound views of the *Avatar*-like karst landscape, set to Red Hot Chili Peppers. Inside it's pool, cheap beer (Tsingtao ¥20) and rather cramped quarters; outside, on long summer evenings especially, it's astonishing views in all directions.

---

### Courses in Yángshuò

Yángshuò is an excellent place to expand your skills: **Omeida Chinese Academy** (欧美达书院; Ōuměidá Shūyuàn; ☎0773 881 2233; www.omeida.com.cn; 49 Longyue Lu; 龙岳路49号) offers Chinese-language courses, or cook up some Guǎngxī cuisine at **Yángshuò Cooking School** (阳朔烹饪学校; Yángshuò Pēngrèn Xuéxiào; ☎137 8843 7286; Cháolóng Village).

### Where to Stay

Yángshuò teems with hotels run by English-speaking staff, and virtually all provide wi-fi access. While the Xijie neighbourhood is stuffed with choices, quieter and more attractive lodgings lie on the outskirts.

Find your way to 18 Xijie, the Alshan Hotel, and take the lift to the 4th floor before walking up the last two flights to Mojo Bar.

##  ENTERTAINMENT

### Impressions Liú Sānjiĕ
Performing Arts

(印象刘三姐; Yìnxiàng Liú Sānjiĕ; ☑0773 881 7783; tickets ¥200-680; ☺7.30-8.30pm & 9.30-10.30pm) The busiest show in town is directed by filmmaker Zhang Yimou, who also directed acclaimed films such as *Raise the Red Lantern* and *House of Flying Daggers*. Six hundred performers take to the Lí River each night with 12 illuminated karst peaks serving as a backdrop. Book at your hotel for discounts and transport to/from the venue (1.5km from town).

##  INFORMATION

Travel agencies can be found all over town. Backpacker-oriented cafes and most hotels can also often dispense good advice. Shop around for the best deals.

**Bank of China** (中国银行; Zhōngguó Yínháng; Xijie; 西街; ☺9am-5pm) Foreign exchange and 24-hour ATM for international cards.

> *Unfolding before you is a beautiful panorama of karst peaks*

##  GETTING THERE & AWAY

### AIR

The closest airport is in Guìlín. Your hotel should be able to organise taxi rides directly to the airport (about ¥240, one hour).

### BUS

Yángshuò has two bus stations: **Shímă South bus station** (汽车南站; qìchē nánzhàn; courtyard of the Agriculture Mechanisation Management Bureau, 321 Guodao; 国道321号, 农业机械化管理局) and **Dàcūnmén North station** (汽车北站; qìchē bĕizhàn; fishery market next to Dàcūnmén Provincial Government Service Centre, Qingquan Lu; 大村门开发区清泉路, 大村门县政务服务中心, 水产批发市场处).

Direct bus links include Guìlín (¥20, one hour, every 15 to 20 minutes, leaves when full), Guìlín Airport (¥70, 1½ hours, eight daily) and Xìngpíng (¥8, one hour, every 15 minutes from 6.30am to 6pm).

### TRAIN

Yángshuò town itself has no train station, but there is a station called Yángshuò station servicing high-speed trains in Fànzèng Shān (饭甑山), near Xìngpíng, 14km away. Regular buses (¥20) connect the train station with Yángshuò, travelling via Xìngpíng. Destinations include Guìlín (2nd/1st class ¥21/25, 30 minutes, seven daily).

##  GETTING AROUND

Most places in town can be reached by pedicab for less than ¥20. Bicycles can be rented at almost all hostels and from streetside outlets for ¥10 to ¥25 per day. A deposit of ¥200 to ¥500 is standard, but don't hand over your passport. For better-quality bikes, head to **Bike Asia** (☑0773 882 6521; www.bikeasia.com; 8 Guihua Lu; 桂花路8号; ☺8.30am-6.30pm).

Bike rental operators will rent you an electric scooter (from ¥150 per day) or petrol scooter (from ¥200) without asking to see a driver's licence. Scooters can make the going easier, but be aware that if you don't have a Chinese driver's licence, you will probably not be insured (international drivers' licences are not accepted in China) and things could get complicated and costly in the event of an accident.

Bus 5 (¥1) links the two bus stations and will also get you to Xijie from either bus station.

## Guìlín

Guìlín (桂林) was China's first city to develop tourism after 1949. No matter where you're going in Guǎngxī, you're likely

to spend a night or two here – Guìlín is a convenient base to plan trips to the rest of the province. It's clean and modern, with a high percentage of English-speaking locals, but you'll have to put up with touts and high admission fees to sights.

## ◉ SIGHTS

Guìlín's sights are built around scraggly karst peaks that dot the bustling city. Some, owing to exorbitant admission prices, can be skipped, especially if you are

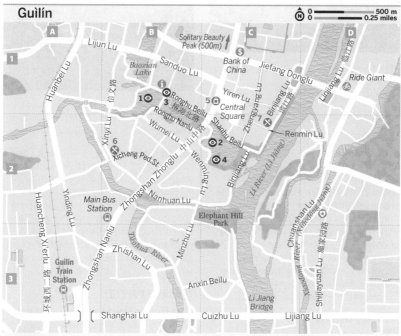

## Guìlín

From left: Guìlín Night Market; Sun & Moon Twin Pagodas; Guìlín rice noodles

heading to Yángshuò (which is the whole point).

### Sun & Moon Twin Pagodas                 Pagoda

(日月双塔; Rìyuè Shuāng Tǎ; admission ¥45; ⊙8am-10.30pm) Elegantly embellishing the scenery of **Shān Lake** (杉湖; Shān Hú), the Sun and Moon Twin Pagodas, beautifully illuminated at night, are the highlight of a stroll around Guìlín's two central lakes. The octagonal, seven-storey Moon Pagoda (月塔; Yuè Tǎ) is connected by an underwater tunnel to the 41m-high Sun Pagoda (日塔; Rì Tǎ), one of the few pagodas with a lift.

### Solitary Beauty Peak                 Park

(独秀峰; Dúxiù Fēng; 1 Wangcheng; 王城1号; admission ¥130; ⊙7.30am-6pm; 🚍1, 2) This park is a peaceful, leafy retreat from the city centre. The entrance fee for the famous lone pinnacle includes admission to an underwhelming 14th-century Ming prince's

mansion (oversold as a 'palace'). The 152m peak affords fine views of Guìlín.

### South Gate                 Gate, Lake

(Nán Mén; 南门) On the northern shore of **Róng Lake** (榕湖; Róng Hú), and strikingly illuminated at night, the South Gate is the only surviving section of the original Song dynasty city wall (城墙; *chéng qiáng*). The area is abuzz with activity and is a good place to watch locals practising taichi, calligraphy and dancing.

## 🟢 ACTIVITIES

### Two Rivers Four Lakes                 Boating

(二江四湖; Èr Jiāng Sì Hú) This boat ride around Guìlín does a loop of the Lí River and the city's lakes. Prices vary from ¥150 to ¥340 for 90 minutes, depending on the time of day (it costs more at night). Pretty much every Guìlín hotel and tourist information service centre can arrange the tour.

FREER / SHUTTERSTOCK ©

 **SHOPPING**

### Guìlín Night Market Market

(夜市; Yèshì; Zhongshan Zhonglu; 中山中
路; ⏱from 7pm) For souvenirs, check out
Guìlín's night market, which runs along
Zhongshan Zhonglu from Ronghu Beilu to
Sanduo Lu.

## **EATING**

Local specialities include Guìlín rice noodles (桂林米粉; Guìlín mǐfěn), beer duck
(啤酒鸭; píjiǔ yā) and snails (田螺; tiánluó).
The pedestrianised Zhengyang Lu and its
surrounding lanes are the busiest dining
areas.

### Kali Mirch Indian ¥¥

(黑胡椒印度餐厅; Hēi Hújiāo Yìndù Cāntīng; 15
Binjiang Lu, Zhengyang Jie; 正阳步行街滨江路
15号; mains from ¥30; 🛜) Tucked away behind
the Sheraton, this fantastic restaurant
is run by an affable and well-travelled
man from Darjeeling, who speaks perfect
English and ensures that every dish is true
to form. The vegetable samosas, onion
pakoras, butter chicken and lamb biryani
are just a few excellent dishes from a tried-
and-tested menu, with all spices imported
from India.

### Céngsān
### Jiāwèiguǎn Guangxi ¥¥

(曾三家味馆; 🕿0773 286 3781; 10 Xinyi Lu,
near junction with Xicheng Lu; dishes ¥20-158;

---

### 🛎 Where
to Stay

Guìlín is well supplied with accommodation options, from good youth hostels, to riverside inns and top-ranking
international-standard hotels. Book
ahead, especially at weekends and
during the busy summer months.

## Lí River
## Boating Trip

The popular Lí River trip from Guìlín
to Yángshuò lasts about 4½ hours and
includes a wonderfully scenic boat trip
to Yángshuò, lunch and a bus ride back
to Guìlín. Expect to pay ¥350 to ¥450
for a boat with an English-speaking
guide. Many Guìlín hotels and the tourist
information service centre can arrange
these tours.

Lí River
E X P O S E / SHUTTERSTOCK ©

⊙11am-2pm & 5-9pm) A modern restaurant
jam-packed with middle-class locals who
come for the generously plated wild boar,
rabbit and cured meat dishes. If you prefer
tamer flavours, there are other great
options in the phone book of a menu. For
weekend dinner, go before 6.15pm to snag
a table. There's a Chinese picture menu.

##  DRINKING & NIGHTLIFE

Guìlín's streets are dotted with trendy
cafes – Zhengyang Lu has a short stretch
of bars with outdoor seating, while Binjiang
Lu alongside the river has a slew of cute
drinking spots, most with free wi-fi.

##  INFORMATION

**Bank of China** (中国银行; Zhōngguó Yínháng)
Branches on Zhongshan Nanlu (near the main
bus station) and Jiefang Donglu change money,
give credit-card advances and have 24-hour
ATMs.

**Guìlín Tourist Information Service Centre** (桂
林旅游咨询服务中心; Guìlín Lǚyóu Zīxún Fúwù
Zhōngxīn; ☑0773 280 0318; South Gate, Ronghu
Beilu; 榕湖北路; ⊙8am-10pm) These helpful
centres dot the city. There's a good one just west
of the South Gate on Róng Lake.

## ℹ GETTING THERE & AWAY

### AIR

Direct flights from Guìlín Liǎngjiāng Inter-
national Airport (两江国际机场; Liǎngjiāng
Guójì Jīchǎng) include Běijīng, Chéngdū,
Chóngqìng, Hǎikǒu, Guǎngzhōu, Hong Kong,
Kūnmíng, Shànghǎi and Xī'ān. International
destinations include Seoul and Osaka.

The airport is 30km west of the city.
Half-hourly shuttle buses (¥20) run from the
CAAC office between 6.30am and 9pm. From the
airport, shuttle buses meet every arrival. A taxi
(40 minutes) costs about ¥120.

### BUS

Guìlín's **main bus station** (桂林汽车客运总站;
Guìlín qìchē kèyùn zǒngzhàn; ☑0773 386 2358;
65 Zhongshan Nanlu; 中山南路65号; ☐3, 9, 10,
11, 16, 25, 51, 88, 91, 99) has regular buses to
Sānjiāng (¥43, four hours, hourly) and Yángshuò
(¥25, 1½ hours, every 15 to 20 minutes).

The **North bus station** (桂林汽车客北站;
Guìlín qìchē běizhàn; 76 Beichen Lu; 北辰路76
号; ☐18, 32, 99, 100) has buses to Zīyuán (¥31,
every 20 minutes 6.40am to 5.50pm).

Buses to Lóngshèng and the Lóngjǐ Rice
Terraces depart from the North bus station (¥34,
two hours, four daily) and **Qíntán bus
station** (琴潭汽车站; Qíntán qìchē zhàn; 31
Cuizhu Lu; 翠竹路31号; ☐2, 12, 26, 32, 85, 91;
¥34, two hours, every 40 min, 6.10am-7pm).

### TRAIN

Few trains start in Guìlín, which means it's often
tough to find tickets, so get them a few days in
advance. Most trains leave from Guìlín station
(桂林站; Guìlín zhàn), but some may leave from
Guìlín North train station (桂林北站; Guìlín
běizhàn), 9km north of the city centre.

Solitary Beauty Peak (p198), Guìlín

Direct services include Běijīng West (2nd/1st class ¥806/1250, 10½ hours, two daily), Chóngqìng (¥280, 20 hours, two daily), Kūnmíng (¥280, 18½ to 24 hours, four daily), Shànghǎi (G-class train 2nd/1st class ¥660/1049, 9½ hours, daily) and Xī'ān (¥367, 27 hours, daily).

## ⓘ GETTING AROUND

### BICYCLE

Guìlín's sights are all within cycling distance. Many hostels rent bicycles (about ¥20 per day). For decent bikes, head to **Ride Giant** (捷安特 自行车; Jié'āntè Zìxíngchē; ☏ 0773 286 1286; 28

Dongjiang Lu; 东江路28号; per day ¥70, deposit ¥500; ☉ 9.30am-9pm).

### BUS

Buses numbered 51 to 58 are all free but run very infrequently. Regular buses cost ¥1 to ¥2. The following are the most useful:

**Bus 2** Runs past Elephant Trunk Hill and Folded Brocade Hill.

**Bus 51** Starts at the train station and heads north along the length of Zhongshan Lu to the Bird Flower Market and beyond.

**Bus 58** Goes to Elephant Trunk Hill, Seven Stars Park, Wave-Subduing Hill, Folded Brocade Hill and Reed Flute Cave.

# YÚNNÁN

# Yúnnán at a Glance...

*Yúnnán (云南) is the most diverse province in all China, both in its extraordinary mix of peoples (more than half of the country's minority groups reside here) and in the splendour of its landscapes. From dense jungle sliced by the Mekong River in the far south and soul-recharging glimpses of the sun over rice terraces in the southeastern regions to snowcapped mountains as you edge towards Tibet, Yúnnán's eye-catching contrasts are endlessly fascinating.*

### Two Days in Yúnnán

From the provincial capital Kūnmíng, jump on a bus to **Dàlǐ** (p216) to experience the fun Bai minority town and its gorgeous natural scenery, which affords plenty of hiking opportunities. Spend the night in Dàlǐ before making the journey to **Lìjiāng** (p213) to discover its old Naxi town and the magnificent spectacle of **Yùlóng Xuěshān** (p213).

### Four Days in Yúnnán

Stay overnight in Lìjiāng and then tackle **Tiger Leaping Gorge** (p210) the following day; either spend the night in the gorge or back in Lìjiāng before flying to Kūnming early the next day to then take the bus to **Yuányáng Rice Terraces** (p206) in the south of Yúnnán province, and enjoy its beautiful scenery and stunning treks.

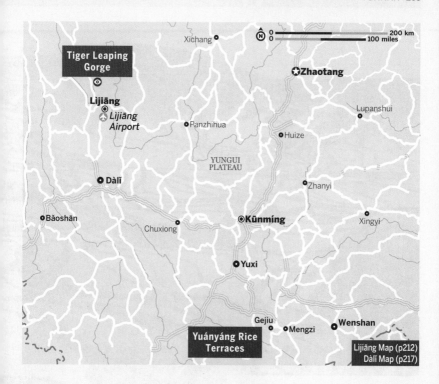

## Arriving in Yúnnán

**Air** Kūnmíng's newish airport is the fourth-largest and seventh-busiest in China and has daily flights to most cities, as well as to an increasing number of international destinations. Lìjiāng is also well connected to a number of Chinese cities, while Dàlǐ has many more flights than before.

**Train** Railways link Yúnnán to Guìzhōu, Guǎngxī, Sìchuān and beyond. The main route for travellers is the line from Kūnmíng to Dàlǐ and Lìjiāng.

## Where to Stay

Yúnnán's busiest destinations offer the full range of accommodation options: hostels and guesthouses, budget and midrange places, and boutique and upmarket hotels. Smaller towns sometimes have guesthouses, but you are mostly reliant on standard budget and midrange hotels. In remote villages, homestays are the norm.

# Yuányáng Rice Terraces

*Picture hilltop villages above rolling fog and cloud banks, an artist's palette of colours at sunrise and sunset and spirit-recharging treks through centuries-old rice-covered hills.*

Hewn out of hills that stretch off into the far distance, the rice terraces of Yuányáng are testimony to the wonderfully intimate relationship the local Hani people have with the sublime landscape they live in. Covering roughly 12,500 hectares, and one of Yúnnán's most stunning sights, it's hard not to become indulgent when describing this remarkable topography.

### Yuányáng

Yuányáng (元阳) is actually split into two: Nánshà, the new town, and Xīnjiē, the old town, an hour's bus or minivan ride up a nearby hill. Either can be labelled Yuányáng, depending what map you use. Xīnjiē is the one you want, so make sure you get off there.

### Great For...

☑ **Don't Miss**

Seeing the rice terraces at sunrise or sunset for the best visuals.

Yuányáng Rice Terraces

## ℹ️ Need to Know

A combined ¥100 ticket gets you access to Duōyīshù, Bádá, Quánfúzhuāng and Měngpǐn.

## 🍴 Take a Break

Almost all restaurants are concentrated in Xīnjiē. In Pǔgāolǎo, all guesthouses serve meals, though they can be pricey.

## ★ Top Tip

Avoid visiting during Chinese public holidays, when prices for minibuses go sky-high (¥600 or more per day).

○ **Měngpǐn Rice Terrace** (勐品; Měngpǐn Tītián) Měngpǐn, also known as Lǎohǔzuǐ (老虎嘴), is one of Yuányáng's most mesmerising places to watch the sunset.

○ **Bádá Rice Terrace** (坝达; Bádá Tītián) Another one of the finest rice terraces at Yuányáng to catch a sunset.

## Getting There

Xīnjiē is the main transport hub for Yuányáng, with daily buses from the bus station to and from Kūnmíng.

While buses run to all the villages from the bus station, you are much better off arranging your own transport, or hooking up with other travellers to split the cost of a sunrise–sunset drive. Minivans and motor-rickshaws congregate around Yúntī Shùnjié Dàjiǔdiàn and on the street west of the bus station. Expect to pay ¥400 to ¥500 in peak season for a minivan. Less comfortable motor-rickshaws can be got for ¥250.

## The Rice Terraces

The terraces around dozens of outlying villages have their own special characteristics, often changing with the daylight. Bilingual maps are available at all hotels in town. Bear in mind that the *tītián* (梯田; rice terraces) are at their most extraordinary in winter when they are flooded with water, which the light bounces off in spectacular fashion.

○ **Duōyīshù Rice Terrace** (多依树; Duōyīshù Tītián) Located about 25km from Xīnjiē, Duōyīshù has the most awesome sunrises and, of all those at Yuányáng, is the one you should not miss.

○ **Quánfúzhuāng Rice Terrace** (全福庄; Quánfúzhuāng Tītián) A less-crowded alternative to Duōyīshù, and has easy access via trails that reach the terraces.

EFIRED / SHUTTERSTOCK ©

# Lìjiāng's Old Town

*A Unesco World Heritage Site since 1997, Lìjiāng is a city of two halves: the old town and the very modern new town. The remarkable old town is where you'll be spending your time.*

## Great For...

### ☑ Don't Miss

Joining the locals in Zhōngyì Market for its old-time flavours.

How popular is this time-locked place? Lìjiāng's maze of cobbled streets, rickety (or rickety-looking, given gentrification) wooden buildings and gushing canals suck in over *eight million* people a year. So thick are the crowds in the narrow alleys that it can feel like that they've all arrived at the same time.

But remember the 80/20 rule: 80% of the tourists will be in 20% of the places. Get up early enough and you can often beat the crowds.

### Old Town

The old town is centred on the busy and touristy **Old Market Sq** (四方街; Sìfāng Jiē). The surrounding lanes are dissected by a web of artery-like canals that once brought the city's drinking water from Yuquan Spring, on the far outskirts of what

Looking at the Past Pavillion

APHOTOSTORY / SHUTTERSTOCK ©

Fuhui Lu

Minzhu Lu 民主路

Dong Dajie

Jinhong Lu

**Lìjiāng's Old Town**

Wuyi Jie

### ❶ Need to Know

古城; Old Town; admission ¥80

### ✗ Take a Break

There are plenty of choices in the old town to sit down and snack; try **Tiāntiān Xiān** (p213).

### ★ Top Tip

When the crowds appear, that's the cue to hop on a bike and cycle out to one of the nearby villages.

is now Black Dragon Pool Park. Several wells and pools are still in use around town (but hard to find). **White Horse Dragon Pool** (白马龙潭; Báimǎlóng Tán) is one such pool, still used by the locals to wash veggies bought from the nearby market. Where there are three pools, these were designated into pools for drinking, washing clothes and washing vegetables.

## Looking at the Past Pavillion

The **Looking at the Past Pavillion** (望古楼; Wànggǔ Lóu; incl in ¥80 old town entrance ticket; ⊘8.30am-6pm) was raised for tourists at a cost of more than ¥1 million. It's famed for a unique design using dozens of four-storey pillars – unfortunately these were culled from northern Yúnnán old-growth forests. A path (with English signs) leads from Old Market Sq. It acts as a sentinel of sorts

for the town. Sit on the slope in the early morning and watch the mist clearing as the old town comes to life.

## Mu Family Mansion

The former home of a Naxi chieftain, the **Mu Family Mansion** (木氏土司府; Mùshì Tǔsīfǔ; admission ¥60; ⊘8.30am-5.30pm) was heavily renovated (more like built from scratch) after the devastating earthquake that struck Lìjiāng in 1996. Mediocre captions do a poor job of introducing the Mu family, but many travellers find the beautiful grounds reason enough to visit. Bizarrely, the mansion is not covered by the old town entrance ticket.

## Zhōngyì Market

This **market** (忠义市场; Zhōngyì Shìchǎng; Xianghe Lu; 祥和路; ⊘6am-5pm) sells produce, copper items and livestock. If you are craving a slice of old Lìjiāng, this is where you'll find it.

# Hiking Tiger Leaping Gorge

*One of the deepest gorges in the world, Tiger Leaping Gorge measures 16km long and, despite the odd danger, it's gorgeous almost every single step of the way.*

### Great For...

### ☑ Don't Miss

Taking the detour down to Tiger Leaping Stone.

## Hike Practicalities

There are two trails: the higher and the lower. The latter follows the road and is best avoided, unless you enjoy being enveloped in clouds of dust from passing tour buses and 4WDs. While the scenery is stunning wherever you are in the gorge, it's absolutely sublime from the high trail. Make sure you don't get too distracted by all that beauty, though, and so miss the blue signs and red arrows that help you avoid getting lost on the way.

From the Qiáotóu ticket office, it's seven hours to Běndiwān, nine hours to Middle Gorge (Tina's Guesthouse) or 10 hours to Walnut Garden. It's much more fun, and a lot less exhausting, to do the trek over two days, stopping overnight at one of the many guesthouses along the way.

Bridge over the gorge

PHOTONGPIX / GETTY IMAGES ©

### ❶ Need to Know

虎跳峡; Hǔtiào Xiá; admission ¥65

### ✕ Take a Break

All the guesthouses double as restaurants and shops, where you can have meals or pick up water and snacks.

### ★ Top Tip

If you plan to hike the route alone, assume you'll need all provisions and equipment for extremes of weather.

## The Higher Road

The main hiking route along the higher road starts at **Jane's Tibetan Guesthouse** (峡谷行客栈; Xiágǔ Xíng Kèzhàn; ☎0888 880 6570; janetibetgh@163.com; dm ¥35, d with/without bathroom ¥120/70; ☎). Walk away from **Qiáotóu** (桥头), past the school, for five minutes or so, then head up the paved road branching to the left; there's a sign to guide you. After about 2.5km on the road, look for the blue sign pointing to the high-trail diversion. The serious climbing starts straight away thanks to the diversion, with a steep ascent and then descent into **Nuòyú** (诺余) village.

The toughest section of the trek comes after Nuòyu, when the trail winds through the 28 agonising bends, or turns, that lead to the highest point of the gorge. Count on

six hours at normal pace to get through here and to reach **Yāchà** (牙叉) village. It's a relatively straightforward walk on to **Běndìwān** (本地湾). About 1½ hours on from here, you begin the descent to the road on slippery, poor, precarious paths. Watch your step here; if you twist an ankle, it's a long hop down.

After the path meets the road at **Tina's Guesthouse** (中峡旅店; Zhōngxiá Lǚdiàn; ☎0888 820 2258; tina999@live.com; 8-/4-bed dm ¥30/40, d ¥120-280; @☎), there's a good detour that leads down to the middle rapids and **Tiger Leaping Stone** (admission ¥15), where a tiger is once said to have leapt across the Yangzi, thus giving the gorge its name. From one of the lower rest points another trail (¥15) heads downstream for a one-hour walk to **Walnut Garden** (核桃园).

Most hikers stop at Tina's, have lunch and head back to Qiáotóu.

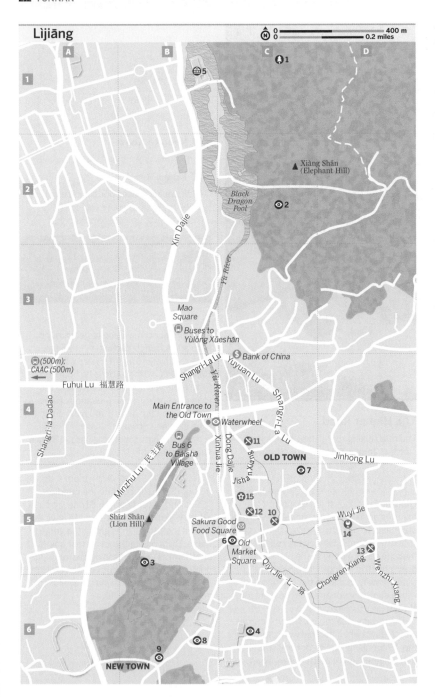

# Lìjiāng

⊕N 0 ———— 400 m
0 ———— 0.2 miles

**A** **B** **C** **D**

**1**

🏛 5

🌲 1

Xiàng Shān
(Elephant Hill) ▲

**2**

Black
Dragon
Pool

◉ 2

*Xin Dajie*

*Yu River*

**3**

Mao
Square

🚌 Buses to
Yùlóng Xuěshān

💲 Bank of China

🚌 (500m);
CAAC (500m)
←

Fuhui Lu  福慧路

*Shangri-La Lu*

*Yu River*

*Yuyuan Lu*

*Shangri-La Lu*

**4**

Main Entrance to
the Old Town

◉ Waterwheel

✕ 11

**OLD TOWN**

Jinhong Lu

◉ 7

🏛 Bus 6
to Báishā
Village

*Xinhua Jie*

*Dong Dajie*

*Minzhu Lu 民主路*

*Shangri-la Dadao*

*Jisha*

*Xinyi*

**5**

Shīzi Shān ▲
(Lion Hill)

✪ 15

✉ 12
◉ 10
✕

Sakura Good
Food Square

Wuyi Jie

🏛 14

◉ 3

6 ◉ Old
Market
Square

13 ✕

*Qiyi Jie 七一路*

*Chongren Xiang*

*Wenzhi Xiang*

**6**

◉ 8
◉ 4

9 ◉

**NEW TOWN**

# Lìjiāng

# Lìjiāng

## ◉ SIGHTS

Visitors to Lìjiāng's **old town** (admission ¥80) have long been required to buy a 'protection fee' ticket, allegedly for preservation projects, but now proof of payment is being enforced much more rigidly. The ticket is valid for 15 days and you'll need to hang onto it, as there are now ticket checks at the entrances leading into the old town. You will also need it to gain free entry to the Black Dragon Pool Park, as well as to other sites such as Yùlóng Xuěshān.

### Black Dragon Pool Park     Park
(黑龙潭公园; Hēilóngtán Gōngyuán; Xin Dajie; admission free with ¥80 town entrance ticket; ⊙7am-8pm) On the northern edge of town is the Black Dragon Pool Park; its view of Yùlóng Xuěshān is an obligatory photo shoot in southwestern China. Note that the pool has dried up in recent years and without water some visitors are disappointed with this site; ask at your guesthouse first if the pool has water before deciding whether or not to visit.

### Dōngbā Research Institute     Cultural Centre
(东巴文化研究室; Dōngbā Wénhuà Yánjiūshì; admission free with ¥80 old town entrance ticket; ⊙8am-5pm Mon-Fri) The Dōngbā Research Institute is part of a renovated complex on the hillside north of the old town. Here you can see Naxi cultural artefacts and scrolls featuring a unique pictograph script.

### Yùlóng Xuěshān     Mountain
(玉龙雪山; Jade Dragon Snow Mountain; admission ¥135, plus Lijiang old town entrance ticket ¥80) Also known as Mt Satseto, Yùlóng Xuěshān soars to some 5500m. Its peak was first climbed in 1963 by a research team from Běijīng and now, at some 35km from Lìjiāng, it is regularly mobbed by hordes of Chinese tour groups and travellers, especially in the summer.

## ◉ ACTIVITIES

### Keith Lyons     Tour
(✆137 6900 1439; keithalyons@gmail.com; per day from ¥200) Lìjiāng-based guide Keith Lyons runs tours and treks, specialising in the area outside Lìjiāng.

## ◉ TOURS

It is possible to see most of Lìjiāng's environs on your own, but a few agencies in Lìjiāng, such as Keith Lyons, offer half- or full-day tours, starting from ¥200, plus fees.

## ◉ EATING

There are many, many eateries around the old town, and almost every menu will have both Chinese and Western dishes.

### Tiāntiān Xiān     Yunnan ¥
(天天鲜; ✆0888 518 4933; 47 Wangjiazhuang Xiang, Wuyi Jie; 五一街王家庄巷47号; dishes from ¥12; ⊙11am-9pm) Locals flock here for

# The Naxi
# of Lìjiāng

Lìjiāng has been the homeland of the Naxi (纳西; pronounced 'na-shee', also spelle Nakhi and Nahi) minority for about the last 1400 years. The Naxi descend from ethnically Tibetan Qiang tribes and lived until recently in matrilineal families. Since local rulers were always male it wasn't truly matriarchal, but women still seemed to run the show.

The Naxi matriarchs maintained their hold over the men with flexible arrangements for love affairs. The *azhu* (friend) system allowed a couple to become lovers without setting up joint residence. Both partners would continue to live in their respective homes; the boyfriend would spend the nights at his girlfriend's house but return to live and work at his mother's house during the day. Any children born to the couple belonged to the woman, who was responsible for bringing them up. The man provided support, but once the relationship was over, so was the support. Children lived with their mothers and no special effort was made to recognise paternity. Women inherited all property, and disputes were adjudicated by female elders.

There are strong matriarchal influences in the Naxi language. Nouns enlarge their meaning when the word for 'female' is added; conversely, the addition of the word for 'male' will decrease the meaning. For example, 'stone' plus 'female' conveys the idea of a boulder; 'stone' plus 'male' conveys the idea of a pebble.

Naxi man in traditional dress
APHOTOSTORY / SHUTTERSTOCK ©

the superb, grilled fish and chicken and soy-bean-paste dishes (get here before 7pm or it will have run out). But all the Naxi specialities on offer are fantastic and great value. No English spoken, but there is an English menu. To find it, look for the three characters with 'Daily Fresh' written in English underneath them.

**Prague Cafe**          Cafe ¥¥
(布拉格咖啡馆; Bùlāgé Kāfēiguǎn; 80 Mishi Xiang; 密士巷80号; breakfast from ¥30, mains from ¥40; 🕗8am-11pm; 🛜) Something of an oasis in the heart of the old town, with good coffee and tea, solid breakfasts and a selection of Western and Japanese dishes, as well as books to read. They serve alcohol, too.

**Āmāyì Nàxī Snacks**      Yunnan ¥¥
(阿妈意纳西饮食院; Āmāyì Nàxī Yǐnshí Yuàn; 📱0888 530 9588; Wuyi Jie; dishes from ¥18; 🕗11am-10pm) The name doesn't do justice to the small but select and very authentic selection of Naxi cuisine on offer at this calm courtyard restaurant. There are fantastic mushroom dishes, when in season, as well as *zhútǒng fàn* (rice packed in bamboo). It's down an alley off Wuyi Jie, close to the Stone Bridge.

**Lamu's House
of Tibet**                Tibetan ¥¥
(西藏屋西餐馆; Xīzàngwū Xīcāntīng; 📱0888 511 5776; 56 Xinyi Jie; dishes from ¥20; 🕗9.30am-10.30pm; 🛜) Friendly Lamu has been serving up smiles and hearty Tibetan and international fare for more than a decade. Ascend the little wooden staircase to the 2nd-floor dining area, a great spot for people-watching, and try the excellent Naxiburger, or choose from the selection of Tibetan dishes. There's also a good selection of paperback books to thumb through.

# 🍷 DRINKING & NIGHTLIFE
Xinhua Jie, just off Old Market Sq, is packed out with Chinese-style drinking dens, most with live music of some form. Western-type

bars are in much shorter supply. There are many cafes around the old town.

### Stone the Crows  Bar
(134-2 Wenzhi Xiang; beers from ¥25; ⊙6pm-late) Worth checking out is this foreign-owned, endearingly ramshackle bar with a good range of local and foreign beers and a mixed crowd of locals (many musicians who play in the nearby bars come here) and Westerners. There's a pool table and they do decent pub food: pizza, pies and burgers. It gets going later rather than earlier.

### ⭐ ENTERTAINMENT

### Nàxī Orchestra  Live Music
(纳西古乐会; Nàxī Gǔyuè Huì, Nàxī Music Academy; Xinhua Jie; 新华街; tickets ¥120-160; ⊙8pm) Attending a performance of this orchestra inside a beautiful building in the old town is a good way to spend an evening in Lìjiāng. Not only are all two dozen or so members Naxi, but they play a type of Taoist temple music (known as *dòngjīng*) that has been lost elsewhere in China.

### Where to Stay

Rising rents mean that most guesthouses have relocated to just outside the old town, either north or south. Nevertheless, there are still well over a thousand places to stay in the old town, with more appearing all the time. Many have fewer than 10 rooms. In peak season (especially over public holidays), prices double (or more).

The pieces they perform are said to be faithful renditions of music from the Han, Song and Tang dynasties, and are played on original instruments.

### Impression Lìjiāng  Dance
(tickets ¥230; ⊙1pm daily) This big song and dance show, squarely aimed at local tour groups, takes place at the foot of Yùlóng Xuěshān (p213).

Nàxī Orchestra

## Naxi Script

The Naxi created a written language more than 1000 years ago using an extraordinary system of pictographs – the only hieroglyphic language still in use. The most famous Naxi text is the Dongba classic *Creation,* and ancient copies of it and other texts can still be found in Lìjiāng, as well as in the archives of some US universities. The Dongba were Naxi shamans who were caretakers of the written language and mediators between the Naxi and the spirit world. The Dongba religion, itself an offshoot of Tibet's pre-Buddhist Bon religion, eventually developed into an amalgam of Tibetan Buddhism, Islam and Taoism.

Useful phrases in the Naxi language are *nuar lala* (hello) and *jiu bai sai* (thank you).

##  INFORMATION

**Bank of China** (中国银行; Zhōngguó Yínháng; Yuyuan Lu; ⏱9am-5pm) This branch has an ATM and is convenient for the old town. There are many ATMs in the old town too.

**China Post** (中国邮政; Zhōngguó Yóuzhèng; Minzhu Lu; ⏱8.30am-6pm) In the old town just north of Old Market Sq.

##  GETTING THERE & AWAY

### AIR

Lìjiāng's airport is 28km east of town. Tickets can be booked at **CAAC** (中国民航; Zhōngguó Mínháng; cnr Fuhui Lu & Shangrila Dadao; ⏱8.30am-9pm). Most hotels in the old town also offer an air-ticket booking service.

From Lìjiāng there are 13 daily flights to Kūnmíng, as well as daily flights to Běijīng, Chéngdū, Chóngqìng and Shànghǎi.

Buses to the airport (¥25) leave from outside the CAAC office from 6.30am to 10pm.

### BUS

The main long-distance bus station (客运站; kèyùnzhàn) is south of the old town; to get here, take bus 8 or 11 (¥1; the latter is faster) from along Minzhu Lu. Destinations include Chéngdū (¥317, 24 hours, daily), Kūnmíng (¥217, seven hours, seven daily), Qiáotóu (¥22, 1½ hours, daily; Lìjiāng to Shangri-la buses also stop here) and Xiàguān (¥56 to ¥87, three hours, every 30 minutes from 7.10am to 7pm).

In the north of town, the **express bus station** (高快客运站; gāo kuài kèyùnzhàn; Shangrila Dadao) is where many of the above buses originate, but it's usually more convenient to catch your bus from the long-distance bus station.

### TRAIN

There are seven trains daily to Dàlǐ (¥34 to ¥69, two to three hours, 8am to 9.50pm) and seven trains to Kūnmíng (hard sleeper ¥141, eight to nine hours, 8am to 11.50pm). The line will be extended to reach Shangri-la by 2019.

##  GETTING AROUND

Bus 6 runs to Báishā Village from Minzhu Lu, close to the main entrance to the old town. Buses to Yùlóng Xuěshān run from Mao Sq, a few hundred metres north of the old town.

Taxi flagfall is ¥7. Taxis are not allowed into the old town. Bike hire is available at most hostels (¥30 per day).

## Dàlǐ

Dàlǐ (大理), the original backpacker hangout in Yúnnán, was once *the* place to chill, with its stunning location sandwiched between mountains and Ěrhǎi Lake (Ěrhǎi Hú). Loafing here for a couple of weeks was an essential part of the Yúnnán experience.

In recent years, domestic tourists have discovered Dàlǐ in a big way and the scene has changed accordingly. Instead of dreadlocked Westerners, it's young Chinese who walk around with flowers in their hair. Still, Dàlǐ has not been overwhelmed by visitors like nearby Lìjiāng and remains a reason-

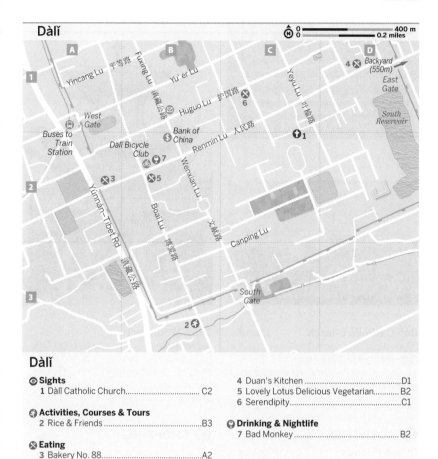

# Dàlǐ

## Dàlǐ

ably relaxed destination, with the local Bai population very much part of daily life.

Surrounding Dàlǐ there are fascinating possibilities for exploring, especially by bicycle and in the mountains above the lake, or you can do what travellers have done for years – eat, drink and make merry.

## ⊙ SIGHTS

### Three Pagodas                           Pagoda
(三塔寺; Sān Tǎ Sì; admission ¥120; ☉8.30am-6.30pm) Absolutely *the* symbol of the town and region, these pagodas, a 2km walk

north of the north gate, are among the oldest standing structures in southwestern China. The tallest of the three, Qiānxún Pagoda, has 16 tiers that reach a height of 70m. It was originally erected in the mid-9th century by engineers from Xī'ān. It is flanked by two smaller 10-tiered pagodas, each of which is 42m high.

While the price is cheeky considering you can't go inside the pagodas, Chóngshèng Temple (Chóngshèng Sì) behind them has been restored and converted into a relatively worthy museum.

★ **Dai Temple Etiquette**
Take off shoes when entering, and don't take photos of monks or the inside of temples without permission.

Never raise yourself higher than a Buddha figure or rub the head of, or point your feet at, anyone.

From left: Three pagodas (p217), Dàlǐ; Dàlǐ Catholic Church; Old Town (p208), Lìjiāng

### Dàlǐ Catholic Church          Church
(off Renmin Lu) It's worth checking out Dàlǐ's Catholic Church. Dating back to 1927, it's a unique mix of Bai-style architecture and classic European church design. Mass is held here every Sunday at 9.30am.

### 🟢 ACTIVITIES
**Rice & Friends**          Cooking
(📞151 2526 4065; www.riceandfriends.com) Recommended cooking school that includes trips to markets to purchase ingredients and tips on preparation, as well as cooking classes.

### 🟢 TOURS
**China Minority Travel**   Cultural Tour
(📞138 8723 5264; chinaminoritytravel@gmail.com) Henriette, a Dutch expat, can offer a long list of trips, including tours to Muslim and Yi minority markets as well as through remote areas of Yúnnán and Guìzhōu.

### Tibet Motorcycle
### Adventures          Motorcycle Tour
(📞151 8499 9452; www.tibetmoto.de) Motorbikes can be rented for ¥150 per day and tours (although not to Tibet) arranged. Contact Hendrik Heyne.

### 🔒 SHOPPING
Dàlǐ is famous for its marble blue-and-white batik printed on cotton and silk. There are many clothes shops around Dàlǐ. Most can also make clothes to your specifications – which will come as a relief when you see how small some of the items of ready-made clothing are.

### 🍴 EATING
Bai food makes use of local flora and fauna – many of which are unrecognisable! Specialities include *rǔbǐng* (goat's cheese) and *ěr kuài* (饵块; toasted rice 'cakes'). Given the proximity of Ěrhǎi Lake, try *shāguō yú* (沙锅鱼), a claypot fish stew made from

OUTCAST85 / GETTY IMAGES ©

salted Ěrhǎi Lake carp – and, as a Bai touch, magnolia petals.

### Lovely Lotus
### Delicious Vegetarian           Chinese ¥

(爱莲说素膳; Ài Lián Shuō Sùshàn; ☑0872 533 7737; B2, Jiulongju, west side of Fuxing Lu; 复兴路西侧九隆居B2号; buffet ¥20; ⊘11.30am-1.30pm & 6-8pm; ✍) No menu here; instead you choose from a tempting buffet of all-vegetarian dishes. It bustles at lunchtimes and there's a small outside area to eat at. It's just off Boai Lu on the right-hand side of a forecourt.

### Duan's Kitchen                  Yunnan ¥¥

(小段厨房; Xiǎoduàn Chúfáng; ☑153 0872 7919; 12 Renmin Lu; 人民路12号; dishes from ¥38; ⊘11am-2pm & 5.30-9pm; ♠) Now so popular that you can expect to queue for a table, this place is set around a cosy and cute courtyard. The dishes are an interpretation of Bai cuisine rather than 100% the real deal, but the ingredients are absolutely local. It's at the far eastern end of Renmin Lu.

### Serendipity                   American ¥¥

(大理美国小馆; Dàlǐ Měiguó Xiǎoguǎn; 53 Guangwu Lu; 广武路53号; mains from ¥38; ⊘8am-11.30pm; ♠) Busy, American-run diner with a traditional counter to sit around and a solid menu of properly cooked burgers, steaks, pasta and salad, as well as hefty, top-notch breakfasts. Some outdoor seating on an alley that is rather quieter than Dàlǐ's main drag.

### Bakery No. 88                  Western ¥¥

(88号西点店; Bāshíbā Hào Xīdiǎndiàn; ☑0872 267 9129; 17 Renmin Lu; 人民路17号; sandwiches

---

### Where
### to Stay

There's heaps of accommodation in Dàlǐ, but the popular places fill up quickly during peak summer months. Increasingly, the most in-demand guesthouses are located just outside the west gate of the old town, or close to the east gate.

pastas and soups, all prepared with local produce, as well as fine breads and cakes. It also sells German sausages and beer.

## 💭 Markets Around Dàlǐ

Travellers have a market to go to nearly every day of the week. Every Monday at **Shāpíng** (沙坪), about 30km north of Dàlǐ, there is a colourful Bai market (Shāpíng Gǎnjí). From 10am to 2.30pm you can buy everything from food products and clothing to jewellery and local batik.

Regular buses to Shāpíng (¥11, one hour) leave from just outside the west gate. By bike, it will take about two hours at a good clip.

Markets also take place in **Shuāngláng** (双廊; Tuesday), **Shābā** (沙坝; Wednesday), **Yòusuǒ** (右所; Friday morning; the largest in Yúnnán) and **Jiāngwěi** (江尾; Saturday). **Xǐzhōu** (喜州) and **Zhōuchéng** (州城) have daily morning and afternoon markets, respectively. **Wāsè** (挖色) also has a popular market every five days with trading from 9am to 4.30pm. Thanks to the lack of boats, travellers now have to slog to Xiàguān's east bus station for buses to Wāsè (¥20).

Many guesthouses and hostels in Dàlǐ offer tours or can arrange transport to these markets for around ¥150 for a half day.

Spices, Xǐzhōu market
PETER STUCKINGS / SHUTTERSTOCK ©

& breakfast from ¥25; ⏰8.30am-10pm; 🛜) Spread across two floors and with a small garden, this popular, smoke-free haven of tranquillity has excellent sandwiches,

## 🍷 DRINKING & NIGHTLIFE

There are many Chinese-style bars, with live music, as well as a couple of long-standing Western places and numerous cafes.

### Backyard                          Bar
(后院酒吧; Hòuyuàn Jiǔbā; 27 Hongwu Lu; 洪武路27号; beers from ¥15; ⏰6pm-late, closed Thu; 🛜) Dàlǐ's most laid-back and hidden bar attracts locals and expats with a fine selection of foreign beers and alcohol and a bar set in a garden (hence the name). It shows live European football on the weekends, there are pool, table football and darts, and it serves the best chips and spaghetti bolognese in town.

To find it, turn right at the east gate and walk along Hongwu Lu for 300m. It's down a small alley to the right of a motor repair shop. Look for the light.

### Bad Monkey                        Bar
(坏猴子; Huài Hóuzi; 📱136 8882 4871; 59 Renmin Lu; 人民路59号; beers from ¥15; ⏰9am-late; 🛜) The eternally happening, Brit-run Bad Monkey brews its own strong ales (from ¥30; the IPA packs a punch), and has nightly live music and endless drink specials. There's also reasonable pub grub (pizzas, burgers and shepherd's pie) and Sunday roast for ¥55. A couple of doors down is a second Bad Monkey, which is more of a music venue than a bar.

## ℹ️ INFORMATION

**Bank of China** (中国银行; Zhōngguó Yínháng; Fuxing Lu) Changes cash and travellers cheques, and has an ATM that accepts all major cards.

**China Post** (中国邮政; Zhōngguó Yóuzhèng; cnr Fuxing Lu & Huguo Lu; ⏰8am-8pm) Dàlǐ's main post office.

## ❶ GETTING THERE & AWAY

The golden rule: almost all buses advertised to Dàlǐ actually go to Xiàguān. Coming from Lìjiāng and Shangri-la, Xiàguān-bound buses stop at the eastern end of Dàlǐ to let passengers off before continuing on to Xiàguān's north bus station.

From Kūnmíng's west bus station there are numerous buses to Dàlǐ (¥110 to ¥137, four to five hours, every 15 minutes from 7.20am to 8.20pm). Heading north, it's easiest to pick up a bus on the roads outside the west or east gates; buy your ticket in advance from your guesthouse or a travel agent and they'll make sure you get on the right one. (You could hail one yourself to save a surcharge but you're not guaranteed a seat.)

From the old town (near the west gate) you can catch a 30-seater bus to Kūnmíng for ¥130; it runs seven times a day, departing 8.30am, 9.30am, 10.30am, 11.30am, 1.30pm, 2.30pm and 4.30pm. There are also frequent buses from the old town to Lìjiāng (¥85) and Shangri-la (¥117).

Buses run regularly to Shāpíng (¥11), Xǐzhōu (¥7) and other local destinations from outside the west gate.

## ❶ GETTING AROUND

From Dàlǐ, a taxi to Xiàguān airport takes 45 minutes and costs around ¥100; to Xiàguān's train station it costs ¥50.

Bikes are the best way to get around and can be hired at numerous places from ¥25 to ¥40 per day. Try **Dàlǐ Bicycle Club** (大理自行车俱乐部; Dàlǐ Zìxíngchē Jùlèbù; 41 Boai Lu; ◷7.30am-8pm), which rents bikes and scooters.

Buses (marked 大理; ¥2, 30 minutes) run between the old town and Xiàguān from as early as 6.30am; wait along the highway and flag one down. Bus 8 runs between Dàlǐ and central Xiàguān (¥2, 30 minutes), close to the express bus station and the Xīngshèng bus station. Bus

 **Festival Fun**

**Third Moon Fair** (三月节; Sānyuè Jié) Merrymaking – along with endless buying, selling and general horse-trading (but mostly partying) – takes place during the third moon fair, which begins on the 15th day of the third lunar month (usually April) and ends on the 21st day.

**Torch Festival** (火把节; Huǒbǎ Jié) The Torch Festival is held on the 24th day of the sixth lunar month (normally July) and is likely to be the best photo op in the province. Flaming torches are paraded at night through homes and fields. Locals throw pine resin at the torches causing minor explosions everywhere. According to one local guesthouse owner, 'It's total madness'.

Torch Festival

4 also travels between Dàlǐ and central Xiàguān (¥2, 30 minutes). There is also an unmarked bus that runs past the west gate to and from the train station every 15 minutes from 6.30am (¥2, 30 minutes).

*Dàlǐ is the original backpacker hang-out in Yúnnán*

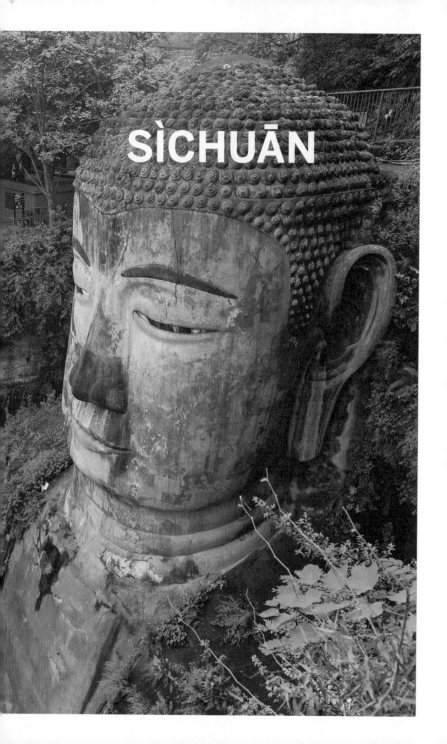

SÌCHUĀN

# Sìchuān at a Glance...

*It's fitting that an ancient form of opera and magic called biànliǎn (face-changing) originated here, for Sìchuān (四川) is a land of many guises. The capital, Chéngdū, shows a modern face, but just beyond its bustling ring roads you'll find a more traditional landscape of mist-shrouded mountains, and a countryside scattered with ancient villages and cliffs of carved Buddhas. Central Sìchuān is also home to the giant panda, the most famous face in China.*

### Two Days in Sìchuān

Spend your first day exploring Chéngdū – get up close to the cuddly creatures at the **Giant Panda Breeding Research Base** (p230), visit the **Wénshū Temple** (p231), explore the **Chéngdū Museum** (p231) and discover the signature dish of **Chén Mápó Dòufu** (p233). On day two, make a day trip to **Lè Shān** (p228) to size up its colossal Buddha.

### Four Days in Sìchuān

From Lè Shān, hop on a bus or a train for the short journey to the sacred Buddhist Mountain of **Éméi Shān** (p226). Aim to spend the night here so you can fully enjoy the scenery and the temple heritage and catch the sunrise. Spend the next day further exploring the mountain before returning to Chéngdū for a hotpot feast at **Chóngqìng Yúan-lǎosì Old Hotpot** (p233).

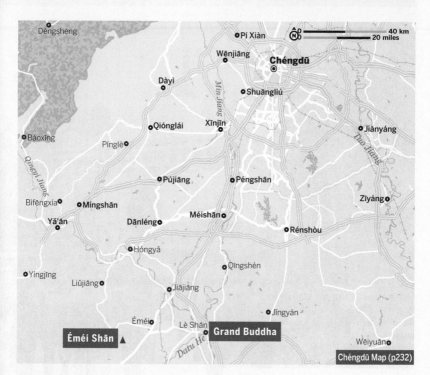

Déngshēng • Pí Xiàn
Wénjiāng •
**Chéngdū**
Dàyì • Shuāngliú •
Qióngái • Xīnjīn • Jiānyáng •
Pínglè •
Bǎoxīng • Pújiāng • Péngshān •
Ziyáng •
Bìfēngxiá • Míngshān • Méishān •
Yǎ'ān • Dānléng • Rénshòu •
Hóngyǎ •
Qīngshén •
Yíngjīng • Liújiāng •
Jiājiāng •
Jīngyán •
Éméi • Lè Shān **Grand Buddha**
**Éméi Shān** ▲
Wēiyuán •
Chéngdū Map (p232)

## Arriving in Sìchuān

Chéngdū serves as the province's transit hub (see p236 for more information). Smooth expressways to eastern and southern Sìchuān make for short trips to many destinations, but heading north or west is a different story; many roads are in poor shape or are under construction. Weather conditions are unpredictable at high elevations, and hazards ranging from landslides to overturned semis are common.

## Where to Stay

The province has an inspiring variety of sleeping options, from restored courtyard homes and wooden mansions in Chéngdū and the Sìchuān Basin, to Tibetan homestays in the west, and mountain-top temples in between. If you're feeling adventurous, there are also several national parks where you can throw a tent down on the banks of a mountain river and fend for yourself.

Wànnián Temple

BEIBAOKE / SHUTTERSTOCK ©

# Éméi Shān

*A cool, misty retreat from the Sìchuān basin's heat, stunning Éméi Shān (3099m) is one of China's four sacred Buddhist Mountains.*

## Great For...

### ☑ Don't Miss

The views at sunset (and sunrise) from Jīndǐng Temple on the highest peak.

Beyond its rich cultural heritage, the mountain also stands on the edge of the eastern Himalayan highlands and hosts a diverse range of plants and animals.

## Visiting Éméi Shān

Most rewarding is walking the whole way starting from Bàoguó Temple, but most opt to ride to Wànnián depot (for easy access to the cable car) or to Wǔxiǎngǎng depot (an easy walk to poetic Qīngyīn Pavilion and other important sights). The Léidòngpíng bus drops off closest to the summit, just a few hours short of Jīndǐng Peak.

## Wànnián Temple

Reconstructed in the 9th century, **Wànnián Temple** (万年寺; Wànnián Sì; admission ¥10), at 1020m, is the oldest surviving Éméi temple. It's dedicated to the man on the white

Bodhisattva Pǔxián statue, Wànnián Temple

BLEAKSTAR / SHUTTERSTOCK ©

### ℹ️ Need to Know

峨眉山; admission adult/student & seniors ¥185/¥90, winter ¥110/55

### ✕ Take a Break

The unexpected and very welcome **Hard Wok Cafe** (晓雨小餐店; Xiǎoyǔ Xiǎocāndiàn; ⏱hours vary) is one of few that has an English menu.

### ★ Top Tip

The best time to visit is June to October, when the mist burns off by early afternoon.

elephant, the Bodhisattva Pǔxián (also known as Samantabhadra), the Buddhist Lord of Truth and patron of the mountain. Somewhere between Qīngyīn Pavilion and Hóngchūn Píng (Venerable Trees Terrace), you will at some point encounter the mountain's infamous monkeys. Many before you have teased this merry band into grabby monsters.

## Jīndǐng Temple

The magnificent **Jīndǐng Temple** (金顶 寺; Jīndǐng Sì) is at the Golden Summit (Jīndǐng; 3077m), commonly referred to as the mountain's highest peak. This temple is a striking modern renovation, covered with glazed tiles and surrounded by white marble balustrades. The views at sunset and sunrise, as golden light illuminates the clouds below, are a highlight of any visit to Émǎi.

## Getting There

Émǎi town (峨眉山市; Émǎi Shān Shì) is the transport hub, lying 6.5km east of the park entrance. Most buses terminate at Émǎi Shān central station (峨眉山客运中心; Émǎi Shān kèyùn zhōngxīn), opposite Émǎi railway station (峨眉山火车站; Émǎi huǒchēzhàn). The newly finished high-speed-train station (高速列车站; gāosù lièchē zhàn) is closest to Bàoguó Village, around 4km away. A taxi from Émǎi town to Bàoguó Village is about ¥25, or many guesthouses will pick you up if you arrange it in advance. Local bus 8 (¥1) connects the Émǎi town train station with the park entrance.

You cannot travel directly to Bàoguó from most long-distance destinations, although some long-distance buses do leave from Bàoguó including Chéngdū South (¥50, 2½ hours, five daily) and Lè Shān (¥11, 45 minutes, every 30 minutes from 8am to 5.30pm). Trains run from Bàoguó to Chéngdū (C/K&T ¥65/24, 1½ to 2¾ hours, 13 daily) and Lè Shān (C ¥11, 15 minutes, seven daily).

# Lè Shān's Grand Buddha

*With fingernails larger than the average human, the world's biggest ancient Buddha draws plenty of tourists to the relaxed riverside town of Lè Shān (乐山).*

This Unesco World Heritage Site is an easy day trip from Chéngdū or stopover en route to or from Éméi Shān, but the laid-back vibe and newly opened higher-quality accommodation options may convince you to linger.

## History of the Buddha

Lè Shān's serene, 1200-year-old Grand Buddha sits in repose, carved from a cliff face overlooking the confluence of three busy rivers: the Dàdù, Mín and Qīngyì. The Buddhist monk Haitong conceived the project in AD 713, hoping that Buddha would protect the boats and calm the lethal currents.

## Dimensions

At 71m tall, he is indeed grand. His shoulders span 28m, and each of his big toes is

---

**Great For...**

 **Don't Miss**

Getting an up-close look at the head, then descending the steep, winding stairway for the lilliputian view.

Wŭyóu Temple

### ℹ Need to Know

大佛; Dàfó; adult ¥90, students & seniors ¥45; ◷7.30am-6.30pm Apr-early Oct, 8am-5.30pm early Oct-Mar

### ✕ Take a Break

**Sū's Garden** (苏园), just above the entry and exit area to the Buddha, has a cliffside teahouse.

---

### ★ Top Tip

Avoid visiting on weekends and holidays, when traffic on the staircase can come to a complete standstill and queues can top two hours or more.

---

ing an incredible variety of postures and facial expressions.

## Getting There

Lè Shān has three main bus stations, all within 5km of each other. Buses from Chéngdū's Xīnnánmén station usually arrive at **Xiàobà bus station** (肖坝旅游车站; Xiàobà lǚyóu chēzhàn), the main tourist station.

Note: if you're heading to Éméi Shān, it's better to use Xiàobà bus station, as buses from there go all the way to Bàoguó (¥11, 45 minutes, every 30 minutes from 7am to 5pm). Other services from Xiàobà include Chéngdū (¥45, two hours, every 30 minutes from 7am to 7pm) and Éméi Town (¥8, 30 minutes, every 30 minutes from 7.30am to 6pm).

High-speed trains depart Lè Shān for Chéngdū's South and East train stations (¥54, 1¼ hours, 12 daily) and Éméi Shān (¥11, 15 minutes, five daily).

---

8.5m long. His ears are 7m. Their length symbolises wisdom and the conscious abandonment of materialism. Inside the body, hidden from view, is a water-drainage system to prevent weathering, although he is showing his age and soil erosion is an ongoing problem.

### Caves & Temples

Admission to the site also includes access to a number of caves and temples on the grounds, though they are a decent hike from the main attraction. Wŭyóu Temple, like the Buddha, dates from the Tang dynasty, and has Ming and Qing renovations. This monastery contains calligraphy and artefacts, with the highlights in the Luóhàn Hall – 1000 terracotta *arhat* (Buddhist celestial beings, similar to angels) display-

# Chéngdū

Chéngdū (成都) is perennially popular. It could be the relaxing teahouse culture, with favourite local institutions serving the same brews for generations. Maybe it's the lively nightlife, with a strong showing of local partiers bolstered by large student and expat populations. It might just be the food, famous both for heat and history even in this cuisine-rich culture. Then there are the pandas, both the live versions in the local Research Base and the plush, stuffed, cuddly kind for sale on seemingly every street.

## ◉ SIGHTS

### Giant Panda Breeding Research Base
Wildlife Reserve

(大熊猫繁育基地; Dàxióngmāo Fányù Jīdì; ☏028 8351 0033; www.panda.org.cn; 1375 Xiongmao Dadao; 熊猫大道1375号; adult/student ¥58/29; ☺8am-5.30pm) One of Chéngdū's most popular attractions, this reserve 18km north of the city centre is the easiest way to glimpse Sìchuān's most famous residents outside of a zoo. The enclosures here are large and well maintained. Home to nearly 120 giant and 76 red pandas, the base focuses on getting these shy creatures to breed.

March to May is the 'falling in love period' (wink wink). If you visit in autumn or winter, you may see tiny newborns in the nursery.

Try to visit in the morning, when the pandas are most active. Feeding takes place around opening time at 8am, although you'll see them eating in the late afternoon too. They spend most of their afternoons sleeping, particularly during the height of midsummer, when they sometimes disappear into their (air-conditioned) living quarters.

Catch bus 49 (¥2, 40 minutes) and transfer at Zhāojué Hénglù stop (昭觉横路站) to bus 87 (¥2, 20 minutes) to the Panda Base stop (熊猫基地站; Xióngmāo Jīdì). Alternatively, from North train station take bus 9 (¥2, 60 minutes) to the Zoo stop (动物园站; Dòngwùyuán) and switch to 198 (¥2, 20 minutes). Hostels run trips here, too. Metro line 3 will run directly here when it is completed.

From left: Giant panda; Wénshū Temple; Teahouse, People's Park

NELIK / SHUTTERSTOCK ©

TRAVELER1116 / GETTY IMAGES ©

**Wénshū Temple**     Buddhist Temple
(文殊院; Wénshū Yuàn; 66 Wenshuyuan Lu; 文
殊院路66号; ⊗6am-9pm; M1) FREE This
Tang dynasty monastery is dedicated to
Wénshū (Manjushri), the Bodhisattva of
Wisdom, and is Chéngdū's largest and
best-preserved Buddhist temple. The air
is heavy with incense and the low murmur
of chanting; despite frequent crowds of
worshippers, there's still a sense of serenity
and solitude.

**Chéngdū Museum**          Museum
(成都博物馆; Chéngdū Bówùguǎn; www.cd
museum.com; west side of Tiānfǔ Sq; 天府广场
西侧; ⊗9am-5pm Tue-Sun) FREE Spanning
ancient Shu and pre-Qin to the Revolutionary era and modern Chéngdū, this brand-
new five-storey museum is packed with
historical and cultural relics of the city's
past. Don't miss the 'Puppetry and Shadow
Plays of China' gallery on the top floor, with
excellent examples of the art from across
the country.

**People's Park**                    Park
(人民公园; Rénmín Gōngyuán; 9 Citang Jie; 祠堂
街9号; ⊗6.30am-10pm; M2) FREE On weekends, locals fill this park with dancing, song
and taichi. There's a small, willow-tree-lined
boating lake and a number of teahouses:
Hè Míng Teahouse (p233) is the most
popular and atmospheric.

## 🛍 SHOPPING

Fancy-pants shopping centres dot the city,
with the highest concentration around the
**Chūnxī Lù shopping district** (春熙路步行
街; Chūnxīlù Bùxíngjiē; M2) east of Tiānfǔ Sq.
At the south end of town sprawls the **New
Century Global Center** (新世纪环球中心;
Xīn Shìjì Huánqiú Zhōngxīn; ☎028 6273 2888;
1700 Tianfu Bei Dadao; 天府北大道1700号; M1
to Jincheng Square), the world's largest mall.
  For traditional Tibetan shopping options,
try the **shops** (藏族用品一条街; Zàngzú
Yòngpǐn Yītiáo Jiē) in the Tibetan neighbourhood southeast of Wǔhóu Temple.

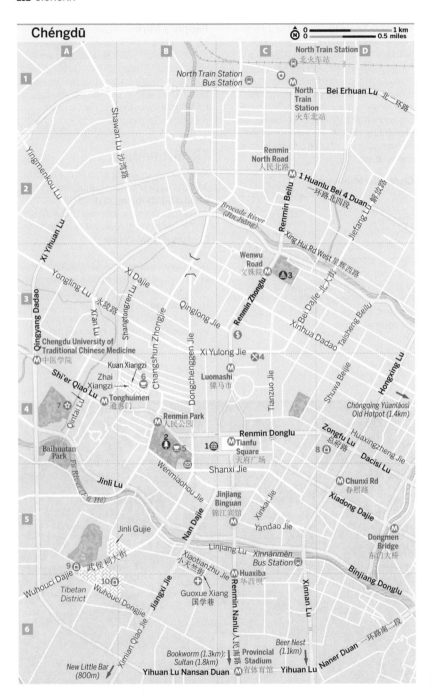

# Chéngdū

0 ————— 1 km
0 ————— 0.5 miles

A | B | C | D

North Train Station
北火车站

North Train Station
Bus Station

North
Train
Station

Bei Erhuan Lu 北二环路

Renmin
North Road
人民北路

1 Huanlu Bei 4 Duan
一环路北四段

North
Train
Station
火车北站

Renmin Beilu

Jiefang Lu 解放路

Xing Hui Rd West 星辉西路

Yingmenkou Lu

Shawan Lu 沙湾路

Brocade River
(Jǐn Jiāng)

Wenwu
Road
文殊院

🔺3

Xi Yihuan Lu

Yongling Lu

Qingyang Dadao

Xi Dajie

Shangtongren Lu

Renmin Zhonglu

Bei Dajie 北大街

Xinhua Dadao

Taisheng Beilu

Hongxing Lu

Xi'an Lu

Qinglong Jie

Changshun Zhongjie

Xi Yulong Jie

✖4

Shuwa Beijie

Chengdu University of
Traditional Chinese Medicine
中医学院

Kuan Xiangzi

Zhai
Xiangzi

🛒6

Dongchengen Jie

Luomashi
骡马市

Tianzuo Jie

Chóngqìng Yúanlǎosi
Old Hotpot (1.4km)

Shi'er Qiao Lu

7🟊

Tonghuimen
通惠门

Renmin Park
人民公园

Renmin Donglu

Tianfu
Square
天府广场

Zongfu Lu 总府路

Huaxingzheng Jie

Qintai Lu

Baihuatan
Park

🅰2
📮5

1🏛️

8🅰

Dacisi Lu

Shanxi Jie

Chunxi Rd
春熙路

Jinli Lu

Wenmiaohou Jie

Nan Dajie

Jinjiang
Binguan
锦江宾馆

Xinkai Jie

Xiadong Dajie

Dongmen
Bridge
东门大桥

Jinli Gujie

Yandao Jie

9🏛️ 武侯祠大街

Linjiang Lu

Xīnnánmén
Bus Station

Binjiang Donglu

10🏛️

Wuhouci Dajie

Wuhouci Dongjie

Jiangxi Jie

Tibetan
District

Xiaotianzhu Jie
小天竺街

Renmin Nanlu人民南路

Huaxiba
华西坝

Xinnan Lu

Guoxue Xiang
国学巷

Ximin Qiao Jie

New Little Bar
(800m)

Bookworm (1.3km);
Sultan (1.8km)

Yihuan Lu Nansan Duan

Beer Nest
(1.1km)

Provincial
Stadium
省体育馆

Yihuan Lu

Naner Duan 一环路南二段

# Chéngdū

Outdoor enthusiasts gearing up for mountains trips should head to **Sanfo Outdoors** (三夫户外; Sānfū Hùwài; ☎028 8507 9586; www.sanfo.com; 243 Wuhouci Dajie; 武侯词大街243号; ◷10am-8.30pm) or **Decathlon** (迪卡侬运动超市; Díkǎnóng Yùndòng Chāoshì; ☎028 8531 0388; 9 Zhanhua Lu, Gaoxin District; 高新区站华路9号; ◷10am-10pm; M1).

## ✴ EATING

Chéngdū has reportedly the highest density of restaurants and teahouses of any city in the world, and is the first city in Asia to be named a Unesco City of Gastronomy, so your most memorable moments here are likely to involve food.

Several monasteries, including Wénshū Temple, have popular vegetarian restaurants that are generally open only for lunch.

### Chén Mápó Dòufu          Sichuan ¥¥

(陈麻婆豆腐; ☎028 8674 3889; 197 Xi Yulong Jie; 西玉龙街197号; mains ¥22-58; ◷11.30am-2.30pm & 5.30-9pm) The plush flagship of this famous chain is a great place to experience *mápó dòufu* (麻婆豆腐; small/large ¥12/20) – soft, house bean curd with a fiery sauce of garlic, minced beef, fermented soybean, chilli oil and Sìchuān pepper. It's one of Sìchuān's most famous dishes and is this restaurant's specialty. Non-spicy choices, too.

### Chóngqìng Yúanlǎosì
### Old Hotpot          Hotpot ¥¥

(重庆袁老四老火锅; Chóngqìng Yúanlǎosì Lǎohuǒguǒ; ☎028 8444 5220; 66 Mengzhuiwan Jie; 猛追湾街66号; pot ¥88, dishes from ¥10; ◷11am-10pm) Though it may seem like sacrilege to eat Chóngqìng-style hotpot in rival Chéngdū, this place is cleaner than most and the flavour and ingredient quality speak for themselves (plus the beer is cold).

### Sultan          Middle Eastern ¥¥¥

(苏坦土耳其餐吧; Sūtǎn Tǔ'ěrqí Cānba; ☎028 8555 4780; 25-12 Fanghua Jie; 芳华街25号附12号; mains from ¥50; ◷noon-11pm; 🛜) Crowd-pleasing fare from the western reaches of the Silk Road, including lamb kebabs, hummus, house-made yoghurt, Turkish coffee, and warm naan. Hook into the free wi-fi outside on the patio, or into a sheesha pipe (¥50) in a private room piled with cushions.

## ● DRINKING & NIGHTLIFE

### Hè Míng Teahouse          Teahouse

(鹤鸣茶馆; Hèmíng Cháguǎn; People's Park; ◷6am-9pm) Always lively, this century-old spot is most pleasant for whiling away an afternoon with a bottomless cup of tea (¥12 to ¥30). Neat tea-pouring performances happen on Saturdays from 2pm to 3pm. Ear cleanings (¥20) available daily.

## The Art of Tea

The art of tea – brewing, serving and savouring – dates back 3000 years, and teahouses have long been the centres of neighbourhood social life. In Chéngdū, they are as they always have been – people gossip, play cards, watch opera, get haircuts and even have their ears cleaned! Try a Sìchuān-grown green tea such as *máofēng* (毛峰), which uses tender, downy tea leaves, or *zhúyèqīng* (竹叶青), which looks like tiny bamboo leaves.

Today you'll find crowded teahouses all over the city, particularly in parks and temple grounds. There are also pleasant ones along the river banks. Tea is generally served by the cup (¥15 to ¥40) and is topped up for free as often as you like, but do note that most places enforce a policy of one cup per person (so no sharing).

Tea ceremony, Chéngdū
OSTILL / SHUTTERSTOCK ©

### Kǎi Lú Lǎo Zhái Cháyuán
Teahouse

(庐恺老宅茶园; ☎180 3041 6632; 11 Kuan Xiangzi; 宽巷子11号; ☺10am-11pm; 🛜) For 200 years, one of the city's most venerable teahouses has been tucked away in a peaceful courtyard behind a stone archway off frenetic Kuan Alley, the distant hum of which is more than countered by the sound of zither music that plays in the background. These days there's wi-fi, but that seems to be about all that has changed. Tea from ¥38; snacks ¥12.

### Bookworm
Cafe

(老书虫; Lǎo Shūchóng; ☎028 8552 0177; www.chengdubookworm.com; 2 Yujie Dongjie, 28 Renmin Nanlu; 人民南路28号、玉洁东街2号; ☺9am-1am) This hopping bookstore-cafe, like its branches in Běijīng and Sūzhōu, is a gathering place for expats and a pleasant spot for a beer or coffee (from ¥30). It also serves decent Western food (mains ¥35 to ¥95), though service can be painfully slow. You can buy or borrow from the English-language section, or stop by for author talks, live music and other events.

### Beer Nest
Bar

(啤酒窝酒吧; Píjiǔ Wō Jiǔbā; ☎151 0836 0121; info@thebeernest.com; 34-7 Jinxiu Li; 锦绣路34号附7号; ☺2pm-late) Owned by a real-life Belgian brewing his own beer, this place is an instant favourite. There's a daily 'Buy-2-Get-1' Happy Hour (2pm to 8pm) and specials every day of the week, but Tuesday (three-beer sampler for ¥40), Thursday (beer pong 8pm to 11pm, free beer!) and Sunday (¥30 craft beers) are among the best. They can also get Tex-Mex delivered (¥15 to ¥38).

## ⊛ ENTERTAINMENT

### Shǔfēng Yǎyùn Teahouse
Sìchuān Opera

(蜀风雅韵; Shǔfēng Yǎyùn; ☎028 8776 4530; www.shufengyayun.net; inside Culture Park; 文化公园内面; tickets ¥140-500; ☺ticket office 3-9.30pm, nightly shows 8-9.30pm) This famous century-old theatre and teahouse puts on excellent 1½-hour shows that include music, puppetry and Sìchuān opera's famed fire breathing and face changing. Come at around 7.15pm to watch performers putting on their elaborate make-up and costumes. For ¥50 to ¥100, kids (and adults) can try on garb and have a costume artist paint their face.

### New Little Bar
Live Music

(小酒馆(芳沁店); Xiǎo Jiǔguǎn (Fāngqìn Diàn); ☎028 8515 8790; http://site.douban.com/littlebar; 47 Yongfeng Lu & Fangqin Jie; 永丰路

Hotpot (p236)

47号丰尚玉林商务港5楼,芳沁街; ⊙6pm-2am)
This small pub-like venue is *the* place in
Chéngdū to catch live local bands; they
play most Fridays and Saturdays, and occasional weekdays, usually from 8pm. Live
music carries a cover charge of around ¥15,
depending on who's playing. Check online
for the schedule.

is among the most well regarded. Foreigners
should head for the International Hospital here,
where doctors and some staff speak English.
Note that some treatments without qualifying
insurance may require a deposit.

# ℹ️ INFORMATION

**Bank of China** (中国银行; Zhōngguó Yínháng;
35 Renmin Zhonglu, 2nd Section; 人民中路二段
35号; ⊙8.30am-5.30pm Mon-Fri, to 5pm Sat &
Sun) The bank's main Chéngdū branch changes
money and travellers cheques, and offers cash
advances on credit cards.

**China Post** (中国邮政; Zhōngguó Yóuzhèng; 151
Wenweng Lu; 文翁路151号; ⊙9am-5pm)

**West China Hospital SCU** (四川大学华西医院;
Sìchuān Dàxué Huáxī Yīyuàn; ☏24hr emergency
assistance in Chinese & English 028 8542 2761,
for appointment 028 8542 2408; http://eng.
cd120.com; 37 Guoxue Xiang; 国学巷37号; 🚌1)
This hospital complex is China's largest and

## Where to Stay

The once-limited hostel scene has
blossomed in recent years. For many
travellers these places will be the best
value and they're also a great way to
meet locals, as more young Chinese are
beginning to travel independently.

The midrange offers private rooms at
affordable rates, but not always in great
locations or with the level of service that
might be expected in other countries.

At the top end, stay in restored historic buildings or luxury properties.

### ¡@¡ Local Specialities

One popular speciality is *chuànchuàn xiāng* (串串香), the skewer version of the famous Chóngqìng hotpot (火锅; *huǒguō*) that is just as spicy. First, choose the broth – usually either *hóng guō* (红锅; spicy) or *yuānyang guō* (鸳鸯锅; half-spicy, half-not) – then your meats, vegetables and whatnot. Skewers generally cost ¥1, platters ¥2. There are restaurants specialising in this quintessential local eating experience all over the city.

*Chuànchuàn xiāng*
JEAN-PAUL GALICHET / GETTY IMAGES ©

## ❶ GETTING THERE & AWAY

### AIR

You can fly directly to **Chéngdū Shuāngliú International Airport** (☏028 8520 5555; www. cdairport.com/front_en/index.jsp), 18km west of the city, from nearly any other major Chinese city in less than three hours. There are also numerous direct international flights into Chéngdū.

From the airport, shuttle buses cover five routes, reaching all corners of the city. A taxi will cost ¥70 to ¥90. Most guesthouses offer airport pick-up services for slightly more.

### BUS

The main bus station for tourists is Xīnnánmén (新南门汽车站; Xīnnánmén qìchēzhàn) – officially the central tourist station; 旅游客运中心.

Destinations from Xīnnánmén bus station include Éméi Shān (¥41, 2½ hours, every 20 minutes from 7.20am to 7.20pm) and Lè Shān (¥49, two hours, every 20 minutes from 7.20am to 7.35pm).

### TRAIN

Chéngdū's two main train stations are Chéngdū North train station (火车北站; *huǒchē běizhàn*) and the newer Chéngdū East train station (火车东站; *huǒchē dōngzhàn*), both of which connect directly to the metro.

Sìchuān's newly completed high-speed train line stops at the airport (双流机场; Shuāngliú *jīchǎng*) on the way to two of the province's major tourist destinations – Lè Shān (2nd/1st class ¥46/55, one hour, six daily) and Éméi Shān (2nd/1st class ¥56/68, one hour, six daily).

## ❶ GETTING AROUND

### BICYCLE

Chéngdū is nice and flat, with designated biking lanes, although the traffic can be a strain for cyclists. Youth hostels rent out bikes for around ¥20 per day.

### METRO

Line 1 links Chéngdū North and South train stations, running the length of Renmin Lu and beyond. East–west Line 2 links Chéngdū East train station with the city centre, meeting Line 1 at Tiānfǔ Sq before continuing west to Chádiànzì bus station.

Line 3, which will run to the Giant Panda Breeding Research Base and Xīnnánmén bus station, and Line 4, for the new Chéngdū West train station, are slated for completion in 2017.

Rides cost ¥2 to ¥6 depending on the distance covered.

### TAXI

Taxis are ¥8 (¥9 from 11pm to 6am) for the first 2km, then ¥1.90 (¥2.20 at night) per kilometre thereafter.

Traditional *biànliǎn*, or face-changing, performance (p234)

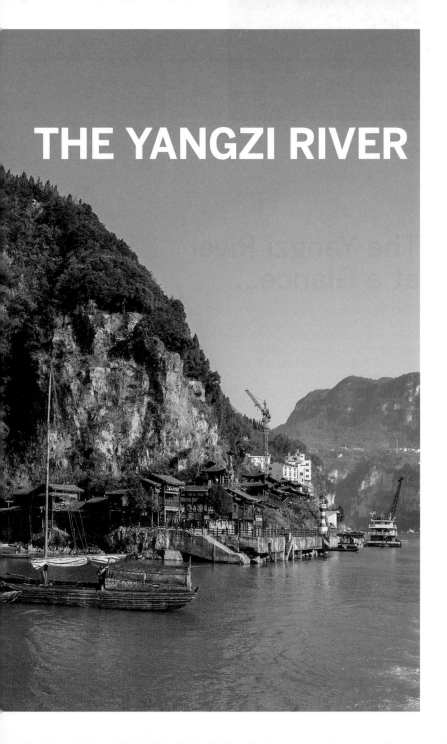

# THE YANGZI RIVER

# The Yangzi River at a Glance...

*Starting life as trickles of snow melt in the Tánggǔlā Shān of south-western Qīnghǎi, the Yangzi River (长江; Cháng Jiāng) then spills from Tibet, swells through seven Chinese provinces, sucks in water from hundreds of tributaries and rolls powerfully into the Pacific Ocean north of Shànghǎi. Taking a boat down the river is all about the journey rather than the destination. It isn't just an escape from marathon train trips and bumpy bus rides, but a chance for contemplation and relaxation as an astonishing panorama slides by at a sedate pace.*

**Two Days on the Yangzi River**

Arrive in **Chóngqìng** (p246) and spend a day exploring the Yangzi River port city, the splendid Buddhist grottoes at **Dàzú** (p252) and **Cíqìkǒu Ancient Town** (p246). Fill up on hotpot at **Liúyīshǒu Huǒguō** (p247). On the second day, get aboard a boat for the journey through the **Three Gorges** (p242). Try to get a ticket for the **Little Three Gorges** (p245), one of the highlights of the journey.

**Four Days on the Yangzi River**

Drift through the **Three Gorges** (p242) – Qútáng Gorge, Wū Gorge and Xīlíng Gorge – heading downstream in the direction of Wǔhàn, Nánjīng and Shànghǎi. After pulling into **Yíchāng** (p250), take a trip to the **Three Gorges Dam** (p251). For dinner, feast on views of Xīlíng Gorge from **Fàngwēng Restaurant** (p251).

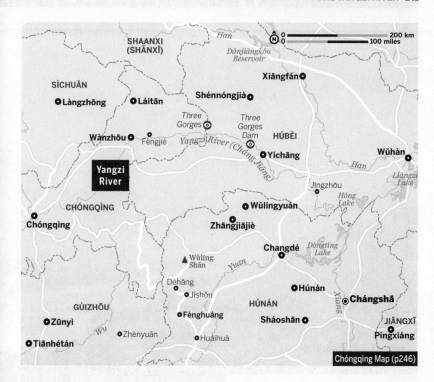

Chóngqìng Map (p246)

## Arriving at the Yangzi River

**Jiāngběi Airport, Chóngqìng** Metro Line 3 runs into the city (¥7, 45 minutes). A taxi is ¥55 to ¥70.

Chóngqìng is the starting (or concluding) point for hugely popular boat cruises through the magnificent Three Gorges. The city has several long-distance bus stations; most buses use Càiyuánbà Bus Station beside the main (old) train station. Chóngqìng's new North Station has fast trains including trains to and from Chéngdū.

## Where to Stay

Chóngqìng has a huge choice of accommodation options, from backpacker hostels to very smart international hotels, although Yíchāng is less well provided. Sleeping options aboard ferries and tourist boats for the journey through the Three Gorges vary from the highly frugal to the very comfortable.

# Cruising the Yangzi River

*Get ready to shift down a gear or two as you float past the awe-inspiring Three Gorges.*

Cruising the Yangzi is a truly unique experience, one that gets you up close with mostly domestic travellers allowing time for real interaction. The journey puts you adrift on China's mightiest – and, at 6300km, the world's third-longest – river.

## The Three Gorges

Apocryphally the handiwork of the Great Yu, a legendary architect of the river, the **Three Gorges** (三峡, Sānxiá) – Qútáng, Wū and Xīlíng – commence just east of Fèngjié in Chóngqìng province and level out west of Yíchāng in Húběi province, a distance of around 200km. The principal route for those cruising the Yangzi River is therefore between the cities of Chóngqìng and Yíchāng.

The route can be travelled in either direction, but most passengers journey

## Great For...

☑ **Don't Miss**

The Little Three Gorges – a splendid diversion from the main sweep, but book ahead.

Yangzi River

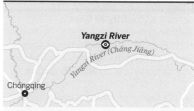

### ⓘ Need to Know

In Chóngqìng or Yíchāng, most hotels, hostels and travel agents can sell you a Three Gorges trip.

### ✖ Take a Break

Top-end cruises feature daily buffet meals, tourist boats have restaurants serving standard Chinese fare, while passenger boats have Chinese-style canteens.

### ★ Top Tip

April and May have the best weather, with fewer crowds than summer.

Effects of the Three Gorges Dam

The dwarfing chasms of rock, sculpted over aeons by the irresistible volume of water, are the Yangzi River's most fabled stretch. Yet the construction of the controversial and record-breaking **Three Gorges Dam** (三峡大坝; Sānxiá Dàbà) cloaked the gorges in as much uncertainty as their famous mists: have the gorges been humbled or can they somehow shrug off the rising waters?

In brief, the gorges have been undoubtedly affected by the rising waters. The peaks are not as towering as they once were, nor are the flooded chasms through which boats travel as narrow and pinched. The effect is more evident to seasoned boat hands or repeat visitors. For first-timers the gorges still put on a dramatic show.

## Chóngqìng to Wànzhōu

Passing the drowned town of **Fúlíng** (涪陵), the first port of call is at **Fēngdū** (丰都),

downstream from Chóngqìng. Travelling upstream does ensure a less crowded boat, but somehow feels less dramatic.

The gorges these days can get mixed press. To some, the gorges' dramatic appearance can become rather repetitive, especially overlong Xīlíng Gorge (Xīlíng Xiá). The reservoir built up behind the Three Gorges Dam – a body of water almost the length of England – has certainly taken its toll as much more is now inundated. If you don't expect to swoon at every bend in the river, however, journeying downriver is a stimulating and relaxing adventure, not least because of the change of pace and perspective.

The only ticket truly worth buying in advance is for the popular and worthwhile Little Three Gorges tour, which is often full.

170km from Chóngqìng city. Long nicknamed the **City of Ghosts** (鬼城; Guǐchéng), the town is just that: inundated in 2009, its residents were moved across the river. This is the stepping-off point for crowds to clamber up **Míng Mountain** (名山; Míng Shān; adult ¥120, cable car ¥20), with its theme-park crop of ghost-focused temples.

Drifting through the county of Zhōng-zhōu, the boat takes around three hours to arrive at **Shíbǎozhài** (石宝寨, Stone Treasure Stockade; adult ¥70; ⊗8am-4pm) on the northern bank of the river. A 12-storey, 56m-high wooden pagoda built on a huge, river-water-encircled rock bluff, the structure dates to the reign of Qing dynasty emperor Kangxi (1662–1722).

Most morning boats moor for the night at partially inundated **Wànzhōu** (万州; also

called Wànxiàn). Travellers aiming to get from A to B as fast as possible while taking in the gorges can skip the Chóngqìng to Wànzhōu section by hopping on a 3½-hour bus and then taking a passenger ship from the Wànzhōu jetty.

## Wànzhōu to Yíchāng

The ancient town of **Fèngjié** (奉节), capital of the state of Kui during the periods known as the 'Spring and Autumn' (722–481 BC) and 'Warring States' (475–221 BC), overlooks Qútáng Gorge, the first of the three gorges.

**Qútáng Gorge** (瞿塘峡; Qútáng Xiá), also known as Kui Gorge (夔峡; Kuí Xiá), rises dramatically into view, towering into huge vertiginous slabs of rock, its cliffs jutting out in jagged and triangular chunks. The shortest and narrowest of the

Qútáng Gorge (p242)

three gorges, 8km-long Qútáng Gorge is over almost as abruptly as it starts, but is considered by many to be the most awe-inspiring.

After Qútáng Gorge the terrain folds into a 20km stretch of low-lying land before boats pull in at the riverside town of **Wūshān** (巫山), situated high above the river. Most boats stop at Wūshān for five to six hours so passengers can transfer to smaller boats for trips along the **Little Three Gorges** (小三峡, Xiǎo Sānxiá; ticket

¥200) on the **Dàníng River** (大宁河; Dàníng Hé).

Back on the Yangzi River, boats pull away from Wūshān to enter the penultimate Wū Gorge, under a bright-red bridge.

**Wū Gorge** (巫峡; Wū Xiá) – the Gorge of Witches – is stunning, cloaked in green and carpeted in shrubs, its sides frequently disappearing into ethereal layers of mist.

At 80km, **Xīlíng Gorge** (西陵峡; Xīlíng Xiá) is the longest and perhaps least spectacular gorge; sections of the gorge in the west have been submerged.

Apart from the top-end luxury cruises, tour boats no longer pass through the monumental **Three Gorges Dam**, although many tours offer the option of a visit to the dam by bus. The passenger ferries and hydrofoils tend to finish (or begin) their journey at **Tàipíng Creek Port** (太平溪港; Tàipíngxī Gǎng), upstream from the dam. From here, two types of shuttle bus wait to take you into Yíchāng (one hour).

## Best Top-End Cruises

◦ **Viking River Cruises** (www.vikingriver cruises.com; from US$3010) Very luxurious cruise, offering five-day cruises from Chóngqìng to Wǔhàn, as part of a larger 13-day tour of China.

◦ **Century Cruises** (www.centuryrivercruises. com; from US$450) Claims to be the most luxurious cruise service on the Yangzi. Ships are new, service is first class and facilities are top notch.

◦ **Victoria Cruises** (www.victoriacruises.com; from US$550) Comfortable four-day trips between Chóngqìng and Yíchāng. Older boats than some other operators, but has excellent English-speaking guides.

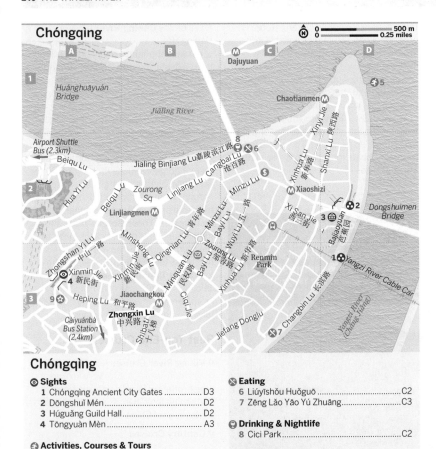

# Chóngqìng

# Chóngqìng

## ◉ SIGHTS

Chóngqìng is not especially heavy on world-class sights. Those that do exist are spread fairly evenly around the city.

### Cíqìkǒu Ancient Town    Old Town

(磁器口古镇; Cíqìkǒu Gǔzhèn; Shapingba; Ciqikou, exit 1) The opportunity to snatch a glimpse of old Chóngqìng makes it worth riding out to Shapingba district, on the Jiālíng River west of the centre. Through the archway that is the entrance to the

town, most of the buildings in this sprawling complex – many dating to the late Ming dynasty – have been restored. The main drag can feel like a carnival, complete with candied fruits and neon fairy wands for sale, especially on weekends, but away from the central street, a living, working village remains.

### Húguǎng Guild Hall    Museum

(湖广会馆; Húguǎng Huìguǎn; ☎6393 0287; Dongshuimen Zhengjie; 东水门正街; admission ¥30; ◷9am-5pm; MXiaoshizi) You could spend several hours poking around the beautifully restored buildings in this gorgeous museum complex, which once served as a community headquarters for immigrants from the Hú (Húnán and Húběi) and Guǎng (Guǎngdōng and Guǎngxī) provinces, who arrived in Chóngqìng several hundred years ago. There are rooms filled with artwork and furniture, a temple, a teahouse and several stages for Chinese opera performances.

### Chóngqìng Ancient City Gates
Ruins

(古城门; Gǔchéngmén) Sadly, only fragments remain of Chóngqìng's once magnificent Ming dynasty city wall, which stretched 8km around the Jiěfàngbēi peninsula and was more than 30m tall in places. Of the 17 gates that punctuated the wall before demolition began in 1927, two are still standing. The charming, moss-hewn **Dōngshuǐ Mén** (东水门) is on a pathway beside the Yangtze River Hostel. Larger, and partly restored is **Tōngyuán Mén** (通远门; ⓂQixinggang, exit 1), a short walk from Qixinggang metro station.

## 🅕 TOURS

Chóngqìng looks best from the water, especially at night when the city flashes with neon. The so-called two-river cruises last for 60 to 90 minutes, leaving every afternoon (2pm to 3pm) and evening (7pm to 8pm) from Cháotiānmén Dock, and can be a fun way of getting an alternative view of this unique metropolis

### Cháotiānmén Cruise Boat
Boating

(朝天门; Cháotiānmén; Chaotianmen Guang-chang; 朝天门广场; evening cruise ¥158) This company is a popular choice for cruising the rivers in ye olde boats. Tours are less than two hours.

## 🅧 EATING

Chóngqìng is all about hotpot (火锅; huǒguō): a fiery cauldron of head-burning làjiāo (辣椒; chillies) and mouth-numbing

huājiāo (花椒; Sìchuān peppers) into which is dipped deliciously fresh ingredients, from vegetables and tofu to all types of fish and meat. It's a dish best sampled with a group. Indeed, hotpot restaurants tend to be among the liveliest you'll find.

### Liúyīshǒu Huǒguō
Hotpot ¥

(刘一手火锅; ☏023 6161 8555; 46 Cangbai Lu, 3rd fl; 沧白路46号南国丽景大夏3楼; dipping ingredients ¥5-34; ⊗10am-midnight; ⓂXiaoshizi) The hotpot here is excellent, and the atmosphere is congenial, but the real attraction is the view; you dine as you gaze out across the Jiālíng River. You'll be pushed to find a river-view table at peak eating times, so perhaps come earlier or later than you'd usually eat. Take the lift to the right of Motel 168.

### Suzie's Pizza
Pizza ¥¥

(苏蕊比; Sū Ruǐ Bǐ; ☏023 6531 2929; Three Gorges Square, 12/f UME Bldg; room 27 沙坪坝三峡广场玄地广场; pizza from ¥28-55; ⊗11am-10pm; ⓂShapingba) English-speaking Suzie makes what many regard as the best pizza in town. The location, in a renovated apartment on the 12th floor of a residential tower, adds to the charm, as do the fake brick walls and pictures of loyal customers chowing down on cheesy, gooey pies. To get here, enter the building lobby to the right of the McDonald's in Shapingba's Three Gorges Square, and go to the second elevator lobby to get to the 12th floor.

---

### 🛎 Where to Stay

Chóngqìng has an enormous variety of sleeping options, from top-end international brands to backpacker hostels. Since the city attracts relatively few tourists, prices vary little throughout the year. Jiěfàngbēi is the most central neighbourhood for sightseeing and eating; many of the best 'deals' on hotels found online mean you'll wind up in a far-flung business district.

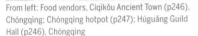

From left: Food vendors, Cíqìkǒu Ancient Town (p246), Chóngqìng; Chóngqìng hotpot (p247); Húguǎng Guild Hall (p246), Chóngqìng

### Zēng Lǎo Yāo Yú Zhuāng
Hotpot ¥¥

(曾老幺鱼庄; ☑023 6392 4315; Changbin Lu; 长滨路 (洞子邮亭鲫鱼); mains from ¥38-68; ☺24hr) Outside, it's a seething mass of people crowded around tables. Inside, it's even more packed as you descend into a former bomb shelter – white-tiled walls and a rock roof. This Chóngqìng institution is a unique, utilitarian dining experience, with all strata of society in search of the signature fish dish (鲫鱼; jìyú; carp) and the simply sublime spare ribs (排骨; páigǔ).

## 🍺 DRINKING & NIGHTLIFE

There are a string of riverside bars (酒吧; jiǔbā), cafes and restaurants on Nan'an Binjiang Lu (南岸滨江路); take the cable car over the Yangzi, then walk down to the river and turn left. From there, walk 15 minutes along the river or hop on any bus for one stop. Note: the cable car stops running at 10pm.

### Cici Park
Bar

(西西公园; Xīxī Gōngyuán; 1/F Hongyadong, Jiabin Lu; 洪崖洞, 嘉滨路; beer from ¥15; ☺5pm-late; Ⓜ Xiaoshizi) The most amenable bar in Chóngqìng, Cici's has a very chilled vibe and bohemian furnishings. Beers are affordable, mixers start at ¥30 and sometimes there are DJs and live music. It attracts a mixed crowd of both locals and expats, some of whom like to roll their own cigarettes.

## ⭐ ENTERTAINMENT

### Chóngqìng Sìchuān Opera House
Theatre

(重庆市川剧院; Chóngqìngshì Chuānjùyuàn; ☑6371 0153; 76 Jintang Jie; 金汤街76号; tickets ¥20; ☺2pm Sat) Holds a 2½-hour performance of Sìchuān opera every Saturday afternoon.

BLEAKSTAR / SHUTTERSTOCK ©

# ℹ️ INFORMATION

**China International Travel Service** (CITS; 中国
国际旅行社; Zhōngguó Guójì Lǚxíngshè; ☏023
6383 9777; www.cits.net; 8th fl, 151 Zourong
Lu; 邹容路151号; ⏱9.30am-5.30pm Mon-Fri)
Friendly English-speaking staff can arrange train
tickets, flights and Three Gorges cruises.

**China Post** (中国邮政; Zhōngguó Yóuzhèng;
Minquan Lu; 民权路; ⏱9am-6pm; Ⓜ Jiaochang-
kou) You can top up your Chinese phone and buy
SIM cards at the China Mobile store (open 9am
to 9pm) on the 1st floor.

# ℹ️ GETTING THERE & AWAY

## AIR

Chóngqìng's Jiāngběi Airport (重庆江北飞机
场) lies 25km north of the city centre, and is
connected to the metro system. Direct flights
include Běijīng, Kūnmíng, Shànghǎi and Xī'ān.

Metro Line 3 goes from the airport (机场;
jīchǎng) into town (¥7, 45 minutes, 6.22am to
10.30pm). Note that the metro is signposted as
'light rail' (轻轨; qīngguǐ) at the airport.

The **airport shuttle bus** (机场大巴, jīchǎng
dàbā; Shangqingsi Lu; ¥15, 45 min) meets all arriving planes and takes you to Meizhuanxiao Jie
(美专校街), a small road off Zhongshan Sanlu
(中山三路), via a couple of stops in the north
of the city. Bus 461 goes from Zhongshan Sanlu
to Chaotianmen (朝天门). To get to the metro,
turn left onto Zhongshan Sanlu and go straight
over the large roundabout. Niujiaotuo (牛角沱)
station will be on your left.

Shuttle buses going to the airport run from
6am to 8pm.

A taxi is ¥55 to ¥70.

## BOAT

Chóngqìng is the starting point for hugely popular cruises down the Yangzi River through the
magnificent Three Gorges.

## BUS

Chóngqìng has several long-distance bus
stations, but most buses use **Càiyuánbà bus
station** (菜园坝汽车站; Càiyuánbà qìchēzhàn;
Ⓜ Lianglukou) beside the main (old) train station.
There is no English spoken nor English signage,

so you're best off buying tickets via an agency or a hostel. Destinations include Chéngdū (¥98, four hours, hourly 6.30am to 8.30pm) and Dàzú (¥43, 2½ hours, every 30 minutes 7am to 7pm).

Buses for Jiāngjīn (¥24, 70 minutes, every 30 minutes 7am to 9pm) and Fèngjié (¥160, four to five hours, hourly 7.30am to 8.30pm), where you can catch the Three Gorges ferry, leave from **Lóngtóusì bus station** (龙头寺汽车站; Lóngtóusì qìchēzhàn), which is on metro Line 3 (station name: 龙头寺; Longtousi).

### TRAIN

New, faster trains, including the D class 'bullet' train to and from Chéngdū, use Chóngqìng's new **North station** (重庆北站; Chóngqìng běizhàn; Kunlun Dadao; 昆仑大道), but some others, such as the train to Kūnmíng use the older train station at Càiyuánbà (菜园坝). There is no English in the stations, so if you don't speak Chinese, try buying tickets ahead via an agency or hostel.

Destinations include Běijīng West (hard sleeper ¥393, 23 to 31 hours, five daily), Chéngdū East (hard seat from ¥97, 1½ to two hours, 20 daily), Guìlín (hard sleeper ¥270, 20 hours, one daily), Kūnmíng (hard sleeper from ¥245, 18 to 19 hours, three daily), Shànghǎi (hard sleeper from ¥510, 28 to 40 hours, three daily) and Xī'ān (hard sleeper from ¥184, 10 to 11 hours, three daily).

### ❶ GETTING AROUND

#### BUS

Local bus fares are ¥1 or ¥2.

#### METRO

Chóngqìng's part-underground, part-overground metro system has four lines and links the Jiěfàngbēi peninsula with many parts of the city, including the airport and the two train stations. Fares are ¥2 to ¥10 and trains run 6.30am to 11.30pm.

#### TAXI

Taxi flagfall is ¥10. A taxi from Jiěfàngbēi to Shapingba should cost around ¥45.

## Yíchāng

Yíchāng (宜昌) is a small, compact city known as the culmination point for many a Three Gorges cruise. It's a remarkable feel-

From left: Yangzi River (p242); Xīlíng Gorge (p242); Three Gorges Dam

VIEW STOCK / GETTY IMAGES ©

BLEAKSTAR / SHUTTERSTOCK ©

ing to glide through this iconic geological formation and quickly becomes the highlight for many travellers to China. There is not a lot to do for the waylaid traveller in Yíchāng – other than get psyched for, or decompress from, the boat trip – but the Yangzi offers an attractive backdrop to the unpretentious urban hum and a vibrant street-food scene.

## ◉ SIGHTS

### Three Gorges Dam          Architecture

(三峡大坝; Sānxiá Dàbà; ¥105) The huge, hulking Three Gorges Dam is the world's largest dam due to its length (2.3km) rather than its height (101m), and while it isn't the most spectacular dam, it is worth a peek. You can't walk on it, but there's a tourist viewing area to the north. The view from the south is much the same, and free.

Take a bus from the long-distance station to Máopíng (茅坪; ¥15, 8.30am to 3pm), but get off at Bālù Chēzhàn (八路车战). Alternatively, bus 8 (¥20, one hour, 8am to 4pm) leaves from Yíchāng's east train station.

Day trips can also be taken by boat (¥280 including entrance fee and lunch) from the old ferry port (老码头; lǎo mǎtóu). Boats leave at 7.30am and return around 5pm. Buy tickets from Yangtze River International Travel at the port.

## ✖ EATING

### Xiǎo Hú Niú          Hubei ¥

(小胡牛; 73 Shangshu Xiang, Běimén; 北门尚书巷73号; ingredients ¥8-26; ⊘4pm-2am) Our favourite restaurant in Běimén specialises in a local beef hotplate called xiǎo hú niú. Order that first, stipulating how spicy you want your beef (¥25 for 250g) or lamb (¥26 for 250g) – mild (微辣; wēi là), medium (中辣; zhōng là) or hot (麻辣; mǎ là) – before ordering other raw ingredients to fry with it on your hotplate.

### Fàngwēng Restaurant          Hubei ¥¥

(放翁酒家; Fàngwēng Jiǔjiā; ☑0717 886 2179; Nanjin Guan Sanyoudong Bridge; 南津关三游洞桥头; dishes ¥60-160; ⊘9am-9.30pm) At Xīlíng Gorge (西陵峡; Xīlíng Xiá), 12km north of Yíchāng, is a peculiar restaurant perched

## ⌐⃗⌐ Dàzú Buddhist Caves

Two hours from Chóngqìng, some 50,000 Buddhist cliff carvings and statues dating as far back as the 9th century are scattered amid the flat countryside. A Unesco World Heritage Site, **Dàzú** (大足石窟; Dàzú Shíkū) is a fascinating stop for anyone interested in Chinese art and history. It's also simply impressive for having survived the Cultural Revolution intact, largely because of its isolation.

You can visit the carvings independently, though getting to some of the smaller sites is challenging for non-Chinese speakers, or join a group tour from Chóngqìng. Be aware that the tours, which run about ¥200, include several stops at 'museums' where you'll be given the hard sell on buying products like locally made knives.

Dàzú is usually visited as a day trip from Chóngqìng. If you plan to stay overnight, there are several hotels in Dàzú city, though many don't accept foreigners.

Buddha statues
SUDALIM / SHUTTERSTOCK ©

precariously against a cliff. Claimed to be the ninth 'cave restaurant' in the world, the cuisine is distinctly Húběi, the service brisk and the view quite amazing. Taxis know it well (for about ¥80 one way).

## 🍷 DRINKING & NIGHTLIFE

A handful of reasonable bars are found in the streets parallel to the river.

## ℹ️ INFORMATION

**China International Travel Service** (CITS; 中国国际旅行社; Zhōngguó Guójì Lüxíngshè; ☎0717 625 3088; www.cits.net; Yunji Lu; 云集路; ⊗8am-6pm) Sells luxury cruises (from ¥2800) and tourist boat tickets (¥880 to ¥900) to Chóngqìng, but not hydrofoil tickets. Some English is spoken.

**Three Gorges Tourist Centre** (三峡游客中心; Sānxiá Yóukè Zhōngxīn; ☎0717 696 6116; Yanjiang Dadao; 沿江大道; ⊗7am-8pm) Commission-free, so cheaper than CITS. Sells hydrofoil tickets to Fèngjié (¥245) plus passenger ferry tickets to various destinations between Yíchāng and Chóngqìng. Minimal English is spoken, but staff members are helpful. Enter the modern tourist centre (no English sign) and head to the ticket counters at the far right of the building.

**Yangtze River International Travel** (宜昌长江国际旅行社; Yíchāng Chángjiāng Guójì Lüxíngshè; ☎0717 692 1808; Yanjiang Dadao; 沿江大道; ⊗7am-8pm) Marginally cheaper than CITS for ordinary tourist-boat tickets to Chóngqìng (from ¥890). Also sells luxury cruises. Housed inside the Three Gorges Tourist Centre, but has a separate desk beside the passenger-boat ticket counters.

## ℹ️ GETTING THERE & AROUND

### AIR

Daily flights from Three Gorges Airport (三峡机场; Sānxiá Jīchǎng) include Běijīng, Guǎngzhōu, Shànghǎi and Xī'ān.

Airport shuttle buses (¥20, 50 minutes) run to and from the Qīngjiāng building (清江大

厦; Qīngjiāng *dàshà*), leaving two hours before outgoing flights and meeting all incoming flights.

## BUS

There are three main long-distance bus stations: Yíchāng long-distance bus station (长途汽车站; *chángtú qìchēzhàn*), plus one at the east train station and one at the old ferry port. All are modern and well run, and offer very similar bus services. Services from the Yíchāng long-distance bus station include Wǔhàn (Wǔchāng) (¥78 to ¥110, 4½ hours, every hour from 7am to 8pm).

Local buses cost ¥1.

## TRAIN

Yíchāng's East train station (火车东站; *huǒchē dōngzhàn*) is the station that almost all trains use. Train tickets (¥5 service charge) can also

## Where to Stay

Yíchāng has a few good business hotels, especially near the river.

be bought at window 1 of Yíchāng long-distance bus station. Destinations include Běijīng West (G train 2nd/1st class ¥606/931, eight hours, four daily), Chéngdū (D train 2nd/1st class ¥259/311, seven hours, 11 daily, with some to Chéngdū East), Chóngqìng North (D train 2nd/1st class ¥162/195, four hours, regular), Shànghǎi Hóngqiáo (D train 2nd/1st class ¥348/416, eight hours, six daily), Wǔhàn (D train 2nd/1st class ¥96/116, 2½ hours, regular) and Xī'ān (hard sleeper ¥200, 11 hours, daily).

Chóngqìng (p246)

# GĀNSÙ &
# THE SILK ROAD

# Gānsù & the Silk Road at a Glance...

*Synonymous with the Silk Road, the slender province of Gānsù (甘肃) flows east to west along the Héxī Corridor, the gap through which goods and ideas once streamed between China and Central Asia. The constant flow of commerce left Buddhist statues, beacon towers, forts, chunks of the Great Wall and ancient trading towns in its wake. Alongside an astonishing ethnic and cultural diversity, Gānsù also offers an entrancingly rich geographic diversity, with eerie deserts, colossal dunes and wide grasslands.*

## Two Days in Gānsù & the Silk Road

Pass through **Lánzhōu** (p270) and jump on a bus to Xiàhé to spend the night in the monastery town. Devote the next day to exploring **Labrang Monastery** (p260) before returning to Lánzhōu for dinner at **Mǎzilù Beef Noodles** (p272) then preparing for the journey northwest to Jiāyùguān and Dūnhuáng .

## Four Days in Gānsù & the Silk Road

Travel from Lánzhōu to **Jiāyùguān** (p268) to journey beyond town to its namesake **fort** (p262) and to explore sections of the **Great Wall** (p263); spend the night in town. Continue on to **Dūnhuáng** (p264) to visit the outstanding **Mògāo Grottoes** (p258) and the awe-inspiring **Singing Sands Dune** (p264), followed up with a sundowner on the rooftop at **Zhāixǐng Gé** (p266).

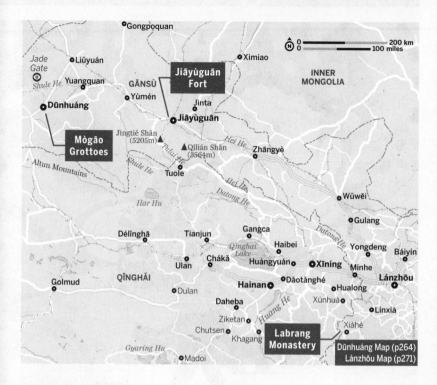

## Arriving in Gānsù & the Silk Road

**Lánzhōu Zhōngchuān Airport** Take a shuttle bus to the centre (¥30, one hour, hourly), or an intercity train to Lánzhōu Station (40 to 50 minutes, ¥21.50 to ¥26) or Lánzhōu West Railway Station (30 to 40 minutes, ¥18.50 to ¥22), both of which serve the Lánzhōu–Xīnjiāng high-speed rail line.

**Dūnhuáng Airport** Take a taxi to town (¥40, 20 minutes).

## Where to Stay

There is a wide variety of accommodation options in Gānsù, ranging from international-quality hotels in the larger cities such as Lánzhōu, to backpacker hostels and even no-frills sand-dune camping in Dūnhuáng. Accommodation is mostly in 2- and 3-star Chinese-style hotels, where private or shared bathrooms are available. In many smaller towns, it's customary to ask to see a room before committing.

Mural, Northern Wei caves

ZORAZHUANG / GETTY IMAGES ©

# Mògāo Grottoes

*The stunning Mògāo Grottoes are considered one of the most important collections of Buddhist art in the world.*

## Great For...

### ☑ Don't Miss

Visiting as many caves as you can; of the 492 grottoes, 20 'open' caves are rotated fairly regularly.

Wealthy traders and important officials were the primary donors responsible for creating new caves, as caravans made the long detour past Mògāo to pray or give thanks for a safe journey through the treacherous wastelands to the west. The traditional date ascribed to the founding of the first cave is AD 366.

The caves fell into disuse for about 500 years after the collapse of the Yuan dynasty and were largely forgotten until the early 20th century, when they were 'rediscovered' by a string of foreign explorers.

## Northern Wei, Western Wei & Northern Zhou Caves

These, the earliest of the Mògāo Caves, are distinctly Indian in style and iconography. All contain a central pillar, representing a stupa (symbolically containing the ashes of

Pagoda

KEITH LEVIT / SHUTTERSTOCK ©

**ⓘ Need to Know**

莫高窟; Mògāo Kū; www.mgk.org.cn/index.
htm; low/high season ¥120/220; ⊘8am-6pm
May-Oct, 9am-5.30pm Nov-Apr

**✗ Take a Break**

You'll need to return to Dūnhuáng to
find a restaurant or cafe.

**★ Top Tip**

Advance purchase of tickets is necessary. Go to the Mògāo Grottoes Reservation and Ticket Center (p267) in
Dūnhuáng when you arrive.

Some 230 caves were carved during the
religiously diverse Tang dynasty, including
two impressive grottoes containing enormous, seated Buddha figures.

the Buddha), which the devout would circle
in prayer. Paint was derived from malachite
(green), cinnabar (red) and lapis lazuli
(blue), expensive minerals imported from
Central Asia.

## Tang Caves

The Tang dynasty (AD 618–907) was
Mògāo's high point, when the site housed
18 monasteries, more than 1400 monks
and nuns, and countless artists, translators
and calligraphers. Painting and sculpture
techniques became much more refined, and
some important aesthetic developments,
notably the sex change (from male to
female) of Guanyin and the flying apsaras,
took place. The beautiful murals depicting
the Buddhist Western Paradise offer rare
insights into the court life, music, dress and
architecture of Tang China.

## Tours

Tours by excellent English-speaking guides
at 9am, noon and 2.30pm are included in
the admission price, and you should be
able to arrange tours in other languages as
well. Many of the guides are students or re-
searchers at the Dūnhuáng Academy, which
administers the caves.

## Getting to the Caves

The Mògāo Grottoes are 25km (30 minutes)
southeast of Dūnhuáng, but tours start and
end at the visitor centre, about 5km from
Mingshan Lu near the train station. A green
minibus (one way ¥3) leaves for the visitor
centre every 30 minutes from 8am to 5pm
from outside the **Silk Road Hotel** (丝路宾馆;
Sīlù Bīnguǎn). A taxi costs ¥15 one way, and
taxis generally wait outside the visitor centre,
so it's easy to find one on the way back.

BOISVIEUX CHRISTOPHE / HEMIS.FR / GETTY IMAGES ©

# Labrang Monastery

*With its succession of squeaking prayer wheels (3km in total), hawks circling overhead, and the throb of Tibetan longhorns resonating from the surrounding hills, Labrang is a monastery town unto itself.*

## Great For...

☑ **Don't Miss**

The inner *kora*, which brings the monastery alive to visitors as a place of devout pilgrimage.

Many of the monastery's chapel halls are illuminated in a yellow glow by yak-butter lamps, their strong-smelling fuel scooped out from voluminous tubs. Even if Tibet is not on your itinerary, the monastery sufficiently conveys the mystique of its devout persuasions, leaving indelible impressions of a deeply sacred domain.

## The Main Buildings

The only way to visit the interior of the most important buildings is on a tour (no photos allowed inside buildings), which generally includes the Institute of Medicine, the Manjushri Temple, the Serkung (Golden Temple) and the main Prayer Hall (Grand Sutra Hall), plus a museum of relics and yak-butter sculptures.

English-language **tours** (per person ¥40) leave the monastery's ticket office around

Prayer wheels

BEIBAOKE / SHUTTERSTOCK ©

### ❶ Need to Know

拉卜楞寺; Lābǔléng Sì; Renmin Xilu; 人民西
路; tour ¥40

### ✕ Take a Break

Pop into **Nirvana Restaurant & Bar**
(德古园; Dégǔyuán; ☎0941 718 1702; 247
Yagetang; 雅鸽塘247号; dishes ¥15-35;
⊙9am-9pm; 🅿🛜) for Tibetan dishes,
liquid refreshment and a fine vibe.

### ★ Top Tip
It's best to show up at around 6am
or 7am, when the monks come out to
pray and chant.

10.15am and 3.15pm most days, and
although they give you plenty to see, they
can feel a bit rushed.

Outside these times you can latch on to
a Chinese tour, with little lost even if you
don't understand the language, but be
aware you must purchase the ¥40 ticket
to gain entrance to any of the building
interiors. At dusk the hillside resonates with
the throaty sound of sutras being chanted
behind the wooden doors.

### Other Buildings

The rest of the Labrang can be explored
by walking the inner *kora* (pilgrim path).
Although many of the temple halls are
padlocked shut, there are a couple of separate smaller chapels you can visit, though
they can often be closed for unexplained
reasons. Some charge admission. Among

the most popular are the three-storey
**Barkhang** (人民西路; admission ¥10), the
monastery's traditional printing temple, as
well as the **Hall of Hayagriva** (马头明王殿;
Mǎtóu Míngwáng Diàn, Hall of Horsehead Buddha;
人民西路; admission ¥10) with its enchanting
murals, and the golden **Gòngtáng Pagoda**
(贡唐宝塔; Gòngtáng Bǎotǎ, Gòngtáng Chörten;
人民西路; admission ¥20), which offers
incredible views over the whole monastery
from its roof.

Access to the rest of the monastery area
is free, and you can easily spend several
hours just walking around and soaking up
the atmosphere in the endless maze of
mud-packed walls. The Tibetan greeting
in the local Amdo dialect is *Cho day mo?*
('How do you do?') – a great icebreaker.

The best morning views of the monastery come from the Thangka Display Terrace, a popular picnic spot, or the forested
hills south of the main town.

# Jiāyùguān Fort

*One of the classic images of western China, this fort once guarded the narrow pass between the snowcapped Qílián Shān peaks and the Hēi Shān (Black Mountains) of the Mǎzōng Shān range.*

## Great For...

### ☑ Don't Miss

Photographing the fort against the backdrop of snowcapped mountains.

You approach Jiāyùguān (嘉峪关) through the forbidding lunar landscape of north Gānsù. It's a fitting setting, as Jiāyùguān marks the symbolic end of the Great Wall, the western gateway of China proper and, for imperial Chinese, the beginning of the back of beyond. One of the defining points of the Silk Road, a Ming dynasty fort was erected here in 1372 and Jiāyùguān came to be colloquially known as the 'mouth' of China, while the narrow Héxī Corridor, leading back towards the *nèidì* (inner lands), was dubbed the 'throat'.

Built in 1372, the fort was named the 'Impregnable Defile Under Heaven'. Although the Han Chinese often controlled territory far beyond here, this was the last major stronghold of imperial China – the end of their 'civilised world', beyond which lay only desert demons and the barbarian armies of Central Asia.

Jiāyùguān Museum of the Great Wall

SURA ARK / GETTY IMAGES ©

**Jiāyùguān Fort** ⊚

Jiāyùguān ●

Jiǔquán ●

## ⓘ Need to Know

嘉峪关城楼; Jiāyùguān Chénglóu; Guancheng Nanlu; 关城南路; admission ¥120; ⊙8.30am-8pm, to 6pm in winter

## ✕ Take a Break

Grab a noodle lunch from one of the small stands that line the entryways to Jiāyùguān Fort and the Overhanging Great Wall.

## ★ Top Tip

With the exception of the Wèijìn Tombs (p269), all the sites are covered by purchasing a through ticket (通票; *tōngpiào*) to Jiāyùguān Fort

## The Gates of the Fort

Towards the eastern end of the fort is the **Gate of Enlightenment** (光化楼; Guānghuá Lóu) and on the west side is the **Gate of Conciliation** (柔远楼; Róuyuǎn Lóu), from where exiled poets, ministers, criminals and soldiers would have ridden off into oblivion. Each gate dates from 1506 and has 17m-high towers with upturned flying eaves and double gates that would have been used to trap invading armies. On the inside are horse lanes leading up to the top of the inner ramparts. The fort received major refurbishments in 2015, brightening up wood with coats of paint and reinforcing foundations and cracked walls.

## Jiāyùguān Museum

Located inside Jiāyùguān Fort, the excellent **Jiāyùguān Museum of the Great Wall**

(嘉峪关长成博物馆; Jiāyùguān Chángchéng Bówùguǎn; incl in through ticket to Jiāyùguān Fort; ⊙8.30am-6pm) FREE contains photos, artefacts, maps, Silk Road exhibits and models to show just how the fort and the Great Wall of China influenced the history of the Héxī Corridor and China as a whole.

## Overhanging Great Wall

Running north from Jiāyùguān Fort, this section of the **Great Wall** (悬壁长城; Xuánbì Chángchéng; adult ¥21, incl in through ticket to Jiāyùguān Fort; ⊙8.30am-8pm, to 6pm winter) is believed to have been first constructed in 1539, though it was reconstructed in 1987. It's quite an energetic hike up the equivalent of 55 flights of stairs to excellent views of the desert and the glittering snowcapped peaks in the distance (though views can be a little mired by Jiāyùguān's increasingly polluted air). The Wall is about 9km north of the fort.

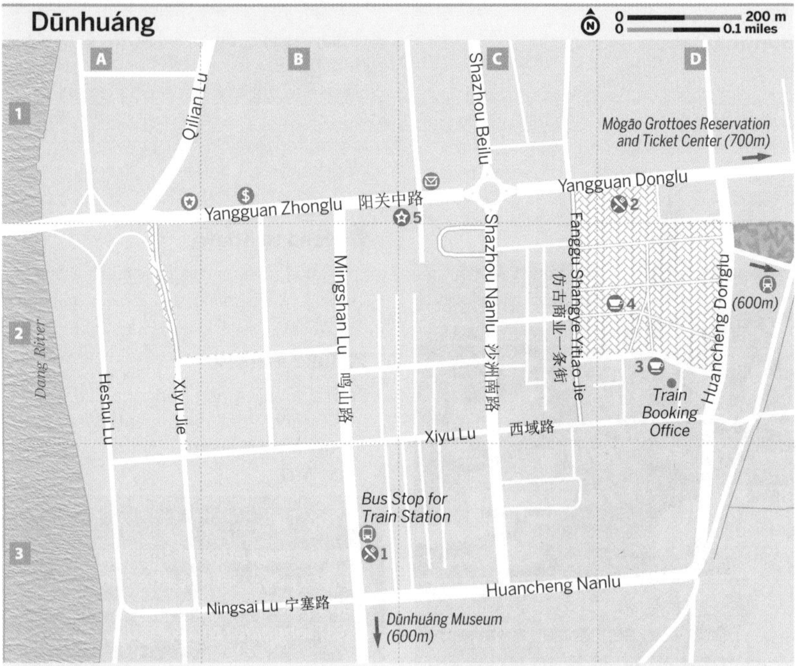
Dūnhuáng
0 200 m
0 0.1 miles
A
B
C
D
1
2
3
Qilian Lu
Mògāo Grottoes Reservation and Ticket Center (700m)
Shazhou Beilu
Yangguan Zhonglu 阳关中路
Yangguan Donglu
Fanggu Shangye Yitiao Jie 仿古商业一条街
Mingshan Lu 鸣山路
Shazhou Nanlu 沙洲南路
Huancheng Donglu
(600m)
Train Booking Office
Dang River
Heshui Lu
Xiyu Jie
Xiyu Lu 西域路
Bus Stop for Train Station
Huancheng Nanlu
Ningsai Lu 宁塞路
Dūnhuáng Museum (600m)

## Dūnhuáng

**Eating**
1 Charley Johng's Cafe .......... B3
2 Shāzhōu Night Market .......... D1

**Drinking & Nightlife**
3 Brown Sugar Cafe .......... D2
4 Memory Box Cafe .......... D2

**Entertainment**
Dūnhuáng Goddess .......... (see 5)
5 Dūnhuáng Theatre .......... C1

## Dūnhuáng

### SIGHTS

**Singing Sands Dune** Oasis

(鸣沙山; Míngshā Shān; admission ¥120; 6am-7.30pm) Six kilometres south of Dūnhuáng at Singing Sands Dune, the desert meets the oasis in most spectacular fashion. From the sheer scale of the dunes, it's easy to see how Dūnhuáng gained its moniker, 'Shāzhōu' (Town of Sand). The view across the undulating desert and green poplar trees below is awesome.

You can cycle to the dunes in 20 minutes from the centre of Dūnhuáng. Bus 3 (¥2) shuttles between Shazhou Lu and Mingshan Lu and the dunes from 7.30am to 9pm. A taxi costs ¥20 one way.

**Jade Gate Pass** Historic Site

(玉门关, Yùmén Guān & 阳关, Yáng Guān; Jade Gate ¥60, South Pass ¥40) The Jade Gate Pass, 78km west of Dūnhuáng, was originally a military station, and together with **Sun Pass** (阳关; Yángguān; admission ¥50; 8am-8pm), formed part of the Han dynasty series of beacon towers that extended to the garrison town of Lóula'n in Xīnjiāng. Admission includes entry to a section of Han dynasty Great Wall (101 BC), impressive for its antiquity and lack of restoration; and the ruined city walls of Hécāng Chéng, 15km down a side road.

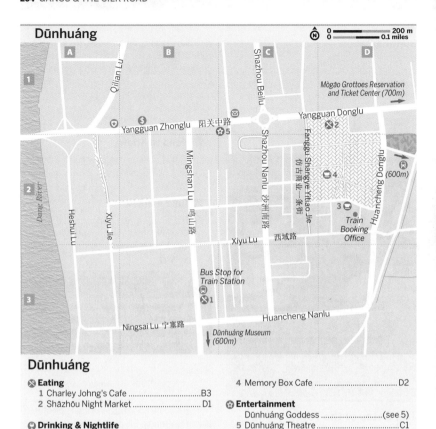

## Western Thousand Buddha Caves
Buddhist Site

(西千佛洞; Xī Qiānfó Dòng; admission ¥40; ⊙8.30am-5pm) Located 35km west of Dūn-huáng, there are 16 caves hidden in the cliff face of the Dǎng Hé gorge, ranging from the Northern Wei to the Tang dynasties. Take an afternoon departure to witness a glorious desert sunset. You will need to arrange a private driver to take you here, or enquire at Charley Johng's Cafe for current bus tours.

## Yǎdān National Park
Desert

(雅丹国家地质公园; Yǎdān Guójiā Dìzhì Gōngyuán; admission ¥120; ⊙8am-5.30pm) The weird, eroded desert landscape of Yǎdān National Park is 180km northwest of Dūnhuáng, in the middle of the Gobi Desert's awesome nothingness. A former lake bed that eroded in spectacular fashion some 12,000 years ago, the strange rock formations provided the backdrop to the last scenes of Zhang Yimou's film *Hero*. Tours (included in the price) are confined to group minibuses (with regular photo stops) to preserve the natural surrounds, but the desert landscape here is so dramatic you will still feel like you're at the ends of the Earth.

To get to Yǎdān you have to pass through (and buy a ticket to) the Jade Gate and Sun Passes. The best way to get here is to take one of two daily minibus tours (¥100 per person): the first departs at 7am and can be booked through Charley Johng's Cafe; the other leaves at 12.30pm and is organised through the **Shazhouyi International Youth Hostel** (敦煌沙州驿国际 青年旅舍; Dūnhuáng Shāzhōuyì Guójì Qīngnián Lǚshě; ☑0937 880 8800; 8 Qilian Lu; 祁连路8号 – 北辰市场对面). Tour prices don't include entrance fees to the individual sights. The 10- to 12-hour tours include a stop at the Jade Gate and Sun Passes and the Western Thousand Buddha Caves.

## Dūnhuáng Museum
Museum

(敦煌博物馆; Dūnhuáng Bówùguǎn; ☑0937 882 2981; Mingshan Lu; ⊙8am-6pm) FREE Outside of town on the road to Singing Sands Mountain is this sparkling museum

that takes you on an artefact-rich journey through the Dūnhuáng area (from pre-historic to Qing dynasty times) via hallways designed to make you feel as if you were in a cave. You can easily walk here in 15 minutes from the centre of town. Bring your passport for admission.

## ☞ TOURS

Ask at any hostel or Charley Johng's Cafe for tourist info; they can also help with tours, from camel treks to overnight camping excursions and day trips. Bus tours (¥100) that include visits to Yǎdān National Park and Jade Gate Pass and Sun Pass depart daily from Dūnhuáng and can also be arranged at Charley Johng's. Be aware you'll have to pay for admission to each site separately during the tour.

## ✖ EATING

### Charley Johng's Cafe
Breakfast, Chinese ¥

(风味餐馆; Fēngwèi Cānguǎn; ☑0937 388 2411; Mingshan Lu; 名山路; dishes ¥6-36; ⊙8am-10pm; 🛜) Tasty Western-style breakfasts including scrambled eggs, muesli with yoghurt, and pancakes are available all day either à la carte or as a set. There are also sandwiches, and a host of Chinese dishes such as stir-fries and dumplings. They also arrange daily tours to surrounding sights, including Yǎdān National Park (p265),

---

### Where to Stay

Competition among Dūnhuáng's hotels is fierce, and you should get significant discounts (50% or more) outside of summer.

There are a dozen or so smaller business-type hotels along Mingshan Lu and Yangguan Zhonglu. They tend to be around ¥200 in the low season and ¥300 to ¥400 in the height of summer.

From left: Western Thousand Buddha Caves (p265); Detail of a dragon mural; Singing Sands Dune (p264) and Cresent Lake

and are a good source of traveller information. English spoken.

### Zhāixīng Gé
Chinese, International ¥¥

(摘星阁; Silk Road Dūnhuáng Hotel; Dunyue Lu; dishes ¥18-38; ☺7am-1pm & 4.30pm-midnight) Part of the Silk Road Dūnhuáng Hotel, this rooftop restaurant is ideal for a meal (the Western buffet breakfast is excellent) or a sundowner gazing out over the golden sand dunes. Dishes do not cost much more than places in town. Try the Uighur bread or the surprisingly good thick-crust pizza.

### Shāzhōu Night Market
Market ¥¥

(沙洲夜市; Shāzhōu Yèshì; btwn Yangguan Donglu & Xiyu Lu; ☺morning-late) Extending from Yangguan Lu south to Xiyu, this market is both a place to eat and to socialise, night and day. Off Yanguang Donglu are dozens of well-organised stalls with English signs: expect Sìchuān, Korean noodles, dumplings, claypot, barbecue including *ròujiāmó* (肉夹馍; pulled-pork sandwich) and Lánzhōu noodles. Also look out for cooling cups of *xìngpíshuǐ* (杏皮水; apricot juice; ¥5).

### 🍷 DRINKING & NIGHTLIFE

The streets around Shāzhōu Night Market, particularly the ones near Dūnhuáng Mosque, have cafes that also serve as bars in the evening. In summer, the **Silk Road Dūnhuáng Hotel** (敦煌山庄; Dūnhuáng Shānzhuāng; ☎0937 888 2088; www.dunhuang resort.com; Dunyue Lu; 敦月路) hosts a **beer garden** (丝路酒坊; Sīlù Jiǔfáng; ☺12.30-4pm & 6pm-1am) at the entrance to the grounds, while their stylish rooftop Zhāixīng Gé offers peerless views over the desert to go with a beer or a glass of local ice wine.

### Memory Box Cafe
Cafe, Bar

(时光盒子咖啡馆; Shíguāng Hézi Kāfēi Guǎn; ☎0937 8819911; room 106A, 7th Bldg, Fengqing City; juice ¥25, beer ¥15) This comfy cafe serves a range of drinks and Chinese and Western snacks, including Illy coffee and some imported beers. They also have a few nice seats out front in warmer weather.

### Brown Sugar Cafe
Cafe

(黑糖咖啡; Hēitáng Kāfēi; ☎0937 881 7111; 28 Tianma Jie; 天马街28号; tea ¥25-38, bottle of wine ¥78-198; ☺1pm-midnight; 🛜) This friend-

LUCA FEBRAIO / 500PX ©

ly cafe mixes modern with crafty decor and cafe classics with a Dūnhuáng twist. Try a cup of fresh-leaf Chinese tea to balance out a sweet black-rice muffin. Things turn smoky at night when fashionable locals come to sip beer and Mògāo wine.

## ⭐ ENTERTAINMENT

**Dūnhuáng Goddess**          Theatre
(敦煌神女; Dūnhuáng Shénnǚ; Dūnhuáng Theater, Yangguan Zhonglu; 敦煌大剧院阳关中路; ticket ¥220; ⏱8.30pm) An 80-minute acrobatic dramatisation of stories on the walls of the Mògāo Grottoes. It's held at the Dūnhuáng Theatre (敦煌大剧院; Dūnhuáng Dàjùyuàn); English subtitles are provided.

## ℹ INFORMATION

**Bank of China** (中国银行; Zhōngguó Yínháng; Yangguan Zhonglu; 阳关中路; ⏱8am-noon & 2-6pm Mon-Fri) Has a 24-hour ATM.

**China Post** (中国邮政; Zhōngguó Yóuzhèng; Yangguan Donglu; 阳关中路; ⏱8.30am-6pm daily) Sells stamps and delivers packages internationally.

**Mògāo Grottoes Reservation and Ticket Center** (莫高窟参观预约售票中心; Mògāo Kū Cānguān Yùyuē Shòupiào Zhōngxīn; Yangguan Dadao; 阳关大道迎宾花园北区15号楼102号)

## ℹ GETTING THERE & AWAY

### AIR

Apart from November to March, when there are only flights to/from Lánzhōu and Xī'ān, there are regular flights to/from Běijīng, Lánzhōu, Shàng-hǎi, Ürümqi and Xī'ān from Dūnhuáng Airport. Seats can be booked at the air ticket office in the lobby of the Yóuzhèng Bīnguǎn hotel (邮政宾馆), on Yangguan Donglu west of China Post.

The airport is 13km east of town; a taxi to/from the airport costs ¥40 and takes 20 minutes.

### BUS

From Dūnhuáng's **bus station** (长途汽车站; Zhángtú qìchēzhàn; ☏0937 885 3746; Xiyu Lu; ⏱7am-8pm daily), you can catch buses to Jiāyùguān and Lánzhōu (though trains are cheaper and faster), as well as to Golmud (¥99, nine hours, two daily), Liǔyuán (¥20, three hours, eight daily) and Ürümqi (sleeper ¥198, 14 hours, daily; may stop in Turpan).

## TRAIN

Dūnhuáng's station is 10km east of town, but for some destinations, such as Běijīng West and Ürümqi, you'll have to leave from Liǔyuán station, a crazy 180km away. Destinations include Jiāyùguān (seat/hard sleeper ¥53/112, 4½ hours, seven daily), Lánzhōu (hard/soft sleeper ¥141/276, 14 hours, three daily; more trains leave from Liǔyuán station), Turpan (from Liǔyuán station; hard/soft sleeper ¥93/184, six to eight hours; high-speed trains go to Turpan North) and Ürümqi (from Liǔyuán station; hard/ soft sleeper/high-speed 2nd-class seat ¥112/219/247, five to nine hours; high-speed trains leave from Liǔyuán South).

Tickets can be booked at the **train booking office** (火车票发售点; *huǒchē piào fāshòu diǎn*; Tianma Jie; 天马街; ⊘8am-noon & 1-4pm, to 8pm summer) **south of the mosque.**

##  GETTING AROUND

The train station is 14km from the centre of town, on the same road as the airport. Bus 1 runs to the train station from the bus stop on Mingshan Lu from 7.30am to 9pm.

If you are heading to Liǔyuán train station (for trains to Ürümqi and high-speed rail), catch a bus or shared taxi (per person ¥45) from the front of the bus station. Give yourself at least three hours to get to Liǔyuán station (including waiting time for the taxi to fill up with other passengers).

You can rent bikes from travellers' cafes for ¥5 per hour, while taxis around town start at ¥5.

## Jiāyùguān

## ⊙ SIGHTS

### First Beacon Platform of the Great Wall          Historic Site

(长城第一墩; Chángchéng Dìyī Dūn; admission ¥22, incl in through ticket to Jiāyùguān Fort; ⊘8.30am-8pm, to 6pm winter) Atop a 56m-

Market food, Jiāyùguān

MARTIN MOOS / GETTY IMAGES ©

high cliff overlooking the Tǎolài River south of Jiāyùguān, a crumbling pile of packed earth is all that remains of this beacon platform, believed to be the first signalling tower along the western front of the Great Wall. Views over the river and bare gorge below are impressive and you can walk alongside attached vestiges of adobe Ming-era Great Wall.

### Wèijìn Tombs
Tomb

(新城魏晋壁画墓; Xīnchéng Wèijìn Bìhuàmù; admission ¥35; ☉8.30am-8pm) These tombs date from approximately AD 220–420 (the Wei and Western Jin periods) and contain extraordinarily fresh brick-wall paintings (some ineptly retouched) depicting scenes of everyday life, from making tea to picking mulberries for silk production. There are thousands of tombs in the desert 20km east of Jiāyùguān, but only one is currently open to visitors, that of a husband and wife.

 **EATING**

### Jìngtiě Market
Market ¥

(镜铁小吃城; Jìngtiě Xiǎochīchéng; Xinhua Zhonglu; 新华中路; ☉10am-10pm) At this busy market, load up on lamb kebabs, *ròujiāmó* (肉夹馍; pork sandwiches), beef noodles, roast duck and more. There are a handful of small restaurants on the north side of the market that offer sit-down meals.

### Yuànzhōngyuàn Restaurant
Sichuanese ¥¥

(苑中苑酒店; Yuànzhōngyuàn Jiǔdiàn; Jingtie Xilu; 镜铁西路; dishes ¥15-50; ☉9am-9pm) Directly across from the bus station on the far side of a small park is this pleasant Sìchuān restaurant. Try its *gōngbǎo jīdīng* (宫保鸡丁; spicy chicken and peanuts), *tiěbǎn dòufu* (铁板豆腐; fried tofu) or a *yúxiāng ròusī* (鱼香肉丝; stir-fried pork and vegetable strips).

 **DRINKING & NIGHTLIFE**

There is very little in the way of nightlife in Jiāyùguān, apart from the night markets.

 **Where to Stay**

Jiāyùguān's hotel landscape is rather bland, with a number of just-fine business- or international-style hotels lining its main streets. There is a very clean, friendly outlet of the popular Jǐnjiāng Inn (锦江之星; Jǐnjiāng Zhīxīng) chain on Lanxin Lu.

These are the best places to find a beer. A few Chinese-style bars and nightclubs line Xinhua Nanlu across from the stadium (体育场; tǐyùchǎng).

 **INFORMATION**

**Bank of China** (中国银行; Zhōngguó Yínháng; 42 Xinhua Zhonglu; 新中中路42号; ☉9.30am-5.30pm Mon-Fri, 10am-4pm Sat & Sun) Has an ATM and can change money. It's south of Lanxin Xilu intersection.

**China Post** (中国邮政; Zhōngguó Yóuzhèng; Xinhua Zhonglu; 新华中路; ☉8am-6pm) Doubles as a train ticket booking office.

**ICBC** (工商银行; Gōngshāng Yínháng; 1493 Xinhua Zhonglu; 新华中路1493号) Has a 24hr ATM.

**People's No 1 Hospital** (第一人民医院; Dìyī Rénmín Yīyuàn; 26 Xinhua Zhonglu) This hospital can only be used by Chinese nationals.

 **GETTING THERE & AWAY**

### AIR

Jiāyùguān has an airport with flights to Běijīng, Shànghǎi and Lánzhōu, but most people arrive by bus or train.

### BUS

Jiāyùguān's **bus station** (嘉峪关汽车站; Jiāyùguān qìchēzhàn; 312 Lanxin Xilu; 兰新西路312号) is by a busy four-way junction on Lanxin Xilu, next to the main budget hotels. It is cheaper and quicker to take a train, but bus destinations include Dūnhuáng, Lánzhōu, Wǔwēi and Zhāngyè.

## TRAIN

Jiāyùguān has two train stations. The main train station (嘉峪关站; Jiāyùguān *zhàn*) is south-west of the town centre. Bus 1 runs here from Xinhua Zhonglu (¥1). A taxi costs ¥10.

Jiāyùguān South station (嘉峪关南站; Jiāyùguān *nánzhàn*) serves the high-speed rail line that connects Lánzhōu to Xīnjiāng. It is located 8km southeast of the town centre. A taxi costs ¥30.

Direct trains to Dūnhuáng are labelled as such. Beware of the more frequently scheduled trains to Liǔyuán – a lengthy 180km away from Dūnhuáng. Train tickets can be booked in town at the post office (p269) on Xinhua Zhonglu. Destinations include Dūnhuáng (seat/hard sleeper ¥53/112, five hours), Lánzhōu (seat/hard sleeper ¥98/201, six to eight hours; high-speed 2nd-class seat ¥215, five hours) and Ürümqi (hard/soft sleeper ¥287/449, 10 to 14 hours; high-speed 2nd-class seat ¥336, 6½ hours).

## ⓘ GETTING AROUND

Bus 1 (¥2) runs from the train station to the bus station. A taxi to the airport (25 minutes) costs ¥50.

A taxi to all the sights in the area, which are all outside town, is likely to cost ¥240, or ¥60 per sight. A taxi just to the sites covered by the Jiāyùguān Fort (p262) ticket will cost ¥180. Touts ply the train and bus stations offering rides; bargain hard. Alternately, most hotels can arrange a taxi to pick you up, which takes the hassle out of having to bargain for the price.

## Lánzhōu

Sandwiched between mountains, the city of Lánzhōu sprawls in an east–west concrete melange for more than 20km along the banks of the Yellow River. There are some attractive neighbourhoods along the northwest, and a pleasant riverside promenade, but travellers moving onward to other places in Gānsù may find them-selves spending a lot of time around the train station, where there is an assortment of hotels and eateries.

## ◉ SIGHTS

### Gānsù Provincial Museum
Museum

(甘肃省博物馆; Gānsù Shěng Bówùguǎn; ☏0931 233 9131; www.gansumuseum.com; 3 Xijin Xilu; 西津西路3号; ⊙9am-5pm Tue-Sun) **FREE** This museum has an intriguing collection of Silk Road artefacts with English descriptions, including inscribed Han dynasty wooden tablets used to relay messages along the Silk Road, and dinosaur skeletons.

The graceful Eastern Han (25 BC–AD 220) bronze horse galloping upon the back of a swallow is known as the 'Flying Horse of Wǔwēi'. Unearthed at Léitái near Wǔwēi, it has been proudly reproduced across northwestern China. Bring your passport for admission.

Take bus 1 (¥1, 40 minutes) here from Lánzhōu train station.

### White Pagoda Temple
Buddhist Site

(白塔寺; Báitǎ Sì; White Pagoda Park, Binhe Zhonglu; 白塔山公园滨河中路; ⊙7am-8pm) **FREE** This temple, built during the Yuan dynasty (1206–1368) for a fallen Tibetan monk, stands on a hilltop in **White Pagoda Park** (白塔山公园; Báitǎ Shān Gōngyuán) on the northern bank of the Yellow River and provides excellent city and river views on a clear day. Enter from a gate on the north side of Zhōngshān Bridge and walk up the stairs or catch the **cable car** (黄河索道; huánghé suǒdào; down/up/return adult ¥25/35/45, child ¥10/15/20; ⊟34) on the south side a few blocks to the east.

### White Cloud Temple
Taoist Temple

(白云观; Báiyún Guān; Binhe Zhonglu; 宾河中路; admission ¥10; ⊙7am-6.30pm) Founded in the 8th century, this largely rebuilt Taoist tem-ple features five halls and was among the most important Quanzhen order temples during the Qing dynasty.

### Water Wheel Park
Historic Site

(水车园; Shuǐchē Yuán; Binhe Donglu; 宾河东路; ⊙8am-6pm, to 8pm summer) **FREE** Lánzhōu is the only city centre that the Yellow River flows through and these massive wooden

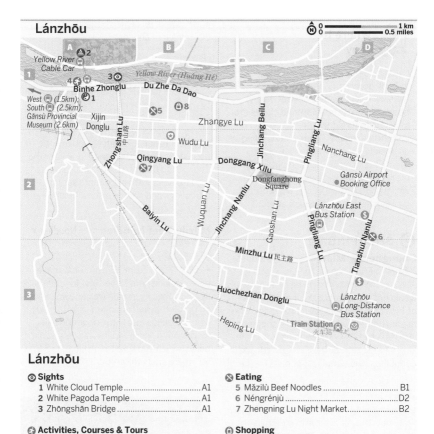

# Lánzhōu

⊙ **Sights**

| | |
|---|---|
| 1 White Cloud Temple | A1 |
| 2 White Pagoda Temple | A1 |
| 3 Zhōngshān Bridge | A1 |

⊕ **Activities, Courses & Tours**

| | |
|---|---|
| 4 Lánzhōu Beach | A1 |

⊗ **Eating**

| | |
|---|---|
| 5 Mǎzilù Beef Noodles | B1 |
| 6 Néngrénjù | D2 |
| 7 Zhengning Lu Night Market | B2 |

⊜ **Shopping**

| | |
|---|---|
| 8 Chénghuáng Miào | B1 |

copies of irrigation devices give a taste of what once lined the banks. They have been turned into a pleasant, if small, riverside park. A few kilometres east, look for a larger collection of about a dozen wheels.

Sheep-skin rafting (one way ¥60) is available from inside the park.

### Zhōngshān Bridge                    Bridge

(Zhōngshān Qiáo; 中山桥; Zhongshan Lu; 中山路) FREE OK, so it's not the world's most beautiful bridge, but it's a Lánzhōu landmark and, when backlit by White Pagoda

Temple each evening, the Yellow River never looked better.

## ⊕ ACTIVITIES

### Lánzhōu Beach          Water Sports

(兰州河滩; Lánzhōu Hétān; btwn Yellow River & Binhe Zhonglu; 宾河中路) FREE Not so much a beach as a dirt embankment, this riverside area is bursting on weekends with volleyball games, kites, speedboats and coracle (lambskin) raft trips (¥30 to ¥40) across the river.

# Where to Stay

Lánzhōu can be a frustrating place to book accommodation, especially if you're travelling on a budget. Many budget hostels and midrange places are off limits to foreigners, including some nationwide chains. Often, places billed as hostels are actually private apartments that have been fitted out with bunk beds. There is a useful branch of Jǐnjiāng Inn (锦江之星; Jǐnjiāng Zhīxīng) on Tianshui Nanlu if you get stuck.

## SHOPPING

### Chénghuáng Miào                    Antiques

(城隍庙; City God Temple; 202 Zhangye Lu; 张掖路202号; ☉9am-6pm daily) The gods probably would not approve, but this former house of Taoist worship has been turned into one of Lánzhōu's most atmospheric shopping venues. Vendors sell everything from Mao kitsch to tea sets, pottery, woodwork and antiquities. The temple is set back on the north side of Buxingjie (pedestrian-only), 500m east of Zhongshan Lu.

## EATING

Lánzhōu is famous for its *niúròu lāmiàn* (牛肉拉面), beef soup with hand-pulled noodles and a spicy topping. There are plenty of places to try the dish, including on Huochezhan Xilu (left as you exit the train station) and Dazhong Xiang near the Zhōngshān Bridge (p271). These streets are also lined with restaurants serving dumplings and noodle dishes. Most have picture menus.

### Mǎzilù Beef Noodles            Noodles ¥

(马子禄牛肉面; Mǎzilù Niúròu Miàn; ☎0931 845 0505; 86 Dazhong Xiang; 大众巷86号; noodles ¥7; ☉6.30am-2.30pm) Locals have been flocking here since 1954 for steaming bowls of the city's most well-known export: spicy hand-pulled noodles (拉面; *lāmiàn*). Join the queue inside the door and ask for *niúròu miàn* (牛肉面). You'll be given a ticket, which you take to the kitchen counter where chefs will prepare your noodles

From left: White Pagoda Temple (p270); Great Wall near Jiāyùguān (p268); Traditional water wheels (p270)

fresh. Grab chopsticks from machines at the ticket counter.

### Zhèngníng Lù
### Night Market                     Market ¥
(正宁路小吃夜市; Zhèngníng Lù Xiǎochī Yèshì; Zhengning Lu; 正宁路; lamb sticks ¥1) One of Lánzhōu's best night markets, this small pedestrian street is lined with vendors on both sides cooking up all manner of Silk Road delights. The mix of Huí, Han and Uighur stalls offer everything from goat's-head soup to steamed snails, *ròujiābǐng* (肉夹饼; mutton served inside a 'pocket' of flat bread), lamb dishes seasoned with cumin, *dàpán jī* (大盘鸡; large plate of spicy chicken, noodles and potatoes), dumplings, spare-rib noodles and more.

### Néngrénjù                        Hotpot ¥¥
(能仁聚; 216 Tianshui Nanlu; 天水南路216号; hotpot from ¥35; ☉11am-10pm) At this Běijīng-style *shuàn yángròu* (涮羊肉; traditional lamb hotpot) restaurant, the pot of broth costs ¥25, after which you can add sliced mutton (¥30), greens (¥10) and various other dishes. The restaurant is about 100m past the intersection with Minzhu Lu.

## 🍷 DRINKING & NIGHTLIFE

Much of Lánzhōu's nightlife is centred on its night markets, which heave with people, especially at weekends. Vendors ply the markets with bottles of the local beer and spirits.

Several permanently docked 'beer boats' line the banks of the Yellow River near Zhōngshān Bridge (p271). These open-air boats are pleasant places to while away an afternoon or evening sipping on a Huang He beer on its eponymous river.

## ℹ️ INFORMATION

**Bank of China** (中国银行; Zhōngguó Yínháng; 525 Tianshui Nanlu; 天水南路525号; ☉9am-5pm) Has a 24-hour ATM.

**China Post** (中国邮政; Zhōngguó Yóuzhèng; 381 Huochezhan Donglu; 火车站东路381号; ☉9am-5pm) Look for the green China Post sign to your right as you exit the train station.

**ICBC** (中国工商银行; Zhōngguó Gōngshāng Yínháng; 475 Dingxi Nanlu; 定西南路475号) Has a 24-hour ATM

Lánzhōu noodles (p272)

# ℹ️ GETTING THERE & AWAY

## AIR

Lánzhōu Zhōngchuān Airport has flights to Běijīng, Dūnhuáng, Jiāyùguān, Kūnmíng, Shànghǎi and Xī'ān. **Gānsù Airport Booking Office** (甘肃机场集团售票中心; Gānsù Jīchǎng Jítuán Shòupiào Zhōngxīn; ☑0931 888 9666; 616 Donggang Xilu; 东岗西路616号; ⏲9am-6pm) can book all air tickets at discounted prices.

The airport is 70km north of the city. Airport shuttle buses (¥30, one hour) leave hourly from 5.30am to 7pm in front of the Gānsù Airport Booking Office on Donggang Xilu, near the **JJ Sun Hotel** (锦江阳光酒店; Jǐnjiāng Yángguāng Jiǔdiàn; ☑0931 880 5511; 589 Donggang Xilu; 东岗西路589号). A taxi costs around ¥150.

A high-speed intercity rail line opened in 2015 connecting the airport with Lánzhōu's main railway station (¥21.50 to ¥26, 40 to 50 minutes) and Lánzhōu West railway station (¥18.50 to ¥22, 30 to 40 minutes), where you can get high-speed rail connections to Jiāyùguān.

## BUS

Lánzhōu has several bus stations, all with departures for Xīníng. The **main long-distance bus station** (兰州汽车站; Lánzhōu qìchē zhàn; 129 Pingliang Lu; 平凉路129号) is just a ticket office, outside which you catch a shuttle bus 30 minutes before departure for the **East bus station** (汽车东站; qìchē dōngzhàn; ☑0931 841 8411; 276 Pingliang Lu; 平凉路276号). Most bus journeys back into Lánzhōu end up at the east bus station; if you want to rough it on a sleeper to Zhāngyè or Jiāyùguān, buy a ticket directly at that station.

Journeys to and from the south of Gānsù, including to Xiàhé, go through the South bus station (汽车南站; qìchē nánzhàn). A taxi to the train station costs ¥45 and takes 45 minutes, or take bus 111 (¥1).

The service to Xiàhé (¥75, four hours, five daily) departs from the South bus station. Frustratingly tickets can only be purchased there, though can be bought just before departure.

*Lánzhōu is the only city centre that the Yellow River flows through*

Note: there is no direct bus from Lánzhōu to Lángmùsì. Go to Hézuò and change.

### TRAIN

Lánzhōu is the major rail link for trains heading to and from western China. The city has two train stations: the centrally located Lánzhōu station (兰州火车站; Lánzhōu *huǒchē zhàn*) and Lánzhōu West railway station (兰州火车西站; Lánzhōu *huǒchē xīzhàn*). Both stations serve the Lánzhōu–Xīnjiāng high-speed rail line and airport trains, though the most frequent departures go from Lánzhōu station.

In high season, buy your onward tickets at least a couple of days in advance to guarantee a sleeper berth. For Dūnhuáng, double check whether you are getting a train to the town itself or Liǔyuán, which is 180km away.

From Lánzhōu station, there are frequent trains to Dūnhuáng (hard/soft sleeper ¥276/430, 13 to 15 hours, two daily direct to Dūnhuáng at 5.25pm and 5.50pm, the rest go to Liǔyuán), Jiāyùguān (2nd/1st class seat ¥215/258, four hours; hard/soft sleeper ¥193/297, seven to ten hours), Ürümqi (hard/soft sleeper ¥418/659, 19 to 24 hours) and Xī'ān (hard/soft sleeper ¥184/283, eight to nine hours).

From Lánzhōu West railway station, there are trains to Jiāyùguān South (2nd/1st class seat ¥215/258, 4½ hours).

### ❶ GETTING AROUND

At the time of writing, Lánzhōu's streets were even more clogged than ever, owing to the construction of a new metro, due to open in 2017. Give yourself plenty of time to get around,

### Silk Road Raiders

In 1900, the self-appointed guardian of the Mògāo Grottoes (p258), Wang Yuanlu, discovered a hidden library filled with tens of thousands of immaculately preserved manuscripts and paintings, dating as far back as AD 406.

It's hard to describe the exact magnitude of the discovery, but stuffed into the tiny cave were texts in rare Central Asian languages, military reports, music scores, medical prescriptions, Confucian and Taoist classics, and Buddhist sutras copied by some of the greatest names in Chinese calligraphy – not to mention the oldest printed book in existence, the *Diamond Sutra* (AD 868). In short, it was an incalculable amount of original source material regarding Chinese, Central Asian and Buddhist history.

Word of the discovery quickly spread and Wang Yuanlu, suddenly the most popular bloke in town, was courted by rival archaeologists Aurel Stein and Paul Pelliot, among others. Following much pressure to sell the cache, Wang Yuanlu finally relented and parted with an enormous hoard of treasure. On his watch, close to 20,000 of the cave's priceless manuscripts were whisked off to Europe for the paltry sum of £220.

especially if you have a morning bus or train to catch, as both taxis and city buses tend to get caught in traffic.

Public buses cost ¥1; taxis are ¥7 for the first 3km. There is no bus from the train station to the south bus station, so you are better off taking a taxi for ¥35 for 45 minutes.

# In Focus

# China Today

*An idiosyncratic mix of can-do entrepreneurs, inward-looking Buddhists, textbook Marxists, overnight million-aires, the out-of-pocket, leather-faced farmers, unflagging migrant workers and round-the-clock McJobbers, China today is as multifaceted as its challenges are diverse.*

Běijīng's ultramodern Galaxy SOHO building, designed by Zaha Hadid Architects
ZHAOJIANKANG / GETTY IMAGES ©

## The Economy: Speed Bump or Cul-de-Sac?

China's eye-watering growth appears to be nearing the end of its blinding three-decade run, although experts remain divided over long-term implications for its US$11 trillion economy. Confronting high levels of debt, chronic overcapacity in manufacturing, a constellation of real-estate bubbles dotted around the land and a stock market prone to sudden dives, the days of easy, double-digit growth have given way to more sober fore-casts. The economy may not be coming off the rails, but China's ambitious proposals in its current five-year plan could take a bruising, including its commitment to hugely expand social security and feed the country's large and demanding military budget. The latter expenditure is perhaps most crucial, to satisfy a growing domestic appetite for a strong nation when rivalries within the region and with the United States are at their keenest.

## belief systems
(% of population)

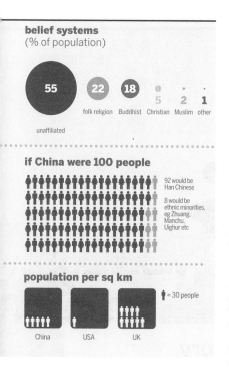

**55**  **22**  **18**  5  2  1

folk religion  Buddhist  Christian  Muslim  other

unaffiliated

## if China were 100 people

92 would be
Han Chinese

8 would be
ethnic minorities,
eg Zhuang,
Manchu,
Uighur etc

## population per sq km

≈ 30 people

China    USA    UK

While a bust is perhaps unlikely, China may need to prepare for a period of middle-income blues with fewer jobs, reduced expectations and the days of double-digit growth a thing of the past.

## China Goes Travelling

China's crashing stock market seems to have done little to stop the Chinese from joining the top league of travelling nations for the first time in their tumultuous and predominantly inward-looking recent history. So while the world goes to China, China is increasingly going to the world. In 2015, a record 120 million outbound visitors left China. In the same year, Chinese arrivals to the UK were up by 40% in the first nine months. Chinese travellers spent a staggering US$215 billion abroad in the same year (more than the GDP of Portugal), up 53% on the previous 12 months, while Chinese tourism is predicted to account for 14% of worldwide tourism revenue by 2020. Relaxed visa rulings from several nations, including the US and UK, have helped get Chinese feet into their outbound travelling shoes. It doesn't quite mean you'll find China deserted when you get there – the Chinese are more actively travelling around their home nation, too: Běijīng is hoping that domestic travellers will outlay ¥5.5 trillion on travel around China by 2020.

## Troubled Waters & Restive Borderlands

China's dazzling economic trajectory over the last three decades has been watched with awe by the West and increasing consternation by the Middle Kingdom's neighbours. By virtue of its sheer size and population, a dominant China will ruffle some East Asian feathers. The long-festering dispute between China and Vietnam, the Philippines and other nations over the control of waters, islands, reefs, atolls and rocky outcrops of the Paracel (Xīshā) and Spratly (Nánshā) Islands in the South China Sea worsened in recent years when China unilaterally began reclaiming land around, and building on, contested reefs. China has attempted to enforce a 12-nautical-mile exclusion zone around these reefs, which has been tested by the US Navy conducting 'freedom of navigation' exercises. The possibility of miscalculation that could lead to conflict has never been greater. Meanwhile, the seemingly intractable spat over the contested and uninhabited Diàoyú Islands (Senkaku Islands to the Japanese) continues to sour relations between China and Japan. While keeping an eye on maritime issues, at home President Xi Jinping has had to deal with unrest in Xīnjiāng province, where Uighur disquiet has prompted an increasingly harsh security clampdown from Běijīng, which may threaten to inflame sentiments further.

# History

*China's history can suggest prolonged epochs of peace occasionally convulsed by sudden break-up, internecine division or external attack; yet for much of its history China has been in conflict. The Middle Kingdom's size and shape may have continuously changed, but an un-interrupted thread of history runs from its earliest roots to the full flowering of Chinese civilisation.*

Left: Hall of Prayer for Good Harvests, Temple of Heaven Park (p48), Běijīng
NINO H. PHOTOGRAPHY / GETTY IMAGES ©

Right: Terracotta Warriors (p98), Xī'ān
BULE SKY STUDIO / SHUTTERSTOCK ©

| **c 4000 BC** | **551 BC** | **214 BC** |
|---|---|---|
| The first known settlements appear along the Yellow River (Huáng Hé). | The birth of Confucius, who outlines ideas of an ethical society that operates through hierarchy. | Emperor Qin indentures thousands of labourers to link existing city walls into one Great Wall, made of tamped earth. |

## From Oracle Bones to Confucius

The earliest 'Chinese' dynasty, the Shang, was long considered apocryphal. However, archaeological evidence – cattle bones and turtle shells in Hénán covered in mysterious scratches, recognised by a scholar as an early form of Chinese writing – proved that a society known as the Shang developed in central China from around 1766 BC.

Sometime between 1050 and 1045 BC, a neighbouring group known as the Zhou conquered Shang territory. A constant theme of the first millennium BC was conflict, particularly the periods known as the 'Spring and Autumn' (722–481 BC) and 'Warring States' (475–221 BC).

From this disorder emerged the thinking of Confucius (551–479 BC), whose system of thought and ethics underpinned Chinese culture for 2500 years.

| c 100 BC | AD 755–763 | 1215 |
|----------|------------|------|
| Buddhism first arrives in China from India. This religious system ends up thoroughly assimilated into Chinese culture. | An Lushan rebels against the Tang court. His rebellion is subdued, but the court cedes immense military power to provincial leaders. | Genghis Khan conquers Běijīng as part of his creation of a massive Eurasian empire under Mongol rule. |

The Great Wall (p68)

AUTOMATON / GETTY IMAGES ©

## Early Empires

The Warring States period ended decisively in 221 BC. The Qin kingdom conquered other states in the central Chinese region and Qin Shi Huang proclaimed himself emperor. The first in a line of dynastic rulers that would last until 1912, Qin Shi Huang has been portrayed in later histories as particularly cruel and tyrannical, but the distinction is dubious: the ensuing Han dynasty (206 BC–AD 220) adopted many of the short-lived Qin's practices of government.

Qin Shi Huang oversaw vast public works projects, including walls built by some 300,000 men, connecting defences into what would become the Great Wall. He unified the currency, measurements and written language, providing the basis for a cohesive state.

Establishing a trend that would echo through Chinese history, a peasant, Liu Bang (256–195 BC), rose up and conquered China, founding the Han dynasty.

## Disunity Restored

Between the early 3rd and late 6th centuries AD, north China witnessed a succession of rival kingdoms vying for power, while a potent division formed between north and south. Riven by warfare, the north succumbed to non-Chinese rule, most successfully by the northern Wei dynasty (386–534), founded by the Tuoba, a northern people who embraced Buddhism and left behind some of China's finest Buddhist art, including the famous caves outside Dūnhuáng. A succession of rival regimes followed until nobleman Yang Jian (d 604) reunified China under the fleeting Sui dynasty (581–618). His son Sui Yangdi contributed greatly to the unification of south and north through construction of the Grand Canal, which was later extended and remained China's most important communication route between south and north until the late 19th century. After instigating three unsuccessful incursions onto Korean soil, resulting in disastrous military setbacks, Sui Yangdi faced revolt and was assassinated in 618 by one of his high officials.

●

**1298–99**

Marco Polo pens his famous account of his travels to China. Inconsistencies in his story have led some scholars to doubt his tale.

●

**1406**

Ming emperor Yongle begins construction of the 800 buildings of the Forbidden City.

●

**1644**

Běijīng falls to peasant rebel Li Zicheng and the last Ming emperor, Chongzhen, hangs himself in Jǐngshān Park.

## The Tang: China Looks West

Tang rule (618–907) was an outward-looking time, when China embraced the culture of its neighbours – marriage to Central Asian people or wearing Indian-influenced clothes was part of the era's cosmopolitan élan – and distant nations that reached China via the Silk Road.

The Tang was founded by the Sui general Li Yuan, his achievements consolidated by his son Taizong (r 626–49). Cháng'ān (modern Xī'ān) became the world's most dazzling capital, with its own cosmopolitan foreign quarter, a population of one million, a market where merchants from as far away as Persia mingled with locals, and an astonishing city wall that eventually enveloped 83 sq km.

Taizong was succeeded by a unique figure: Chinese history's sole reigning woman emperor, Wu Zetian (r 690–705). In 705 she was forced to abdicate in favour of Xuanzong, who would preside over the greatest disaster in the Tang's history: the rebellion of An Lushan. The fighting lasted from 755 to 763, and although An Lushan was defeated, the Tang's control over China was destroyed forever.

## The Song: Conflict & Prosperity

Further disunity – the fragmentary-sounding Five Dynasties or Ten Kingdoms period – followed the fall of the Tang until the northern Song dynasty (960–1127) was established. The Song dynasty existed in a state of constant conflict with its northern neighbours. In 1126 the Song lost its capital, Kāifēng, to a third non-Chinese people, the Jurchen (previously an ally against the Liao). The Song was driven to its southern capital of Hángzhōu for the period of the southern Song (1127–1279), yet the period was culturally rich and economically prosperous.

## Mongols to Ming

Genghis Khan (1167–1227) was beginning his rise to power, turning his gaze on China; he took Běijīng in 1215, destroying and rebuilding it; his successors seized Hángzhōu, the southern Song capital, in 1276. The court fled and, in 1279, southern Song resistance finally crumbled. Kublai Khan, grandson of Genghis, now reigned over all of China as emperor of the Yuan dynasty.

The Mongols ultimately proved less adept at governance than warfare, their empire succumbing to rebellion and eventual vanquishment within a century. Ruling as Ming emperor Hongwu, Zhu Yuanzhang established his capital in Nánjīng, but by the early 15th century the court had begun to move back to Běijīng, where a hugely ambitious reconstruction project was inaugurated by Emperor Yongle (r 1403–24), building the Forbidden City and devising the layout of the city we see today.

| 1842 | 1898 | 1904–05 |
|---|---|---|
| The Treaty of Nanking concludes the First Opium War. China is forced to hand over Hong Kong Island to the British. | The New Territories adjoining Kowloon in Hong Kong are leased to the British for 99 years. | The Russo–Japanese War is fought entirely on Chinese territory. |

Tram (p180), Causeway Bay, Hong Kong

WIBOWO RUSLI / GETTY IMAGES ©

Emperor Yongle, having usurped power from his nephew, was keen to establish his own legitimacy. In 1405 he launched the first of seven great maritime expeditions. The Great Wall was re-engineered and clad in brick, while ships also arrived from Europe, presaging an overseas threat that would develop from entirely different directions.

The Ming was eventually undermined by internal power struggles. Natural disasters, including drought and famine, combined with a menace from the north: the Manchu, a nomadic warlike people, who saw the turmoil within China and invaded.

## The Qing: the Path to Dynastic Dissolution

After conquering just a small part of China and assuming control in the disarray, the Manchu named their new dynasty the Qing (1644–1911). They enforced strict rules of social separation between the Han and Manchu, and tried to maintain – not always very successfully – a culture that reminded the Manchu of their nomadic warrior past. The Qing flourished most greatly under three emperors who ruled for a total of 135 years: Kangxi, Yongzheng and Qianlong. For the Manchu, the single most devastating incident was not either of the Opium Wars, but the far more destructive anti-Qing Taiping Rebellion of 1850–64, an insurgency motivated partly by a foreign credo (Christianity).

## The Path to Rebellion

The Cantonese revolutionary Sun Yatsen (1866–1925) remains one of the few modern historical figures respected in both China and Taiwan. Sun and his Revolutionary League made multiple attempts to undermine Qing rule in the late 19th century, raising sponsorship and support from a wide-ranging combination of the Chinese diaspora, the newly emergent middle class, and traditional secret societies.

The end of the Qing dynasty arrived swiftly. Throughout China's southwest, popular resentment against the dynasty had been fuelled by reports that railway rights in the region were being sold to foreigners. A local uprising in the city of Wǔhàn in October 1911

| 1911 | 1916 | 1930s |
|:---:|:---:|:---:|
| Revolution spreads across China as local governments withdraw support for the dynasty. | Yuan Shikai tries to declare himself emperor. He is forced to withdraw and re-main president, but dies of uraemia later in the year. | Cosmopolitan Shànghǎi is the world's fifth-largest city, supporting a polyglot population of four million people. |

was discovered early, leading the rebels to take over command in the city and hastily declare independence from the Qing dynasty. Within a space of days, then weeks, most of China's provinces did likewise. Provincial assemblies across China declared themselves in favour of a republic, with Sun Yatsen (who was not even in China at the time) as their candidate for president.

## The Republic: Instability

The Republic of China lasted less than 40 years on the mainland (1912–49) and continues to be regarded as a dark chapter in modern Chinese history, when the country was under threat from what many described as 'imperialism from without and warlordism from within'.

Sun Yatsen returned to China and only briefly served as president, before having to make way for militarist leader Yuan Shikai. However, after Yuan's death in 1916, the country split into rival regions ruled by militarist warlord-leaders.

## The Northern Expedition & the Long March

Sun died of cancer in 1925. The succession battle in the party coincided with a surge in antiforeign feeling that accompanied the May Thirtieth Incident when 13 labour demonstrators were killed by British police in Shànghǎi on 30 May 1925. Under Soviet advice, the Kuomintang and CCP prepared for their 'Northern Expedition', the big 1926 push north that was supposed to finally unite China. In 1926–27, the Soviet-trained National Revolutionary Army made its way

 **Dirty Foreign Mud**

Although trade in opium had been banned in China by imperial decree at the end of the 18th century, the *cohong* (local merchants' guild) in Guǎngzhōu helped ensure that the trade continued, and fortunes were amassed on both sides. When the British East India Company lost its monopoly on China trade in 1834, imports of the drug increased to 40,000 chests a year.

In 1839, the Qing government sent Imperial Commissioner Lin Zexu to stamp out the opium trade once and for all. Lin successfully blockaded the British in Guǎngzhōu and publicly burned the 'foreign mud' in Hǔmén. Furious, the British sent a Royal Navy expeditionary force of 4000 men to exact reparations and secure favourable trade arrangements.

What would become known as the First Opium War began in June 1840 when British forces besieged Guǎngzhōu and forced the Chinese to cede five ports to the British. With the strategic city of Nanking (Nánjīng) under immediate threat, the Chinese were forced to accept Britain's terms in the Treaty of Nanking.

The treaty abolished the monopoly system of trade, opened the 'treaty ports' to British residents and foreign trade, exempted British nationals from all Chinese laws and ceded the island of Hong Kong to the British 'in perpetuity'. The treaty, signed in August 1842, set the scope and character of the unequal relationship between China and the West for the next half-century.

**1931**
Japan invades northeast China, provoking an international crisis and forcing Chiang to consider anti-Japanese strategies.

**1937**
The Japanese and Chinese clash at Wanping, near Běijīng, sparks the conflict that the Chinese call the 'War of Resistance'.

**1946**
Communists and the Kuomintang fail to form a coalition government, plunging China back into civil war.

Ruins of the Church of St Paul (p166), Macau

slowly north, fighting, bribing or persuading its opponents into accepting Kuomintang control.

The most powerful military figure turned out to be an officer from Zhèjiāng named Chiang Kaishek (1887–1975). Trained in Moscow, Chiang moved steadily forward and finally captured the great prize, Shànghǎi, in March 1927. However, a horrific surprise was in store for his communist allies. The Soviet advisers had not impressed Chiang and he was increasingly convinced that the communists aimed to use their cooperation with the Kuomintang to seize control themselves. Instead, Chiang struck first. Using local thugs and soldiers, Chiang organised a lightning strike by rounding up CCP activists and union leaders in Shànghǎi and killing thousands of them.

Chiang Kaishek's Kuomintang government officially came to power in 1928 through a combination of military force and popular support. The communists had not stood still and after Chiang's treachery, most of what remained of the CCP fled to the countryside. However, by 1934, Chiang's previously ineffective 'extermination campaigns' were making the CCP's position in Jiāngxī untenable, as the Red Army found itself increasingly encircled by Nationalist troops. The CCP commenced its Long March, travelling over 6400km. It seemed possible that within a matter of months, however, Chiang would attack again and wipe them out.

Events came to a head in December 1936, when the Chinese militarist leader of Manchuria (General Zhang Xueliang) and the CCP kidnapped Chiang. As a condition of his release, Chiang agreed to an openly declared United Front: the Kuomintang and communists would put aside their differences and join forces against Japan.

## War & the Communists

China's status as a major participant in WWII is often overlooked or forgotten in the West. The Japanese invasion of China, which began in 1937, was merciless, with the notorious Nánjīng Massacre (also known as the Rape of Nánjīng) just one of a series of war crimes committed by the Japanese Army during its conquest of eastern China.

### 1949

Mao Zedong stands on top of the Gate of Heavenly Peace in Běijīng on 1 October and announces the formation of the PRC.

### 1950

China joins the Korean War, helping Mao to consolidate his regime with mass campaigns that inspire (or terrify) the population.

### 1966

The Cultural Revolution breaks out, and Red Guards demonstrate in cities across China.

The real winners from WWII, however, were the communists. By the end of the war with Japan, the communist areas had expanded massively, with some 900,000 troops in the Red Army, and party membership at a new high of 1.2 million.

The Kuomintang and communists then plunged into civil war in 1946 and after three long years the CCP won. On 1 October 1949 in Běijīng, Mao declared the establishment of the People's Republic of China.

## Mao's China & the Great Leap Forward

Mao's experiences had convinced him that only violent change could shake up the relationship between landlords and their tenants, or capitalists and their employees, in a China that was still highly traditional. The first year of the regime saw some 40% of the land redistributed to poor peasants. At the same time, some one million or so people condemned as 'landlords' were persecuted and killed.

As relations with the Soviets broke down in the mid-1950s, the CCP leaders' thoughts turned to economic self-sufficiency. Mao, supported by Politburo colleagues, proposed the policy known as the Great Leap Forward (Dàyuèjìn), a highly ambitious plan to harness the power of socialist economics to boost production of steel, coal and electricity.

However, the Great Leap Forward was a horrific failure. Its lack of economic realism caused a massive famine that killed tens of millions.

## Cultural Revolution

Still the dominant figure in the CCP, Mao used his prestige to undermine his own colleagues. In summer 1966, prominent posters in large, handwritten characters appeared at prominent sites, including Peking University, demanding that figures such as Liu Shaoqi (president of the PRC) and Deng Xiaoping (senior Politburo member) must be condemned as 'takers of the capitalist road'. Meanwhile, an all-pervasive cult of Mao's personality took over. One million youths at a time, known as Red Guards, would flock to hear Mao in Tiān'ānmén Sq. Immense violence permeated throughout society: teachers, intellectuals and landlords were killed in their thousands.

Worried by the increasing violence, the army forced the Red Guards off the streets in 1969. Slowly, the Cultural Revolution began to cool down, but its brutal legacy survives today.

## Reform

Mao died in 1976, to be succeeded by the little-known Hua Guofeng (1921–2008). Within two years, Hua had been outmanoeuvred by the greatest survivor of 20th-century Chinese politics, Deng Xiaoping. The party's task would be to set China on the right path in four areas: agriculture, industry, national defence, and science and technology.

| **1976** | **1989** | **1997** |
|---|---|---|
| Mao Zedong dies, aged 83. The Gang of Four are arrested by his successor and put on trial. | Hundreds of civilians are killed by Chinese troops in the streets around Tiān'ānmén Sq. | Hong Kong is returned to the People's Republic of China. |

The first highly symbolic move of the 'reform era' (as the post-1978 period is known) was the breaking down of the collective farms. As part of this encouragement of entrepreneurship, Deng designated four areas on China's coast as Special Economic Zones (SEZs), which would be particularly attractive to foreign investors.

After student protests demanding further opening up of the party in 1985–86, the prime minister (and relative liberal) Hu Yaobang was forced to resign in 1987 and take responsibility for allowing social forces to get out of control. In April 1989, Hu Yaobang died, and students around China used the occasion of his death to organise protests against the continuing role of the CCP in public life. In spring 1989, Tiān'ānmén Sq was the scene of an unprecedented demonstration. Martial law was imposed and on the night of 3 June and early hours of 4 June, tanks and armoured personnel carriers were sent in. The death toll in Běijīng has never been officially confirmed, but it seems likely to have been in the high hundreds or even more.

Faced with a multitude of social problems brought on by inequalities spawned by the Deng years, President Jiang Zemin, with Zhu Rongji as premier, sought to bring economic stability to China while strengthening the centralised power of the state and putting off much-needed political reforms.

## 21st-Century China

Jiang Zemin was succeeded in 2002 by President Hu Jintao, who made further efforts to tame growing regional inequality and the poverty scarring rural areas.

The question of political reform found itself shelved, partly because economic growth was bringing prosperity to so many, albeit unevenly. For many, the first decade of the 21st century was marked by spectacular riches for some – the number of dollar billionaires doubled in just two years – and property prices began moving dramatically beyond the reach of the less fortunate, while bringing wealth to the more fortunate. This period coincided with the greatest migration of workers to the cities the world has ever seen.

Vice-president from 2008, Xi Jinping replaced Hu Jintao as president in 2013. Pledging to root out corruption, Xi has also sought to instigate reforms, including the abolition of both the one-child policy and the *láojiào* (re-education through labour) system. These reforms, however, were matched by a growing zeal for internet and social media controls and a domestic security budget that sucked in more capital than national defence. Political reform found itself even more on the back burner as economic considerations took centre stage and storm clouds gathered above the competing claims over the reefs, shoals and islands of the South China Sea.

| **2008** | **2013** | **2015** |
|---|---|---|
| Běijīng hosts the 2008 Summer Olympic Games and Paralympics. The Games go smoothly and are considered a great success. | The total length of China's national high-speed rail network reaches a staggering 10,000km, the world's longest. | Satellite imagery reveals that China has been rapidly constructing an airfield at Fiery Cross Reef in the Spratly (Nánshā) Islands. |

# People of China

*The stamping ground of roughly one-fifth of humanity, China is often regarded as largely homogeneous, at least from a Western perspective. This is probably because Han Chinese – the majority ethnic type in this energetic and bustling nation – constitute over nine-tenths of the population. You only have to travel a bit further, however, to come face-to-face with a surprising mix of ethnicities.*

Minority Miao women in traditional clothing, Yúnnán (p202)
OUTCAST85 / GETTY IMAGES ©

## Ethnicity

### Han Chinese

Han Chinese (汉族; Hànzú) – the predominant clan among China's 56 recognised ethnic groups – make up the lion's share of China's people, 92% of the total figure. When we think of China – from its writing system to its visual arts, calligraphy, history, literature, language and politics – we tend to associate it with Han culture.

Distributed throughout China, the Han Chinese are, however, predominantly concentrated along the Yellow River, Yangzi River and Pearl River basins. Taking their name from the Han dynasty, the Han Chinese themselves are not markedly homogeneous. China was

Lóngjǐ Rice Terraces (p192)

ruled by non-Han Altaic (Turk, Tungusic or Mongolian) invaders for long periods, most demonstrably during the Yuan dynasty (Mongols) and the long Qing dynasty (Manchu), but also under the Jin, the Liao and other eras. This Altaic influence is more evident in northern Chinese with their larger and broader frames and rounder faces, compared to their slighter and thinner southern Han Chinese counterparts, who are physically more similar to the southeast Asian type. Shànghǎi Chinese, for example, are notably more southern in appearance; with their rounder faces, Běijīng Chinese are quite typically northern Chinese. With mass migration to the cities from rural areas and the increased frequency of marriage between Chinese from different parts of the land, these physical differences are likely to diminish slightly over time.

The Han Chinese display further stark differences in their rich panoply of dialects, which fragments China into a frequently baffling linguistic mosaic, although the promotion of Mandarin has blurred this considerably. The common written form of Chinese using characters (汉字; Hànzi – or 'characters of the Han'), however, binds all dialects together.

## Non-Han Chinese

A glance at the map of China reveals that the core heartland regions of Han China are central fragments of modern-day China's huge expanse. The colossal regions of Tibet, Qīnghǎi, Xīnjiāng, Inner Mongolia and the three provinces of the northeast (Manchuria – Hēilóngjiāng, Jílín and Liáoníng) are all historically non-Han regions, some areas of which remain essentially non-Han today.

Many of these regions are peopled by some of the remaining 8% of the population: China's 55 other ethnic minorities, known collectively as *shǎoshù mínzú* (少数民族; minority nationals). The largest minority groups in China include the Zhuang (壮族; Zhuàng zú), Manchu (满族; Mǎn zú), Miao (苗族; Miáo zú), Uighur (维吾尔族; Wéiwú'ěr zú), Yi (彝族; Yí zú), Tujia (土家族; Tǔjiā zú), Tibetan (藏族; Zàng zú), Hui (回族; Huízú), Mongolian (蒙古族; Ménggǔ zú), Buyi (布依族; Bùyī zú), Dong (侗族; Dòng zú), Yao (瑶族; Yáo zú), Korean (朝鲜族; Cháoxiǎn zú), Bai (白族; Bái zú), Hani (哈尼族; Hāní zú), Li (黎族; Lí zú), Kazak (哈萨克族; Hāsàkè zú) and Dai (傣族; Dǎi zú). Population sizes differ dramatically, from the sizeable Zhuang in Guǎngxī to small numbers of Menba (门巴族; Ménbā zú) in Tibet. Ethnic labelling can be quite fluid: the roundhouse-building Hakka (客家; Kèjiā) were once regarded as a separate minority, but are today considered Han Chinese. Ethnic groups also tell us a lot about the historic movement of peoples around China: the Bonan minority, found in small numbers in a few counties of Qīnghǎi and Gānsù, are largely Muslim, but show marked Tibetan influence and are said to be descended from Mongol troops once stationed in Qīnghǎi during the Yuan dynasty.

China's minorities tend to cluster along border regions, in the northwest, the west, the southwest, the north and northeast of China, but are also distributed throughout the country. Some groups are found in just one area (such as the Hani in Yúnnán); others, such as the Muslim Hui, live all over China.

Wedged into the southwest corner of China between Tibet, Myanmar (Burma), Vietnam and Laos, fecund Yúnnán province alone is home to more than 20 ethnic groups, making it one of the most ethnically diverse provinces in the country.

## The Chinese Character

Shaped by Confucian principles, the Chinese are thoughtful and discreet, subtle but also pragmatic. Conservative and rather introverted, they favour dark clothing over bright or loud colours, while their body language is usually reserved and undemonstrative, yet attentive.

### China's Demographics

- Population: 1.37 billion
- Birth rate: 12.49 births per thousand people
- People over 65: 10%
- Urbanisation rate: 3.05%
- Male to female ratio: 1.17 to 1 (under 15s)
- Life expectancy: 75.4 years

The Chinese can be both delightful and mystifyingly contradictory. One moment they will give their seat to an elderly person on the bus or help someone who is lost, and the next moment they will entirely ignore an old lady who has been knocked over by a motorbike.

Particularly diligent, the Chinese are inured to the kind of hours that may prompt a workers' insurrection elsewhere. This is partly due to a traditional culture of hard work, but is also a response to insufficient social-security safety nets and an anxiety regarding economic and political uncertainties. The Chinese impressively save much of what they earn, emphasising the virtue of prudence. Despite this restraint, however, wastefulness can be breathtaking when 'face' is involved: mountains of food are often left on restaurant dining tables, particularly if important guests are present.

Chinese people are deeply generous. Don't be surprised if a person you have just met on a train invites you for a meal in the dining carriage; they will almost certainly insist on paying, grabbing the bill from the waitress at blinding speed and tenaciously resisting your attempts to help out.

## China's One-Child Policy

The 'one-child policy' (in effect a misnomer) was railroaded into effect in 1979 in a bid to keep China's population to one billion by the year 2000 (a target it failed to meet); the population is expected to peak at around 1.5 billion in 2028. In a momentous reversal, in 2015 it was announced that the policy would be abolished and in January 2016 the regulation was officially amended to a two-child policy.

The policy was harshly implemented at first, but rural revolt led to a softer stance; nonetheless, it generated much bad feeling between local officials and the rural population. All non-Han minorities were exempt from the one-child policy; Han Chinese parents who were both single children could have a second child and this was later expanded to all couples if at least one of them was a single child. Rural families were allowed to have two children if the first child was a girl, but some had upwards of three or four kids. Additional children often resulted in fines, with families having to shoulder the cost of education themselves, without government assistance. Official stated policy opposed

## Nationalism or Patriotism?

In today's China, '-isms' (主义; *zhǔyì* or 'doctrines') are often frowned upon. Any *zhǔyì* may suggest a personal focus that the CCP would prefer people channel into hard work instead. Intellectualism is considered suspect as it may ask difficult questions. Idealism is deemed nonpragmatic and potentially destructive, as Maoism showed.

China's one-party state has reduced thinking across the spectrum via propaganda and censorship, dumbing down an educational system that emphasises patriotic education. This in turn, however, helped spawn another '-ism': nationalism.

Nationalism is not restricted to Chinese youth but it is this generation – with no experience of the Cultural Revolution's terrifying excesses – that most closely identifies with its message. The *fènqīng* (angry youth) have been swept along with China's rise; while they are no lovers of the CCP, they yearn for a stronger China that can stand up to 'foreign interference' and dictate its own terms.

The CCP actively encourages strong patriotism, but is nervous about its transformation into aggressive nationalism and the potential for disturbance. Much nationalism in the PRC has little to do with the CCP but everything to do with China; while the CCP has struggled at length to identify itself with China's civilisation and core values, it has been only partially successful. With China's tendency to get quickly swept along by passions, nationalism is an often unseen but quite potent force, most visibly flaring up into the periodic anti-Japanese demonstrations that can convulse large towns and cities.

---

forced abortion or sterilisation, but allegations of coercion continued as local officials strived to meet population targets.

Families who abided by the one-child policy often went to horrifying lengths to ensure their child was male, with female infanticide, sex-selective abortion and abandonment becoming commonplace. In parts of China, this resulted in a serious imbalance of the sexes – in 2010, 118 boys were born for every 100 girls. In some provinces the imbalance has been even higher. By 2020, potentially around 35 million Chinese men may be unable to find wives.

As women could have a second child abroad, this also led to large numbers of mainland women giving birth in Hong Kong (where the child also qualified for Hong Kong citizenship). The Hong Kong government eventually used legislation to curb this phenomenon, dubbed 'birth tourism', as government figures revealed that almost half of babies born in the territory in 2010 were born to mainland parents. In 2013, the Hong Kong government prohibited mainland women from visiting Hong Kong to give birth, unless their husband is from the territory.

Another consequence of the one-child policy has been a rapidly ageing population, with over a quarter of the populace predicted to be over the age of 65 by 2050. The 2016 abolition of the one-child policy has sought to adjust these profound imbalances, but some analysts argue it has come too late.

# Women in China

## Equality & Emancipation

Growing up in a Confucian culture, women in China traditionally encountered great prejudice and acquired a far lowlier social status to men. The most notorious expression of female subservience was footbinding, which became a widespread practice in the Song dynasty.

Women in today's China officially share complete equality with men; however, as with other nations that profess sexual equality, the reality is often far different. Chinese women do not enjoy strong political representation and the Chinese Communist Party remains a largely patriarchal organisation. Iconic political leaders from the early days of the Chinese Communist Party were men and the influential echelons of the party persist as a largely male domain.

The Communist Party after 1949 tried to outlaw old customs and put women on equal footing with men. It abolished arranged marriages and encouraged women to get an education and join the workforce. Women were allowed to keep their maiden name upon marriage and leave their property to their children. In its quest for equality during this period, however, the Communist Party seemed to 'desexualise' women, fashioning instead a kind of idealised worker/mother/peasant paradigm.

## Chinese Women Today

High-profile, successful Chinese women are very much in the public eye, but the relative lack of career opportunities for females in other fields also suggests a continuing bias against women in employment.

Women's improved social status today has meant that more women are putting off marriage until their late 20s or early 30s, choosing instead to focus on education and career opportunities. This has been enhanced by the rapid rise in house prices, further encouraging women to leave marriage (and having children) till a later age. Premarital sex and cohabitation before marriage are increasingly common in larger cities and lack the stigma they had 10 or 15 years ago.

## Rural Women in China

A strong rural–urban divide exists. Urban women are far more optimistic and freer, while women from rural areas, where traditional beliefs are at their strongest, fight an uphill battle against discrimination. Rural Chinese mores are heavily biased against females, where a marked preference for baby boys still exists. This results in an ever greater shift of Chinese women to the city from rural areas. China's women are more likely to commit suicide than men (in the West it is the other way around), while the suicide rate for rural Chinese women is around five times the urban rate.

# Chinese Cuisine

*Food plays a central role in both Chinese society and the national psyche. The catalysts for all manner of enjoyment, meals are occasions for pleasure and entertainment, to clinch deals, strike up new friendships and rekindle old ones. To fully explore this tasty domain on home soil, all you need is an explorative palate and a passion for the unusual and unexpected.*

Selection of Chinese dishes
ITS_AL_DENTE / SHUTTERSTOCK ©

## Real Chinese Food

Because the nation so skilfully exported its cuisine abroad, your very first impressions of China were probably via your taste buds. Chinatowns the world over teem with the aromas of Chinese cuisine, ferried overseas by China's versatile and hard-working cooks.

But what you see – and taste – abroad is usually just a wafer-thin slice of a very hefty and wholesome pie. To get an idea of the size of its diverse menu, remember that China is not that much smaller than Europe. Just as Europe is a patchwork of different nation states, languages, cultural traditions and climates, China is also a smorgasbord of dialects, languages, ethnic minorities and extreme geographic and climatic differences, despite the common Han Chinese cultural glue.

Following your nose (and palate) around China is one of the exciting ways to journey the land, so pack a sense of culinary adventure along with your travelling boots!

# Regional Cuisines

The evolution of China's wide-ranging regional cuisines has been influenced by the climate, the distribution of crop and animal varieties, the type of terrain, proximity to the sea, the influence of neighbouring nations and the import of ingredients and aromas. Naturally seafood is prevalent in coastal regions of China, while in Inner Mongolia and Xīnjiāng there is a dependence on meat such as beef and lamb.

Many Chinese regions lay claim to their own culinary conventions, which may overlap and cross-pollinate each other. The cooking traditions of China's ethnic minorities aside, Han cooking has traditionally been divided into eight schools (中华八大菜系; *zhōnghuá bādàcàixì*): Chuān (川; Sìchuān cuisine), Huī (徽; Ānhuī cuisine), Lǔ (鲁; Shāndōng cuisine), Mǐn (闽; Fújiàn cuisine), Sū (苏; Jiāngsū cuisine), Xiāng (湘; Húnán cuisine), Yuè (粤; Cantonese/Guǎngdōng cuisine) and Zhè (浙; Zhèjiāng cuisine).

Although each school is independent and well defined, it is possible to group these eight culinary traditions into northern, southern, western and eastern cooking.

## Northern Cooking

With Shāndōng (鲁菜; *lǔcài*) – the oldest of the eight regional schools of cooking – at its heart, northern cooking also embraces Běijīng, northeastern (Manchurian) and Shānxī cuisine, creating the most time-honoured and most central form of Chinese cooking.

In the dry north Chinese wheat belt, an accent falls on millet, sorghum, maize, barley and wheat rather than rice (which requires lush irrigation by water to cultivate). Particularly well suited to the harsh and hardy winter climate, northern cooking is rich and wholesome (northerners partially attribute their taller size, compared to southern Chinese, to its effects). Filling breads – such as *mántou* (馒头) or *bǐng* (饼; flat breads) – are steamed, baked or fried, while noodles may form the basis of any northern meal. (The ubiquitous availability of rice means it can always be found, however.) Northern cuisine is frequently quite salty, and appetising dumplings (饺子; *jiǎozi*) are widely eaten – usually boiled and sometimes fried.

As Běijīng was the principal capital through the Yuan, Ming and Qing dynasties, Imperial cooking is a chief characteristic of the northern school. Peking duck is Běijīng's signature dish, served with typical northern ingredients – pancakes, spring onions and fermented bean paste. You can find it all over China, but it's only true to form in the capital, roasted in ovens fired up with fruit-tree wood.

With China ruled from 1644 to 1911 by non-Han Manchurians, the influence of northeast cuisine *(dōngběi cài)* has naturally permeated northern cooking, dispensing a legacy of rich and hearty stews, dense breads, preserved foods and dumplings.

Meat roasting is also more common in the north than in other parts of China. Meats in northern China are braised until falling off the bone, or slathered with spices and barbecued until smoky. Pungent garlic, chives and spring onions are used with abandon and also employed raw. Also from the northwest is the Muslim Uighur cuisine.

The nomadic and carnivorous diet of the Mongolians also infiltrates northern cooking, most noticeably in the Mongolian hotpot and the Mongolian barbecue.

Some hallmark northern dishes:

| | | |
|---|---|---|
| *Běijīng kǎoyā* | 北京烤鸭 | Peking duck |
| *jiāo zhá yángròu* | 焦炸羊肉 | deep-fried mutton |
| *jiǎozi* | 饺子 | dumplings |

Peking duck

★ **Best Restaurants**
Jīngzūn Peking Duck (p60)
Georg (p60)
Mr & Mrs Bund (p129)
Lung King Heen (p175)
Jian Guo 328 (p130)

| *mántou* | 馒头 | steamed buns |
|---|---|---|
| *qīng xiāng shāo jī* | 清香烧鸡 | chicken wrapped in lotus leaf |
| *ròu bāozi* | 肉包子 | steamed meat buns |
| *sān měi dòufu* | 三美豆腐 | sliced bean curd (tofu) with Chinese cabbage |
| *shuàn yángròu* | 涮羊肉 | lamb hotpot |
| *sì xǐ wánzi* | 四喜丸子 | steamed and fried pork, shrimp and bamboo-shoot balls |
| *yuán bào lǐ jí* | 芫爆里脊 | stir-fried pork tenderloin with coriander |
| *zào liū sān bái* | 糟溜三白 | stir-fried chicken, fish and bamboo shoots |

## Southern Cooking

The southern Chinese – particularly the Cantonese – historically spearheaded successive waves of immigration overseas, leaving aromatic constellations of Chinatowns around the world. Consequently, Westerners most often associate this school of cooking with China.

Typified by Cantonese (粤菜; *yuècài*) cooking, southern cooking lacks the richness and saltiness of northern cooking and instead coaxes more subtle aromas to the surface. The Cantonese astutely believe that good cooking does not require much flavouring, for it is the *xiān* (natural freshness) of the ingredients that marks a truly high-grade dish. Hence the near-obsessive attention paid to the freshness of ingredients in southern cuisine.

The hallmark Cantonese dish is dim sum (点心; Mandarin: *diǎnxīn*). Yum cha (literally 'drink tea') – another name for dim-sum dining – in Guǎngzhōu and Hong Kong can be enjoyed on any day of the week. Dishes, often in steamers, are wheeled around on trolleys so you can see what's available to order.

Rice is the primary staple of southern cuisine.

Some Southern-school dishes:

| *bái zhuó xiā* | 白灼虾 | blanched prawns with shredded scallions |
|---|---|---|
| *dōngjiāng yánjú jī* | 东江盐焗鸡 | salt-baked chicken |
| *gālí jī* | 咖喱鸡 | curried chicken |
| *háoyóu niúròu* | 蚝油牛肉 | beef with oyster sauce |
| *kǎo rǔzhū* | 烤乳猪 | crispy suckling pig |
| *mì zhī chāshāo* | 密汁叉烧 | roast pork with honey |
| *shé ròu* | 蛇肉 | snake |
| *tángcù lǐjī/gǔlǎo ròu* | 糖醋里脊/咕老肉 | sweet-and-sour pork fillets |
| *tángcù páigǔ* | 糖醋排骨 | sweet-and-sour spare ribs |

## Western Cooking

The cuisine of landlocked western China, a region heavily dappled with ethnic shades and contrasting cultures, welcomes the diner to the more scarlet end of the culinary spectrum. The trademark ingredient of the western school is the fiercely hot red chilli, a potent firecracker of an ingredient that floods dishes with an all-pervading spiciness. Aniseed, coriander, garlic and peppercorns are thrown in for good measure to add extra pungency and bite.

The standout cuisine of the western school is fiery Sìchuān (川菜; *chuāncài*) food, one of China's eight regional cooking styles, renowned for its eye-watering peppery aromas. One of the things that differentiates Sìchuān cooking from other spicy cuisines is the use of 'flower pepper' (*huājiāo*), a numbing, peppercorn-like herb that floods the mouth with an anaesthetising fragrance in a culinary effect termed *málà* (numb and hot). A Sìchuān dish you can find cooked up by chefs across China is the delicious sour-cabbage fish soup (酸菜鱼; *suāncàiyú*), which features wholesome fish chunks in a spicy broth. The Chóngqìng hotpot is a force to be reckoned with, but must be approached with a stiff upper lip (and copious amounts of liquid refreshment).

Another of China's eight regional schools of cooking, dishes from Húnán (湘菜; *xiāngcài*) are similarly pungent, with a heavy reliance on chilli. Unlike Sìchuān food, flower pepper is not employed and instead spicy flavours are often sharper, fiercer and more to the fore.

Some Western-school dishes:

### Dining Options

China has a broad range of eating options from street food to fine dining; if you don't speak Chinese, you'll find photo menus are common. In most areas it's possible to hunt down specialities from other regions.

**Cheap eats** China is the master of good-value snacks and meals at food courts (much better than their Western counterparts), street stands and family-run restaurants.

**Cafes** Modern Chinese cities now have good coffee and tea in chic surrounds with Chinese (and Western) lunches or sweet treats, plus speedy wi-fi.

**Restaurants** An elevated, modern spin on classic regional dishes is available at every budget.

| | | |
|---|---|---|
| *bàngbàng jī* | 棒棒鸡 | shredded chicken in a hot pepper and sesame sauce |
| *Chóngqìng huǒguō* | 重庆火锅 | Chóngqìng hotpot |
| *dāndan miàn* | 担担面 | spicy noodles |
| *gānshāo yán lǐ* | 干烧岩鲤 | stewed carp with ham and hot-and-sweet sauce |
| *málà dòufu* | 麻辣豆腐 | spicy tofu |
| *Máoshì Hóngshāoròu* | 毛氏红烧肉 | Mao family braised pork |
| *shuǐ zhǔ niúròu* | 水煮牛肉 | spicy fried and boiled beef |
| *suāncàiyú* | 酸菜鱼 | sour-cabbage fish soup |
| *yú xiāng ròusī* | 鱼香肉丝 | fish-flavour pork strips |
| *zhàcài ròusī* | 榨菜肉丝 | stir-fried pork or beef tenderloin with tuber mustard |

## The East is Red (Wine)

Wine is hot in China. A bottle of red is an obvious status symbol for a burgeoning, wining and dining Chinese middle class: in 2013, China became the world's largest red-wine consumer, overtaking France and Italy by glugging (or at least purchasing) 155 million cases of the stuff. In 2015, China leapfrogged France to become the world's second-largest wine-growing region (behind Spain). Consumption per capita in China remains lower than in Europe, but sales of the tipple tripled from 1997 to 2013.

In China, the colour red (*hóng*) is a positive and vibrant colour: associated with wealth, power and good fortune, so red wine is the way to go (especially for men; Chinese women incline more to white). Despite the clear cachet of imported overseas wines, around 80% of wine drunk in China is more affordable red wine produced in China itself, in Níngxià.

Since the late '90s, the local government has been pumping water into the slopes of the Hèlán Shān mountains, which stand against the Gobi Desert. By the end of 2013, the transformed, fertile soil was feeding 23,500 hectares of vines. It's still early days, however – the vines are young, difficult to keep protected from Hèlán Shān's fluctuating temperatures and propagation standards are low.

## Eastern Cooking

The eastern school of Chinese cuisine derives from a fertile region of China, slashed by waterways and canals, glistening with lakes, fringed by a long coastline and nourished by a subtropical climate. Jiāngsū province itself is the home of Jiāngsū (苏菜; *sūcài*) cuisine – one of the core regions of the eastern school – and is famed as the 'Land of Fish and Rice', a tribute to its abundance of food and produce. The region has been historically prosperous, and in today's export-oriented economy the eastern provinces are among China's wealthiest. This combination of riches and bountiful food has created a culture of epicurism and gastronomic enjoyment.

South of Jiāngsū, Zhèjiāng (浙菜; *zhècài*) cuisine is another cornerstone of Eastern cooking. The Song dynasty saw the blossoming of the restaurant industry here; in Hángzhōu, the southern Song dynasty capital, restaurants and teahouses accounted for two-thirds of the city's business during a splendidly rich cultural era.

Generally more oily and sweeter than other Chinese schools, the eastern school revels in fish and seafood, reflecting its geographical proximity to major rivers and the sea. Fish is usually *qīngzhēng* (清蒸; steamed), but can be stir-fried, pan-fried or grilled. Hairy crabs (*dàxiàxiè*) are a Shànghǎi speciality between October and December. Eaten with soy, ginger and vinegar and downed with warm Shàoxīng wine, the best crabs come from Yangcheng Lake. The crab is believed to increase the body's *yīn* (coldness), so *yáng* (warmth) is added by imbibing lukewarm rice wine with it. It is also usual to eat male and female crabs together.

As with Cantonese food, freshness is a key element in the cuisine, and sauces and seasonings are only employed to augment essential flavours. Stir-frying and steaming are also used, the latter with Shànghǎi's famous *xiǎolóngbāo,* steamer buns filled with nuggets of pork or crab swimming in a scalding meat broth.

Famous dishes from the eastern school:

| | | |
|---|---|---|
| *gōngbào jīdīng* | 宫爆鸡丁 | spicy chicken with peanuts, aka *kung pao* chicken |
| *háoyóu niúròu* | 蚝油牛肉 | beef with oyster sauce |
| *hóngshāo páigǔ* | 红烧排骨 | red-braised spare ribs |
| *hóngshāo qiézi* | 红烧茄子 | red-cooked aubergine |
| *hóngshāo yú* | 红烧鱼 | red-braised fish |
| *huǒguō* | 火锅 | hotpot |
| *húntùn tāng* | 馄饨汤 | wonton soup |
| *jiācháng dòufu* | 家常豆腐 | 'homestyle' tofu |
| *jiǎozi* | 饺子 | dumplings |
| *jīdànmiàn* | 鸡蛋面 | noodles and egg |
| *qīngjiāo ròupiàn* | 青椒肉片 | pork and green peppers |
| *shāguō dòufu* | 沙锅豆腐 | bean curd (tofu) casserole |
| *suānlàtāng* | 酸辣汤 | hot-and-sour soup |
| *tiěbǎn niúròu* | 铁板牛肉 | sizzling beef platter |
| *xīhóngshì chǎojīdàn* | 西红柿炒鸡蛋 | fried egg and tomato |
| *xīhóngshì jīdàntāng* | 西红柿鸡蛋汤 | egg and tomato soup |
| *xīhóngshì niúròu* | 西红柿牛肉 | beef and tomato |
| *yúxiāng qiézi* | 鱼香茄子 | fish-flavoured aubergine |

## Dining: the Ins & Outs

### Tipping

Tipping is never done at cheap restaurants in mainland China. Smart, international restaurants will encourage tipping, but it is not obligatory and it's uncertain whether wait staff receive their tips at the end of the night.

Hotel restaurants automatically add a 15% service charge; some high-end restaurants may do the same.

### Dining Times

The Chinese eat early. Lunch usually commences from around 11.30am, either self-cooked or a takeaway at home, or in a streetside restaurant. Dinner kicks off from around 6pm. Reflecting these dining times, some restaurants open at around 11am, close for an afternoon break at about 2.30pm, open again around 5pm and then close in the late evening. Street-food vendors then take over the duty of feeding the late-night hungry folk.

### Table Manners

Chinese meal times are generally relaxed affairs with no strict rules of etiquette. Meals can commence in a Confucian vein before spiralling into total Taoist mayhem, fuelled by incessant toasts with *báijiǔ* (a white spirit) or beer and furious smoking by the men.

Meals typically unfold with one person ordering a selection of dishes to share on behalf of a group. As the dishes arrive, they are placed communally in the centre of the table or on a lazy Susan, which may be revolved by the host so that the principal guest gets first choice of whatever dish arrives. It is common practice and not impolite (unless messy) to

*Mápó dòufu*

★ **Sichuanese Dishes**

*Gōngbǎo jīdīng* (宫保鸡丁)

*Huíguō ròu* (回锅肉)

*Mápó dòufu* (麻婆豆腐)

*Shuǐzhǔyú* (水煮鱼)

*Zhāngchá yā* (樟茶鸭)

PAUL BRIGHTON / SHUTTERSTOCK ©

use your own chopsticks to serve yourself straight from each dish. Soup may appear midway through the meal or at the end. Rice often arrives at the end of the meal; if you would like it earlier, just ask. Chinese diners will often slurp their noodles quite noisily, which is not considered to be impolite.

It is good form to fill your neighbours' tea cups or beer glasses when they are empty. To serve yourself tea or any other drink without serving others first is bad form; appreciation to the pourer is indicated by gently tapping the middle finger on the table.

When your teapot needs a refill, signal this to the waiter by simply taking the lid off the pot.

It's best to wait until someone announces a toast before drinking your beer; if you want to get a quick shot in, propose a toast to the host. The Chinese do in fact toast each other much more than in the West – often each time they drink. A formal toast is conducted by raising your glass in both hands in the direction of the toastee and crying out *gānbēi* – literally, 'dry the glass' – which is the cue to drain your glass in one hit – this can be quite a challenge if your drink is 65% *báijiǔ*. Your glass will be rapidly refilled to the top after you drain it, in preparation for the next toast (which may rapidly follow).

Don't use your chopsticks to point at people or gesticulate with them – and never stick your chopsticks upright in bowls of rice (it's a portent of death).

Last but not least, don't insist on paying for the bill if someone else is tenaciously determined to pay – usually the person who invited you to dinner. By all means offer to pay, but then raise your hands in mock surrender when resistance is met: to pay for a meal when another person is determined to do it is to make them lose face.

Chinese toothpick etiquette is similar to that found in other Asian nations: one hand excavates with the toothpick, while the other hand shields the mouth.

## Menus

In Běijīng, Shànghǎi and other large cities, you may be proudly presented with an English menu (英文菜谱; *Yīngwén càipǔ*). In smaller towns and out in the sticks, don't expect anything other than a Chinese-language menu and a hovering waitress with no English-language skills. The best is undoubtedly the ever-handy photo menu. If you like the look of what other diners are eating, just point at it (我要那个; *wǒ yào nèi gè;* 'I want that' – a very handy phrase). Alternatively, pop into the kitchen and point out the meats and vegetables you would like to eat.

## Vegetarianism

If you'd rather chew on a legume than a leg of lamb, it can be hard to find truly vegetarian dishes. China's history of famine and poverty means the consumption of meat has always been a sign of status, and is symbolic of health and wealth. Eating meat is also considered to enhance male virility, so vegetarian men raise eyebrows. Partly because of this, there is virtually no vegetarian movement in China, although Chinese people may forgo meat for Buddhist reasons. For the same reasons, they may avoid meat on certain days of the month but remain carnivorous at other times.

You will find that vegetables are often fried in animal-based oils; vegetable soups are often made with chicken or beef stock, so simply choosing 'vegetable' items on the menu is ineffective. A dish that you are told does not contain meat may still mean it is riddled with tiny pieces of meat. In Běijīng and Shànghǎi you will, however, find a generous crop of vegetarian restaurants to choose from, alongside outfits such as Element Fresh, which has a decent range of healthy vegetarian options.

Out of the large cities, your best bet may be to head to a sizeable active Buddhist temple or monastery, where Buddhist vegetarian restaurants are often open to

### What's in a Cup?

An old Chinese saying identifies tea as one of the seven basic necessities of life, along with firewood, oil, rice, salt, soy sauce and vinegar. The Chinese were the first to cultivate tea, and the art of brewing and drinking it has been popular since Tang times (AD 618–907). Tea is to the Chinese what fine wine is to the French: a beloved beverage savoured for its fine aroma, distinctive flavour and pleasing aftertaste.

China has three main types of tea: green tea (*lǜ chá*), black tea (*hóng chá*) and *wūlóng* (a semifermented tea, halfway between black and green tea). In addition, there are other variations, including jasmine (*cháshuǐ*) and chrysanthemum (*júhuā chá*). Some famous regional teas of China are Fújiàn's *tiě guānyīn*, *pú'ěrh* from Yúnnán and Zhèjiāng's *lóngjǐng* tea. Eight-treasure tea (*bābǎo chá*) consists of rock sugar, dates, nuts and tea combined in a cup; it makes a delicious treat.

the public. Buddhist vegetarian food typically consists of 'mock meat' dishes created from tofu, wheat gluten, potato and other vegetables. Some of the dishes are almost works of art, with vegetarian ingredients sculpted to look like spare ribs or fried chicken. Sometimes the chefs go to great lengths to create 'bones' from carrots and lotus roots.

If you want to say 'I am a vegetarian' in Chinese, the phrase to use is *wǒ chī sù* (我吃素).

## Desserts & Sweets

The Chinese do not generally eat dessert, but fruit – typically watermelon (*xīguā*) or oranges (*chéng*) – often concludes a meal. Ice cream can be ordered in some places, but in general sweet desserts (*tiánpǐn*) are consumed as snacks and are seldom available in restaurants.

# Arts & Architecture

*China is custodian of one of the world's richest cultural and artistic legacies. Until the 20th century, China's arts were deeply conservative, but revolutions in technique and content over the last century have fashioned a dramatic transformation. Despite this evolution, China's arts – whatever the period – embrace a common aesthetic that embodies the very soul and lifeblood of the nation.*

Left: Sìchuān opera performance, Chéngdū (p230)
JACK / SHUTTERSTOCK ©
Right: National Centre for the Performing Arts (p63), Běijīng
GUOZHONGHUA / SHUTTERSTOCK ©

## Aesthetics

In reflection of the Chinese character, Chinese aesthetics have traditionally been marked by restraint and understatement, a preference for oblique references over direct explanation, vagueness in place of specificity and an avoidance of the obvious in place of a fondness for the veiled and subtle. Traditional Chinese aesthetics sought to cultivate a more reserved artistic impulse, principles that compellingly find their way into virtually every Chinese art form, from painting and sculpture to ceramics, calligraphy, film, poetry, literature and beyond.

As one of the central strands of the world's oldest civilisation, China's aesthetic traditions are tightly woven into Chinese cultural identity. For millennia, Chinese aesthetics were highly traditionalist and, despite coming under the influence of occupiers from the Mongols to the Europeans, defiantly conservative. It was not until the fall of the Qing dynasty in 1911 and

the appearance of the New Culture Movement that China's great artistic traditions began to rapidly transform. In literature the stranglehold of classical Chinese loosened to allow breathing space for *báihuà* (colloquial Chinese) and a progressive new aesthetic started to flower, ultimately leading to revolutions in all of the arts, from poetry and theatre to painting and music.

It is hard to square China's great aesthetic traditions with the devastation inflicted upon them since 1949. Confucius advocated the edifying role of music and poetry in shaping human lives, but 5th-century philosopher Mozi was less enamoured with them, seeing music and other arts as extravagant and wasteful. The communists took this a stage further, enlisting the arts as props in their propaganda campaigns, and permitting the vandalism and destruction of much traditional architecture and heritage.

## Painting

### Traditional Painting

Despite its symbolism, obscure references and occasionally abstruse philosophical allusions, Chinese painting is highly accessible. For this reason, traditional Chinese paintings – especially landscapes – have long been treasured in the West for their beauty.

Early painters dwelt on the human figure and moral teachings, while also conjuring up scenes from everyday life. By the time of the Tang dynasty, a new genre, known as landscape painting, had begun to flower. Reaching full bloom during the Song and Yuan dynasties, landscape painting meditated on the surrounding environment. Towering mountains,

★ **Art Museums & Galleries**

Shànghǎi Museum (p124)

Rockbund Art Museum (p124), Shànghǎi

National Museum of China (p47), Běijīng

M50 (p125), Shànghǎi

798 (p60), Běijīng

*Q Confucius No 2* by Zhang Huan, Rockbund Art Museum (p124), Shànghǎi

ethereal mists, open spaces, trees and rivers, and light and dark were all exquisitely presented in ink washes on silk. Landscape paintings attempted to capture the metaphysical and the absolute, drawing the viewer into a particular realm where the philosophies of Taoism and Buddhism found expression. Humanity is typically a small and almost insignificant subtext to the performance.

On a technical level, the success of landscapes depended on the artists' skill in capturing light and atmosphere. Blank, open spaces devoid of colour create light-filled voids, contrasting with the darkness of mountain folds and forests, filling the painting with *qì* (life energy) and vaporous vitality. Specific emotions are not aroused, but instead nebulous sensations permeate. Painting and classical poetry often went hand in hand, best exemplified by the work of Tang dynasty poet/artist Wang Wei (AD 699–759).

## Modern Art

After 1949, classical Chinese techniques were abandoned and foreign artistic techniques imported wholesale. Washes on silk were replaced with oil on canvas and China's traditional obsession with the mysterious and ineffable made way for concrete attention to detail and realism.

By 1970, Chinese artists had aspired to master the skills of socialist realism, a vibrant communist-endorsed style that drew from European neoclassical art, the lifelike canvases of Jacques-Louis David and the output of Soviet Union painters. The style had virtually nothing to do with traditional Chinese painting techniques. Saturated with political symbolism and propaganda, the blunt artistic style was manufactured on an industrial scale (and frequently on industrial themes).

It was only with the death of Mao Zedong in September 1976 that the shadow of the Cultural Revolution – when Chinese aesthetics were conditioned by the threat of violence – began its retreat and the individual artistic temperament was allowed to thrive afresh.

Painters such as Luo Zhongli employed the realist techniques gleaned from China's art academies to depict the harsh realities etched in the faces of contemporary peasants. Others escaped the suffocating confines of socialist realism to navigate new horizons. A voracious appetite for Western art brought with it fresh concepts and ideas, while the ambiguity of precise meaning in the fine arts offered a degree of protection from state censors.

The Tiān'ānmén Square protests in 1989 fostered a deep-seated cynicism that permeated artworks with loss, loneliness and social isolation. An exodus of artists to the West commenced. This period also coincided with an upsurge in the art market as investors increasingly turned to artworks and money began to slosh about.

Much post-1989 Chinese art dwelt obsessively on contemporary socioeconomic realities, with consumer culture, materialism, urbanisation and social change a repetitive focus. More universal themes became apparent, however, as the art scene matured. Meanwhile, many artists who left China in the 1990s have returned, setting up private studios and galleries. Government censorship remains, but artists are branching out into other areas and moving away from overtly political content and China-specific concerns.

## Contemporary Directions

Ai Weiwei, who enjoys great international fame partly due to his disobedient stand, best exemplifies the dangerous overlap between artistic self-expression, dissent and conflict with the authorities. Arrested in 2011 and charged with tax evasion, Ai Weiwei gained further publicity for his temporary *Sunflower Seeds* exhibition at the Tate Modern in London.

Working collaboratively as Birdhead, Shànghǎi analogue photographers Ji Weiyu and Song Tao record the social dynamics and architectural habitat of their home city in thoughtful compositions. Běijīng-born Ma Qiusha works in video, photography, painting and installations on themes of a deeply personal nature. In her video work *From No.4 Pingyuanli to No.4 Tianqiaobeili*, the artist removes a bloody razor blade from her mouth after narrating her experiences as a young artist in China.

Born in 1982, Ran Huang works largely in film but across a spectrum of media, conveying themes of absurdity, the irrational and conceptual. Shànghǎi artist Shi Zhiying explores ideas of a more traditional hue in her sublime oil-paint depictions on large canvases of landscapes and religious and cultural objects. Also from Shànghǎi, Xu Zhen works with provocative images to unsettle and challenge the viewer. Xu's *Fearless* (2012), a large mixed-media work on canvas, is a powerful maelstrom of symbolism and the fragments of cultural identity.

Xīnjiāng-born Zhao Zhao – once an assistant to Ai Weiwei – communicates provocative sentiments in his work, exploring ideas of freedom and themes of a non-conformist nature.

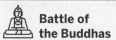

### Battle of the Buddhas

China's largest ancient Buddha gazes out over the confluence of the waters of the Dàdù River and the Mín River at Lè Shān in Sìchuān. When the even bigger Buddha at Bamyan in Afghanistan was demolished by the Taliban, the Lèshān Buddha enjoyed instantaneous promotion to the top spot as the world's largest. The vast (and modern) reclining Buddha at Lèshān is a whopping 170m long and the world's largest 'alfresco' reclining Buddha. The Buddha in the Great Buddha Temple at Zhāngyè in Gānsù province may not take it lying down, though: he is China's largest 'housed reclining Buddha'. Chinese children once climbed inside him to scamper about within his cavernous tummy.

Lounging around in second place is the reclining Buddha in the Mògāo Grottoes. Bristling with limbs, the Thousand Arm Guanyin statue in the Pǔníng Temple's Mahayana Hall in Chéngdé also stands up to be counted: she's the largest wooden statue in China (and possibly the world). Not to be outdone, Hong Kong fights for its niche with the Tian Tan Buddha Statue, the world's 'largest outdoor seated bronze Buddha statue'.

## Architecture

### Traditional Architecture

Four principal styles governed traditional Chinese architecture: imperial, religious, residential and recreational. The imperial style was naturally the most grandiose, overseeing the design of buildings employed by successive dynastic rulers; the religious style was employed for the

CCTV Building, Běijīng (p34)

LU JINRONG / SHUTTERSTOCK ©

★ **Modern Achitecture**

Shànghǎi World Financial Center (p126)

National Centre for the Performing Arts (p63)

HSBC Building (p164)

Shànghǎi Tower (p125)

construction of temples, monasteries and pagodas; while the residential and recreational style took care of the design of houses and private gardens.

Whatever the style, Chinese buildings traditionally followed a similar basic ground plan, consisting of a symmetrical layout oriented around a central axis – ideally running north–south to conform with basic feng shui (风水; *fēngshuǐ*) dictates and to maximise sunshine – with an enclosed courtyard (院; *yuàn*) flanked by buildings on all sides.

In many aspects, imperial palaces are glorified courtyard homes (south-facing, a sequence of courtyards, side halls and perhaps a garden at the rear) completed on a different scale. Apart from the size, the main dissimilarity would be guard towers on the walls and possibly a moat, imperial yellow roof tiles, ornate dragon carvings (signifying the emperor), the repetitive use of the number nine and the presence of temples.

## Modern Architecture

Architecturally speaking, anything goes in today's China. You only have to look at the Pǔdōng skyline to discover a melange of competing designs, some dramatic, inspiring and novel, others rash. The display represents a nation brimming over with confidence, zeal and cash.

The coastal areas are an architect's dreamland – no design is too outrageous, zoning laws have been scrapped, and the labour force is large and inexpensive. Planning permission can be simple to arrange – often all it requires is sufficient connections. Even the once cash-strapped interior provinces are getting in on the act. Opening in Chéngdū in 2013, the staggeringly large New Century Global Center is the world's largest free-standing building: big enough to swallow up 20 Sydney Opera Houses!

Many of the top names in international architecture – IM Pei, Rem Koolhaas, Norman Foster, Kengo Kuma, Jean-Marie Charpentier, Herzog & de Meuron – have all designed at least one building in China in the past decade. Other impressive examples of modern architecture include the National Stadium (aka the 'Bird's Nest'), the National Aquatics Center (aka the 'Water Cube') and Běijīng South train station, all in Běijīng; and the art deco–esque Jīnmào Tower, the towering Shànghǎi World Financial Center, Tomorrow Square and the Shànghǎi Tower in Shànghǎi. In Guǎngzhōu, the Zaha Hadid–designed Guǎngzhōu Opera House is an astonishing contemporary creation, both inside and out. In Hong Kong, the glittering 2 International Finance Center on Hong Kong Island and the International Commerce Center in Kowloon are each prodigious examples of modern skyscraper architecture.

## Traditional Garden Design

Classical Chinese gardens can be an acquired taste – there are generally no lawns and precious few long and ranging views, and misshapen, grey rocks and architectural features jostle for space. Yet a stroll in Shànghǎi's Yùyuán Gardens, for example, is a walk through many different facets of Chinese civilisation where architecture, philosophy, art and literature all converge.

The Chinese for 'landscape' is *shānshuǐ* (山水), literally 'mountain-water'. Mountains and rivers constitute a large part of China's geography, and are fundamental to Chinese life, philosophy, religion and art. So the central part of any garden landscape is a pond surrounded by rock formations. This also reflects the influence of Taoist thought. Contrary to geometrically designed formal European gardens, where humans saw themselves as masters, Chinese gardens seek to create a microcosm of the natural world through an asymmetrical layout of streams, hills, plants and pavilions (they symbolise humanity's place in the universe – never in the centre, just a part of the whole).

Plants are chosen as much for their symbolic meaning as their beauty (the pine for longevity, the peony for nobility) while the use of undulating 'dragon walls' brings good fortune. The names of gardens and halls are often literary allusions to ideals expressed in classical poetry. Painting, too, goes hand in hand with gardening, its aesthetics reproduced in gardens through the use of carefully placed windows and doors that frame a particular view. The central precept of feng shui (literally 'wind water') is also paramount, so rockeries and ponds are deliberately arranged to maximise positive *qì* (energy).

Finally, it's worth remembering that gardens in China have always been lived in. Generally part of a residence, they weren't so much contemplative (as in Japan) as they were a backdrop for everyday life: family gatherings, late-night drinking parties, discussions of philosophy, art and politics – it's the people who spent their leisure hours there that ultimately gave the gardens their unique spirit.

## Chinese Opera

Chinese opera, best known for Běijīng opera (京剧; Jīngjù), has a rich and continuous history of some 900 years. Evolving from a convergence of comic and ballad traditions in the Northern Song period, the art brought together a range of forms: acrobatics, martial arts, poetic arias and stylised dance.

Operas were usually performed by travelling troupes, who had a low social status in traditional Chinese society. Chinese law forbade mixed-sex performances, forcing actors to act out roles of the opposite sex. Opera troupes were frequently associated with homosexuality in the public imagination, contributing further to their lowly status.

Formerly, opera was performed mostly on open-air stages in markets, streets, teahouses or temple courtyards.

More than 100 varieties of opera coexist in China today, including Shanghainese opera (沪剧; Hùjù), sometimes called flower-drum opera, which is sung in the local dialect and has its origins in the folk songs of Pǔdōng. Yueju opera (越剧; Yuèjù) was born in and around Shàoxīng County in neighbouring Zhèjiāng (the ancient state of Yue) province in the early 20th century. Yuèjù roles are normally played by women. Kunju opera (昆剧; Kūnjù) or Kunqu opera (昆曲; Kūnqǔ) originates from Kūnshān, near Sūzhōu in neighbouring Jiāngsū.

Actors portray stylised stock characters who are instantly recognisable to the audience. Most stories are derived from classical literature and Chinese mythology and tell of disasters, natural calamities, intrigues or rebellions. The musicians usually sit on the stage in plain clothes and play without written scores.

# Religion & Beliefs

*Ideas have always possessed a potency and vitality in China.
The 19th-century Taiping Rebellion fused Christianity with revolutionary principles, almost sweeping away the Qing dynasty
in the process. The incandescence of the Boxer Rebellion drew on
a cocktail of martial-arts practices and superstition, while the
chaos of the Cultural Revolution indicated what can happen in
China when beliefs assume the full supremacy they seek.*

Left: Temple, Hong Kong (p158)

## Buddhism

Although not an indigenous faith, Buddhism (佛教; Fójiào) is the religion most deeply
associated with China and Tibet. Although Buddhism's authority has long ebbed, the faith
still exercises a powerful sway over China's spiritual inclinations. Many Chinese may not
be regular temple-goers, but they harbour an interest in Buddhism; they may merely be
'cultural Buddhists', with a strong affection for Buddhist civilisation.

Chinese towns with any history usually have several Buddhist temples, but the number
is well down on pre-1949 figures. The small Héběi town of Zhèngdìng, for example, has
four Buddhist temples, but at one time had eight. Běijīng once had hundreds, compared
to the 20 or so you can find today.

# Taoism

A home-grown philosophy-cum-religion, Taoism (道教; Dàojiào) is also perhaps the hardest of all China's faiths to grasp. Controversial, paradoxical, and – like the Tao itself – impossible to pin down, it is a natural counterpoint to rigid Confucianist order and responsibility.

Taoism predates Buddhism in China and much of its religious culture connects to a distant animism and shamanism, despite the purity of its philosophical school. In its earliest and simplest form, Taoism draws from *The Classic of the Way and Its Power* (Taote Jing; Dàodé Jìng), penned by the sagacious Laotzu (Laozi; c 580–500 BC) who left his writings with the gatekeeper of a pass as he headed west on the back of an ox. Some Chinese believe his wanderings took him to a distant land in the west where he became Buddha.

*The Classic of the Way and Its Power* is a work of astonishing insight and sublime beauty. Devoid of a god-like being or deity, Laotzu's writings instead endeavour to address the unknowable and indescribable principle of the universe, which he calls Dao (道; dào), or 'the Way'. Dao is the way or method by which the universe operates, so it can be understood to be a universal or cosmic principle.

One of Taoism's most beguiling precepts, *wúwéi* (inaction) champions the allowing of things to naturally occur without interference.

# Confucianism

The very core of Chinese society for the past two millennia, Confucianism (儒家思想; Rújiā Sīxiǎng) is a humanist philosophy that strives for social harmony and the common good. In China, its influence can be seen in everything from the emphasis on education and respect for elders to the patriarchal role of the government.

Confucianism is based upon the teachings of Confucius (Kongzi), a 6th century BC philosopher who lived during a period of constant warfare and social upheaval. While Confucianism changed considerably throughout the centuries, some of the principal ideas remained the same – namely an emphasis on five basic hierarchical relationships: father–son, ruler–subject, husband–wife, elder–younger and friend–friend. Confucius believed that if each individual carried out his or her proper role in society (a son served his father respectfully while a father provided for his son, a subject served his ruler respectfully while a ruler provided for his subject, and so on) social order would be achieved. Confucius' disciples later gathered his ideas in the form of short aphorisms and conversations, forming the work known as *The Analects* (Lúnyǔ).

# Christianity

The explosion of interest in Christianity (基督教; Jīdūjiào) in China over recent years is unprecedented except for the wholesale conversions that accompanied the tumultuous rebellion of the pseudo-Christian Taiping in the 19th century.

Christianity first arrived in China with the Nestorians, a sect from ancient Persia that split from the Byzantine Church in 431 AD, who arrived in China via the Silk Road in the 7th century. A celebrated tablet – the Nestorian Tablet – in Xī'ān records their arrival. Much later, in the 16th century, the Jesuits arrived and were popular figures at the imperial court, although they made few converts.

Large numbers of Catholic and Protestant missionaries established themselves in the 19th century, but left after the establishment of the People's Republic of China in 1949. One missionary, James Hudson Taylor from Barnsley in England, immersed himself in

Thousand arm Guanyin statue, Shuānglín Temple (p85)

Chinese culture and is credited with helping to convert 18,000 Chinese Christians and building 600 churches during his 50 years in 19th-century China.

In today's China, Christianity is a burgeoning faith, perhaps uniquely placed to expand due to its industrious work ethic, associations with developed nations and its emphasis on human rights and charitable work.

Some estimates point to as many as 100 million Christians in China. However, the exact number is hard to calculate, as many groups – outside the four official Christian organisations – lead a strict underground existence (in what are called 'house churches') out of fear of a political clampdown.

## Islam

Islam (伊斯兰教; Yīsīlán Jiào) in China dates to the 7th century, when it was first brought to China by Arab and Persian traders along the Silk Road. Later, during the Mongol Yuan dynasty, maritime trade increased, bringing new waves of merchants to China's coastal regions, particularly the port cities of Guǎngzhōu and Quánzhōu. The descendants of these groups – now scattered across the country – gradually integrated into Han culture, and are today distinguished primarily by their religion. In Chinese, they are referred to as the Hui.

Other Muslim groups include the Uighurs, Kazaks, Kyrgyz, Tajiks and Uzbeks, who live principally in the border areas of the northwest. It is estimated that 1.5% to 3% of Chinese today are Muslim.

# China's Landscapes

*The world's third-largest country – on a par size-wise with the USA – China swallows up an immense 9.5 million sq km, only surpassed in area by Russia and Canada. So whatever floats your boat – verdant bamboo forests, sapphire Himalayan lakes, towering sand dunes, sublime mountain gorges, huge glaciers or sandy beaches – China's landscapes offer a jaw-dropping diversity.*

Huángshān (p138)

## The Land

Straddling natural environments as diverse as subarctic tundra in the north and tropical rainforests in the south, this massive land ranges from the world's highest mountain range and one of its hottest deserts in the west to the steamy, typhoon-lashed coastline of the South China Sea. Fragmenting this epic landscape is a colossal web of waterways, including one of the world's mightiest rivers – the Yangzi (长江; Cháng Jiāng).

## Mountains

China has a largely mountainous and hilly topography, commencing in precipitous fashion in the vast and sparsely populated Qīnghǎi–Tibetan plateau in the west and levelling out

Tiger Leaping Gorge (p210)

MARTINHO SMART / SHUTTERSTOCK ©

gradually towards the fertile, well-watered, populous and wealthy provinces of eastern China.

This mountainous disposition sculpts so many of China's scenic highlights: from the glittering Lóngjǐ (Dragon's Backbone) Rice Terraces and sublime karst geology of Yángshuò of Guǎngxī to the incomparable stature of Mt Everest, the stunning beauty of Jiǔzhàigōu National Park in Sìchuān, the ethereal peaks of misty Huángshān in Ānhuī, the vertiginous inclines of Huá Shān in Shǎnxī and the volcanic drama of Heaven Lake in Jílín.

Averaging 4500m above sea level, the Qīnghǎi–Tibetan region's highest peaks thrust up into the Himalayan mountain range along its southern rim. This vast high-altitude region (Tibet alone constitutes one-eighth of China's landmass) is home to an astonishing 37,000 glaciers, the third-largest mass of ice on the planet after the Arctic and Antarctic. This enormous body of frozen water ensures that the Qīnghǎi–Tibetan region is the source of many of China's largest rivers, including the Yellow (Huáng Hé), Mekong (Láncāng Jiāng), and Salween (Nù Jiāng) Rivers and, of course, the mighty Yangzi, all of whose headwaters are fed by snow-melt from here.

## Deserts

China contains head-spinningly huge – and growing – desert regions that occupy almost one-fifth of the country's landmass, largely in its mighty northwest. North towards Kazakhstan and Kyrgyzstan from the plateaus of Tibet and Qīnghǎi is Xīnjiāng's Tarim Basin, the largest inland basin in the world. This is the location of the mercilessly thirsty Taklamakan Desert – China's largest desert and the world's second-largest mass of sand after the Sahara Desert.

The Silk Road into China steered its epic course through this entire region, ferrying caravans of camels laden with merchandise, languages, philosophies, customs and peoples from the far-flung lands of the Middle East. The harsh environment shares many topographical features in common with the neighbouring nations of Afghanistan, Kyrgyzstan and Kazakhstan, and is almost the exact opposite of China's lush and well-watered southern provinces.

China's most famous desert is, of course, the Gobi, although most of it lies outside the country's borders.

## Rivers & Plains

At about 5460km long and the second-longest river in China, the Yellow River (黄河; Huáng Hé) is touted as the birthplace of Chinese civilisation and has been fundamental in the development of Chinese society. From its source in Qīnghǎi, the river runs through North China, meandering past or near many famous towns, including Lánzhōu, Yínchuān, Bāotóu, Hánchéng, Jìnchéng, Luòyáng, Zhèngzhōu, Kāifēng and Jǐ'nán in Shāndōng, before exiting China north of Dōngyíng (although the watercourse often runs dry nowadays before it reaches the sea).

The Yangzi (the 'Long River') is one of the longest rivers in the world (and China's longest). Its watershed of almost 2 million sq km – 20% of China's land mass – supports 400 million people. Dropping from its source high on the Tibetan plateau, it runs for 6300km to the sea, of which the last few hundred kilometres is across virtually flat alluvial plains. In the course of its sweeping journey, the river (and its tributaries) fashions many of China's scenic spectacles, including Tiger Leaping Gorge and the Three Gorges, and cuts through a string of huge and historic cities, including Chóngqìng, Wǔhàn and Nánjīng, before surging into the East China Sea north of Shànghǎi.

# Wildlife

China's vast size, diverse topography and climatic disparities support an astonishing range of habitats for animal life. The Tibetan plateau alone is the habitat of more than 500 species of birds, while half of the animal species in the northern hemisphere exist in China.

It is unlikely you will see many of these creatures in their natural habitat unless you are a specialist, or have a lot of time, patience, persistence, determination and luck. But there are plenty of pristine reserves within relatively easy reach of travellers' destinations such as Chéngdū and Xī'ān, and even if you don't get the chance to see animals, the scenery is terrific.

## Mammals

China's towering mountain ranges form natural refuges for wildlife, many of which are now protected in parks and reserves that have escaped the depredations of loggers and dam-builders.

The Himalayan foothills of western Sìchuān support the greatest diversity of mammals in China. Aside from giant pandas, other mammals found in this region include the panda's small cousin – the raccoon-like red panda – as well as Asiatic black bears and leopards. Among the grazers are golden takin, a large goat-like antelope with a yellowish coat and a reputation for being cantankerous, argali sheep and various deer species, including the diminutive mouse deer.

Overall, China is unusually well endowed with big and small cats. The world's largest tiger, the Manchurian tiger (Dōngběihǔ) – also known as the Siberian Tiger – only numbers a few hundred in the wild, its remote habitat being one of its principal saviours. Three species of leopard can also be found, including the beautiful clouded leopard of tropical rainforests, plus several species of small cat, such as the Asiatic golden cat and a rare endemic species, the Chinese mountain cat.

Rainforests are famous for their diversity of wildlife, and the tropical south of Yúnnán province, particularly the area around Xīshuāngbǎnnà, is one of the richest in China. These forests support Indo-Chinese tigers and herds of Asiatic elephants.

The giant panda (xióngmāo – literally 'bear cat') is western Sìchuān's most famous denizen, but the animal's solitary nature makes it elusive for observation in the wild, and even today, after decades of intensive research and total protection in dedicated reserves, sightings are rare.

### Best Books on China's Environment

o *When a Billion Chinese Jump* (2010) Jonathan Watts' sober and engaging study of China's environmental issues.

o *China's Environmental Challenges* (2012) Judith Shapiro's excellent primer for understanding China's manifold environmental problems.

o *The River Runs Black: The Environmental Challenge to China's Future* (2010; 2nd edition) Elizabeth Economy's frightening look at the unhappy marriage between breakneck economic production and environmental degradation.

o *The China Price: The True Cost of Chinese Competitive Advantage* (2008) Alexandra Harney's telling glimpse behind the figures of China's economic rise.

o *China's Water Crisis* (2004) Ma Jun rolls up his sleeves to fathom China's water woes.

## Birds

Most of the wildlife you'll see in China will be birds, and with more than 1300 species recorded, including about 100 endemic or near-endemic species, China offers some fantastic birdwatching opportunities. Spring is usually the best time, when deciduous foliage buds, migrants return from their wintering grounds and nesting gets into full swing. BirdLife International (www.birdlife.org/datazone/country/china), the worldwide bird conservation organisation, recognises 14 Endemic Bird Areas (EBAs) in China, either wholly within the country or shared with neighbouring countries.

## Plants

China is home to more than 32,000 species of seed plant and 2500 species of forest tree, plus an extraordinary plant diversity that includes some famous 'living fossils' – a diversity so great that Jílín province in the semifrigid north and Hǎinán province in the tropical south share few plant species.

Apart from rice, the plant probably most often associated with China and Chinese culture is bamboo, of which China boasts some 300 species. Bamboos grow in many parts of China, but bamboo forests were once so extensive that they enabled the evolution of the giant panda, which eats virtually nothing else, and a suite of small mammals, birds and insects that live in bamboo thickets. Most of these species are found in the subtropical areas south of the Yangzi, and the best surviving thickets are in southwestern provinces such as Sìchuān.

A growing number of international wildlife travel outfits arrange botanical expeditions to China, including UK-based Naturetrek (www.naturetrek.co.uk), which arranges tours to Yúnnán, Sìchuān and the Tibetan Plateau.

## Endangered Species

Almost every large mammal you can think of in China has crept onto the endangered species list, as well as many of the so-called 'lower' animals and plants. The snow leopard, Manchurian tiger, Indo-Chinese tiger, chiru antelope, crested ibis, Asiatic elephant, red-crowned crane and black-crowned crane are all endangered.

Deforestation, pollution, hunting and trapping for fur, body parts and sport are all culprits. The Convention on International Trade in Endangered Species of Wild Fauna and Flora (CITES) records legal trade in live reptiles and parrots, and high numbers of reptile and wildcat skins. The number of such products collected or sold unofficially is anyone's guess.

Despite the threats, a number of rare animal species cling to survival in the wild. Notable among them are the Chinese alligator in Ānhuī, the giant salamander in the fast-running waters of the Yangzi and Yellow Rivers, the Yangzi River dolphin in the lower and middle reaches of the river (although there have been no confirmed sightings since 2002), and the pink dolphin of the Hong Kong islands of Sha Chau and Lung Kwu Chau. The giant panda is confined to the fauna-rich valleys and ranges of Sìchuān.

# A Greener China?

China is painfully aware of its accelerated desertification, growing water shortages, shrinking glaciers, acidic rain, contaminated rivers, caustic urban air and polluted soil. The government is keenly committed, on a policy level, to the development of greener and cleaner energy sources. China's leaders are also seeking to devise a more sustainable and less wasteful economic model for the nation's future development.

There is evidence of ambitious and bold thinking: in 2010, China announced it would pour billions into developing electric and hybrid vehicles (although the goal of 30% of car sales going to electric vehicles seemed wildly optimistic); Běijīng committed itself to over-taking Europe in renewable energy investment by 2020; wind-farm construction (in Gānsù, for example) continues apace; and China leads the world in the production of solar cells. Coal use is also declining: in 2015, China imported 30% less and consumed 3.7% less coal, aiming to shut 1000 mines by the end of 2016. Some analysts say China has already surpassed 'peak coal', however, two-thirds of China's power still comes from the fossil fuel.

Rafting near Guilín (p197)

FEIYUEZHANGJIE / SHUTTERSTOCK ©

# Survival Guide

# Directory A–Z

## Accommodation

China's accommodation choices are impressive but enormously varied. Top-tier cities have a rich variety of sleeping options; other towns can have a poor supply, despite being inundated with visitors. Rural destinations are largely a patchwork of homesteads and hostels, with the occasional boutique-style choice in big-ticket villages.

**Hotels** From two-star affairs with very limited English and simple rooms to international-level, five-star towers and heritage hotels.

**Hostels** Exist across China in growing numbers, usually

### Book Your Stay Online

For accommodation reviews by Lonely Planet authors, check out http://hotels.lonely planet.com/china. You'll find independent reviews, as well as recommendations on the best places to stay. Best of all, you can book online.

offering dorm beds and double rooms and dispensing useful travel advice.

**Homestays** In rural locations, you can often find double rooms in converted houses, with meals provided.

## Hotel Discounts

Always ignore the rack rate and ask for the discounted price or bargain for a room, as discounts usually apply everywhere but youth hostels (except for hostel members) and the cheapest accommodation. Discounts of 10% to 60% off the tariff rate (30% is typical) are the norm, available by simply asking at reception on arrival, by phoning in advance to reserve a room or by booking online at Ctrip.

Apart from during the busy holiday periods (the end of April and first few days of May; the first week of October; Chinese New Year), rooms should be priced well below the rack rate and are rarely booked out.

## Reservations

Accommodation prices vary across China. Rooms are generally easy to procure, but phone ahead to reserve a room in popular tourist towns, especially for weekend visits. Booking online can help you secure a room and obtain a good price. To secure accommodation, always plan ahead and book your room in advance during the high season. Airports at major cities often have

hotel-booking counters that offer discounted rates.

**Ctrip** (www.english.ctrip.com) Excellent hotel booking, air and train ticketing website, with English helpline. Useful app available.

**Elong** (www.elong.net) Hotel and air ticket booking, with English helpline.

**Travel Zen** (www.travel zen.com) Air tickets and hotel bookings; Chinese-only website. English helpline.

## Bargaining

Haggling is standard procedure in markets and shops (outside of department stores and malls) where prices are not clearly marked. There's no harm in coming in really low, but remain polite at all times. In touristy markets in Shànghǎi and Běijīng, vendors can drop as low as 25% of the original price.

## Customs Regulations

Chinese customs generally pay tourists little attention. 'Green channels' and 'red channels' at the airport are clearly marked. You are not allowed to import or export illegal drugs, or animals and plants (including seeds). Pirated DVDs and CDs are illegal exports from

China – if found they will be confiscated. You can take Chinese medicine up to a value of ¥300 when you depart China.

Duty free, you're allowed to import:

o 400 cigarettes (or the equivalent in tobacco products)

o 1.5L of alcohol

o 50g of gold or silver.

Also note:

o Importation of fresh fruit and cold cuts is prohibited.

o There are no restrictions on foreign currency, but you should declare any cash exceeding US$5000 or its equivalent in another currency.

Objects considered antiques require a certificate and a red seal to clear customs when leaving China. Anything made before 1949 is considered an antique, and if it was made before 1795 it cannot legally be taken out of the country. To get the proper certificate and red seal, your antiques must be inspected by the **State Administration of Cultural**

**Heritage** (Guójiā Wénwù Jú; Map p56; ☏010 5679 2211; www.sach.gov.cn; 83 Beiheyan Dajie; ☺8.30am-5pm; ⑤Lines 6, 8 to Nanluoguxiang, exit B or Line 5 to Zhangzizhonglu, exit D) in Běijīng.

## Electricity

There are three types of plugs used in China – three-pronged angled pins, two flat pins (the most common) or two narrow round pins. Electricity is 220 volts, 50 cycles AC.

## Climate

### Běijīng

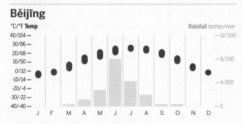

### Hong Kong

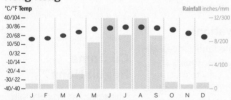

### Shànghǎi

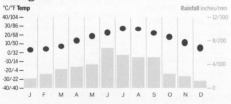

220V/50Hz

220V/50Hz

# Food

Unless otherwise noted, price ranges in the guide are for mains.

**Běijīng**
(prices for a two-course meal)
**$** less than ¥40
**$$** ¥40 to ¥100
**$$$** more than ¥100

**Shànghǎi**
(prices for a two-course meal)
**$** less than ¥60
**$$** ¥60 to ¥160
**$$$** more than ¥160

**Rest of Mainland China**
(prices for a two-course meal)
**$** less than ¥40
**$$** ¥40 to ¥60
**$$$** more than ¥60

**Hong Kong** (prices for a two-course meal with drinks)
**$** less than HK$200
**$$** HK$200 to HK$500
**$$$** more than HK$500

**Macau** (prices for a two-course meal with drinks)
**$** less than MOP$200
**$$** MOP$200 to MOP$400
**$$$** more than MOP$400

# Health

China is a reasonably healthy country to travel in, but some health issues should be noted. Outside of the major cities, medical care is often inadequate, and food and waterborne diseases are common.

The following advice is a general guide only and does not replace the advice of a doctor trained in travel medicine.

## Before You Go

It's usually a good idea to consult your government's travel advisory website for health warnings before departure (if one is available).

**Australia** (www.dfat.gov.au/travel)

**Canada** (www.travelhealth.gc.ca)

**New Zealand** (www.safetravel.govt.nz)

**UK** (www.gov.uk/foreign-travel-advice) Search for travel in the site index.

**USA** (www.cdc.gov/travel)

## Recommended Vaccinations

The World Health Organization (WHO) recommends the following vaccinations for travellers to China:

**Adult diphtheria and tetanus (ADT)** Single booster recommended if you've not received one in the previous 10 years. Side effects include a sore arm and fever. An ADT vaccine that immunises against pertussis (whooping cough) is also available and may be recommended by your doctor.

**Hepatitis A** Provides almost 100% protection for up to a year; a booster after 12 months provides at least another 20 years' protection. Mild side effects such as a headache and sore arm occur in 5% to 10% of people.

**Hepatitis B** Now considered routine for most travellers. Given as three shots over six months; a rapid schedule is also available. There is also a combined vaccination with hepatitis A. Side effects are mild and uncommon, usually a headache and sore arm. Lifetime protection results in 95% of people.

**Measles, mumps and rubella (MMR)** Two doses of MMR is recommended unless you have had the diseases. Occasionally a rash and a flulike illness can develop a week after receiving the vaccine. Many adults under 40 require a booster.

**Typhoid** Recommended unless your trip is less than a week. The vaccine offers around 70% protection, lasts for two to three years and comes as a single shot. Tablets are also available; however, the injection is usually recommended as it has fewer side effects. A sore arm and fever may occur. A vaccine combining hepatitis A and typhoid in a single shot is now available.

**Varicella** If you haven't had chickenpox, discuss this vaccination with your doctor.

The following immunisations are recommended for travellers spending more than one month in the country or those at special risk:

**Influenza** A single shot lasts one year and is recommended for those over 65 years of age or with underlying medical conditions such as heart or lung disease.

**Japanese B encephalitis** A series of three injections with a booster after two years. Recommended if spending more than one month in rural areas in the summer months, or more than three months in the country.

**Pneumonia** A single injection with a booster after five years is recommended for all travellers over 65 years of age or with underlying medical conditions that compromise immunity, such as heart or lung disease, cancer or HIV.

**Rabies** Three injections in all. A booster after one year will then provide 10 years' protection. Side effects are rare – occasionally a headache and sore arm.

**Tuberculosis** A complex issue. High-risk, adult, long-term travellers are usually recom-

mended to have a TB skin test before and after travel, rather than vaccination. Only one vaccine is given in a lifetime. Children under five spending more than three months in China should be vaccinated.

Pregnant women and children should receive advice from a doctor who specialises in travel medicine.

## Medical Checklist

Recommended items for a personal medical kit:

o antibacterial cream, eg mucipirocin

o antibiotics for diarrhoea, including norfloxacin, ciprofloxacin or azithromycin for bacterial diarrhoea; or tinidazole for giardia or amoebic dysentery

o antibiotics for skin infections, eg amoxicillin/clavulanate or cephalexin

o antifungal cream, eg clotrimazole

o antihistamine, eg cetrizine for daytime and promethazine for night-time

o anti-inflammatory, eg ibuprofen

o antiseptic, eg Betadine

o antispasmodic for stomach cramps, eg Buscopan

o decongestant, eg pseudoephedrine

o diamox if going to high altitudes

o bandages, gauze, thermometer (but not mercury),

sterile needles and syringes, safety pins and tweezers

o indigestion tablets, such as Quick-Eze or Mylanta

o insect repellent containing DEET

o iodine tablets to purify water (unless you're pregnant or have a thyroid problem)

o laxative, eg coloxyl

o oral-rehydration solution (eg Gastrolyte) for diarrhoea, diarrhoea 'stopper' (eg loperamide) and anti-nausea medication (eg prochlorperazine)

o paracetamol

o permethrin to impregnate clothing and mosquito nets

o steroid cream for rashes, eg 1% to 2% hydrocortisone

o sunscreen

o thrush (vaginal yeast infection) treatment, eg clotrimazole pessaries or Diflucan tablet

o urinary infection treatment, eg Ural

## Websites

**Centers for Disease Control & Prevention** (www.cdc.gov)

**MD Travel Health** (www.mdtravelhealth.com) Provides complete travel-health recommendations for every country; updated daily.

**World Health Organization** (www.who.int/ith) Publishes the excellent *International Travel & Health*, revised annually and available online.

## In China

### Availability & Cost of Health Care

Good clinics catering to travellers can be found in major cities. They are more expensive than local facilities but you may feel more comfortable dealing with a Western-trained doctor who speaks your language. These clinics usually have a good understanding of the best local hospital facilities and close contacts with insurance companies should you need evacuation.

### Infectious Diseases

#### Dengue

This mosquito-borne disease occurs in some parts of southern China. There is no vaccine so avoid mosquito bites – the dengue-carrying mosquito bites day and night, so use insect-avoidance measures at all times. Symptoms include high fever, severe headache and body ache. Some people develop a rash and diarrhoea. There is no specific treatment – just rest and paracetamol. Do not take aspirin.

#### Hepatitis A

A problem throughout China, this food- and water-borne virus infects the liver, causing jaundice (yellow skin and eyes), nausea and lethargy. There is no specific treatment for hepatitis A; you just need to allow time for the liver to heal. All travellers to China should be vaccinated.

#### Hepatitis B

The only sexually transmitted disease that can be prevented by vaccination, hepatitis B is spread by contact with infected body fluids. The long-term consequences can include liver cancer and cirrhosis. All travellers to China should be vaccinated.

#### Japanese Encephalitis

Formerly known as 'Japanese B encephalitis', this is a rare disease in travellers; however, vaccination is recommended if you're in rural areas for more than a month during summer months, or if spending more than three months in the country. No treatment is available; one-third of infected people die, another third suffer permanent brain damage.

#### Malaria

Malaria has been nearly eradicated in China; it is not generally a risk for visitors to the cities and most tourist areas. It is found mainly in rural areas in the southwestern region bordering Myanmar, Laos and Vietnam, principally Hǎinán, Yúnnán and Guǎngxī. More limited risk exists in the remote rural areas of Fújiàn, Guǎngdōng, Guìzhōu and Sìchuān. Generally, medication is only advised if you are visiting rural Hǎinán, Yúnnán or Guǎngxī.

#### Rabies

An increasingly common problem in China, this fatal disease is spread by the bite or lick of an infected animal, most commonly a dog. Seek medical advice immediately after any animal bite and commence postexposure treatment. The pretravel vaccination means the post-bite treatment is greatly simplified.

#### Schistosomiasis (Bilharzia)

This disease occurs in the central Yangzi River (Cháng Jiāng) basin, carried in water by minute worms that infect certain varieties of freshwater snail found in rivers, streams, lakes and, particularly, behind dams. The infection often causes no symptoms until the disease is well established (several months to years after exposure); any resulting damage to internal organs is irreversible. Effective treatment is available.

○ Avoid swimming or bathing in fresh water where bilharzia is present.

○ A blood test is the most reliable way to diagnose the disease, but the test will not show positive until weeks after exposure.

#### Typhoid

Typhoid is a serious bacterial infection spread via food and water. Symptoms include headaches, a high and slowly progressive fever, perhaps accompanied by a dry cough and stomach pain. Vaccination is not

100% effective, so still be careful what you eat and drink. All travellers spending more than a week in China should be vaccinated against typhoid.

### Environmental Hazards

#### Air Pollution

Air pollution is a significant and worsening problem in many Chinese cities. People with underlying respiratory conditions should seek advice from their doctor prior to travel to ensure they have adequate medications in case their condition worsens. Take treatments such as throat lozenges, and cough and cold tablets.

#### Tap Water

In general, you should never drink the tap water in China, even in 5-star hotels. Boiling water makes it safe to drink, but you might still prefer to buy bottled water for the taste or mineral make-up.

Follow these tips to avoid becoming ill:

○ Never drink unboiled tap water.

○ Bottled water is generally safe – check that the seal is intact at purchase.

○ Avoid ice.

○ Avoid fresh juices – they may have been watered down.

○ Boiling water is the most efficient method of purifying water.

○ The best chemical purifier is iodine. It should not be used by pregnant women or those with thyroid problems.

#### Traveller's Diarrhoea

Between 30% and 50% of visitors will suffer from traveller's diarrhoea within two weeks of starting their trip. In most cases, the ailment is caused by bacteria and responds promptly to treatment with antibiotics.

Treatment consists of staying hydrated; rehydration solutions such as Gastrolyte are best. Antibiotics such as norfloxacin, ciprofloxacin or azithromycin will kill the bacteria quickly. Loperamide is just a 'stopper' and doesn't cure the problem; it can be helpful, however, for long bus rides. Don't take loperamide if you have a fever, or blood in your stools.

#### Amoebic Dysentery

Amoebic dysentery is actually rare in travellers and is over-diagnosed. Symptoms are similar to bacterial diarrhoea – fever, bloody diarrhoea and generally feeling unwell. Always seek reliable medical care if you have blood in your diarrhoea. Treatment involves two drugs: tinidazole or metronidazole to kill the parasite in your gut, and then a second drug to kill the cysts. If amoebic dysentery is left untreated, complications such as liver or gut abscesses can occur.

#### Giardiasis

Giardiasis is a parasite relatively common in travellers. Symptoms include nausea, bloating, excess gas, fatigue and intermittent diarrhoea. 'Eggy' burps are often attributed solely to giardia, but are not specific to the parasite. Giardiasis will eventually go away if left untreated, but this can take months. The treatment of choice is tinidazole, with metronidazole a second option.

#### Intestinal Worms

These parasites are most common in rural, tropical areas. Some may be ingested in food such as undercooked meat (eg tapeworms) and some enter through your skin (eg hookworms). Consider having a stool test when you return home.

### Women's Health

Pregnant women should receive specialised advice before travelling. The ideal time to travel is in the second trimester (between 14 and 28 weeks), when the risk of pregnancy-related problems is at its lowest and pregnant women generally feel at their best. During the first trimester, miscarriage is a risk; in the third trimester, complications such as premature labour and high blood pressure are possible. Travel with a companion and carry a list of quality medical facilities for your destination, ensuring you continue your standard antenatal care at these facilities. Avoid rural areas with poor transport and medical facilities. Above all, ensure travel insurance covers all pregnancy-related possibilities, including premature labour.

Malaria is a high-risk disease in pregnancy. The World Health Organization recommends that pregnant women do not travel to areas with chloroquine-resistant malaria.

Heat, humidity and antibiotics can all contribute to thrush. Treatment is with antifungal creams and pessaries such as clotrimazole. A practical alternative is a single tablet of fluconazole (Diflucan). Urinary tract infections can be precipitated by dehydration or long bus journeys without toilet stops; bring suitable antibiotics.

Supplies of sanitary products may not be readily available in rural areas. Birth-control options may be limited, so bring adequate supplies of your own form of contraception.

## Insurance

Carefully consider a travel insurance policy to cover theft, loss, trip cancellation and medical eventualities. Travel agents can sort this out for you, although it is often cheaper to find good deals with an insurer online or with a broker.

Paying for your airline ticket with a credit card often provides limited travel accident insurance – ask your credit-card company what it's prepared to cover.

Worldwide travel insurance is available at www.lonelyplanet.com/travel-insurance. You can buy, extend and claim online anytime – even if you're already on the road.

## Internet Access

Wi-fi accessibility in hotels, cafes, restaurants and bars is generally good. The best option is to bring a wi-fi equipped smartphone, tablet or laptop or use your hotel computer or broadband internet connection. Chain restaurants and cafes with free wi-fi often still require a Chinese phone number to receive a login code.

The Chinese authorities remain mistrustful of the internet, and censorship is heavy-handed. Around 10% of websites are blocked; the list is constantly changing but includes sites and apps such as Facebook, Twitter, Instagram, Google-owned sites (YouTube, Google Maps, Gmail, Google Drive), Dropbox and Telegram, so plan ahead. Google's search function is blocked, but a limited Chinese version of Yahoo and Bing are accessible. Newspapers such as the *New York Times* are also blocked, as is Bloomberg, though the *Guardian* is allowed.

Users can gain access to blocked websites by using a VPN (Virtual Private Network) service such as VyperVPN (www.golden frog.com). Be aware that using VPNs can be slow, and often are blocked sites themselves so must be installed before arriving in China – and not all even work in China.

Many internet cafes only accept customers with Chinese ID, thus barring foreigners. In large cities and towns, the area around the train station generally has internet cafes.

The internet icon @ in hotel reviews indicates the presence of an internet cafe or a terminal where you can get online; wi-fi areas are indicated with a wi-fi 🛜 icon.

## Legal Matters

China does not officially recognise dual nationality or the foreign citizenship of children born in China if one of the parents is a PRC national. If you have Chinese and another nationality you may, in theory, not be allowed to visit China on your foreign passport. In practice, Chinese authorities are not switched-on enough to know if you own two passports, and should accept you on a foreign passport. Dual-nationality citizens who enter China on a Chinese passport are subject to Chinese laws and are legally not allowed consular help. If over 16 years of age, carry your passport with you at all times as a form of ID.

Gambling is officially illegal in mainland China, as is distributing religious material.

China takes a particularly dim view of opium and all its derivatives; trafficking in more than 50g of heroin can lead to the death penalty. Foreign passport holders have been executed in China for drug offences. The Chinese criminal justice system does not necessarily ensure a fair trial and defendants are not presumed innocent until proven guilty. If arrested, most foreign citizens have the right to contact their embassy.

## LGBT Travellers

Greater tolerance exists in the big cities than in the more conservative countryside, but even in urban areas, gay and lesbian public displays of affection can raise an eyebrow. You will often see Chinese friends of the same sex holding hands or putting their arms around each other, but this usually has no sexual connotation.

There are gay bars and clubs in the major cities, but it is far more common for people to socialise on apps.

**Dànlán** (淡蓝; www.danlan.org) Chinese-only news and lifestyle.

**Spartacus International Gay Guide** (www.spartacusworld. com/en) Best-selling guide for gay travellers; also available as an iPhone App.

**Utopia** (www.utopia-asia.com/tipschin.htm) Tips on travelling in China and a complete listing of gay bars nationwide.

## Money

ATMs in big cities and towns. Credit cards less widely used; carry cash.

### ATMs

Bank of China and the Industrial & Commercial Bank of China (ICBC) 24-hour ATMs are plentiful, and you can use Visa, Master-Card, Cirrus, Maestro Plus and American Express to withdraw cash. All ATMs accepting international cards have dual-language ability. The network is largely found in sizeable towns and cities.

The exchange rate on ATM withdrawals is similar to that for credit cards, but there is a maximum daily withdrawal amount. Note that banks can charge a withdrawal fee for using the ATM network of another bank, so check with your

bank before travelling. Bank of Nanjing ATMs waive the withdrawal fee for members of the Global ATM Alliance (enquire with your bank).

To have money wired from abroad, visit Western Union or Moneygram (www. moneygram.com).

### Cash

The Chinese currency is the rénmínbì (RMB), or 'people's money'. The basic unit of RMB is the yuán (元; ¥), which is divided into 10 jiǎo (角), which is again divided into 10 fēn (分). Colloquially, the yuán is referred to as kuài and jiǎo as máo (毛). The fēn has so little value these days that it is rarely used.

The Bank of China issues RMB bills in denominations of ¥1, ¥2, ¥5, ¥10, ¥20, ¥50 and ¥100. Coins come in denominations of ¥1, 5 jiǎo, 1 jiǎo and 5 fēn. Paper versions of the coins remain in circulation.

Hong Kong's currency is the Hong Kong dollar (HK$). The Hong Kong dollar is divided into 100 cents. Bills are issued in denominations of HK$10, HK$20, HK$50, HK$100, HK$500 and HK$1000. Copper coins are worth 50c, 20c and 10c, while the $5, $2 and $1 coins are silver and the $10 coin is nickel and bronze. The Hong Kong dollar is pegged to the US dollar at a rate of US$1 to HK$7.80, though it is allowed to fluctuate a little.

Macau's currency is the pataca (MOP$), which is divided into 100 avos. Bills are issued in denominations of MOP$10, MOP$20, MOP$50, MOP$100, MOP$500 and MOP$1000. There are copper coins worth 10, 20 and 50 avos and silver-coloured MOP$1, MOP$2, MOP$5 and MOP$10 coins. The pataca is pegged to the Hong Kong dollar at a rate of MOP$103.20 to HK$100. In effect, the two currencies are interchangeable and Hong Kong dollars, including coins, are accepted in Macau. Chinese rénmínbì is also accepted in many places in Macau at one-to-one. You can't spend patacas anywhere else, however, so use them before you leave Macau. Prices quoted are in yuán unless otherwise stated.

## Credit Cards

In large tourist towns, credit cards are relatively straightforward to use, but don't expect to be able to use them everywhere, and always carry enough cash. The exception is in Hong Kong, where international credit cards are accepted almost everywhere (although some shops may try to add a surcharge to offset the commission charged by credit companies, which can range from 2.5% to 7%).

## Exchange Rates

| Australia | A$1 | ¥4.9 |
|---|---|---|
| Canada | C$1 | ¥5.1 |
| Euro zone | €1 | ¥7.4 |
| Hong Kong | HK$1 | ¥0.8 |
| Japan | ¥100 | ¥6.3 |
| New Zealand | NZ$1 | ¥4.7 |
| UK | UK£1 | ¥9.7 |
| US | US$1 | ¥6.6 |

For current exchange rates see www.xe.com.

## Moneychangers

It's best to wait till you reach China to exchange money as the exchange rate will be better. Foreign currency and travellers cheques can be changed at border crossings, international airports, branches of the Bank of China, tourist hotels and some large department stores; hours of operation for foreign exchange counters are 8am to 7pm (later at hotels). Top-end hotels will generally change money for hotel guests only. The official rate is given almost everywhere and the exchange charge is standardised, so there is little need to shop around for the best deal.

Keep at least a few of your exchange receipts. You will need them if you want to exchange any remaining RMB you have at the end of your trip.

## Taxes & Refunds

When shoppping, tax is already included on the dis-played prices. Nearly all of the major cities offer a tax refund for foreign tourists on purchases made in the previous 90 days; the list of provinces keeps expanding.

The 11% tax is refunded at the airport and all items must leave China with you. Goods have a minimum purchase of ¥500 from the one store.

## Tipping

**Hotels** Porters may expect a tip.

**Restaurants** Tipping is never expected at cheap, and many midrange, restaurants. In general there is no need to tip if a service charge has already been added, so check your bill for one.

**Taxis** Drivers do not expect tips.

## Travellers Cheques

With the prevalence of ATMs across China, travellers cheques are not as useful as they once were and cannot be used everywhere, so always ensure you carry enough ready cash. You should have no problem cashing travellers cheques at tourist hotels, but they are of little use in budget hotels and restaurants. Most hotels will only cash the cheques of guests. If cashing them at banks, aim for larger banks such as the Bank of China or ICBC.

Stick to the major companies such as Thomas Cook, Amex and Visa.

## Opening Hours

China officially has a five-day working week; Saturday and Sunday are public holidays.

**Banks** Open Monday to Friday 9am to 5pm (or 6pm); may close for two hours in the afternoon. Many also open Saturday and maybe Sunday. Same for offices and government departments.

**Bars** Open in the late afternoon, shutting around midnight or later.

**Post Offices** Generally open daily.

**Restaurants** Open from around 10.30am to 11pm; some shut at around 2pm and reopen at 5pm or 6pm.

**Shops** Open daily 10am to 10pm. Same for department stores and shopping malls.

## Passports

Chinese law requires foreign visitors to carry their passport (护照; *hùzhào*) with them at all times; it is the most basic travel document and all hotels (and internet cafes) will insist on seeing it. You also need it to buy train tickets or to get into some tourist sights, particularly those that are free.

It's a good idea to bring an ID card with your photo in case you lose your passport. Even better, make photocopies, or take digital photos of your passport – your embassy may need these before issuing a new one. You should also report the loss to the local Public Security Bureau (PSB). Be careful whom you pass your passport to, as you may never see it again.

## Public Holidays

The People's Republic of China has a number of national holidays. Some of the following are nominal holidays that do not result in leave. It's not a great idea to arrive in China or go travelling during the big holiday periods as hotel prices reach their maximum and transport can become very tricky. It is also possible to contact a hotel and ask when large conferences occur in the area.

**New Year's Day** 1 January

**Chinese New Year** 16 February 2018, 5 February 2019; a week-long holiday for most.

**International Women's Day** 8 March

**Tomb Sweeping Festival** First weekend in April; a popular three-day holiday period.

**International Labour Day** 1 May; for many it's a three-day holiday.

**Youth Day** 4 May

**International Children's Day** 1 June

**Dragon Boat Festival** 30 May 2017, 18 June 2018, 7 June 2019

**Birthday of the Chinese Communist Party** 1 July

**Anniversary of the Founding of the People's Liberation Army** 1 August

**Mid-Autumn Festival** 4 October 2017, 24 September 2018, 13 September 2019

**National Day** 1 October; the big one – a weeklong holiday.

## Safe Travel

China is relatively safe and non-violent. Unrest is mostly contained to certain areas, as noted in those chapters. Most crime, such as pickpocketing, is preventable by taking precautions.

## Telephone

Nearly everybody in China has a mobile phone (you may be judged on your model). Landlines and calling cards are rare. Some hotels will give you unlimited local or national calls.

Country code:
China ☎86
Hong Kong ☎852
Macau ☎853
International access code ☎00
Directory assistance ☎114

### Mobile Phones

A mobile phone should be the first choice for calls, but ensure your mobile is unlocked for use in China if

## Government Travel Advice

The following government websites offer travel advisories and information on current hot spots:

**Australian Department of Foreign Affairs & Trade** (www. smarttraveller.gov.au)

**British Foreign & Commonwealth Office** (www.gov.uk/foreign-travel-advice)

**Canadian Department of Foreign Affairs & International Trade** (http://travel.gc.ca/travelling/advisories)

**New Zealand Ministry of Foreign Affairs and Trade** (www.safetravel.govt.nz)

**US State Department** (http://travel.state.gov)

taking your own. SIM cards can be bought at the arrivals at major airports.

If you have the right phone (eg Blackberry, i-Phone, Android), you can use Skype (www.skype. com), Viber (www.viber. com) and Whatsapp (www. whatsapp.com) to make either very cheap or free calls with wi-fi access, even if your phone is network-locked or you have no phone credit. Communication through Chinese app WeChat (微信, Wēixìn; www. wechat.com), which boasts half a billion users, is standard practice between both friends and small businesses and is not considered unprofessional. (Note that although Chinese also use the word 'app', they spell it out as 'a-p-p'.)

Consider buying a data SIM card plan in China for constant network access away from wi-fi hot spots; plans start at under ¥70 for 500MB of data and 200 minutes of China calls per month. You will be warned about cancelling this service before leaving the country to avoid a hefty bill should you return. For this reason and the language barrier, it can be more convenient (if more expensive) to pick up a SIM card on arrival at an airport in the major cities. Though more expensive, 3G Solutions (www.3g solutions.com.cn) offers a range of mobile data and voice packages with prebooking online, and will have the SIM card delivered to your accommodation on the day you arrive in China.

If you want to get a SIM card independently, China Unicom offers the most reliable service with the greatest coverage. China Mobile or China Unicom outlets can sell you a standard prepaid SIM card, which cost sfrom ¥60 to ¥100 and includes ¥50 of credit. (You'll be given a choice of phone numbers. Choose a number without the unlucky number 4, if you don't want to irk Chinese colleagues.)

When your prepaid credit runs out, top up by buying a credit-charging card (充值 卡; *chōngzhí kǎ*) from outlets. Cards are also available from newspaper kiosks and shops displaying the China Mobile sign.

Cafes, restaurants and bars in larger towns and cities frequently offer wi-fi.

## Landlines

If making a domestic call, look out for very cheap public phones at newspaper stands (报刊亭; *bàokāntíng*) and hole-in-the-wall shops (小卖部; *xiǎomàibù*); you make your call and then pay the owner. Domestic and international long-distance phone calls can also be made from main telecommunications offices and 'phone bars' (话吧; *huàbā*). Cardless international calls are expensive and it's far cheaper to use an internet phone (IP) card (p327).

Public telephone booths are rarely used now in China but may serve as wi-fi hot spots (as in Shànghǎi).

## Phone Cards

Beyond Skype or Viber, using an internet phone card on your mobile or a landline phone is much cheaper than calling direct, but they can be hard to find outside the big cities.

## Time

The 24-hour clock is commonly used in China. Despite China's breadth, there is one single time zone in China: UTC+8. (You can also find UTC+6 used in Tibet and Xīnjiāng, though it is not official.)

## Toilets

Toilets in China can be a challenge for visitors, especially the common squat style (it may help to keep in mind that they're actually healthier for the body.)

It is useful to carry around tissues with you as paper is often not supplied in public toilets. Public toilets are either very cheap or free.

## Tourist Information

Tourist information continues to improve, with modern booths with pamphlets springing up even in smaller cities. The quality of spoken English can be hit-and-miss, though.

**China National Tourist Office**
www.cnto.org

## Travellers with Disabilities

China is not easy to navigate for travellers with limited mobility, but travel in a wheelchair is possible in the large cities at top-end accommodation (with lots of preparation and prebooking). Even still, expect plenty of stares.

Download Lonely Planet's free *Accessible Travel* guide from http://lptravel.to/AccessibleTravel.

## Visas

Needed for all visits to China except Hong Kong, Macau and 72-hour-and-under trips to Shànghǎi, Běijīng, Chángshā, Chéngdū, Chóngqìng, Dàlián, Guǎngzhōu, Guìlín, Harbin, Kūnmíng, Qīngdǎo, Shěnyáng, Tiānjīn, Wǔhàn, Xiàmén and Xī'ān.

### Applying for Visas

#### For China

Citizens from Japan, Singapore, Brunei, San Marino, Mauritius, the Seychelles and the Bahamas do not require a visa to visit China.

Your passport must be valid for at least six months after the expiry date of your visa (nine months for a double-entry visa) and you'll need at least one entire blank page in your passport for the visa. For children under the age of 18, a parent must sign the application form on their behalf.

At the time of writing, the visa application process had become more rigorous and applicants were required to provide the following:

○ a copy of flight confirmation showing onward/return travel

○ for double-entry visas, flight confirmation showing all dates of entry and exit

○ if staying at a hotel in China, confirmation from the hotel (this can be cancelled later if you stay elsewhere and often just showing the first night is enough)

○ if staying with friends or relatives, a copy of the information page of their passport, a copy of their China visa and a letter of invitation from them.

At the time of writing, prices for a standard single-entry 30-day visa were as follows:

○ UK£85 for UK citizens

○ US$140 for US citizens

○ US$40 for citizens of other nations.

Double-entry visas:

○ UK£85 for UK citizens

○ US$140 for US citizens

○ US$60 for all other nationals.

Six-month multiple-entry visas:

○ UK£85 for UK citizens

○ US$140 for US citizens

○ US$80 for all other nationals.

A standard, 30-day single-entry visa can be issued in four to five working days. In many countries, the visa service has been outsourced from the Chinese embassy to a compulsory Chinese Visa Application Service Centre (www.visaforchina.org), which levies an extra administration fee.

In the case of the UK, a single-entry visa costs UK£85, but the standard administration charge levied by the centre is an additional UK£66 (three-day express UK£78, postal service UK£90).

In some countries, such as the UK, France, the US and Canada, there is more than one service centre nationwide. Visa Application Service Centres are open Monday to Friday.

A standard 30-day visa is activated on the date you enter China, and must be used within three months of the date of issue. Travel visas of 60 days and 90 days are harder to get but possible just by applying. To stay longer, you can extend your visa in China.

Visa applications require a completed application form (available from the embassy, visa application service centre or downloaded from its website) and at least one photo (normally 51mm x 51mm). You generally pay for your visa when you collect it. A visa mailed to you will take up to three weeks. In the US and Canada, mailed visa applications have to go via a visa agent, at extra cost. In the US, many people use the **China Visa Service Center** (☑in the US 800 799 6560; www.mychinavisa.com), which offers prompt service.

## Visa-Free Transits

Citizens from 51 nations (including the US, Australia, Canada, France, Brazil and the UK) can stay in Běijīng for 72 hours without a visa as long as they are in transit to other destinations outside China, and have a third-country visa and an air ticket out of Běijīng. Similarly, citizens from the same nations can also transit through Chángshā, Chéngdū, Chóngqìng, Dàlián, Guǎngzhōu, Guìlín, Harbin, Kūnmíng, Qīngdǎo, Shěnyáng, Tiānjīn, Wǔhàn, Xiàmén and Xī'ān for 72 hours visa-free, with the same conditions.

For visa-free transit:

● You must inform your airline at check-in.

● Upon arrival, look for the dedicated immigration counter.

● Your transit time is calculated from just after mid-night, so you may actually be permitted a little over 72 or 144 hours in Shànghǎi.

● If you are not staying at a hotel, you must register with a local police station within 24 hours of arriving.

● Hong Kong, Macau and Taiwan are eligible third countries.

● Visitors on the 72-hour visa-free transit must leave the country from the same airport of entry.

Check your eligibility as the rules change quickly and new cities are being added.

The procedure takes around 10 to 14 days. CIBT (www.uk.cibt.com) offers a global network and a fast and efficient turnaround.

Hong Kong is a good place to pick up a China visa. China Travel Service (CTS; 中国旅行社; Zhōngguó Lǚxíngshè) will be able to obtain one for you, or you can apply directly to the **Visa Office of the People's Republic of China** (☑10-11am & 3-4pm Mon-Fri 852 3413 2424, recorded info 852 3413 2300; www.fmcoprc.gov.hk; 7th fl, Lower Block, China Resources Centre, 26 Harbour Rd, Wan Chai; ◷9am-noon & 2-5pm Mon-Fri; Ⓜ Wan Chai, exit A3).

### For Hong Kong

At the time of writing, most visitors to Hong Kong, including citizens of the EU, Australia, New Zealand, the USA and Canada, could enter and stay for 90 days without a visa. British passport holders get 180 days, while South Africans are allowed to stay 30 days visa-free. If you visit Hong

Kong from China, you will need a double-entry, multiple-entry or new visa to re-enter China.

### For Macau

Most travellers, including citizens of the EU, Australia, New Zealand, the USA, Canada and South Africa, can enter Macau without a visa for between 30 and 90 days. British-passport holders get 180 days. Most other nationalities can get a 30-day visa on arrival, which will cost MOP$100/50/200 per adult/child under 12/family. If you're visiting Macau from China and plan to re-enter China, you will need to be on a multiple- or double-entry visa.

### Visa Extensions

The Foreign Affairs Branch of the local Public Security Bureau (PSB) deals with visa extensions.

First-time extensions of 30 days are usually easy to obtain on single-entry tourist visas, but must be done at least seven days before your visa expires; a further extension of a month may be possible, but you may only get another week. Travellers report generous extensions in provincial towns, but don't bank on this. Popping across to Hong Kong to apply for a new tourist visa is another option.

Extensions to single-entry visas vary in price, depending on your nationality. At the time of writing, US trav-

ellers paid ¥185, Canadians ¥165, UK citizens ¥160 and Australians ¥100. Expect to wait up to seven days for your visa extension to be processed.

The penalty for overstaying your visa in China is up to ¥500 per day, and you may even be banned from returning to China for up to 10 years if you overstay by more than 11 days.

# Transport

Flights, cars and tours can be booked online at www.lonelyplanet.com/bookings.

## Getting There & Away

### Air

Hong Kong, Běijīng and Shànghǎi are China's principal international air gateways; Báiyún International Airport in Guǎngzhōu is of lesser, but growing, importance.

#### Báiyún International Airport

(CAN; 白云国际机场; Báiyún Guójì Jīchǎng; ☎020 3606 6999; http://www.gbiac.net) In Guǎngzhōu; receiving an increasing number of international flights.

#### Capital Airport (PEK; 北京首都国际机场; Běijīng Shǒudū

Guójì Jīchǎng; ☎010 6454 1100; www.en.bcia.com.cn) Běijīng's international airport; three terminals.

#### Hong Kong International Airport (HKG; ☎852 2181 8888; www.hkairport.com) On an island off the northern coast of Lantau and connected to the mainland by several spans.

#### Hóngqiáo Airport (SHA; 虹桥国际机场; Hóngqiáo Guójì Jīchǎng; ☎021 5260 4620, flight information 021 6268 8899; www.shairport.com; ⓜHongqiao Airport Terminal 1, ⓜHongqiao Airport Terminal 2) In Shànghǎi's west; domestic flights, some international connections.

#### Pǔdōng International Airport (PVG; 浦东国际机场; Pǔdōng Guójì Jīchǎng; ☎021 6834 7575, flight information 96990; www.shairport.com) In Shànghǎi's east; international flights.

China doesn't have one single national airline, but large airlines that operate both domestic and international flights. The largest are Air China (www.airchina.com); China Eastern Airlines (www.ce-air.com), based in Shànghǎi; and China Southern Airlines (www.cs-air.com), based in Guǎngzhōu. They fly to China from the US, Europe, Australia/New Zealand and other parts of Asia. Multiple international carriers also fly to China along similar routes.

### Land

China shares borders with Afghanistan, Bhutan, India,

Kazakhstan, Kyrgyzstan, Laos, Mongolia, Myanmar (Burma), Nepal, North Korea, Pakistan, Russia, Tajikistan and Vietnam; the borders with Afghanistan, Bhutan and India are closed. There are also official border crossings between China and its special administrative regions, Hong Kong and Macau.

Lonely Planet *China* guides may be confiscated by officials, primarily at the Vietnam–China border.

In addition to the Trans-Siberian and Trans-Mongolian rail services, the following routes can be travelled by train:

o Hung Hom station in Kowloon (Jiǔlóng; Hong Kong; www.mtr.com.hk) to Guǎngzhōu, Shànghǎi, Běijīng

o Pyongyang (North Korea) to Běijīng

o Almaty (Kazakhstan) to Ürümqi

o Astana (Kazakhstan) to Ürümqi

o Běijīng to Ulaanbaatar

o Běijīng to Hanoi

A good resource is the website The Man in Seat Sixty-One (www.seat61.com).

## Sea

There are weekly ferries between Osaka and Kōbe in Japan, and Shànghǎi. There are also twice-weekly boats from Qīngdǎo to Shimonoseki.

International ferries connect the South Korean port of Incheon with Wēihǎi, Qīngdǎo, Yāntái, Dàlián and Dāndōng.

# Getting Around

## Air

China's air network is extensive and growing. The civil aviation fleet is expected to triple in size over the next two decades, up to 70 new airports were planned for construction in recent years alone and 100 more were to be expanded or upgraded. When deciding between flying and using high-speed rail, note that flight delays in China are the worst in the world (according to travel industry monitor Flight-Stats), while trains almost always leave on time.

Planes vary in style and comfort. You may get a hot meal, or just a small piece of cake and an airline souvenir. On-board announcements are delivered in Chinese and English.

Shuttle buses usually run from Civil Aviation Administration of China (CAAC; Zhōngguó Mínháng) offices in towns and cities throughout China to the airport, often running via other stops. For domestic flights, arrive at the airport one hour before departure.

Remember to keep your baggage receipt label on your ticket as you will need to show it when you collect your luggage.

### Tickets

You can use credit cards at most CAAC offices and travel agents. Departure tax is included in the ticket price.

**Ctrip** (www.english.ctrip.com) Excellent hotel booking, air and

## Climate Change & Travel

Every form of transport that relies on carbon-based fuel generates $CO_2$, the main cause of human-induced climate change. Modern travel is dependent on aeroplanes, which might use less fuel per kilometre per person than most cars but travel much greater distances. The altitude at which aircraft emit gases (including $CO_2$) and particles also contributes to their climate change impact. Many websites offer 'carbon calculators' that allow people to estimate the carbon emissions generated by their journey and, for those who wish to do so, to offset the impact of the greenhouse gases emitted with contributions to portfolios of climate-friendly initiatives throughout the world. Lonely Planet offsets the carbon footprint of all staff and author travel.

train ticketing website, with English helpline. Useful app available.

**Elong** (www.elong.net) Hotel and air ticket booking, with English helpline.

**Travel Zen** (www.travelzen. com) Air tickets and hotel bookings. Chinese-only website.

## Bicycle

Bikes (自行车; *zìxíngchē*) are an excellent method for getting around China's cities and tourist sights. They can also be invaluable for exploring the countryside and surrounding towns.

Youth hostels often rent out bicycles – as do many hotels, although the latter are more expensive.

## Boat

Boat services within China are limited, especially with the growth of high-speed rail and expressways.

## Bus

Long-distance bus (长途公共汽车; *chángtú gōnggòng qìchē*) services are extensive and reach places you cannot reach by train; with the increasing number of intercity highways, journeys are getting quicker.

## Car & Motorcycle

Hiring a car in China has always been complicated or impossible for foreign visitors and in mainland China is currently limited to Běijīng and Shànghǎi, cities

that both have frequently gridlocked roads.

## Train

Trains are the best way to travel long distance around China in reasonable speed and comfort. They are also adventurous, exciting, fun, practical and efficient, and ticket prices are reasonable to boot. Colossal investment over recent years has put high-speed rail at the heart of China's rapid modernisation drive. You really don't have to be a trainspotter to find China's railways a riveting subculture; as a plus, you'll get to meet the Chinese people at their most relaxed and sociable.

### Buying Tickets

Ticket offices (售票厅; *shòupiàotīng*) at train stations are usually to one side of the main train station entrance. Automated ticket machines operate on some routes but never accept foreign passports as ID. At large stations there should be a window staffed by someone with basic English skills.

Alternatively, independent train ticket offices usually exist elsewhere in town, where tickets can be purchased for a ¥5 commission without the same kind of queues; we list these where possible. Larger post offices may also sell train tickets. Your hotel will also be able to rustle up a ticket

for you for a commission, and so can a travel agent.

It's cheaper to buy your ticket at the station, but tickets can be bought online at the following (China DIY Travel is the cheapest) and collected from any train before travel:

**China DIY Travel** (www.china-diy-travel.com; 6 Chaoyang Park Nanlu; 朝阳公园南路6号; commission per ticket $10)

**Ctrip** (www.english.ctrip.com)

**China Trip Advisor** (www.chinatripadvisor.com)

You can also find English-language train timetables on these websites.

To get a refund (退票; *tuìpiào*) on an unused ticket, look for the specifically marked windows at large train stations, where you can get from 80% to 95% of your ticket value back, depending on how many days prior to the departure date you cancel.

## Local Transport

Long-distance transport in China is good, but local transport is less efficient, except for cities with metro systems.

### Bus

With extensive networks, buses are an excellent way to get around town, but foreign travellers rarely use them. Boarding a bus, point to your destination on a map and the conductor (seated near the door) will sell you the right ticket. The conductor will usually tell you where to disembark, provided they remember. In conductor-less buses, you put money for your fare into a slot near the driver as you embark.

## Subway, Metro & Light Rail

Going underground or using light rail is fast, efficient and cheap; most networks are either very new or relatively recent and can be found in a rapidly growing number of cities, including Běijīng, Chéngdū, Chóngqìng, Dàlián, Guǎngzhōu, Hángzhōu, Hong Kong, Kūnmíng, Shànghǎi, Shěnyáng, Shēnzhèn, Sūzhōu, Tiānjīn, Wǔhàn, and Xī'ān.

## Taxi

Taxis (出租汽车; *chūzū qìchē*) are cheap and easy to find. Taxi rates per kilometre are clearly marked on a sticker on the rear side window of the taxi; flag fall varies from city to city, and depends upon the size and quality of the vehicle. Most taxis have meters but they may only be switched on in larger towns and cities. If the meter is not used (on an excursion out of town, for example, or when hiring a taxi for the day or half-day), negotiate a price before you set off and write the fare down. If you want the meter used, ask for *dǎbiǎo* (打表). Also ask for a receipt (发票; *fāpiào*); if you leave something in the taxi, you can have the taxi located by its vehicle number printed on the receipt.

Some more tips:

● Congregation points include train and long-distance bus stations, but usually you can just flag taxis down.

● Taxi drivers rarely speak any English – have your destination written down in characters.

● If you have communication problems, consider using your mobile to phone your hotel for staff to interpret.

● You can hire taxis on a daily or half-day basis, often at reasonable rates (always bargain).

# Language

China has eight major dialect groups. It's the language spoken in Běijīng that is considered the official language of China. It's usually referred to as Mandarin, but the Chinese themselves call it Pǔtōnghuà (meaning 'common speech'). With the exception of the western and southernmost provinces, most of the population speaks Mandarin (although it may be spoken there with a regional accent). To enhance your trip with a phrasebook, visit **lonelyplanet.com**.

## Mandarin

In this section we've provided pinyin (the official system of writing Mandarin in the Roman alphabet). The tones are indicated by accent marks on vowels: high (ā), rising (á), falling-rising (ǎ) and falling (à).

### Basics

**Hello./Goodbye.**
你好。/再见。    Nǐhǎo./Zàijiàn.

**Yes./No.**
是。/不是。    Shì./Bùshì.

**Excuse me.**
劳驾。    Láojià.

**Sorry.**
对不起。    Duìbùqǐ.

**Please ...**
请……    Qǐng ...

**Thank you.**
谢谢你。    Xièxie nǐ.

**You're welcome./That's fine.**
不客气。    Bù kèqi.

**How are you?**
你好吗?    Nǐhǎo ma?

**Fine. And you?**
好。你呢?    Hǎo. Nǐ ne?

**Do you speak English?**
你会说英文吗?    Nǐ huìshuō Yīngwén ma?

**I don't understand.**
我不明白。    Wǒ bù míngbai.

**How much is this?**
多少钱?    Duōshǎo qián?

## Accommodation

**Do you have a single/double room?**
有没有单人/    Yǒuméiyǒu dānrén/
套房?    tào fáng?

**How much is it per night/person?**
每天/人多少钱?    Měi tiān/rén duōshǎo qián?

## Eating & Drinking

**I'd like ..., please.**
我想吃……    Wǒ xiǎng chī ...

**That was delicious.**
真好吃。    Zhēn hǎochī.

**The bill/check, please.**
买单。    Mǎidān.

**I'm allergic to (nuts).**
我对(果仁)过敏。    Wǒ duì (guǒrén) guòmǐn.

**I don't eat ...**
我不吃……    Wǒ bùchī ...

| | | |
|---|---|---|
| **fish** | 鱼 | yú |
| **pork** | 猪肉 | zhūròu |
| **red meat** | 牛羊肉 | niúyángròu |

## Emergencies

**I'm ill.**
我生病了。    Wǒ shēngbìng le.

**Help!**
救命!    Jiùmìng!

**Call a doctor!**
请叫医生来!    Qǐng jiào yīshēng lái!

**Call the police!**
请叫警察!    Qǐng jiào jǐngchá!

## Directions

**Where's a/the ...?**
……在哪儿?    ... zài nǎr?

| | | |
|---|---|---|
| **bank** | 银行 | yínháng |
| **market** | 市场 | shìchǎng |
| **museum** | 博物馆 | bówùguǎn |
| **post office** | 邮局 | yóujú |
| **restaurant** | 餐馆 | cānguǎn |
| **toilet** | 厕所 | cèsuǒ |
| **tourist office** | 旅行店 | lǚxíng diàn |

# Cantonese

If you read our pronunciation guides, provided in this section next to the Cantonese script, as if they were English, you'll be understood fine. The tones are indicated by accent marks on 'n' and on vowels: high (à), high rising (á), low falling (à̲), low rising (á̲) and low (a̲).

## Basics

**Hello.**
哈佬。     hàa·ló
**Goodbye.**
再見。     joy·gin
**Yes.**
係。     ha̲i
**No.**
不係。     ǹg·ha̲i
**Excuse me.**
對唔住。     deui·ǹg·jew
**Sorry.**
對唔住。     deui·ǹg·jew
**Please ...**
唔該……     ǹg·gòy ...
**Thank you.**
多謝。     dàw·je
**You're welcome./ That's fine.**
唔駛客氣。     ǹg·sái haak·hay
**How are you?**
你幾好啊嗎？     láy gáy hó à maa
**Fine. And you?**
幾好。     gáy hó
你呢？     láy lè
**Do you speak English?**
你識唔識講     láy sìk·ǹg·sìk gáwng
英文啊？     yìng·mán aa
**I don't understand.**
我唔明。     ngá̲w ǹg mìng
**How much is this?**
幾多錢？     gáy·dàw chín

## Accommodation

**Do you have a (single/double) room?**
有冇(單人/     yáu·mó (dàan·ya̲n/
雙人)房？     sèung·ya̲n) fáwng

**How much is it per (night/person)?**
一(晚/個人)     yàt (má̲an/gaw ya̲n)
幾多錢？     gáy·dàw chín

## Eating & Drinking

**I'd like ..., please.**
我想食……     ngá̲w séung sik ...
**That was delicious.**
真好味。     ja̲n hó·may
**I'd like the bill/check, please.**
唔該我要埋單。     ǹg·gòy ngá̲w yiu ma̲ai·dàan
**I'm allergic to (nuts).**
我對(果仁)     ngá̲w deui (gwá̲w·ya̲n)
過敏。     gaw·má̲n

**I don't eat ...**
我唔吃……     ngá̲w ǹg sik ...
   **fish**    魚    yéw
   **poultry**    雞鴨鵝    gài ngaap ngà̲w
   **red meat**    牛羊肉    ngà̲u yèung yuk

## Emergencies

**I'm ill.**
我病咗。     ngá̲w beng·já̲w
**Help!**
救命！     gau·meng
**Call a doctor!**
快啲叫醫生!     faai·dì giu yì·sàng
**Call the police!**
快啲叫警察!     faai·dì giu gíng·chaat

## Directions

**Where's a/the ...?**
……喺邊度？     ... hái bìn·do̲
   **bank**    銀行    nga̲n·hà̲wng
   **market**    街市    gàai·sí
   **museum**    博物館    bawk·ma̲t·gún
   **post office**    郵局    yàu·gúk
   **restaurant**    酒樓    jáu·là̲u
   **toilet**    廁所    chi·sáw
   **tourist office**    旅行社    léui·hà̲ng·sé

# Behind the Scenes

## Acknowledgements

Climate map data adapted from Peel MC, Finlayson BL & McMahon TA (2007) 'Updated World Map of the Köppen-Geiger Climate Classification', Hydrology and Earth System Sciences, 11, 163344.

Illustrations p44-5, p116-17 by Michael Weldon.

## This Book

This guidebook was curated by Damian Harper, who also researched and wrote for it, along with Piera Chen, Megan Eaves, David Eimer, Helen Elfer, Trent Holden, Stephen Lioy, Emily Matchar, Rebecca Milner, Kate Morgan, Tom Spurling and Phillip Tang.

This guidebook was produced by the following:

**Destination Editor** Megan Eaves

**Product Editor** Amanda Williamson

**Senior Cartographer** Julie Sheridan

**Book Designer** Wibowo Rusli

**Assisting Editors** Helen Koehne, Saralinda Turner

**Cartographers** Hunor Csutoros, Julie Dodkins

**Cover Researcher** Naomi Parker

**Thanks to** James Hardy, Victoria Harrison, Liz Heynes, Sally Howes, Andi Jones, Kate Kiely, Indra Kilfoyle, Linda Limberger, Wayne Murphy, Fiona Powrie, Kirsten Rawlings, Shane Raymond, Dianne Schallmeiner, John Taufa, Sam Trafford, Tony Wheeler, Juan Winata

## Send Us Your Feedback

We love to hear from travellers – your comments keep us on our toes and help make our books better. Our well-travelled team reads every word on what you loved or loathed about this book. Although we cannot reply individually to postal submissions, we always guarantee that your feedback goes straight to the appropriate authors, in time for the next edition. Each person who sends us information is thanked in the next edition, the most useful submissions are rewarded with a selection of digital PDF chapters.

Visit lonelyplanet.com/contact to submit your updates and suggestions or to ask for help. Our award-winning website also features inspirational travel stories, news and discussions.

# Index

HSBC Building (Hong Kong) 164-5
Jade Gate Pass 264
Jiāyùguān Fort 262-3
Jīnmào Tower 125
Labrang Monastery 260-1
Leal Senado 167
Mandarin's House 167
Mid-Lake Pavilion Teahouse 119
Monte Fort 166-7
Mu Family Mansion 209
Muslim Quarter 103, 104
Peace Hotel 114
Senate Library 167
Shànghǎi Tower 125
Shànghǎi World Financial Center 126
Wang Family Courtyard 88
Water Wheel Park 270-1
Xī'ān City Walls 103
historic towns 18-19
history 280-8
  Communism 286-7
  Confucius 281
  Cultural Revolution 287
  dynasties 283-4
  Great Leap Forward 287
  Long March 285-6
holidays 326
Hóngcūn 148-9
Hong Kong 11, 158-80, **161, 168-9, 172, 174, 185**
  accommodation 161, 185
  drinking 176-7
  entertainment 177-8
  food 173, 175-6
  highlights 162-5
  information 178
  itineraries 160
  nightlife 176-7
  shopping 173
  sights 170-3
  travel to/from 161, 178-9
  travel within 179-80
Hong Kong International Airport 330
Hongkong & Shanghai Bank Building 115
Hóngqiáo Airport 330
Huá Shān 100-1
Huángpǔ Park 133
Huángshān 14, 140-57, **141, 152**
  accommodation 141, 145
  highlights 142-5
  itineraries 140
  travel to/from 141
Huīzhōu villages 14, 140-57, **141**
  food 156
  highlights 146-9
  itineraries 140
  travel to/from 141
  travel within 141
*hútòngs* 54-5, **54-5**

**I**

Imperial Vault of Heaven 49
information 328, *see also individual locations*
insurance 323
internet access 323
internet resources 17, 320
Islam 310
itineraries 26-31, **26, 27, 28-9, 30-1**, *see also individual locations*

**J**

Jiànkòu 75-6
Jiāyùguān 268-70
Jiāyùguān Fort 262-3
Jīngjù 307
Jīnmào Tower 125
Jīnshānlǐng 76
Jiǔhuá Shān 155

**K**

Kūnmíng Lake 51

**L**

Labrang Monastery 260-1
lakes
  Kūnmíng Lake 51
  Moon Pond 149
  Róng Lake 198
  Shān Lake 198
  South Lake 149
Lamma 173
languages 16, 334-5
Lantau 172-3
Lánzhōu 270-5, **271**
legal matters 323-4
lesbian travellers 324
LGBT travellers 324
Lìjiāng 208-9, 213-16, **212**
Lí River 8, 187-201
Lí Riverside Path 194
literature 25, 313
Little Goose Pagoda 103-4
Liúgōng 191
local transport 332-3, *see also individual locations*
Lóngjǐ Rice Terraces 192-3

**M**

Macau 11, 158-61, 180-5, **161, 182-3**
  accommodation 161
  entertainment 181
  food 180-1
  highlights 166-7
  information 181
  itineraries 160
  sights 180
  travel to/from 161, 181, 184
  travel within 184
Mandarin language 334

# Symbols & Map Key

## Look for these symbols to quickly identify listings:

- Sights
- Activities
- Courses
- Tours
- Festivals & Events
- Eating
- Drinking
- Entertainment
- Shopping
- Information & Transport

## These symbols and abbreviations give vital information for each listing:

- Sustainable or green recommendation
- FREE No payment required

- Telephone number
- Opening hours
- Parking
- Nonsmoking
- Air-conditioning
- Internet access
- Wi-fi access
- Swimming pool
- Bus
- Ferry
- Tram
- Train
- English-language menu
- Vegetarian selection
- Family-friendly

## Find your best experiences with these Great For... icons.

 Budget

 Food & Drink

 Drinking

 Cycling

 Shopping

 Sport

 Art & Culture

Events

 Photo Op

Scenery

Family Travel

 Short Trip

 Detour

 Walking

 Local Life

 History

 Entertainment

 Beaches

Winter Travel

 Cafe/Coffee

Nature & Wildlife

## Sights

- Beach
- Bird Sanctuary
- Buddhist
- Castle/Palace
- Christian
- Confucian
- Hindu
- Islamic
- Jain
- Jewish
- Monument
- Museum/Gallery/ Historic Building
- Ruin
- Shinto
- Sikh
- Taoist
- Winery/Vineyard
- Zoo/Wildlife Sanctuary
- Other Sight

## Points of Interest

- Bodysurfing
- Camping
- Cafe
- Canoeing/Kayaking
- Course/Tour
- Diving
- Drinking & Nightlife
- Eating
- Entertainment
- Sento Hot Baths/ Onsen
- Shopping
- Skiing
- Sleeping
- Snorkelling
- Surfing
- Swimming/Pool
- Walking
- Windsurfing
- Other Activity

## Information

- Bank
- Embassy/Consulate
- Hospital/Medical
- Internet
- Police
- Post Office
- Telephone
- Toilet
- Tourist Information
- Other Information

## Geographic

- Beach
- Gate
- Hut/Shelter
- Lighthouse
- Lookout
- Mountain/Volcano
- Oasis
- Park
- Pass
- Picnic Area
- Waterfall

## Transport

- Airport
- BART station
- Border crossing
- Boston T station
- Bus
- Cable car/Funicular
- Cycling
- Ferry
- Metro/MRT station
- Monorail
- Parking
- Petrol station
- Subway/S-Bahn/ Skytrain station
- Taxi
- Train station/Railway
- Tram
- Tube Station
- Underground/ U-Bahn station
- Other Transport

## Helen Elfer

Helen Elfer made Shanghai her home between 2007-10, so she was delighted to be able to return and contribute to the latest Lonely Planet *China* and *Shanghai* guides. After a two-year stint in Abu Dhabi, she moved back to London, working as a travel writer for various newspapers and magazines. She's currently Lonely Planet's Destination Editor for the Middle East and North Africa.

## Trent Holden

A Geelong-based writer, located just outside Melbourne, Trent has worked for Lonely Planet since 2005. He's covered 30 plus guidebooks across Asia, Africa and Australia. With a penchant for megacities, Trent's in his element when assigned to cover a nation's capital – the more chaotic the better – to unearth cool bars, art, street food and underground subculture. On the flipside he also writes books to idyllic tropical islands across Asia, in between going on safari to national parks in Africa and the subcontinent. When not travelling, Trent works as a freelance editor, reviewer and spending all his money catching live gigs.

## Stephen Lioy

Stephen is a photographer, writer, hiker, and travel blogger based in Central Asia. A 'once in a lifetime' Eurotrip and post-university move to China set the stage for what would eventually become a semi-nomadic lifestyle based on sharing his experiences with would-be travellers and helping provide that initial push out of comfort zones and into all that the planet has to offer.

## Emily Matchar

A native of Chapel Hill, North Carolina, Emily first caught Relapsing Travel Fever during a high school semester abroad in Argentina. She studied English and Spanish at Harvard University, but the most important part of her education happened during summers in Mexico and Nicaragua researching for the college's Let's Go series of travel guides. Upon graduation, she hightailed it back down South to spend the next three years keeping tabs on local government as a reporter with Raleigh's *The News and Observer*. Office life, however, did not agree with her, and she was soon off gallivanting around the globe for Lonely Planet. To date, Emily has contributed to the following Lonely Planet guides: *USA, Trips: The Carolinas, Georgia and the South, Mexico, Canada, New England* and *Best in Travel 2010*. She also writes about travel, adventure and food for publications including *Men's Journal, Outside, Gourmet, Chow, Forbes Life, BBC History, AOL Food* and many others. When she's not busy rating Memphis barbecue joints, wandering around night markets in Laos, or tramping in New Zealand, she can be found eating fried chicken biscuits in Chapel Hill.

## Rebecca Milner

California born. Longtime Tokyo resident (14 years and counting!). Co-author of Lonely Planet guides to *Tokyo, Japan, Korea* and *China*. Freelance writer covering travel, food & culture. Published in the *Guardian*, the *Independent*, the *Sunday Times Travel Magazine*, the *Japan Times* & more. After spending the better part of her twenties working to travel – doing odd jobs in Tokyo to make money so she could spend months at a time backpacking around Asia – she was fortunate enough to turn the tables in 2010, joining the Lonely Planet team of freelance authors.

## Kate Morgan

Having worked for Lonely Planet for more than a decade now, Kate has been fortunate enough to cover plenty of ground working as a writer on destinations such as Shanghai, Japan, India, Zimbabwe, the Philippines and Phuket. She has had stints living in London, Paris and Osaka but these days she is based in one of her favourite regions in the world – Victoria, Australia.

## Tom Spurling

Tom is an Australian Lonely Planet guidebook writer and high school teacher currently based in Hong Kong in search of the long-lost expatriate package. He's worked on 13 Lonely Planet titles, including *Japan, China, Central America, Turkey, India, South Africa* and *Australia*. When not chasing his tail, he enjoys tucking it under his crossed legs for minutes on end.

## Phillip Tang

Phillip Tang grew up on typically Australian pho and fish'n'chips. A degree in Latin-American and Chinese cultures launched him into travel and writing about it for Lonely Planet's *Canada, China, Japan, Korea, Mexico, Peru* and *Vietnam* guides. More pics and words: philliptang.co.uk. Phillip has made his home in Sydney, Melbourne, London and Mexico City. His travels include most countries in Europe, much of Asia and Latin America, as well as the greatest hits of North America. Phillip has written for the Lonely Planet pictorial and gift books the *Cities Book, Cooks Clowns and Cowboys, Calm, 1000 Ultimate Adventures, Guide to Pride, World's Best Drinks, World's Best Brunches, World's Best Spicy Food, The Best Things in Life are Free* and *Best in Travel 2017*. Phillip writes about travel and the people there, who just call it living. He likes smelling fresh mint in a market in a new town and imagining a parallel life there.

## Our Story

A beat-up old car, a few dollars in the pocket and a sense of adventure. In 1972 that's all Tony and Maureen Wheeler needed for the trip of a lifetime – across Europe and Asia overland to Australia. It took several months, and at the end – broke but inspired – they sat at their kitchen table writing and stapling together their first travel guide, Across Asia on the Cheap. Within a week they'd sold 1500 copies. Lonely Planet was born. Today, Lonely Planet has offices in Franklin, London, Melbourne, Oakland, Dublin, Beijing, and Delhi, with more than 600 staff and writers. We share Tony's belief that 'a great guidebook should do three things: inform, educate and amuse'.

# Our Writers

### Damian Harper

Ten years of British boarding school gave Damian every incentive to explore new horizons beyond home. A degree in History of Art at Leeds University followed in 1995 and a few years later Damian applied to work on the Lonely Planet *China* guide. Since then, Damian has served as coordinating author on seven editions of the guide and has co-authored multiple editions of the *Beijing* and *Shanghai* city guides, *Malaysia, Singapore and Brunei, Vietnam, Thailand, London, Great Britain* and *Ireland*; Damian also wrote the first edition of *Shanghai Encounter* and *Best of Shanghai* and co-wrote *China's Southwest* (3rd edition) and two *Hong Kong* titles.

### Piera Chen

Piera is a travel writer who divides her time among Hong Kong (hometown), Taiwan and Vancouver when not on the road. She has authored over a dozen travel guides. Piera has a BA in literature from Pomona College. Her early life was peppered with trips to Taiwan and China to visit relatives, and then to Southeast Asia where her father was working. But it was during her first trip to Europe that dawn broke. She remembers fresh off a flight, looking around her in Rome, thinking, 'I want to be doing this everyday.' And she has.

### David Eimer

David has been a journalist and writer ever since abandoning the idea of a law career in 1990. After spells working in his native London and in Los Angeles, he moved to Beijing in 2005, where he contributed to a variety of newspapers and magazines in the UK. Since then, he has travelled and lived across China and in numerous cities in Southeast Asia, including Bangkok, Phnom Penh and Yangon. He has been covering China, Myanmar (Burma) and Thailand for Lonely Planet since 2006.

◄───  More Writers  ◄───

**STAY IN TOUCH** LONELYPLANET.COM/CONTACT

**AUSTRALIA** The Malt Store, Level 3, 551 Swanston St, Carlton, Victoria 3053 ☏03 8379 8000, fax 03 8379 8111

**IRELAND** Unit E, Digital Court. The Digital Hub, Rainsford St, Dublin 8, Ireland

**USA** 124 Linden Street, Oakland, CA 94607 ☏510 250 6400, toll free 800 275 8555, fax 510 893 8572

**UK** 240 Blackfriars Road, London SE1 8NW ☏ 020 3771 5100, fax 020 3771 5101

 twitter.com/ lonelyplanet

facebook.com/ lonelyplanet

 instagram.com/ lonelyplanet

 youtube.com/ lonelyplanet

lonelyplanet.com/ newsletter